CLARENDON MEDIEVAL AND
TUDOR SERIES

General Editor
J. A. W. BENNETT

DISCARD

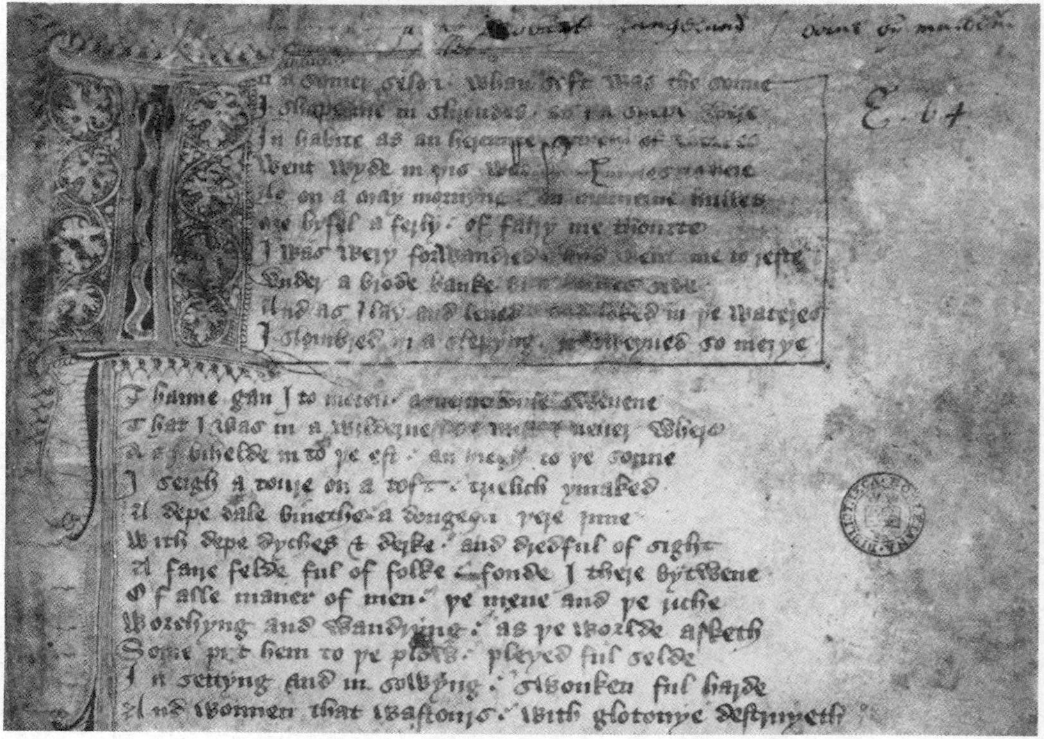

Bodleian MS. Laud. Misc. 581, fol. 1 (in part)

LANGLAND
PIERS PLOWMAN

The Prologue and Passus I-VII
of the B text as found in
Bodleian MS. Laud Misc. 581

Edited with Notes and Glossary by
J. A. W. BENNETT

OXFORD
AT THE CLARENDON PRESS

Oxford University Press, Walton Street, Oxford OX2 6DP

Oxford New York Toronto
Delhi Bombay Calcutta Madras Karachi
Petaling Jaya Singapore Hong Kong Tokyo
Nairobi Dar es Salaam Cape Town
Melbourne Auckland

and associated companies in
Beirut Berlin Ibadan Nicosia

Oxford is a trade mark of Oxford University Press

Published in the United States
by Oxford University Press, New York

© Oxford University Press 1972

First published 1972
Reprinted 1976, 1979, 1988

ISBN 0 19 871090 9

Printed in Great Britain
at the University Printing House, Oxford
by David Stanford
Printer to the University

CONTENTS

PREFACE

THIS volume replaces one prepared by W. W. Skeat over a century ago and many times reprinted with only minor alterations. Thanks primarily to Skeat's editorial labours, *Piers Plowman* is now recognized as a masterpiece. Information about the poem is widely disseminated, critical studies abound (they are even collected and reprinted), and the characteristics of fourteenth-century English have become familiar; so that it seems permissible to devote to additional notes the space that Skeat gave to a general introduction.[1] Even so, an *editio minor* cannot compass all the advances in literary and linguistic history, not to speak of religious, social, and economic history; it can do no more than provide summary elucidation and pertinent references. Nor can it consider textual complexities: they are the province of the editors of the Athlone edition of the three recensions of the poem, in which only Professor Kane's (definitive) edition of the A text has so far appeared, and from which he kindly allows me to quote some selected readings.

Thirty-five years ago R. W. Chambers suggested that Skeat's publication of the first seven passus in a separate edition, by focusing attention on the opening visions, had made for misunderstanding of the poet's main intention. But this, if true then, is true no longer. Indeed, the danger now lies in the opposite direction. Yet attention to every detail in these passus remains a prerequisite for appreciation of the work as a whole.

Skeat's attribution of the three recensions of the poem to William Langland has been accepted by most scholars (even if some have had reservations about the third or C version). Professor Kane has recently set out the evidence in a monograph to which every student must turn (see Bibliography). But we still

[1] For a brief account of the date, authorship, content, and meaning of the poem see the article *Langland* in the current edition of the *Encyclopaedia Britannica*.

PREFACE

know no more of Langland's life—inferences from the text apart
—than is stated in a note in the Dublin MS.[1] to the effect that
he was a son of Stacy de Rokayle, who held land in Shipton-
under-Wychwood, Oxon. This leaves open the possibility that
he took his surname from a different area; and that he cryptically
alludes to this name in B xv. 148 ('I haue lyued in londe, quod I,
my name is Longe Wille') is practically certain. The name *Longe-
londe* (with variants) has recently been found in several Shropshire
documents dating from 1399 onwards, and that may well have
been the form that the poet used.

Pending the appearance of the critical text of 'B', there is no
reason to question Skeat's choice of the Laud MS. as the best
single copy of that version extant. I have collated his printed text
with the MS. (and consulted other MSS.), corrected certain slips,
repunctuated several passages, and restored lines omitted by
Skeat on grounds of indelicacy. Generally I retain Laud readings
whenever they yield sense and grammar, but correct faults that
are evidently purely scribal or that are not found in A. The
alternative or superior readings cited in the Notes and Table of
Variants are selective, and intended chiefly to remind the reader
that the Laud copy cannot be (as Skeat surmised) the poet's
autograph. I have rarely emended on metrical or alliterative
grounds alone, since it is impossible to be sure what variation the
poet (as distinct from the copyists) allowed himself within an
accepted alliterative pattern. By the same token I offer no pro-
nouncements about the dialect of the Laud MS., or of the poet:
these must be left to Professor McIntosh and Professor Samuels;
enough to note that the A texts can now be assigned, on linguistic
grounds, to areas ranging from South Sussex to Durham, the
B texts circulated chiefly in the Worcester and London areas, and
the C texts in the area of the Malvern Hills (Samuels, *English
Studies*, 44, p. 94).

The Glossary has been largely rewritten, and expanded; but
philological lore now incorporated, or corrected, in the *Oxford
English Dictionary* or the *Middle English Dictionary* (Ann Arbor),
is omitted. The Bibliography may serve as a partial supplement

[1] Reproduced and discussed by G. Kane in his monograph.

viii

to that provided in the 1954 reprint of Skeat's parallel-text edition (1886).

My own interest in Langland was first kindled some forty years ago by lectures of the late P. S. Ardern at Auckland University College. To his rigorous scrutiny of the text and of its critics I owe much; some of my notes may retain vestiges of his *ipsissima verba*. A devoted teacher and an impeccable scholar, he worked in isolation and with few of the appurtenances of modern learning. Not to acknowledge his stimulus would be to ignore the poem's closing injunction: *Redde quod debes*.

J. A. W. B.

SELECT BIBLIOGRAPHY

(Including works cited in the Notes by the author's name, or by
other abbreviations, here italicized in brackets)

(i) EDITIONS (for Skeat's editions of B v. pp. ix and 75).

George Kane: *'Piers Plowman': The A Version. Will's Visions of
Piers Plowman and Do-Well*: an edition in the form of Trinity
College Cambridge MS. R. 3. 14 (London: The Athlone Press
1960). (Quotations from this edition are distinguished by *A*.)
(*Kane*)

Thomas A. Knott and David C. Fowler: *'Piers the Plowman':
A Critical Edition of the A-version* (Baltimore 1952, reprinted
1970). (*KF*)

Elizabeth Salter and Derek Pearsall: *Piers Plowman* (London 1967)
(selections from C based on MS. Huntington 143; useful Introduction (58 pp.)).

(ii) MONOGRAPHS, GENERAL STUDIES, AND COLLECTIONS OF
STUDIES

R. J. Blanch (ed.): *Style and Symbolism in 'Piers Plowman': A
Modern Critical Anthology* (Knoxville, Tenn. 1969). The follow-
ing are pertinent items: M. W. Bloomfield: 'Present State of
PPl Studies' (1939+); N. Coghill: 'The Pardon of *PPl*' (1945);
T. P. Dunning: 'The Structure of the B-text of *PPl*' (1956);
J. Lawlor: 'The Imaginative Unity of *PPl*' (1957); Elizabeth
Zeeman (Salter): '*PPl* and the Pilgrimage to Truth' (1958);
P. M. Kean: 'Love, Law and Lewte in *PPl*' (1964); H. W.
Troyer: 'Who is PPL?' (1932); A. G. Mitchell: 'Lady Meed and
the Art of *PPl*' (1956); J. Burrow: 'The Action of Langland's
Second Vision' (1956). (*Blanch*)

M. W. Bloomfield: *'Piers Plowman' as a Fourteenth-century Apoca-
lypse* (New Brunswick, N.J. 1961). (*Bloomfield*)

Christine Brooke-Rose: 'Ezra Pound: Piers Plowman in the
Waste Modern Land', *Review of Eng. Lit.* 2 (1961), 74–88.

SELECT BIBLIOGRAPHY

J. W. Burrow: 'The Audience of *Piers Plowman*', *Anglia* 75 (1957), 373–84.

Ladislav Cejp: 'An Introduction to . . . *Piers Plowman*; the Method of Medieval Allegory and *PPl*', *Acta Univ. Palackianæ* (1956, *Olomucensis* 1961).

N. Coghill: 'Langland's Kind of Poetry', in *English and Mediaeval Studies presented to J. R. R. Tolkien* (London 1962).

Id.: *Langland* (London 1964) (British Council booklet, with sel. bibliog.).

E. T. Donaldson: '*Piers Plowman*', *the C-Text and its Poet* (New Haven, Conn. 1949). (*Donaldson*)

Id.: 'MSS. R and F in the B-Tradition of *PPl*', *Transactions of the Connecticut Academy of Arts and Sciences*, 39 (1955), 177–212. (*Donaldson, TCA*)

T. P. Dunning: '*Piers Plowman*': *An Interpretation of the A-Text* (London 1937). (*Dunning*: new edn. in progress)

D. C. Fowler: '*Piers the Plowman*': *Literary Relations of the A and B Texts* (Seattle 1961).

S. S. Hussey (ed.): '*Piers Plowman*'. *Critical Approaches* (London 1969). A collection of essays previously unpublished, including: G. H. Russell: 'Some Aspects of the Process of Revision in *PPl*'; Rosemary Woolf: 'The Tearing of the Pardon'; J. Burrow: 'Words, Works and Will: Theme and Structure in *PPl*'; Priscilla Jenkin: 'Conscience: the Frustration of Allegory'; Barbara Raw: 'Piers and the Image of God in Man'; D. Mills: 'The Rôle of the Dreamer in *PPl*'; T. P. Dunning: 'Action and Contemplation in *PPl*'; R. W. V. Elliott: 'The Langland Country'; W. O. Evans: 'Charity in *PPl*'; S. T. Knight: 'Satire in *PPl*'; J. A. W. Bennett: 'Chaucer's Contemporary'. (*Hussey*)

S. S. Hussey: 'Langland's Reading of Alliterative Poetry', *Modern Language Review*, 60 (1965), 163–70.

G. Kane: '*Piers Plowman*': *The Evidence for Authorship* (London 1965).

J. Lawlor: '*Piers Plowman*'. *An Essay in Criticism* (London 1962).

Przemysław Mroczkowski: '*PPl*: the Allegory in Motion', *Prace historycznoliterackiez*, 8 (1965).

Elizabeth Salter: '*Piers Plowman*'. *An Introduction* (Oxford 1962).

G. Shepherd: *The Nature of Alliterative Poetry in Late Medieval England* (Gollancz Lecture 1970; London 1971).

SELECT BIBLIOGRAPHY

B. H. Smith: *Traditional Imagery of Charity in 'Piers Plowman'* (The Hague 1966).

A. C. Spearing: 'The Art of Preaching in *PPl*' in his *Criticism and Medieval Poetry* (London 1964).

Elizabeth Suddaby: 'The Poem *PPl*', *Journal of English and Germanic Philology*, 54 (1955), 103.

E. Vasta: *The Spiritual Basis of 'Piers Plowman'* (The Hague 1965).

Translation: J. F. Goodridge: *Piers the Ploughman* (Harmondsworth 1959, 1966) (with useful Introduction.)

(iii) HISTORICAL AND OTHER WORKS

H. S. Bennett: *Life on the English Manor* (Cambridge 1937) (*Bennett*)

E. Lipson: *The Economic History of England*, vol. i (8th edn., London 1945). (*Lipson*)

G. R. Owst: *Literature and Pulpit in Medieval England* (2nd edn., Oxford 1961). (*Owst*)

The Oxford Dictionary of the Christian Church, ed. F. L. Cross (Oxford 1957). (*ODCC*)

W. A. Pantin: *The English Church in the Fourteenth Century* (Cambridge 1955). (*Pantin*)

Register of Edward the Black Prince (London: P.R.O. 1930–3). (*BPR*)

R. W. Southern: *Western Society and the Church in the Middle Ages* (Harmondsworth 1970). (*Southern*)

Sunday Sermons of the Great Fathers (ed. M. F. Toal) (4 vols., London and Chicago 1955 etc.). (*Sunday Sermons*)

R. H. Tawney: *Religion and the Rise of Capitalism* (Pelican edn., Harmondsworth 1938). (Modern criticism of this work does not lessen the value of the quotations collected in its notes.) (*Tawney*)

A. Hamilton Thompson: *The English Clergy and their Organization in the Later Middle Ages* (Oxford 1947, repr. 1966). (*Thompson*)

B. J. Whiting: *Proverbs, Sentences and Proverbial Phrases from English Writings mainly before 1500* (Harvard 1968). (*Whiting*)

John A. Yunck: *The Lineage of Lady Meed* (Notre Dame, Indiana 1963). (*Yunck*)

SELECT BIBLIOGRAPHY

Except where otherwise noted, references to Middle English texts are to editions published by the Early English Text Society and identifiable in its list of titles. References to Chaucer (*CT*, *HF*, *BD*, etc.) are usually made by the abbreviations used in Robinson's edition. Those to Gower's *Confessio Amantis* (*CA*) are to Macaulay's edition. Some ME texts are cited as edited by Bennett and Smithers, *Early Middle English Verse and Prose* (Oxford 1966, 1968) (*EMEVP*); and by K. Sisam, *Fourteenth Century Verse and Prose* (Oxford 1921, etc.) (*Sisam*). The Appendix to the latter book provides a useful account of the English language (including spellings and inflexions) in Langland's time. Shorter texts are cited from *The Oxford Book of Medieval English Verse*, ed. Celia and Kenneth Sisam (Oxford 1970) (*OBMEV*).

DOST = *Dictionary of the Older Scottish Tongue* (in progress)
HM = Huntington Library MS.
JWCI = *Journal of the Warburg and Courtauld Institutes*
MED = *Middle English Dictionary* (in progress)
R.S. = Rolls Series
Sir Gawain = *Sir Gawain and the Green Knight*
Summa = St. Thomas, *Summa Theologiæ*
VCH = Victoria County Histories

Other abbreviations as in Robinson's Chaucer.

* denotes: see Addenda.

xiv

Incipit liber de Petro Plowman

In a somer seson whan soft was the sonne
I shope me in shroudes as I a shepe were;
In habite as an heremite vnholy of workes
Went wyde in þis world wondres to here.
Ac on a May mornynge on Maluerne hulles   5
Me byfel a ferly, of fairy me thouȝte:
I was wery forwandred and went me to reste
Vnder a brode banke bi a bornes side,
And as I lay and lened and loked in þe wateres,
I slombred in a slepyng, it sweyued so merye.   10

   Thanne gan I to meten a merueilouse sweuene,
That I was in a wildernesse, wist I neuer where.
As I bihelde into þe est, an hiegh to þe sonne,
I seigh a toure on a toft trielich ymaked;
A depe dale binethe, a dongeon þereinne   15
With depe dyches and derke and dredful of sight.
A faire felde ful of folke fonde I there bytwene,
Of alle maner of men, þe mene and þe riche,
Worchyng and wandryng as þe worlde asketh.
Some putten hem to þe plow, pleyed ful selde,   20
In settyng and in sowyng swonken ful harde,
And wonnen that wastours with glotonye destruyeth.

   And some putten hem to pruyde, apparailed hem þere-
     after,
In contenaunce of clothyng comen disgised.

   In prayers and in penance putten hem manye,   25
Al for loue of owre Lorde lyueden ful streyte,
In hope forto haue heueneriche blisse;
As ancres and heremites that holden hem in here selles,
And coueiten nought in contre to kairen aboute,
For no likerous liflode her lykam to plese.   30

   And somme chosen chaffare; they cheuen the bettere,
As it semeth to owre syȝt that suche men thryueth;

I

And somme murthes to make as mynstralles conneth,
And geten gold with here glee giltles, I leue.
Ac iapers and iangelers, Iudas chylderen,   35
Feynen hem fantasies and foles hem maketh,
And han here witte at wille to worche, ȝif þei sholde;
That Poule precheth of hem I nel nought preue it here;
Qui turpiloquium loquitur etc. is Luciferes hyne.

Bidders and beggeres fast about ȝede   40
With her bely and her bagge of bred ful ycrammed;
Fayteden for here fode, fouȝten atte ale;
In glotonye, God it wote, gon hij to bedde,
And risen with ribaudye, tho roberdes knaues;
Slepe and sori sleuthe seweth hem eure.   45

Pilgrymes and palmers pliȝted hem togidere
To seke seynt Iames and seyntes in Rome.
Thei went forth in here wey with many wise tales,
And hadden leue to lye al here lyf after.
I seigh somme that seiden þei had ysouȝt seyntes: 50
To eche a tale þat þei tolde here tonge was tempred to lye
More þan to sey soth, it semed bi here speche.

Heremites on an heep, with hoked staues,
Wenten to Walsyngham, and here wenches after;
Grete lobyes and longe that loth were to swynke   55
Clotheden hem in copis, to ben knowen fram othere,
And shopen hem heremites here ese to haue.

I fonde þere freris, alle þe foure ordres,
Preched þe peple for profit of hemseluen,
Glosed þe gospel as hem good lyked,   60
For coueitise of copis construed it as þei wolde.
Many of þis maistres freris mowe clothen hem at lykyng,
For here money and marchandise marchen togideres.
For sith charite haþ be chapman and chief to shryue lordes
Many ferlis han fallen in a fewe ȝeris.   65
But holychirche and hij holde better togideres,
The most myschief on molde is mountyng wel faste.

þere preched a pardonere as he a prest were;
Brouȝte forth a bulle with bishopes seles,

2

And seide þat hymself myȝte assoilen hem alle
Of falshed of fastyng, of vowes ybroken.
   Lewed men leued hym wel and lyked his wordes;
Comen vp knelyng to kissen his bulles.
He bonched hem with his breuet and blered here eyes
And rauȝte with his ragman rynges and broches.   75
Thus þey geuen here golde glotones to kepe.
And leueth such loseles þat lecherye haunten.
Were þe bischop yblissed and worth bothe his eres,
His seel shulde nouȝt be sent to deceyue þe peple.
Ac it is nauȝt by þe bischop þat þe boy precheth,   80
For the parisch prest and þe pardonere parten þe siluer
That þe poraille of þe parisch sholde haue, ȝif þei nere.
   Persones and parisch prestes pleyned hem to þe bischop
þat here parisshes were pore sith þe pestilence tyme,
To haue a lycence and a leue at London to dwelle,   85
And syngen þere for symonye, for siluer is swete.
   Bischopes and bachelers, bothe maistres and doctours,
þat han cure vnder Criste and crounyng in tokne
And signe þat þei sholden shryuen here paroschienes,
Prechen and prey for hem, and þe pore fede,   90
Liggen in London in Lenten, an elles.
Somme seruen þe kyng and his siluer tellen;
In cheker and in chancerye chalengen his dettes
Of wardes and wardmotes, weyues and streyues.
   And some seruen as seruantz lordes and ladyes,   95
And in stede of stuwardes sytten and demen.
Here messe and here matynes and many of here oures
Arn don vndeuoutlych; drede is at þe laste
Lest Crist in constorie acorse ful manye.
I parceyued of þe power þat Peter had to kepe,   100
To bynde and to vnbynde as þe boke telleth;
How he it left wiþ loue, as owre Lorde hight:
Amonges foure vertues þe best of all vertues
þat cardinales ben called and closyng ȝatis,
þere Crist is in kyngdome to close and to shutte,   105
And to opne it to hem and heuene blisse shewe.

3

Ac of þe cardinales atte courte þat cauȝt of þat name
And power presumed in hem a pope to make,
To han þat power þat Peter hadde inpugnen I nelle:
For in loue and letterure þe eleccioun bilongeth—   110
Forþi I can and can nauȝte of courte speke more.

    þanne come þere a kyng, knyȝthod hym ladde,
Miȝt of þe comunes made hym to regne.
And þanne cam Kynde Wytte and clerkes he made
For to conseille þe kyng and þe comune saue.   115

    The kyng and knyȝthode and clergye bothe
Casten þat þe comune shulde hemself fynde.

    þe comune contreued of kynde witte craftes,
And for profit of alle þe poeple plowmen ordeygned
To tilie and trauaile as trewe lyf askeþ.   120
þe kynge and þe comune and kynde witte þe thridde
Shope lawe and lewte, eche man to knowe his owne.

    þanne loked vp a lunatik, a lene þing withalle,
And knelyng to þe kyng clergealy he seyde:
'Crist kepe þe, sire kyng and þi kyngriche,   125
And leue þe lede þi londe so leute þe louye,
And for þi riȝtful rewlyng be rewarded in heuene!'

    And sithen in þe eyre an hiegh an angel of heuene
Lowed to speke in Latyn—for lewed men ne coude
Iangle ne iugge þat iustifie hem shulde,   130
But suffren and seruen, forthi seyde þe angel:
'*Sum rex, sum princeps, neutrum fortasse deinceps;*
O qui iura regis Christi specialia regis,
Hoc quod agas melius iustus es, esto pius!
Nudum ius a te vestiri vult pietate;   135
Qualia vis metere talia grana sere.
Si ius nudatur nudo de iure metatur;
Si seritur pietas de pietate metas!'

    Thanne greued hym a goliardeys, a glotoun of wordes,
And to þe angel an heiȝ answeres after: 140
'*Dum rex a regere dicatur nomen habere,*
Nomen habet sine re nisi studet iura tenere.'

    And þanne gan alle þe comune crye in vers of Latin,

4

To þe kynges conseille, construe hoso wolde:
'*Precepta regis sunt nobis vincula legis.*'   145
  Wiþ þat ran þere a route of ratones at ones,
And smale mys myd hem mo þen a þousande,
And comen to a conseille for here comune profit:
For a cat of a courte cam whan hym lyked,
And ouerlepe hem ly3tlich and lau3te hem at his wille,   150
And pleyde wiþ hem perilouslych and possed hem aboute.
'For doute of dyuerse dredes we dar nou3te wel loke;
And 3if we grucche of his gamen he wil greue vs alle,
Cracche vs, or clowe vs and in his cloches holde,
That vs lotheth þe lyf or he lete vs passe.   155
My3te we wiþ any witte his wille withstonde,
We my3te be lordes aloft and lyuen at owre ese.'
  A raton of renon, most renable of tonge,
Seide for a souereygne help to hymselue:
'I haue ysein segges,' quod he, 'in þe cite of London   160
Beren bi3es ful bri3te abouten here nekkes,
And some colers of crafty werk; vncoupled þei wenden
Boþe in wareine and in waste where hem leue lyketh;
And otherwhile þei aren elleswhere, as I here telle.
Were þere a belle on here bei3, bi Iesu, as me thynketh,   165
Men my3te wite where þei went and awei renne!
And ri3t so,' quod þat ratoun, 'reson me sheweth
To bugge a belle of brasse or of bri3te syluer
And knitten on a colere for owre comune profit,
And hangen it vpon þe cattes hals; þanne here we mowen   170
Where he ritt or rest or renneth to playe.
And 3if him list for to laike þenne loke we mowen
And peren in his presence þerwhile hym plaie liketh,
And 3if him wrattheth be ywar and his weye shonye.'
  Alle þis route of ratones to þis reson þei assented.   175
Ac þo þe belle was ybou3t and on þe bei3e hanged,
þere ne was ratoun in alle þe route for alle þe rewme of
      Fraunce,
þat dorst haue ybounden þe belle aboute þe cattis nekke,
Ne hangen it aboute þe cattes hals, al Engelonde to wynne;

5

And helden hem vnhardy and here conseille feble, 180
And leten here laboure lost and alle here longe studye.
    A mous þat moche good couthe, as me thouȝte,
Stroke forth sternly and stode biforn hem alle,
And to þe route of ratones reherced þese wordes:
'Thouȝ we culled þe catte, ȝut sholde þer come another, 185
To cracchy vs and al owre kynde, þouȝ we croupe vnder
    benches.
Forþi I conseille alle þe comune to lat þe catte worthe,
And be we neuer so bolde þe belle hym to shewe.
For I herde my sire seyn, is seuene ȝere ypassed,
þere þe catte is a kitoun þe courte is ful elyng. 190
þat witnisseth holiwrite, whoso wil it rede:
        Ve terre vbi puer rex est, etc.
For may no renke þere rest haue for ratones bi nyȝte.
þe while he caccheþ conynges he coueiteth nouȝt owre caroyne,
But fet hym al with venesoun, defame we hym neuere.
For better is a litel losse þan a longe sorwe— 195
þe mase amonge vs alle þouȝ we mysse a schrewe.
For many mannus malt we mys wolde destruye,
And also ȝe route of ratones rende mennes clothes,
Nere þat cat of þat courte þat can ȝow ouerlepe.
For had ȝe rattes ȝowre wille ȝe couthe nouȝt reule ȝowre-
    selue. 200
I sey for me,' quod þe mous, 'I se so mykel after,
Shal neuer þe cat ne þe kitoun bi my conseille be greued,
Ne carpyng of þis coler þat costed me neure.
And þouȝ it had coste me catel biknowen it I nolde,
But suffre as hymself wolde to do as hym liketh, 205
Coupled and vncoupled, to cacche what thei mowe.
Forþi vche a wise wiȝte I warne wite wel his owne.'
    What þis meteles bemeneth, ȝe men þat be merye,
Deuine ȝe, for I ne dar, bi dere God in heuene!
    Ȝit houed þere an hondreth in houues of selke, 210
Seriauntȝ, it semed, þat serueden atte barre,
Plededen for penyes and poundes þe lawe,
And nouȝt for loue of owre Lorde vnlese here lippes onis.

6

þow myȝtest better mete þe myste on Maluerne hulles
þan gete a momme of here mouthe, but money were shewed.
   Barones an burgeis and bondemen als   216
I seiȝ in þis assemble, as ȝe shul here after;
Baxsteres and brewesteres and bochcres manye,
Wollewebsteres and weueres of lynnen,
Taillours and tynkeres and tolleres in marketes,   220
Masons and mynours and many other craftes.
Of alkin libbyng laboreres lopen forth somme,
As dykers and delueres þat doth here dedes ille
And dryuen forth þe longe day with '*dieu vous saue, dame
    Emme!*'
Cokes and here knaues crieden, 'hote pies, hote!   225
Gode gris and gess! go we dyne, go we!'
   Tauerners vntil hem tolde þe same:
'White wyn of Oseye and red wyn of Gascoigne!
Of þe Ryne and of þe Rochel, þe roste to defye'—
Al þis seiȝ I slepyng, and seuene sythes more.   230

Passus primus de visione

What this montaigne bymeneth and þe merke dale
And þe felde ful of folke, I shal ȝow faire schewe.
A loueli ladi of lere, in lynnen yclothed,
Come down fram a castel and called me faire,
And seide, 'Sone, slepestow? sestow þis poeple,   5
How bisi þei ben abouten þe mase?
þe moste partie of þis poeple þat passeth on þis erthe,
Haue þei worschip in þis worlde, þei wilne no better;
Of other heuene þan here holde þei no tale.'

I was aferd of her face, þeiȝ she faire were,   10
And seide, 'mercy, madame, what is þis to mene?'
'þe toure vp þe toft,' quod she, 'Treuthe is þereinne,
And wolde þat ȝe wrouȝte as his worde techeth;
For he is fader of feith, fourmed ȝow alle,
Bothe with fel and with face, and ȝaf ȝow fyue wittis   15
Forto worschip hym þerwith þe while þat ȝe ben here.
And þerfore he hyȝte þe erthe to help ȝow vchone
Of wollen, of lynnen, of lyflode at nede,
In mesurable manere to make ȝow at ese.

And comaunded of his curteisye in comune þree þinges;   20
Arne none nedful but þo, and nempne hem I thinke,
And rekne hem bi resoun; reherce þow hem after:
That one is vesture from chele þe to saue,
And mete atte mele for myseise of þiselue,
And drynke whan þow dryest; ac do nouȝt out of resoun,   25
That þow worth þe werse whan þow worche shuldest.
For Loth in his lifdayes for likyng of drynke
Dede bi his douȝtres þat þe deuel lyked;
Delited hym in drynke, as þe deuel wolde,
And lecherye hym lauȝt, and lay bi hem boþe;   30
And al he witt it wyn þat wikkede dede:
  Inebriamus eum vino, dormiamusque cum eo
  Vt seruare possimus de patre nostro semen.

8

Thorw wyn and þorw women þere was Loth acombred
And þere gat in glotonye gerlis þat were cherlis.
Forþi drede delitable drynke, and þow shalt do þe bettere;
Mesure is medcyne þouʒ þow moche ʒerne.   35
It is nauʒt al gode to þe goste þat þe gutte axeþ,
Ne liflode to þi likam þat leef is to þi soule.
Leue not þi likam, for a lyer him techeth,
That is þe wrecched worlde wolde þe bitraye.
For þe fende and þi flesch folweth þe togidere,   40
This and þat sueth þi soule and seith it in þin herte;
And for þow sholdest ben ywar I wisse þe þe beste.'
   'Madame, mercy,' quod I, 'me liketh wel ʒowre wordes,
Ac þe moneye of þis molde þat men so faste holdeth,
Telle me to whom, madame, þat tresore appendeth?'   45
   'Go to þe gospel,' quod she, 'þat God seide hymseluen,
Tho þe poeple hym apposed wiþ a peny in þe temple,
Whether þei shulde þerwith worschip þe kyng Sesar.
And God axed of hem of whome spake þe lettre,
And þe ymage ilyke þat þereinne stondeth   50
"Cesaris," þei seide, "we sen hym wel vchone."
"Reddite Cesari," quod God, "þat Cesari bifalleth.
Et que sunt dei, deo or elles ʒe done ille."
For riʒtful reson shulde rewle ʒowe alle,
And kynde witte be wardeyne, ʒowre welthe to kepe,   55
And tutour of ʒoure tresore and take it ʒow at nede:
For housbonderye and hij holden togideres.'
þanne I frained hir faire, for hym þat hir made:
'That dongeoun in þe dale þat dredful is of siʒte,
What may it be to mene, madame, I ʒow biseche?'   60
   'þat is þe castel of care; whoso cometh þerinne
May banne þat he borne was to body or to soule.
þerinne wonieth a wiʒte þat Wronge is yhote,
Fader of falshed, and founded it hymselue.
Adam and Eue he egged to ille,   65
Conseilled Caym to kullen his brother;
Iudas he iaped with Iuwen siluer,
And sithen on an eller honged hym after.

He is letter of loue and lyeth hem alle;
That trusten on his tresor bitrayeth he sonnest.'   70

   Thanne had I wonder in my witt what womman it were
þat such wise wordes of holy writ shewed,
And asked hir on þe hieʒe name, ar heo þennes ʒeode,
What she were witterli þat wissed me so faire?

   'Holicherche I am,' quod she, 'þow ouʒtest me to know;
I vnderfonge þe firste and þe feyth tauʒte,   76
And brouʒtest me borwes my biddyng to fulfille
And to loue me lelly þe while þi lyf dureth.'

   Thanne I courbed on my knees and cryed hir of grace,
And preyed hir pitousely prey for my synnes,   80
And also kenne me kyndeli on Criste to bileue,
That I miʒte worchen his wille þat wrouʒte me to man:
'Teche me to no tresore, but telle me þis ilke—
How I may saue my soule, þat seynt art yholden.'

   'Whan alle tresores aren tried,' quod she, 'trewthe is þe
     best;   85
I do it on *deus caritas* to deme þe soþe;
It is as derworth a drewery as dere God hymseluen.

   Whoso is trewe of his tonge and telleth none other,
And doth þe werkis þerwith and wilneth no man ille,
He is a god bi þe gospel agrounde and aloft   90
And ylike to owre Lorde, bi seynte Lukes wordes.

   þe clerkes þat knoweþ þis shulde kenne it aboute,
For cristene and vncristne clameþ it vchone.
Kynges and kniʒtes shulde kepe it bi resoun,
Riden and rappe down in reumes aboute,   95
And taken *trangressores* and tyen hem faste,
Til treuthe had ytermyned her trespas to þe ende.
And þat is þe professioun appertly þat appendeth for knyʒtes
And nouʒt to fasten a Fryday in fyue score wynter;
But holden wiþ him and with hir þat wolden al treuthe,   100
And neuer leue hem for loue ne for lacchyng of syluer.

   For Dauid in his dayes dubbed kniʒtes,
And did hem swere on here swerde to serue trewthe euere,
And whoso passed þat poynte was *apostata* in þe ordre.

But Criste, kingene kynge, kniȝted ten,
Cherubyn and seraphin, suche seuene and an othre,
And ȝaf hem myȝte in his maieste, þe muryer hem þouȝte;
And ouer his mene meyne made hem archangeles,
Tauȝte hem bi þe trinitee treuthe to knowe,
To be buxome at his biddyng; he bad hem nouȝte elles. 110
  Lucifer wiþ legiounes lerned it in heuene,
But for he brake buxumnesse his blisse gan he tyne,
And fel fro þat felawship in a fendes liknes
Into a depe derke helle, to dwelle þere for eure;
And mo þowsandes wiþ him þan man couthe noumbre 115
Lopen out wiþ Lucifer in lothelich forme,
For þei leueden vpon hym þat lyed in þis manere:
        '*Ponam pedem in aquilone, et similis ero altissimo.*'
  And alle þat hoped it miȝte be so, none heuene miȝte hem
        holde,
But fellen out in fendes liknesse nyne dayes toglderes
'Til God of his goodnesse gan stable and stynte 120
And garte þe heuene to stekye and stonden in quiete.
  Whan thise wikked went out, wonderwise þei fellen;
Somme in eyre, somme in erthe and somme in helle depe.
Ac Lucifer lowest lith of hem alle;
For pryde þat he pult out his peyne hath none ende. 125
And alle þat worche with wronge wenden hij shulle
After her deth-day and dwelle wiþ þat shrewe.
Ac þo þat worche wel, as holiwritt telleth,
And enden, as I ere seide, in treuthe, þat is þe best,
Mowe be siker þat her soule shal wende to heuene, 130
þer treuthe is in trinitee and troneth hem alle.
Forþi I sey, as I seide ere, bi siȝte of þise textis,
Whan alle tresores arne ytried treuthe is þe beste.
Lereth it þis lewde men, for lettred men it knowen,
þat treuthe is tresore þe triest on erþe.' 135
  'ȝet haue I no kynde knowing,' quod I, 'ȝet mote ȝe kenne
        me better,
By what craft in my corps it comseth, and where.'
  'þow doted daffe,' quod she, 'dulle arne þi wittes;

11

To litel Latyn þow lernedest, lede, in þi ȝouthe;
  Heu michi, quod sterilem duxi vitam iuuenilem!
    It is a kynde knowyng,' quod [s]he, 'þat kenneth in þine
      herte   140
    For to louye þi Lorde leuer þan þiselue;
    No dedly synne to do, dey þouȝ þow sholdest:
    This I trowe be treuthe; who can teche þe better,
    Loke þow suffre hym to sey and sithen lere it after.
      For thus witnesseth his worde, worche þow þereafter: 145
    For Trewthe telleþ þat loue is triacle of heuene;
    May no synne be on him sene þat vseth þat spise,
    And alle his werkes he wrouȝte with loue, as him liste,
    And lered it Moises for þe leuest þing and moste like to heuene,
    And also þe plante of pees, moste precious of vertues.   150
      For heuene myȝte nouȝte holden it, it was so heuy of hymself,
    Tyl it hadde of þe erthe yeten his fylle.
    And whan it haued of þis folde flesshe and blode taken
    Was neuere leef vpon lynde liȝter þerafter,
    And portatyf and persant as þe poynt of a nedle,   155
    That myȝte non armure it lette ne none heiȝ walles.
      Forþi is loue leder of þe lordes folke of heuene,
    And a mene, as þe maire is bitwene þe kyng and þe comune;
    Riȝt so is loue a ledere and þe lawe shapeth;
    Vpon man for his mysdedes þe merciment he taxeth.   160
    And, for to knowe it kyndely, it comseth bi myght,
    And in þe herte þere is þe heuede and þe heiȝ welle;
    For in kynde knowynge in herte þere a myȝte bigynneth,
    And þat falleth to þe fader þat formed vs alle,
    Loked on vs with loue and lete his sone deye   165
    Mekely for owre mysdedes, to amende vs alle.
    And ȝet wolde he hem no woo þat wrouȝte hym þat peyne,
    But mekelich with mouthe mercy he bisouȝte
    To haue pite of þat poeple þat peyned hym to deth.
      Here myȝtow see ensamples in hymselue one,   170
    That he was miȝtful and meke and mercy gan graunte
    To hem þat hongen him an heiȝ and his herte þirled.
      Forthi I rede ȝow riche: haueth reuthe of þe pouere;

Thouȝ ȝe be myȝtful to mote, beth meke in ȝowre werkes.
For þe same mesures þat ȝe mete, amys other elles,   175
Ȝe shullen ben weyen þerwyth whan ȝe wende hennes:
 Eadem mensura qua mensi fueritis, remecietur vobis.

For þouȝ ȝe be trewe of ȝowre tonge and trewliche wynne,
And as chaste as a childe þat in cherche wepeth,
But if ȝe louen lelliche and lene þe poure,
Such good as God ȝow sent godelich parteth,   180
Ȝe ne haue na more meryte in masse ne in houres
þan Malkyn of hire maydenhode þat no man desireth.

For Iames þe gentil iugged in his bokes
That faith withoute þe faite is riȝte no þinge worthi,
And as ded as a dore-tree but ȝif þe dedes folwe: 185
 Fides sine operibus mortua est, etc.
Forthi chastite withoute charite worth cheyned in helle;
It is as lewed as a laumpe þat no liȝte is inne.

Many chapeleynes arne chaste, ac charite is awey;
Aren no men auarousere þan hij whan þei ben auaunced;
Vnkynde to her kyn and to alle cristene,   190
Chewen here charite and chiden after more.
[Such chastite wiþouten charite worth cheyned in helle]

Many curatoures kepen hem clene of here bodies;
Thei ben acombred wiþ coueitise, þei konne nouȝt don it
  fram hem,
So harde hath auarice yhasped hem togideres.   195
And þat is no treuthe of þe trinite but treccherye of helle,
And lernyng to lewde men þe latter for to dele.

Forþi þis wordes ben wryten in þe gospel:
"*Date et dabitur vobis*: for I dele ȝow alle
And þat is þe lokke of loue and lateth oute my grace,   200
To conforte þe careful acombred wiþ synne."
Loue is leche of lyfe and nexte owre Lorde selue,
And also þe graith gate þat goth into heuene;

Forþi I sey, as I seide ere by [siȝte of] þe textis:
Whan alle tresores ben ytryed treuthe is þe beste.   205
Now haue I tolde þe what treuthe is, þat no tresore is bettere.
I may no lenger lenge þe with. Now loke þe owre Lorde!'

Passus II

Yet I courbed on my knees and cryed hir of grace,
And seide, 'mercy, madame, for Marie loue of heuene
That bar þat blisful barne þat bouȝte vs on þe rode,
Kenne me bi somme crafte to knowe þe fals.'

'Loke vppon þi left half, and lo, where he standeth,   5
Bothe Fals and Fauel and here feres manye!'

I loked on my left half as þe lady me taughte,
And was war of a womman wortheli yclothed,
Purfiled with pelure þe finest vpon erthe,
Ycrounede with a corone, þe kyng hath non better.   10
Fetislich hir fyngres were fretted with golde wyre,
And þereon red rubyes as red as any glede,
And diamantz of derrest pris, and double manere safferes,
Orientales and ewages, enuenymes to destroye.
Hire robe was ful riche, of red scarlet engreyned,   15
With ribanes of red golde and of riche stones.
Hire arraye me rauysshed, suche ricchesse saw I neuere;
I had wondre what she was and whas wyf she were.

'What is þis womman,' quod I, 'so worthily atired?'
'That is Mede þe mayde,' quod she, 'hath noyed me ful oft,   20
And ylakked my lemman þat Lewte is hoten,
And bilowen hire to lordes þat lawes han to kepe.
In þe popis paleys she is pryue as myself;
But sothenesse wolde nouȝt so for she is a bastarde.
For Fals was hire fader, þat hath a fykel tonge   25
And neuere sothe seide sithen he come to erthe,
And Mede is manered after hym, riȝte as kynde axeth:
   Qualis pater, talis filius; bona arbor bonum fructum facit.
I auȝte ben herre þan she, I cam of a better:
Mi fader þe grete God is and grounde of alle graces,
O God withoute gynnynge, and I his gode douȝter;   30
And hath ȝoue me Mercy to marye with myself;
And what man be merciful and lelly me loue,

14

Schal be my lorde and I his leef in þe heiȝe heuene.
And what man taketh Mede, myne hed dar I legge,
That he shal lese for hir loue a lappe of *caritatis.* 35

How construeth Dauid þe kynge of men þat taketh Mede,
And men of þis molde þat meynteneth treuthe,
And how ȝe shal saue ȝowself, þe sauter bereth witnesse:
    Domine, quis habitabit in tabernaculo tuo? etc.
And now worth þis Mede ymaried al to a mansed schrewe,
To one Fals Fikel-tonge, a fendes biȝete; 40
Fauel þorw his faire speche hath þis folke enchaunted,
And al is Lyeres ledyng þat she is þus ywedded.

Tomorwe worth ymade þe maydenes bruydale,
And þere miȝte þow wite, if þow wolt, which þei ben alle
That longeth to þat lordeship, þe lasse and þe more. 45
Knowe hem þere, if þow canst, and kepe þi tonge,
And lakke hem nouȝt, but lat hem worth til Lewte be iustice
And haue powere to punyschen hem; þanne put forth þi
    resoun.

Now I bikenne þe Criste,' quod she, 'and his clene moder,
And lat no conscience acombre þe for coueitise of mede.' 50
    Thus left me þat lady liggyng aslepe,
And how Mede was ymaried in meteles me þouȝte,
þat alle þe riche retenauns þat regneth with þe false
Were boden to þe bridale on bothe two sydes,
Of alle maner of men, þe mene and þe riche. 55
To marie þis maydene was many man assembled:
As of kniȝtes and of clerkis and other comune poeple,
As sysours and sompnours, shireues and here clerkes,
Bedelles and bailliues and brokoures of chaffare,
Forgoeres and vitaillers and vokates of þe Arches; 60
I can nouȝt rekene þe route þat ran aboute Mede.

    Ac Symonye and Cyuile and sisoures of courtes
Were moste pryue with Mede of any men, me þouȝte.
Ac Fauel was þe first þat fette hire out of boure,
And as a brokour brouȝte hir to be with Fals enioigned. 65
Whan Symonye and Cyuile seiȝ here beire wille,
Thei assented for siluer to sei as bothe wolde.

15

Thanne lepe Lyer forth, and seide, 'lo, here a chartre
That Gyle with his gret othes gaf hem togidere,'
And preide Cyuile to se and Symonye to rede it.   70
Thanne Symonye and Cyuile stonden forth bothe,
And vnfoldeth þe feffement þat Fals hath ymaked.
And þus bigynneth þes gomes to greden ful heiȝ:
          'Sciant presentes et futuri, etc.

Witeth and witnesseth þat wonieth vpon þis erthe,
þat Mede is ymaried more for here goodis   75
þan for ani vertue or fairenesse or any free kynde.
Falsenesse is faine of hire for he wote hire riche;
And Fauel with his fikel speche feffeth bi þis chartre
To be prynces in pryde and pouerte to dispise,
To bakbite and to bosten and bere fals witnesse,   80
To scorne and to scolde and sclaundere to make,
Vnboxome and bolde to breke þe ten hestes;
     And þe erldome of Enuye and Wratthe togideres,
With þe chastelet of Chest-and-chateryng-oute-of-resoun,
þe counte of Coueitise and alle þe costes aboute,   85
That is, vsure and auarice—alle I hem graunte,
In bargaines and in brokages, with al þe borghe of theft;
And al þe lordeschip of Lecherye in lenthe and in brede,
As in werkes and in wordes and waitynges with eies,
And in wedes and in wisshynges and with ydel thouȝtes,   90
There as wille wolde and werkmanship failleth'.

     Glotonye he gaf hem eke and grete othes togydere,
And alday to drynke at dyuerse tauernes,
And there to iangle and to iape and iugge here euenecristene,
And in fastyng-dayes to frete ar ful tyme were.   95
And þanne to sitten and soupen til slepe hem assaille,
And breden as burghswyn and bedden hem esily
Tyl sleuth and slepe slyken his sides;
And þanne wanhope to awake hym so with no wille to amende,
For he leueth be lost—þis is here last ende.   100
     And þei to haue and to holde, and here eyres after,
A dwellyng with þe deuel and dampned be for eure,
Wiþ al þe purtenaunces of purgatorie into þe pyne of helle.

Ʒeldyng for þis þinge at one Ʒeres ende
Here soules to Sathan, to suffre with hym peynes,   105
And with him to wonye with wo whil God is in heuene.

   In witnesse of which þing Wronge was þe first,
And Pieres þe pardonere of Paulynes doctrine,
Bette þe bedel of Bokynghamshire,
Rainalde þe reue of Rotland sokene,   110
Munde þe mellere and many moo other.
'In þe date of þe deuil þis dede I assele,
Bi siƷte of sire Simonye and Cyuyles leye.'

   þenne tened hym Theologye whan he þis tale herde,
And seide to Cyuile: 'now sorwe mot þow haue,   115
Such weddynges to worche to wratthe with Treuthe;
And ar þis weddyng be wrouƷte, wo þe bityde!

   For Mede is moylere of amendes engendred,
And God graunteth to gyf Mede to Treuthe,
And þow hast gyuen hire to a gyloure. Now God gyf þe
      sorwe!   120
Thi tixt telleth þe nouƷt so, Treuthe wote þe sothe:
For *dignus est operarius* his hyre to haue,
And þow hast fest hire to Fals; fy on þi lawe!
For al by lesynges þow lyuest, and lecherouse werkes;
Symonye and þiself schenden holicherche;   125
þe notaries and Ʒee noyeth þe peple.
Ʒe shul abiggen it bothe, bi God þat me made!
Wel Ʒe witen, wernardes, but if Ʒowre witte faille,
That Fals is faithlees and fikel in his werkes,
And was a bastarde ybore, of Belsabubbes kynne.   130
And Mede is moylere, a mayden of gode,
And myƷte kisse þe kynge for cosyn, an she wolde.

   Forþi worcheth bi wisdome and bi witt also,
And ledeth hire to Londoun þere lawe is yshewed,
If any lawe wil loke þei ligge togederes.   135
And þouƷ iustices iugge hir to be ioigned with Fals,
Ʒet beth war of weddyng: for witty is Truthe,
And Conscience is of his conseille and knoweth Ʒow vchone;
And if he fynde Ʒow in defaute and with þe fals holde,

It shal bisitte ȝowre soules ful soure atte laste!'   140
  Hereto assenteth Cyuile; ac Symonye ne wolde,
Tyl he had siluer for his seruise, and also þe notaries.
  Thanne fette Fauel forth floreynes ynowe,
And bad Gyle to gyue golde al aboute,
And namelich to þe notaries þat hem none ne faille,   145
And feffe false-witnes with floreines ynowe—
'For he may Mede amaistrye and maken at my wille.'
  Tho þis golde was gyue grete was þe þonkynge
To Fals and to Fauel for her faire ȝiftes,
And comen to conforte fram care þe Fals,   150
And seiden, 'certis, sire, cesse shal we neuere
Til Mede be þi wedded wyf þorw wittis of vs alle.
For we haue Mede amaistried with owre mery speche,
That she graunteth to gon with a gode wille
To Londoun to loke ȝif þat þe lawe wolde   155
Iugge ȝow ioyntly in ioye for euere.'
  Thanne was Falsenesse fayne, and Fauel as blithe,
And leten sompne alle segges in schires aboute,
And bad hem alle be bown, beggeres and othere,
To wenden wyth hem to Westmynstre to witnesse þis dede.
  Ac þanne cared þei for caplus to kairen hem þider,   161
And Fauel fette forth þanne folus ynowe;
And sette Mede vpon a schyreue shodde al newe,
And Fals sat on a sisoure þat softlich trotted,
And Fauel on a flaterere, fetislich atired.   165
  Tho haued notaries none; annoyed þei were,
For Symonye and Cyuile shulde on hire fete gange.
  Ac þanne swore Symonye and Cyuile bothe
That sompnoures shulde be sadled and serue hem vchone—
'And lat apparaille þis prouisoures in palfreis wyse;   170
Sir Symonye hymseluen shal sitte vpon here bakkes.
Denes and suddenes drawe ȝow togideres,
Erchdekenes and officiales and alle ȝowre regystreres,
Lat sadel hem with siluer, owre synne to suffre,
As auoutrie and deuorses and derne vsurye,   175
To bere bischopes aboute abrode in visytynge.

Paulynes pryues, for pleyntes in þe consistorie,
Shul serue myself þat Cyuile is nempned;
And cartesadel þe comissarie; owre carte shal he lede
And fecchen vs vytailles at *fornicatores*;   180
And maketh of Lyer a longe carte to lede alle þcse othere,
As freres and faitours þat on here fete rennen.'
And thus Fals and Fauel fareth forth togideres,
And Mede in þe myddes and alle þise men after.

I haue no tome to telle þe taille þat hem folweth,   185
Of many maner man þat on þis molde libbeth;
Ac Gyle was forgoer and gyed hem alle.

Sothenesse seiȝ hym wel and seide but a litel,
And priked his palfrey and passed hem alle,
And come to þe kynges courte and Conscience it tolde,   190
And Conscience to þe kynge carped it after.

'Now, by Cryst,' quod þe kynge, 'and I cacche myȝte
Fals or Fauel or any of his feres,
I wolde be wroke of þo wrecches þat worcheth so ille,
And don hem hange by þe hals and alle þat hem meynteneth!
Shal neure man of molde meynprise þe leste,   196
But riȝte as þe lawe wil loke late falle on hem alle.'
And comanded a constable þat come atte furst,
To attache þo tyrauntz—'for eny thynge, I hote,
And fettereth fals Falsenesse for enykynnes ȝiftes,   200
And gurdeth of Gyles hed and lat hym go no furthere.
And ȝif ȝe lacche lyer late hym nouȝt ascapen
Er he be put on þe pilorye, for eny preyere, I hote;
And bryngeth Mede to me maugre hem alle.'

Drede atte dore stode and þe dome herde,   205
And how þe kynge comaunded constables and seriantz
Falsenesse and his felawschip to fettren an to bynden.
þanne Drede went wiȝtliche and warned þe Fals,
And bad hym flee for fere and his felawes alle.

Falsenesse for fere þanne fleiȝ to þe freres,   210
And Gyle doþ hym to go agast for to dye.
Ac marchantz mette with hym and made hym abide,
And bishetten hym in here shope to shewen here ware,

19

And apparailled hym as a prentice þe poeple to serue.

Liȝtliche Lyer lepe awey þanne,   215
Lorkynge thorw lanes, tolugged of manye.
He was nawhere welcome for his manye tales,
Oueral yhowted and yhote trusse,
Tyl pardoneres haued pite and pulled hym into house.
They wesshen hym and wyped hym and wonden hym in
    cloutes,   220
And sente hym with seles on Sondayes to cherches,
And gaf pardoun for pens poundmel aboute.
Thanne loured leches, and lettres þei sent,
That he sholde wonye with hem, wateres to loke.
Spiceres spoke with hym to spien here ware,   225
For he couth of here craft and knewe many gommes.
Ac mynstralles and messageres mette with hym ones,
And helden hym an half-ȝere and elleuene dayes.
Freres with faire speche fetten hym þennes,
And for knowyng of comeres coped hym as a frere.   230
Ac he hath leue to lepe out as oft as hym liketh,
And is welcome whan he wil and woneth wyth hem oft.

   Alle fledden for fere and flowen into hernes,
Saue Mede þe mayde na mo durst abide.
Ac trewli to telle she trembled for drede,
And ek wept and wronge whan she was attached.   236

Passus tercius

Now is Mede þe mayde, and namo of hem alle,
With bedellus and wiþ bayllyues brou3t bifor þe kyng.
The kyng called a clerke—can I nou3t his name—
To take Mede þe mayde and make hire at ese:
'I shal assaye hir myself and sothelich appose   5
What man of þis molde þat hire were leueste.
And if she worche bi my witte and my wille folwe,
I wil forgyue hir þis gilte, so me God help!'

   Curteysliche þe clerke þanne, as þe kyng hight,
Toke Mede bi þe middel and brou3te hir into chaumbre,   10
And þere was myrthe and mynstralcye, Mede to plese.

   They þat wonyeth in Westmynstre worschiped hir alle;
Gentelliche wiþ ioye þe iustices somme
Busked hem to þe boure þere þe birde dwelled,
To conforte hire kyndely by clergise leue,   15
Ane seiden, 'mourne nought, Mede ne make þow no sorwe,
For we wil wisse þe kynge and þi wey shape,
To be wedded at þi wille and where þe leue liketh,
For al Conscience caste or craft, as I trowe!'

   Mildeliche Mede þanne mercyed hem alle   20
Of þeire gret goodnesse and gaf hem vchone
Coupes of clene golde and coppis of siluer,
Rynges with rubies, and ricchesses manye;
The leste man of here meyne a motoun of golde.
Thanne lau3te þei leue, þis lordes, at Mede.   25

   With that comen clerkis to conforte hir þe same,
And beden hire be blithe: 'for we beth þine owne,
For to worche þi wille þe while þow my3te laste.'
Hendeliche heo þanne bihight hem þe same—
'To loue 3ow lelli and lordes to make,   30
And in þe consistorie atte courte do calle 3owre names;
Shal no lewdnesse lette þe leode þat I louye
That he ne worth first auanced: for I am biknowen

21

þere konnyng clerkes shul clokke bihynde.'
    þanne come þere a confessoure coped as a frere;   35
To Mede þe mayde he mellud þis wordes,
And seide ful softly, in shrifte as it were,
'Theiȝ lewed men and lered men had leyne bi þe bothe,
And falsenesse haued yfolwed þe al þis fyfty wyntre,
I shal assoille þe myselue for a seme of whete,   40
And also be þi bedeman and bere wel þi message
Amonges kniȝtes and clerkis, Conscience to torne.'

    Thanne Mede for here mysdedes to þat man kneled,
And shroue hire of hire shrewednesse, shamelees, I trowe;
Tolde hym a tale and toke hym a noble,   45
Forto ben hire bedeman and hire brokour als.

    Thanne he assoilled hir sone and sithen he seyde:
'We han a wyndowe a wirchyng wil sitten vs wel heigh;
Woldestow glase þat gable and graue þereinne þi name,
Siker sholde þi soule be heuene to haue.'   50
'Wist I that,' quod þat womman, 'I wolde nouȝt spare
For to be ȝowre frende, frere, and faille ȝow neure
Whil ȝe loue lordes þat lechery haunteþ,
And lakkeþ nouȝt ladis þat loueþ wel þe same.
It is a frelete of flesche, ȝe fynde it in bokes,   55
And a course of kynde, wherof we komen alle;
Who may scape þe sklaundre, þe scaþe is sone amended;
It is synne of þe seuene sonnest relessed.
Haue mercy', quod Mede, 'of men þat it haunte,
And I shal keure ȝowre kirke, ȝowre cloystre do maken,   60
Wowes do whiten and wyndowes glasen,
Do peynten and purtraye and paye for þe makynge,
That eury segge shal seyn I am sustre of ȝowre hous.'

    Ac God to alle good folke suche grauynge defendeth,
To writen in wyndowes of here wel dedes,   65
On auenture pruyde be peynted þere and pompe of þe worlde:
For Crist knoweþ þi conscience and þi kynde wille,
And þi coste and þi coueitise and who þe catel ouȝte.
Forþi I lere ȝow, lordes, leueþ suche werkes,
To writen in wyndowes of ȝowre wel dedes,   70

Or to greden after Goddis men whan ȝe delen doles,
An auenture ȝe han ȝowre hire here and ȝoure heuene als:
   Nesciat sinistra quid faciat dextra.
Lat nouȝte þi left half, late ne rathe,
Wyte what þow worchest with þi riȝt syde;
For þus bit þe gospel gode men do here almesse.   75
Meires and maceres that menes ben bitwene
þe kynge and þe comune to kepe þe lawes,
To punyschen on pillories and pynynge-stoles
Brewesteres and bakesteres, bocheres and cokes:
For þise aren men on þis molde þat moste harme worcheth
To þe pore peple þat parcel-mele buggen.   81
For they poysoun þe peple priueliche and oft;
Thei rychen þorw regraterye and rentes hem buggen
With þat þe pore people shulde put in here wombe:
For, toke þei on trewly, þei tymbred nouȝt so heiȝe,   85
Ne bouȝte non burgages, be ȝe ful certeyne.

   Ac Mede þe mayde þe maire hath bisouȝte
Of alle suche sellers syluer to take,
Or presentz withoute pens, as peces of siluer,
Ringes or other ricchesse, þe regrateres to maynetene.   90
'For my loue,' quod that lady, 'loue hem vchone,
And soffre hem to selle somdele aȝeins resoun.'

   Salamon þe sage a sarmoun he made,
For to amende maires and men þat kepen lawes,
And tolde hem þis teme þat I telle thynke: 95
   Ignis deuorabit tabernacula eorum qui libenter accipiunt
     munera, etc.
Amonge þis lettered ledes þis Latyn is to mene
That fyre shal falle and brenne al to blo askes
The houses and þe homes of hem þat desireth
Ȝiftes or ȝeresȝyues bicause of here offices.

   The kynge fro conseille cam and called after Mede,   100
And ofsent hir alswythe with seriauntes manye,
That brouȝten hir to bowre with blisse and with ioye.

   Curteisliche þe kynge þanne comsed to telle,
To Mede þe mayde melleth þise wordes:

23

'Vnwittily, womman, wrou3te hastow oft,   105
Ac worse wrou3testow neure þan þo þow Fals toke.
But I forgyue þe þat gilte and graunte þe my grace;
Hennes to þi deth day do so namore!

   I haue a kny3te, Conscience, cam late fro bi3unde;
3if he wilneth þe to wyf, wyltow hym haue?'   110
'3e, lorde,' quod þat lady, 'Lorde forbede elles!
But I be holely at 3owre heste, lat hange me sone!'

   And þanne was Conscience calde to come and appiere
Bifor þe kynge and his conseille, as clerkes and othere.
Knelynge, Conscience to þe kynge louted,   115
To wite what his wille were and what he do shulde.

   'Woltow wedde þis womman,' quod þe kynge, '3if I wil
    assente?
For she is fayne of þi felawship, for to be þi make.'

   Quod Conscience to þe kynge: 'Cryst it me forbede!
Ar I wedde suche a wyf, wo me bityde!   120
For she is frele of hir feith, fykel of here speche,
And maketh men mysdo many score tymes;
Truste of hire tresore treieth ful manye.
Wyues and widewes wantounes she techeth,
And lereth hem leccherye that loueth hire 3iftes.   125
3owre fadre she felled þorw fals biheste,
And hath apoysounde popis, peired holicherche.
Is nau3t a better baude, bi hym þat me made,
Bitwene heuene and helle, in erthe þough men sou3te.
For she is tikil of hir taile, talwis of hir tonge,   130
As comune as a cartwey to eche a knaue þat walketh,
To monkes, to mynstralles, to meseles in hegges.
Sisoures and sompnoures, suche men hir preiseth;
Shireues of shires were shent 3if she nere,
For she doþ men lese here londe and here lyf bothe.   135
She leteth passe prisoneres and payeth for hem ofte,
And gyueth þe gailers golde and grotes togideres
To vnfettre þe fals, fle where hym lyketh;
And takeþ þe trewe bi þe toppe and tieth hym faste,
And hangeth hym for hatred þat harme dede neure.   140

To be cursed in consistorie she counteth nouȝte a russhe:
For she copeth þe comissarie and coteth his clerkis;
She is assoilled as sone as hirself liketh,
And may neiȝe as moche do in a moneth one
As ȝowre secret seel in syx score dayes.   145
For she is priue with þe pope—prouisoures it knoweth,
For sire Symonye and hirselue seleth hire bulles.

She blesseth þise bisshopes, þeiȝe þey be lewed,
Prouendreth persones and prestes meynteneth,
To haue lemmannes and lotebies alle here lif-dayes,   150
And bringen forth barnes aȝein forbode lawes.
There she is wel with þe kynge wo is þe rewme,
For she is fauorable to the fals and fouleth trewthe ofte.

Bi Ihesus, with here ieweles ȝowre iustices she shendeth,
And lith aȝein þe lawe and letteth hym þe gate,   155
That feith may nouȝte haue his forth, here floreines go so þikke.
She ledeth þe lawe as hire list and louedayes maketh,
And doth men lese þorw hire loue þat lawe myȝte wynne.
þe mase for a mene man, þouȝ he mote hir euere!
Lawe is so lordeliche and loth to make ende,   160
Withoute presentz or pens she pleseth wel fewe.

Barounes and burgeys she bryngeth in sorwe,
And alle þe comune in kare þat coueyten lyue in trewthe;
For clergye and coueitise she coupleth togideres.
þis is þe lyf of that lady. Now Lorde ȝif hir sorwe!   165
And alle that meynteneth here men, meschaunce hem bityde!
For pore men mowe haue no powere to pleyne hem þouȝ þei
    smerte;
Suche a maistre is Mede amonge men of gode.'

Thanne morned Mede and mened hire to the kynge
To haue space to speke, spede if she myȝte.   170

The kynge graunted hir grace with a gode wille:
'Excuse þe, ȝif þow canst. I can namore seggen,
For Conscience acuseth þe to congey þe for euere.'

'Nay, lorde,' quod þat lady, 'leueth hym þe worse,
Whan ȝe wyten witterly where þe wronge liggeth;   175
There þat myschief is grete mede may helpe.

And þow knowest, Conscience, I cam nouȝt to chide,
Ne depraue þi persone with a proude herte.
Wel þow wost, wernard, but ȝif þow wolt gabbe,
þow hast hanged on myne half elleuene tymes,   180
And also griped my golde, gyue it where þe liked;
And whi þow wratthest þe now wonder me thynketh.
Ȝit I may, as I myȝte, menske þe with ȝiftes,
And mayntene þi manhode more þan þow knoweste.

Ac þow hast famed me foule bifor þe kynge here   185
For kulled I neuere no kynge ne conseilled þerafter,
Ne dede as þow demest; I do it on þe kynge!
    In Normandye was he nouȝte noyed for my sake;
Ac þow þiself sothely shamedest hym ofte,
Crope into a kaban for colde of þi nailles,   190
Wendest þat wyntre wolde haue lasted euere,
And draddest to be ded for a dym cloude,
And hiedest homeward for hunger of þi wombe.
    Wiþout pite, piloure, pore men þow robbedest,
And bere here bras at þi bakke to Caleys to selle.   195
There I lafte with my lorde his lyf for to saue,
I made his men meri and mornyng lette.
I batered hem on þe bakke and bolded here hertis,
And dede hem hoppe for hope to haue me at wille.
Had I ben marschal of his men, bi Marie of heuene!   200
I durst haue leyde my lyf, and no lasse wedde,
He shulde haue be lorde of þat londe a lengthe and a brede,
And also kyng of þat kitthe his kynne for to helpe,
þe leste brolle of his blode a barounes pere!
Cowardliche þow, Conscience, conseiledst hym þennes,   205
To leuen his lordeship for a litel siluer,
That is þe richest rewme þat reyne ouer houeth!
    It bicometh to a kynge þat kepeth a rewme
To ȝiue mede to men þat mekelich hym serueth,
To alienes and to alle men, to honoure hem with ȝiftes;   210
Mede maketh hym biloued and for a man holden.
Emperoures and erlis and al manere lordes
For ȝiftes han ȝonge men to renne and to ride.

The pope and alle prelatis presentz vnderfongen,
And medeth men hemseluen to meyntene here lawes.   215
Seruauntz for her seruise, we seth wel þe sothe,
Taken mede of herc maistre as þei mowe acorde.
Beggeres for here biddynge bidden men mcde;
Mynstralles for here murthe mede þei aske.
þe kynge hath mede of his men to make pees in londe.   220
Men þat teche chyldren craue of hem mede,
Prestis þat precheth þe poeple to gode asken mede
And masse-pans and here mete at þe mele tymes.
Alkynnes crafty men crauen mede for here prentis;
Marchauntz and mede mote nede go togideres;   225
No wiȝte, as I wene, withoute mede may libbe.'

Quod þe kynge to Conscience, 'bi Criste, as me thynketh,
Mede is wel worthi þe maistrye to haue'.

'Nay,' quod Conscience to þe kynge, and kneled to þe erthe,
'There aren two manere of medes, my lorde, with ȝowre leue.   230
þat one, God of his grace graunteth in his blisse
To þo þat wel worchen whil þei ben here.
The prophete precheth þerof and put it in þe sautere:
   Domine, quis habitabit in tabernaculo tuo?
"Lorde, who shal wonye in þi wones and with þine holi seyntes,
Or resten on þi holy hilles?". þis asketh Dauid;   235
   And Dauyd assoileth it hymsclf, as þe sauter telleth:
   "*Qui ingreditur sine macula, et operatur iusticiam*:
Tho þat entren of o colour and of on wille,
And han wrouȝte werkis with riȝte and with reson;
And he þat ne vseth nauȝte þe lyf of vsurye,
And enfourmeth pore men and pursueth treuthe: 240
   *Qui pecuniam suam non dedit ad vsuram, et munera super
   innocentem, etc.;*
And alle þat helpeth þc innocent and halt with þe riȝtful,
Withoute mede doth hem gode and þe trewthe helpeth"—
Suche manere men, my lorde, shal haue þis furst mede
Of God at a grete nede whan þei gone hennes.

There is another mede, mesurelees, þat maistres desireth:
To meyntene mysdoers mede þei take;   246

27

And þereof seith þe sauter in a salmes ende:

> *In quorum manibus iniquitates sunt, dextera eorum repleta*
> *est muneribus;*

And he þat gripeth her golde, so me God helpe!
Shal abie it bittere, or þe boke lyeth.

Prestes and persones þat plesynge desireth,   250
That taketh mede and mone for messes þat þei syngeth,
Taketh here mede here as Mathew vs techeth:

> *Amen, amen, receperunt mercedem suam.*

That laboreres and lowe folke taketh of her maistres,
It is no manere mede but a mesurable hire.
In marchandise is no mede, I may it wel avowe;   255
It is a permutacioun apertly, a penyworth for an othre.

Ac reddestow neuere *Regum*, þow recrayed Mede,
Whi þe veniaunce fel on Saul and on his children?
God sent to Saul bi Samuel þe prophete
þat Agage of Amaleke and al his peple aftre   260
Shulde deye for a dede þat done had here eldres.

"Forþi," seid Samuel to Saul, "God hymself hoteth
The be boxome at his biddynge, his wille to fulfille:
Wende to Amalec with þyn oste, and what þow fyndest þere,
  slee it;
Biernes and bestes, brenne hem to ded;   265
Wydwes and wyues, wommen and children,
Moebles and vnmoebles and al þat þow myȝte fynde,
Brenne it, bere it nouȝte awey, be it neuere so riche,
For mede ne for mone; loke þow destruye it,
Spille it and spare it nouȝte; þow shalt spede þe bettere."   270

And for he coueyted her catel and þe kynge spared,
Forbare hym and his bestes bothe, as þe bible witnesseth,
Otherwyse þan he was warned of þe prophete,
God seide to Samuel þat Saul shulde deye,
And al his sede for þat synne shenfullich ende.   275
Such a myschief mede made Saul þe kynge to haue,
That God hated hym for euere and alle his eyres after.
The *culorum* of þis cas kepe I nouȝte to shewe;
An auenture it noyed men, none ende wil I make.

28

For so is þis worlde went wiþ hem þat han powere
That whoso seyth hem sothes is sonnest yblamed.

I, Conscience, knowe þis, for Kynde Witt me it tauʒte,
þat Resoun shal regne and rewmes gouerne;
And riʒte as Agag hadde, happe shul somme:
Samuel shal sleen hym, and Saul shal be blamed,   285
And Dauid shal be diademed and daunten hem alle,
And one cristene kynge kepen hem alle.

Shal na more Mede be maistre, as she is nouthe,
Ac Loue and Lowenesse and Lewte togederes,
þise shul be maistres on molde, Treuthe to saue.   290

And whoso trespasseth ayein Treuthe or taketh aʒein his wille,
Leute shal don hym lawe, and no lyf elles.
Shal no seriaunt for here seruyse were a silke howue,
Ne no pelure in his cloke for pledyng atte barre.

Mede of mysdoeres maketh many lordes,   295
And ouer lordes lawes reuleth þe rewmes.

Ac Kynde Loue shal come ʒit and Conscience togideres,
And make of lawe a laborere, suche loue shal arise,
And such a pees amonge þe peple and a perfit trewthe,
þat Iewes shal wene in here witte and waxen wonder glade
þat Moises or Messie be come into þis erthe,   301
And haue wonder in here hertis þat men beth so trewe.

Alle þat bereth baslarde, brode swerde or launce,
Axe other hachet or eny wepne ellis,
Shal be demed to þe deth but if he do it smythye   30;
Into sikul or to sithe to schare or to kulter:
      Conflabunt gladios suos in vomeres, etc.
Eche man to pleye with a plow, pykoys or spade,
Spynne, or sprede donge or spille hymself with sleuthe.

Prestes and persones with *placebo* to hunte,
And dyngen vpon Dauid eche a day til eue.   310
Huntynge or haukynge if any of hem vse,
His boste of his benefys worth bynome hym after.
Shal neither kynge ne knyʒte, constable ne meire,
Ouerlede þe comune ne to þe courte sompne,
Ne put hem in panel to don hem pliʒte here treuthe;   315

But after þe dede þat is don, one dome shal rewarde,
Mercy or no mercy, as Treuthe wil acorde.

Kynges courte and comune courte, consistorie and chapitele,
Al shal be but one courte, and one baroun be iustice;
That worth Trewe-tonge, a tidy man þat tened me neuere. 320
Batailles shal non be ne no man bere wepne,
And what smyth þat ony smytheth be smyte þerwith to dethe;
>   *Non leuabit gens contra gentem gladium, etc.*

And er þis fortune falle fynde men shal þe worste,
By syx sonnes and a schippe and half a shef of arwes;
And þe myddel of a mone shal make þe Iewes to torne, 325
And Saracenes for þat siȝte shulle synge *gloria in excelsis, etc.*,
For Makomet and Mede myshappe shal þat tyme:
>   For *melius est bonum nomen quam diuicie multe.*'

Also wroth as þe wynde wex Mede in a while,
'I can no Latyn,' quod she, 'clerkis wote þe sothe.
Se what Salamon seith in Sapience bokes, 330
That hij þat ȝiueth ȝiftes þe victorie wynneth,
And moche worschip had þerwith, as holiwryt telleth:
>   *Honorem adquiret qui dat munera, etc.*'

'I leue wel, lady,' quod Conscience, 'þat þi Latyne be trewe;
Ac þow art like a lady þat redde a lessoun ones
Was, *omnia probate*, and þat plesed here herte, 335
For þat lyne was no lenger atte leues ende.
Had she loked þat other half and þe lef torned,
She shulde haue founden fele wordis folwyng þerafter:
Quod bonum est tenete; Treuthe þat texte made!

And so ferde ȝe, madame. Ȝe couthe namore fynde, 340
Tho ȝe loked on Sapience, sittynge in ȝoure studie.
Þis tixte þat ȝe han tolde were gode for lordes,
Ac ȝow failled a cunnyng clerke þat couthe þe lef haue torned.
And if ȝe seche Sapience eft fynde shal ȝe þat folweth
A ful teneful tixte to hem þat taketh mede, 345
And þat is, *animam autem aufert accipientium, etc.*:
And þat is þe taille of þe tixte of þat þat ȝe schewed,
þat, þeiȝe we wynne worschip and wiþ mede haue victorie,
þe soule þat þe sonde taketh bi so moche is bounde.'

'Cesseth,' seith þe kynge, 'I suffre ȝow no lengere.   **Passus**
Ȝe shal sauȝtne, forsothe, and serue me bothe.   **IV**
Kisse hir,' quod þe kynge, 'Conscience, I hote.'
 'Nay, bi Criste,' quod Conscience, 'congeye me for euere!
But Resoun rede me þerto, rather wil I deye!'   5
 'And I comaunde þe,' quod þe kynge to Conscience þanne,
'Rape þe to ride and Resoun þow fecche;
Comaunde hym þat he come my conseille to here.
For he shal reule my rewme and rede me þe beste,
And acounte with þe, Conscience, so me Cryst helpe,   10
How þow lernest þe peple, þe lered and þe lewede.'
 'I am fayne of þat forwarde' seyde þe freke þanne,
And ritt riȝte to Resoun and rowneth in his ere,
And seide as þe kynge badde and sithen toke his leue.
 'I shal arraye me to ride,' quod Resoun, 'reste þe a while'—
And called Catoun his knaue, curteise of speche,   16
And also Tomme Trewe-tonge-tell-me-no-tales-
Ne-lesyng-to-lawȝe-of-for-I-loued-hem-neuere:
'And sette my sadel vppon Suffre-til-I-se-my-tyme,
And lete warrok it wel with witty-wordes gerthes,   20
And hange on hym þe heuy brydel to holde his hed lowe,
For he wil make wche tweye er he be there.'
 Thanne Conscience vppon his caple kaireth forth faste,
And Resoun with hym rit, rownynge togideres
Whiche maistries Mede maketh on þis erthe.   25
 One Waryn Wisdom and Witty his fere
Folwed hem faste, for þei haued to done
In þe cheker and at þe chauncerie to be discharged of þinges;
And riden fast, for Resoun shulde rede hem þe beste,
For to saue hem, for siluer, fro shame and fram harmes. 30
 And Conscience knewe hem wel—þei loued coueitise—
And bad Resoun ride faste and recche of her noither:
'þere aren wiles in here wordes and with Mede þei dwelleth;

There as wratthe and wranglyng is, þere wynne þei siluer;
Ac þere is loue and lewte þei wil nouȝte come þere: 35
> Contricio et infelicitas in vijs eorum, etc.

þei ne gyueth nouȝte of God one gose wynge:
> Non est timor dei ante oculos eorum.

For, wot God, þei wolde do more for a dozeine chickenes,
Or as many cápones, or for a seem of otes,
þan for loue of owre Lorde or alle hise leue seyntes.
Forþi, Resoun, lete hem ride, þo riche, bi hemseluen,   40
For Conscience knoweth hem nouȝte ne Cryst, as I trowe.'
And þanne Resoun rode faste þe riȝte heiȝe gate,
As Conscience hym kenned, til þei come to þe kynge.

Curteisliche þe kynge þanne come aȝein Resoun,
And bitwene hymself and his sone sette hym on benche,   45
And wordeden wel wyseli a gret while togideres.

And þanne come Pees into parlement and put forth a bille,
How Wrong aȝeines his wille had his wyf taken,
And how he rauisshed Rose, Reginoldes loue,
And Margarete of hir maydenhode, maugre here chekis;   50
'Bothe my gees and my grys his gadelynges feccheth;
I dar nouȝte for fere of hym fyȝte ne chyde.
He borwed of me bayard, he brouȝte hym home neure,
Ne no ferthynge þerfore, for nauȝt I couthe plede.
He meyneteneth his men to morther myne hewen,   55
Forstalleth my feyres and fiȝteth in my chepynge,
And breketh vp my bernes dore and bereth aweye my whete,
And taketh me but a taile for ten quarteres of otes;
And ȝet he bet me þerto and lyth bi my mayde;
I nam nouȝte hardy for hym vneth to loke.'   60
The kynge knewe he seide sothe, for Conscience hym tolde
þat Wronge was a wikked luft and wrouȝte moche sorwe.

Wronge was afered þanne and Wisdome he souȝte
To make pees with his pens, and profered hym manye,
And seide, 'had I loue of my lorde þe kynge, litel wolde I
    recche,   65
Theiȝe Pees and his powere pleyned hym eure!'
þo wan Wisdome and sire Waryn þe witty,

For þat Wronge had ywrouȝt so wikked a dede,
And warned Wronge þo with such a wyse tale:
'Whoso worcheth bi wille wratthe maketh ofte;   70
I seye it bi þiself þow shalt it wel fynde.
But if Mede it make, þi myschief is vppe,
For bothe þi lyf and þi londe lyth in his grace.'

Thanne wowed Wronge Wisdome ful ȝerne,
To make his pees with his pens handi-dandi payed.   75
Wisdome and Witte þanne wenten togideres,
And toke Mede myd hem mercy to winne.

Pees put forþ his hed and his panne blody:
'Wythouten gilte, God it wote, gat I þis skaþe,
Conscience and þe comune knowen þe sothe.'   80

Ac Wisdom and Witt were about faste
To ouercome þe kyng with catel, ȝif þei myȝte.

Þe kynge swore bi Crist and bi his crowne bothe
þat Wronge for his werkis sholde wo þolyc,
And comaunded a constable to casten hym in yrens,   85
'And late hym nouȝte þis seuene ȝere seen his feet ones.'

'God wot,' quod Wysdom, 'þat were nauȝte þe beste;
And he amendes mowe make, late meynprise hym haue;
And be borwgh for his bale and biggen hym bote,
And so amende þat is mysdo, and euermore þe bettere.'   90

Witt acorded þerwith and seide þe same:
'Bettere is þat bote bale adoun brynge,
þan bale be ybette and bote neuere þe bettere.'

And þanne gan Mede to mengen here and mercy she bisought,
And profred Pees a present al of pure golde: 95
'Haue þis, man, of me,' quod she, 'to amende þi skaþe,
For I wil wage for Wronge he wil do so namore.'

Pitously Pees þanne prayed to þe kynge
To haue mercy on þat man þat mysdid hym so ofte:
'For he hath waged me wel as Wysdome hym tauȝte,   100
And I forgyue hym þat gilte with a goode wille,
So þat þe kynge assent, I can seye no bettere;
For Mede hath made me amendes, I may namore axe.'

'Nay,' quod þe kynge þo, 'so me Cryst helpe!

Wronge wendeth nouȝte so awaye arst wil I wite more: 105
For loupe he so liȝtly, laughen he wolde,
And efte þe balder be to bete myne hewen;
But Resoun haue reuthe on hym, he shal rest in my stokkes,
And þat as longe as he lyueth, but Lowenesse hym borwe.'

   Somme men redde Resoun þo to haue reuthe on þat
    schrewe,   110
And for to conseille þe kynge and Conscience after;
That Mede moste be meynpernour Resoun þei bisouȝte.

   'Rede me nouȝte,' quod Resoun, 'no reuthe to haue,
Til lordes and ladies louien alle treuthe,
And haten al harlotrye, to heren it, or to mouthen it;   115
Tyl Pernelles purfil be put in here hucche,
And childryn cherissyng be chastyng with ȝerdes,
And harlotes holynesse be holden for an hyne;
Til clerken coueitise be to clothe þe pore and to fede,
And religious romares *recordare* in here cloistres,   120
As seynt Benet hem bad, Bernarde and Fraunceys;
And til prechoures prechyng be preued on hemseluen;
Tyl þe kynges conseille be þe comune profyte;
Tyl bisschopes baiardes ben beggeres chambres,
Here haukes and her houndes helpe to pore religious;   125
And til seynt Iames be souȝte þere I shal assigne,
That no man go to Galis but if he go for euere;
And alle Rome-renneres for robberes of byȝende
Bere no siluer ouer see þat signe of kynge sheweþ,
Noyther graue ne vngraue, golde noither siluer,   130
Vppon forfeture of þat fee whoso fynt hym at Douere,
But if it be marchaunt or his man or messagere with letteres,
Prouysoure or prest or penaunt for his synnes.

   And ȝet,' quod Resoun, 'bi þe rode, I shal no reuthe haue
While Mede hath þe maistrye in þis moot-halle.   135
Ac I may shewe ensaumples, as I se otherwhile;
I sey it by myself,' quod he, 'and it so were
That I were kynge with crowne to kepen a rewme,
Shulde neuere wronge in þis worlde þat I wite myȝte,
Ben vnpunisshed in my powere, for peril of my soule!   140

Ne gete my grace for giftes, so me God saue!
Ne for no mede haue mercy but mekenesse it make.

For *nullum malum* þe man mette with *inpunitum*,
And badde *nullum bonum* be *irremuneratum*.
Late ȝowre confessoure, sire kynge, construe þis vnglosed;   145
And ȝif ȝe worken it in werke I wedde myne eres
That lawe shal ben a laborere and lede afelde donge,
And loue shal lede þi londe as þe lief lyketh'.

Clerkes þat were confessoures coupled hem togideres,
Alle to construe þis clause and for þe kynges profit,   150
Ac nouȝte for conforte of þe comune ne for þe kynges soule.

For I seiȝe Mede in the moot-halle on men of lawe wynke,
And þei lawghyng lope to hire, and lafte Resoun manye.

Waryn Wisdome wynked vppon Mede,
And seide, 'Madame, I am ȝowre man, what so my mouth
    iangleth;   155
I falle in floreines,' quod þat freke, 'an faile speche ofte.'

Alle riȝtful recorded þat Resoun treuthe tolde,
And Witt acorded þerwith and comended his wordes,
And þe moste peple in þe halle and manye of þe grete,
And leten Mekenesse a maistre and Mede a mansed schrewe.

Loue lete of hir liȝte and Lewte ȝit lasse,   161
And seide it so heiȝe þat al þe halle it herde:
'Whoso wilneth hir to wyf for welth of her godis,
But he be knowe for a kokewolde, kut of my nose!'

Mede mourned þo and made heuy chere,   165
For þe moste comune of þat courte called hire an hore.
Ac a sysoure and a sompnoure sued hir faste,
And a schireues clerke byschrewed al þe route.
'For ofte haue I,' quod he, 'holpe ȝow atte barre,
And ȝit ȝeue ȝe me neuere þe worthe of a russhe.'   170

The kynge called Conscience and afterwardes Resoun,
And recorded þat Resoun had riȝtfullich schewed,
And modilich vppon Mede with myȝte þe kynge loked,
And gan wax wrothe with lawe, for Mede almoste had shent it,
And seide, 'þorw ȝowre lawe, as I leue, I lese many chetes;
Mede ouer-maistrieth lawe and moche treuthe letteth.   176

Ac Resoun shal rekene with ȝow ȝif I regne any while,
And deme ȝow, bi þis day, as ȝe han deserued.
Mede shal nouȝte meynprise ȝow, bi þe Marie of heuene!
I wil haue leute in lawe and lete be al ȝowre ianglyng,   180
And, as moste folke witnesseth wel, Wronge shal be demed.'

Quod Conscience to þe kynge; 'but the comune wil assent,
It is ful hard, by myn hed, hereto to brynge it,
Alle ȝowre lige leodes to lede þus euene.'

'By hym þat rauȝte on þe rode', quod Resoun to þe kynge,
'But if I reule þus ȝowre rewme, rende out my ribbes!   186
Ȝif ȝe bidden buxomnes be of myne assente.'

'And I assent,' seith þe kynge, 'by seynte Marie my lady,
Be my conseille comen of clerkis and of erlis.
Ac redili, Resoun, þow shalt nouȝte ride fro me,   190
For as longe as I lyue lete þe I nelle.'

'I am aredy,' quod Resoun 'to reste with ȝow euere,
So Conscience be of owre conseille, I kepe no bettere.'
'And I graunt,' quod the kynge, 'Goddes forbode it faile!
Als longe as owre lyf lasteth lyue we togideres.'   195

Passus quintus de Visione

The kyng and his knightes to the kirke wente
To here matynes of þe day and þe masse after.
þanne waked I of my wynkynge and wo was withalle
þat I ne hadde sleped sadder and yseiȝen more.
Ac er I hadde faren a fourlonge feyntise me hente,   5
That I ne myȝte ferther afoot for defaute of slepynge;
And sat softly adown and seide my bileue,
And so I babeled on my bedes, þei brouȝte me aslepe.

And þanne saw I moche more, þan I bifore tolde,
For I say þe felde ful of folke þat I bifore of seyde,   10
And how Resoun gan arrayen hym, alle þe reume to preche,
And with a crosse afor þe kynge comsed þus to techen.

He preued þat þise pestilences were for pure synne,
And þe southwest wynde on Saterday at eucne
Was pertliche for pure pryde and for no poynt elles.   15
Piries and plomtrees were puffed to þe erthe,
In ensample, ȝe segges, ȝe shulden do þe bettere.
Beches and brode okes were blowen to þe grounde,
Torned vpward her tailles in tokenynge of drede,
þat dedly synne at domesday shal fordon hem alle.   20

Of þis matere I myȝte mamely ful longe,
Ac I shal seye as I saw, so me God helpe!
How pertly afor þe poeple Resoun gan to preche.

He bad Wastoure go worche what he best couthe,
And wynnen his wastyng with somme manere crafte.   25

And preyed Peronelle her purfyle to lete
And kepe it in hir cofre for catel at hire nede.

Thomme Stowue he tauȝte to take two staues,
And fecche Felice home fro þe wyuen pyne.

He warned Watt his wyf was to blame   30
þat hire hed was worth halue a marke, his hode nouȝte worth
    a grote.
And bad Bette kut a bow other tweyne,

And bete Betoun þerwith but if she wolde worche.
And þanne he charged chapmen to chasten her childeren:
'Late no wynnynge hem forweny whil þei be ʒonge,   35
Ne for no pouste of pestilence plese hem nouʒte out of resoun.

My syre seyde so to me, and so did my dame,
þat þe leuere childe þe more lore bihoueth,
And Salamon seide þe same, þat Sapience made:
          Qui parcit virge, odit filium.
þe Englich of þis Latyn is, whoso wil it knowe: 40
Whoso spareth þe sprynge spilleth his children.'

And sithen he preyed prelatz and prestes togideres—
'þat ʒe prechen to þe peple, preue it on ʒowreseluen,
And doth it in dede; it shal drawe ʒow to good;
If ʒe lyuen as ʒe leren vs we shal leue ʒow þe bettere.'   45

And sithen he radde religioun here reule to holde—
'Leste þe kynge and his conseille ʒowre comunes appayre,
And ben stuwardes of ʒowre stedes til ʒe be ruled bettre.'

And sithen he conseilled þe kynge þe comune to louye—
'It is þi tresore, if tresoun ne were, and triacle at þi nede.' 50
And sithen he prayed þe pope haue pite on holicherche,
And er he gyue any grace gouerne firste hymselue—
'And ʒe that han lawes to kepe, late treuthe be ʒowre coueytise,
More þan golde or other gyftes if ʒe wil God plese;
For whoso contrarieth treuthe, he telleth in þe gospel,   55
That God knoweth hym nouʒte, ne no seynte of heuene:
          Amen dico vobis, nescio vos.

And ʒe þat seke seynte Iames and seintes of Rome,
Seketh seynt treuthe for he may saue ʒow alle;
Qui cum patre et filio þat feire hem bifalle
þat suweth my sermon'; and þus seyde Resoun.   60

Thanne ran Repentance and reherced his teme,
And gert Wille to wepe water with his eyen.

Peronelle proude-herte platte hir to þe erthe,
And lay longe ar she loked and 'lorde, mercy!' cryed,
And byhiʒte to hym þat vs alle made   65
She shulde vnsowen hir serke and sette þere an heyre

To affaiten hire flesshe þat fierce was to synne;
'Shal neuere heiȝe herte me hente but holde me lowe,
And suffre to be myssayde—and so did I neuere.
But now wil I meke me and mercy biseche, 70
For al þis I haue hated in myne herte.'

þanne Lecchoure seyde 'allas!' and on owre lady he cryed,
To make mercy for his misdedes bitwene God and his soule,
With þat he shulde þe Saterday seuene ȝere þereafter,
Drynke but myd þe doke and dyne but ones. 75

Enuye with heuy herte asked after sc[h]rifte,
And carefullich *mea culpa* he comsed to shewe.
He was as pale as a pelet, in þe palsye he semed,
And clothed in a caurimaury, I couthe it nouȝte discreue;
In kirtel and kourteby and a knyf bi his syde; 80
Of a freres frokke were þe forsleues.
And as a leke hadde yleye longe in þe sonne,
So loked he with lene chekes, lourynge foule.
His body was tobolle for wratthe þat he bote his lippes,
And wryngynge he ȝede with þe fiste, to wreke hymself he
     þouȝte, 85
With werkes or with wordes whan he seighe his tyme.
Eche a worde þat he warpe was of an addres tonge,
Of chydynge and of chalangynge was his chief lyflode,
With bakbitynge and bismer and beryng of fals witnesse;
þis was al his curteisye where þat euere he shewed hym. 90
'I wolde ben yshryue,' quod þis schrewe, 'and I for shame
     durst;
I wolde be gladder, bi God, þat Gybbe had meschaunce,
Than þouȝe I had þis woke ywonne a weye of Essex chese.
I haue a neighbore neyȝe me; I haue ennuyed hym ofte
And lowen on hym to lordes to don hym lese his siluer, 95
And made his frendes ben his foon thorw my false tonge;
His grace and his good happes greueth me ful sore.
Bitwene many and many I make debate ofte,
þat bothe lyf and lyme is lost þorw my speche.

39

And whan I mete him in market þat I moste hate,   100
I hailse hym hendeliche as I his frende were:
For he is douʒtier þan I, I dar do non other.
Ac hadde I maystrye and myʒte, God wote my wille!

And whan I come to þe kirke and sholde knele to þe rode,
And preye for þe po[e]ple as þe prest techeth,   105
For pilgrimes and for palmers for alle þe poeple after,
þanne I crye on my knees þat Cryste ʒif hem sorwe
þat baren awey my bolle and my broke schete.

Awey fro þe auter þanne turne I myn eyghen,
And biholde how Eleyne hath a newe cote;   110
I wisshe þanne it were myne, and al þe webbe after.

And of mennes lesynge I laughe; þat liketh myn herte;
And for her wynnynge I wepe and waille þe tyme,
And deme þat hij don ille þere I do wel worse;
Whoso vndernymeth me hereof, I hate hym dedly after.   115
I wolde þat vche a wyght were my knaue,
For whoso hath more þan I, þat angreth me sore.
And þus I lyue louelees, lyke a luther dogge,
That al my body bolneth for bitter of my galle.

I myʒte nouʒte eet many ʒeres as a man ouʒte,   120
For enuye and yuel wille is yuel to defye.
May no sugre ne swete þinge asswage my swellynge,
Ne no *diapenidion* dryue it fro myne herte,
Ne noyther schrifte ne shame, but hoso schrape my mawe?'

'ʒus, redili,' quod Repentaunce, and radde hym to þe beste:
'Sorwe of synnes is sauacioun of soules.'   126

'I am sori,' quod þat segge, 'I am but selde other,
And þat maketh me þus megre, for I ne may me venge.
Amonges burgeyses haue I be dwellynge at Londoun,
And gert Bakbitinge be a brocoure to blame mennes ware.
Whan he solde and I nouʒte, þanne was I redy   131
To lye and to loure on my neighbore and to lakke his chaffare.
I wil amende þis, ʒif I may, þorw myʒte of God almyʒty.'

Now awaketh Wratthe with two whyte eyen,
And nyuelynge with þe nose, and his nekke hangynge.   135

'I am Wrath,' quod he, 'I was sumtyme a frere,
And þe couentes gardyner for to graffe ympes;
On limitoures and listres lesynges I ymped,
Tyl þei bere leues of low speche lordes to plese,
And sithen þei blosmed obrode in boure to here shriftes.   140
And now is fallen þerof a frute, þat folke han wel leuere
Schewen her schriftes to hem þan shryue hem to her persones.

And now persones han parceyued þat freres parte with hem,
þise possessioneres preche and depraue freres,
And freres fyndeth hem in defaute, as folke bereth witnes,   145
That whan þei preche þe poeple in many place aboute,
I, Wrath, walke with hem and wisse hem of my bokes.
þus þei speken of spiritualte, þat eyther despiseth other,
Til þei be bothe beggers and by my spiritualte libben,
Or elles alle riche and riden aboute.   150
I, Wrath, rest neuere, þat I ne moste folwe
This wykked folke, for suche is my grace.

I haue an aunte to nonne, and an abbesse bothe;
Hir were leuere swowe or swelte þan suffre any peyne.
I haue be cook in hir kichyne and þe couent serued   155
Many monthes with hem and with monkes bothe.
I was þe priouresses potagere, and other poure ladyes,
And made hem ioutes of iangelynge—þat Iohanne was a
    bastard
And dame Clarice a kniȝtes douȝter, ac a kokewolde was hire
    syre,   159
And dame Peronelle a prestes file; priouresse worth she neuere,
For she had childe in chirityme, al owre chapitere it wiste.

Of wykked wordes I, Wrath, here wortes imade,
Til "þow lixte" and "þow lixte" lopen oute at ones,
And eyther hitte other vnder þe cheke;   164
Hadde þei had knyues, bi Cryst, her eyther had killed other.

Seynt Gregorie was a gode pope and had a gode forwit,
þat no priouresse were prest for þat he ordeigned.
þei had þanne ben *infamis* þe firste day, þei can so yuel hele
    conseille.
Amonge monkes I miȝte be, ac many tyme I shonye:

41

For þere ben many felle frekis my feres to aspye,   170
Bothe prioure an supprioure and owre *pater abbas;*
And if I telle any tales þei taken hem togyderes,
And do me faste Frydayes to bred and to water,
And am chalanged in þe chapitelhous as I a childe were,
And baleised on þe bare ers, and no breche bitwene.   175
Forþi haue I no lykyng with þo leodes to wonye.
I ete there vnthende fisshe and fieble ale drynke;
Ac other while, when wyn cometh whan I drynke wyn at eue,
I haue a fluxe of a foule mouthe wel fyue dayes after.
Al þe wikkednesse þat I wote bi any of owre bretheren,   180
I couth it in owre cloistre þat al owre couent wote it.'

'Now repent þe,' quod Repentaunce, 'and reherce þow neure
Conseille þat þow cnowest, bi contenaunce ne bi riȝte;
And drynke nouȝte ouer delicatly ne to depe noyther,
þat þi wille bi cause þerof to wrath myȝte torne.   185
Esto sobrius,' he seyde, and assoilled me after,
And bad me wilne to wepe, my wikkednesse to amende.

And þanne cam Coueytise. Can I hym nouȝte descryue,
So hungriliche and holwe sire Heruy hym loked.
He was bitelbrowed and baberlipped also,   190
With two blered eyghen as a blynde hagge;
And as a letheren purs lolled his chekes,
Wel sydder þan his chyn þei chiueled for elde;
And as a bondman of his bacoun his berde was bidraueled;
With an hode on his hed, a lousi hatte aboue,   195
And in a tauny tabarde of twelue wynter age,
Al totorne and baudy and ful of lys crepynge;
But if þat a lous couthe haue lopen þe bettre,
She sholde nouȝte haue walked on þat welche, so was it
   thredebare.
   'I haue ben coueytouse,' quod þis caityue, 'I biknowe it
   here;   200
For some tyme I serued Symme-atte-stile,
And was his prentis ypliȝte his profit to wayte.
First I lerned to lye a leef other tweyne,

42

Wikkedlich to weye was my furst lessoun.

To Wy and to Wynchestre I went to þe faire   205
With many manere marchandise as my maistre me hiȝte;
Ne had þe grace of gyle ygo amonge my ware,
It had be vnsolde þis seuene ȝere, so me God helpe!

Thanne drowe I me amonges draperes my donet to lerne,
To drawe þe lyser alonge, þe lenger it semed;   210
Amonge þe riche rayes I rendred a lessoun
To broche hem with a paknedle, and plaited hem togyderes
And put hem in a presse and pynned hem þerinne
Tyl ten ȝerdes or twelue tolled out threttene.

My wyf was a webbe and wollen cloth made;   215
She spak to spynnesteres to spynnen it oute.
Ac þe pounde þat she payed by poised a quarteroun more
Than myne owne auncere, whoso weyȝed treuthe.

I bouȝte hir barly malte; she brewe it to selle,
Peny-ale and podyng-ale she poured togideres   220
For laboreres and for low folke; þat lay by hymselue.
The best ale lay in my boure or in my bedchambre,
And whoso bummed þerof bouȝte it þerafter,
A galoun for a grote, God wote, no lesse;
And ȝit it cam in cupmel; þis crafte my wyf vsed.   225
Rose þe regratere was hir riȝte name;
She hath holden hokkerye al hire lyf-tyme.

Ac I swere now, so the Ik, þat synne wil I lete,
And neuere wikkedliche weye ne wikke chaffare vse,
But wenden to Walsyngham, and my wyf als,   230
And bidde þe rode of Bromeholme brynge me oute of dette.'

    'Repentedestow þe euere,' quod Repentance, 'ne restitucioun
        madest?'
    'Ȝus, ones I was herberwed,' quod he, 'with an hep of
        chapmen;
I roos whan þei were arest and yrifled here males.'
    'That was no restitucioun,' quod Repentance, 'but a rob-
        beres thefte;   235
þow haddest [be] better worthy be hanged þerfore
þan for al þat þat þow hast here shewed.'

43

'I wende ryflynge were restitucioun,' quod he, 'for I lerned
neuere rede on boke,

And I can no Frenche in feith but of þe ferthest ende of
Norfolke.'

'Vsedestow euere vsurie,' quod Repentaunce, 'in alle þi
lyf-tyme?'   240

'Nay, sothly,' he seyde, 'saue in my зouthe.

I lerned amonge Lumbardes and Iewes a lessoun,

To wey pens with a peys and pare þe heuyest,

And lene it for loue of þe crosse, to legge a wedde and lese it;

Suche dedes I did wryte зif he his day breke,   245

I haue mo maneres þorw rerages þan þorw *miseretur et comodat*.

I haue lent lordes and ladyes my chaffare,

And ben her brocour after and bouзte it myself.

Eschaunges and cheuesances, with suche chaffare I dele,

And lene folke þat lese wol a lyppe at euery noble.   250

And with Lumbardes lettres I ladde golde to Rome,

And toke it by taille here and tolde hem þere lasse.'

'Lentestow euere lordes for loue of her mayntenaunce?'

'Зe, I haue lent lordes loued me neuere after,   254

And haue ymade many a knyзte, bothe mercere and drapere

þat payed neuere for his prentishode nouзte a peire gloues.'

'Hastow pite on pore men þat more nedes borwe?'

'I haue as moche pite of pore men as pedlere hath of cattes,

þat wolde kille hem, yf he cacche hem myзte, for coueitise of
here skynnes.'

'Artow manlyche amonge þi neiзbores of þi mete and
drynke?'   260

'I am holden,' quod he, 'as hende as hounde is in kychyne,

Amonges my neighbores namelich, such a name ich haue.'

'Now God leue neure,' quod Repentance, 'but þow repent
þe rather,

þe grace on þis grounde þi good wel to bisette,

Ne þine ysue after þe haue ioye of þat þow wynnest,   265

Ne þi excecutours wel bisett þe siluer þat þow hem leuest;

And þat was wonne with wronge with wikked men be despended.

44

For were I frere of þat hous þere gode faith and charite is,
I nolde cope vs with þi catel ne owre kyrke amende,
Ne haue a peny to my pitaunce of þyne, bi my soule hele, 270
For þe best boke in owre hous, þeiȝe brent golde were þe
    leues,
And I wyst wytterly þow were suche as þow tellest:
[Or elles þat I kouþe knowe it by any kynnes wise.]
Seruus es alterius cum fercula pinguia queris,
Pane tuo pocius vescere, liber eris. 275

    Thow art an vnkynde creature, I can þe nouȝte assoille
Til þow make restitucioun and rekne with hem alle,
And sithen þat Resoun rolle it in þe regystre of heuene
That þow hast made vche man good, I may þe nouȝte assoille:
      Non dimittitur peccatum, donec restituatur ablatum, etc.
    For alle þat haue of þi good, haue God my trouthe! 280
Ben holden at þe heighe dome to helpe þe to restitue.
And whoso leueth nouȝte þis be soth, loke in þe sauter glose,
In *miserere mei deus*, where I mene treuthe:
      Ecce enim veritatem dilexisti, etc.
    Shal neuere werkman in þis worlde þryue wyth þat þow
    wynnest:
Cum sancto sanctus eris; construe me þat on Englische.' 285
    Thanne wex þat shrewe in wanhope and walde haue hanged
    himself
Ne hadde Repentaunce þe rather reconforted hym in þis
    manere:
'Haue mercye in þi mynde and with þi mouth biseche it,
For Goddes mercye is more þan alle hise other werkes:
      Misericordia eius super omnia opera eius, etc.
    And al þe wikkednesse in þis worlde þat man myȝte worche
    or thynke 290
Ne is no more to þe mercy of God þan in þe see a glede:
      Omnis iniquitas quantum ad misericordiam dei, est [quasi]
      sintilla in medio maris.
    Forþi haue mercy in þi mynde, and marchandise, leue it,
For þow hast no good grounde to gete þe with a wastel,
But if it were with thi tonge or ellis with þi two hondes.

For þe good þat þow hast geten bigan al with falsehede, 295
And as longe as þow lyuest þerwith þow ʒeldest nouʒte, but
borwest.
And if þow wite neuere to whiche ne whom to restitue,
Bere it to þe bisschop and bidde hym, of his grace,
Bisette it hymselue as best is for þi soule.
For he shal answere for þe at þe heygh dome, 300
For þe and for many mo þat man shal ʒif a rekenynge,
What he lerned ʒow in Lente, leue þow none other,
And what he lent ʒow of owre Lordes good to lette ʒow fro
synne.'

Now bigynneth Glotoun for to go to schrifte,
And kaires hym to kirke-ward his coupe to schewe. 305
Ac Beton þe brewestere bad hym good morwe
And axed of hym with þat whiderward he wolde.
'To holi cherche,' quod he, 'for to here masse,
And sithen I wil be shryuen and synne namore.'
'I haue gode ale, gossib,' quod she, 'glotown, wiltow assaye?'
'Hastow auʒte in þi purs—any hote spices?' 311
'I haue peper and piones,' quod she, 'and a pounde of
garlike,
A ferthyngworth of fenel-seed for fastyngdayes.'
þanne goth Glotoun in, and Grete Othes after;
Cesse þe souteresse sat on þe benche, 315
Watte þe warner and hys wyf bothe,
Tymme þe tynkere and tweyne of his prentis,
Hikke þe hakeneyman and Hughe þe nedeler,
Clarice of Cokkeslane and þe clerke of þe cherche,
Dawe þe dykere and a dozeine other; 320
Sire Piers of Pridie and Peronelle of Flaundres,
A ribibour, a ratonere, a rakyer of Chepe,
A ropere, a redyngkyng and Rose þe dissheres,
Godfrey of Garlekehithe and Gryfin þe walshe;
And vpholderes an hepe erly bi þe morwe 325
Geuen Glotoun with glad chere good ale to hansel.
Clement þe cobelere cast of his cloke,

And atte new faire he nempned it to selle;
Hikke þe hakeneyman hitte his hood after,
And badde Bette þe bochere ben on his side. 330
þere were chapmen ychose þis chaffare to preise;
Whoso haueth þe hood shuld haue amendes of þe cloke.

Two risen vp in rape and rouned togideres,
And preised þese penyworthes apart bi hemselue;
þei couth nouȝte bi her conscience acorden in treuthe, 335
Tyl Robyn þe ropere aryse þei bisouȝte,
And nempned hym for a noumpere, þat no debate nere,
[For to trye þis chaffare bitwixen hem þre.]

Hikke þe hostellere hadde þe cloke
In coucnaunte þat Clement shulde þe cuppe fille 340
And haue Hikkes hode hostellere and holde hym yserued;
And whoso repented rathest shulde arise after
And grete sire Glotoun with a galoun ale.

þere was laughyng and louryng and 'let go þe cuppe,'
And seten so til euensonge and songen vmwhile 345
Tyl Glotoun had yglobbed a galoun an a iille.
His guttis gunne to godly as two gredy sowes;
He pissed a potel in a paternoster-while,
And blew his rounde ruwet at his rigge-bon ende,
That all þat herde þat horne held her nose after, 350
And wissheden it had be wexed with a wispe of firses.
He myȝte neither steppe ne stonde er his staffe hadde;
And þanne gan he go liche a glewmannes bicche,
Somme tyme aside and somme tyme arrere,
As whoso leyth lynes forto lacche foules. 355

And whan he drowgh to þe dore þanne dymmed his eighen,
He þrumbled on þe thresshewolde an threwe to þe erthe.
Clement þe cobelere cauȝte hym bi þe myddel
For to lifte hym alofte, and leyde him on his knowes;
Ac Glotoun was a gret cherle and a grym in þe liftynge, 360
And coughed up a caudel in Clementis lappe;
Is non so hungri hounde in Hertfordschire
Durst lape of þe leyunges, so vnlouely þei smauȝte.

With al þe wo of þis worlde his wyf and his wenche

47

Baren hym home to his bedde and brou3te hym þerinne. 365
And after al þis excesse he had an accidie,
þat he slepe Saterday and Sonday til sonne 3ede to reste.
þanne waked he of his wynkyng and wiped his eyghen;
þe fyrste worde þat he warpe was, 'where is þe bolle?'
His wif gan edwite hym þo how wikkedlich he lyued, 370
And Repentance ri3te so rebuked hym þat tyme:
    'As þow with wordes and werkes hast wrou3te yuel in þi
        lyue,
Shryue þe and be shamed þerof and shewe it with þi mouth.'
    'I, Glotoun,' quod þe gome, 'gylti me 3elde,
þat I haue trespassed with my tonge I can nou3te telle how
    ofte, 375
Sworen 'Goddes soule' and 'so God me help and halidom'
þere no nede ne was, nyne hundreth tymes;
    And ouerseye me at my sopere and some tyme at nones,
þat I, Glotoun, girt it vp er I hadde gone a myle,
And yspilte þat my3te be spared and spended on somme
    hungrie; 380
Ouerdelicatly on fastyng-dayes drunken and eten bothe,
And sat some tyme so longe þere þat I slepe and ete at ones.
For loue of tales, in tauernes, to drynke þe more, I dyned,
And hyed to þe mete er none whan fastyng-dayes were.'
    'This shewyng shrifte,' quod Repentance, 'shal be meryte
        to þe.' 385
    And þanne gan Glotoun grete and gret doel to make
For his lither lyf þat he lyued hadde,
And avowed to fast, 'for hunger or for thurst
'Shal neuere fisshe on þe Fryday defien in my wombe,
Tyl Abstinence myn aunte haue 3iue me leue; 390
And 3it haue I hated hir al my lyf-time.'

þanne come Sleuthe al bislabered, with two slymy ei3en,
'I most sitte,' seyde þe segge, 'or elles shulde I nappe;
I may nou3te stonde ne stoupe ne withoute a stole knele
Were I brou3te abedde, but if my taille-ende it made, 395
Sholde no ryngynge do me ryse ar I were rype to dyne'.

48

He bygan *benedicite* with a bolke, and his brest knocked,
And roxed and rored, and rutte atte laste.
'What! awake, renke!' quod Repentance, 'and rape þe to
    shrifte.'

'If I shulde deye bi þis day, me liste nouȝte to loke;   400
I can nouȝte perfitly my pater-noster as þe prest it syngeth,
But I can rymes of Robyn Hood and Randolf erle of Chestre,
Ac neither of owre Lorde ne of owre Lady þe leste þat euere
    was made.

I haue made vowes fourty and forȝete hem on þe morne;
I parfourned neure penaunce as þe prest me hiȝte,   405
Ne ryȝte sori for my synnes ȝet was I neuere.
And ȝif I bidde any bedes, but if it be in wrath,
þat I telle with my tonge is two myle fro myne herte.
I am occupied eche day, haliday and other,
With ydel tales atte ale and otherwhile in cherches;   410
Goddes peyne and his passioun ful selde þynke I þereon.

I visited neuere fieble men ne fettered folke in puttes,
I haue leuere here an harlotrie or a somer-game of souteres,
Or lesynges to laughe at and belye my neighbore,
þan al þat euere Marke made, Mathew, John, and Lucas.
And vigilies and fastyng-dayes, alle þise late I passe,   416
And ligge abedde in Lenten an my lemman in myn armes,
Tyl matynes and masse be do, and þanne go to þe freres;
Come I to *ite, missa est*, I holde me yserued.
I nam nouȝte shryuen some tyme, but if sekenesse it make,   420
Nouȝt tweies in two ȝere, and þanne vp gesse I schryue me.

I haue be prest and persoun passynge thretti wynter,
Ȝete can I neither solfe ne synge ne seyntes lyues rede;
But I can fynde in a felde or in a fourlonge an hare,
Better þan in *beatus vir* or in *beati omnes*   425
Construe oon clause wel and kenne it to my parochienes.
I can holde louedayes and here a reues rekenynge,
Ac in canoun ne in þe decretales I can nouȝte rede a lyne.

Ȝif I bigge and borwe it, but ȝif it be ytailled,
I forȝete it as ȝerne; and ȝif men me it axe,   430
Six sithes or seuene I forsake it with othes,

49

And þus tene I trewe men ten hundreth tymes.

    And my seruauntz some tyme her salarye is bihynde,
Reuthe is to here þe rekenynge whan we shal rede acomptes;
So with wikked wille and wraththe my werkmen I paye.   435
    Ȝif any man doth me a benfait or helpeth me at nede,
I am vnkynde aȝein his curteisye and can nouȝte vnder-
    stonde it;
For I haue and haue hadde some dele haukes maneres:
I nam nouȝte lured with loue, but þere ligge auȝte vnder þe
    thombe.
    The kyndenesse þat myne euene-cristene kidde me fern-
    yere,   440
Sixty sythes I, Sleuthe, haue forȝete it sith,
In speche and in sparynge of speche yspilte many a tyme
Bothe flesche and fissche and many other vitailles;
Bothe bred and ale, butter, melke, and chese
Forsleuthed in my seruyse til it myȝte serue noman.   445
    I ran aboute in ȝouthe and ȝaf me nouȝte to lerne,
And euere sith haue be beggere for my foule sleuthe;
Heu michi, quod sterilem vitam duxi iuuenilem!'
    'Repentestow þe nauȝte?' quod Repentance; and riȝte with
    þat he swowned
Til *Vigilate* þe veille fette water at his eyȝen,   450
And flatte it on his face and faste on hym criede,
And seide, 'ware þe fram wanhope wolde þe bitraye.
"I am sori for my synnes", sey so to þiselue,
And bete þiselue on þe breste and bidde hym of grace;
For is no gult here so grete þat his goodnesse nys more.'   455
    þanne sat Sleuthe vp and seyned hym swithe,
And made avowe tofore God for his foule sleuthe:
'Shal no Sondaye be þis seuene ȝere, but sykenesse it lette,
þat I ne shal do me er day to þe dere cherche,
And heren matines and masse as I a monke were.   460
Shal none ale after mete holde me þennes
Tyl I haue euensonge herde, I behote to þe rode.
And ȝete wil I ȝelde aȝein, if I so moche haue,
Al þat I wikkedly wan sithen I wytte hadde.

And þough my liflode lakke, leten I nelle,
þat eche man ne shal haue his ar I hennes wende;
And with þe residue and þe remenaunt, bi þe rode of Chestre,
I shal seke Treuthe arst ar I se Rome!'

Robert þe robbere on *reddite* lokede,
And for þer was nouȝte wherof he wepe swithe sore.   470
Ac ȝet þe synful shrewe seyde to hymselue:
'Cryst, þat on Caluarye vppon þe crosse deydest,
Tho Dismas my brother bisouȝte ȝow of grace,
And haddest mercy on þat man for *memento* sake,
So rewe on þis robbere þat *reddere* ne haue,   475
Ne neuere wene to wynne with crafte þat I owe.
But for þi mykel mercy mitigacioun I biseche;
Ne dampne me nouȝte at domesday for þat I did so ille.'

What bifel of þis feloun I can nouȝte faire schewe;
Wel I wote he wepte faste water with boþe his eyen,   480
And knowleched his gult to Cryst ȝete eftsones,
þat *penitencia* his pyke he shulde polsche newe
And lepe with hym ouer londe al his lyf-tyme,
For he had leyne bi *Latro*, Luciferes aunte.

And þanne had Repentaunce reuthe and redde hem alle to
   knele: 485
'For I shal biseche for al synful owre saueoure of grace,
To amende vs of owre mysdedes and do mercy to vs alle.
  Now God,' quod he, 'þat of þi goodnesse gonne þe worlde
   make,
And of nouȝte madest auȝte, and man moste liche to þiselue,
And sithen suffredest for to synne, a sikenesse to vs alle,   490
And al for þe best, as I bileue, what cuere þe boke telleth;
   O felix culpa! o necessarium peccatum Ade! etc.
For þourgh þat synne þi sone sent was to þis erthe,
And bicam man of a mayde mankynde to saue,
And madest þiself with þi sone and vs synful yliche:
   Faciamus hominem ad ymaginem et similitudinem
      nostram;
   Et alibi: qui manet in caritate, in deo manet, et deus in eo;

And sith with þi self sone in owre sute deydest   495
On godeFryday for mannes sake at ful tyme of þe daye,
þere þiself ne þi sone no sorwe in deth feledest;
But in owre secte was þe sorwe and þi sone it ladde:
  Captiuam duxit captiuitatem.

þe sonne for sorwe þerof les syȝte for a tyme   499
Aboute mydday, whan most liȝte is and meletyme of seintes;
Feddest with þi fresche blode owre forfadres in derknesse;
  Populus qui ambulabat in tenebris, vidit lucem magnam;
And thorw þe liȝte þat lepe oute of þe Lucifer was blent,
And blewe alle þi blissed into þe blisse of paradise.

þe thrydde daye after þow ȝedest in owre sute,
A synful Marie þe seighe ar seynte Marie þi dame,   505
And al to solace synful þow suffredest it so were:
  Non veni vocare iustos, set peccatores ad penitenciam.
And al þat Marke hath ymade, Mathew, Iohan, and Lucas,
Of þyne douȝtiest dedes were don in owre armes:
  Verbum caro factum est, et habitauit in nobis.
And bi so moche, me semeth, þe sikerere we mowe
Bydde and biseche, if it be þi wille   510
þat art owre fader and owre brother, be merciable to vs,
And haue reuthe on þise ribaudes þat repente hem here sore
þat euere þei wratthed þe in þis worlde in worde, þouȝte, or
  dedes.'

þanne hent Hope an horne of *deus, tu conuersus viuificabis
  nos,*
And blew it with *Beati quorum remisse sunt iniquitates,*   515
þat alle seyntes in heuene songen at ones:
  *Homines et iumenta saluabis, quemadmodum multiplicasti
  misericordiam tuam, deus, etc.*

A thousand of men þo thrungen togyderes;
Criede vpward to Cryst and to his clene moder
To haue grace to go with hem Treuthe to seke.

Ac þere was wyȝte non so wys þe wey þider couthe,   520
But blustreden forth as bestes ouer bankes and hilles,
Til late was and longe þat þei a lede mette,
Apparailled as a paynym in pylgrymes wyse.

He bare a burdoun ybounde with a brode liste,
In a withewyndes wise ywounden aboute. 525
A bolle and a bagge he bare by his syde;
An hundreth of ampulles on his hatt seten,
Signes of Synay and shelles of Galice;
And many a cruche on his cloke, and keyes of Rome,
And þe vernicle biforc, for men shulde knowe 530
And se bi his signes whom he souȝte hadde.
    þis folke frayned hym firste fro whennes he come.
    'Fram Synay,' he seyde, 'and fram owre Lordes sepulcre;
In Bethleem and in Babiloyne, I haue ben in bothe,
In Ermonye, in Alisaundre, in many other places. 535
ȝe may se bi my signes þat sitten on myn hatte
þat I haue walked ful wyde in wete and in drye
And souȝte gode seyntes for my soules helth.'
    'Knowestow ouȝte a corseint þat men calle Treuthe?
Coudestow auȝte wissen vs þe weye where þat wy dwelleth?'
    'Nay, so me Gode helpc!' seide þe gome þanne, 541
'I seygh neuere palmere with pike ne with scrippe
Axen after hym er til now in þis place.'
    'Peter!' quod a plowman, and put forth his hed,
'I knowe hym as kyndely as clerke doþ his bokes; 545
Conscience and Kynde Witte kenned me to his place,
And deden me suren hym sikerly to serue hym for euere,
Bothe to sowe and to sette þe while I swynke myghte.
I haue ben his folwar al þis fourty wyntre;
Bothe ysowen his sede and sued his bestes, 550
Withinne and withouten wayted his profyt.
I dyke and I delue, I do þat Treuthe hoteth;
Some tyme I sowe and some tyme I thresche,
In tailoures crafte and tynkares crafte, what Treuthe can
    deuyse,
I weue an I wynde and do what Treuthe hoteth. 555
    For, þouȝe I seye it myself, I serue hym to payc;
Ich haue myn huire of hym wel and otherwhiles more;
Hc is þe prestest payer þat pore men knoweth;
He ne withhalt non hewe his hyre þat he ne hath it at euen.

He is as low as a lombe and loueliche of speche;   560
And ʒif ʒe wilneth to wite where þat he dwelleth,
I shal wisse ʒow witterly þe weye to his place.'
  'ʒe, leue Pieres,' quod þis pilgrymes, and profered hym
    huire
For to wende with hem to Treuthes dwellyng place.
  'Nay, bi my soules helth,' quod Pieres, and gan forto
    swere,   565
'I nolde fange a ferthynge, for seynt Thomas shryne!
Treuthe wolde loue me þe lasse a long tyme þereafter!
Ac if ʒe wilneth to wende wel þis is þe weye thider,
[þat I shal say to yow and sette yow in þe soþe.]
  ʒe mote go þourgh Mekenesse, bothe men and wyues, 570
Tyl ʒe come into Conscience, þat Cryst wite þe sothe
þat ʒe louen owre Lorde God leuest of alle þinges;
And þanne ʒowre neighbores nexte in non wise apeyre
Otherwyse þan þow woldest he wrouʒte to þiselue.
  And so boweth forth bi a broke Beth-buxum-of-speche, 575
Tyl ʒe fynden a forth ʒowre-fadres-honoureth:
        Honora patrem et matrem, etc.:
Wadeþ in þat water and wascheth ʒow wel þere,
And ʒe shul lepe þe liʒloker al ʒowre lyf-tyme.
And so shaltow se Swere-nouʒte-but-if-it-be-for-nede-
And-namelich-an-ydel-þe-name-of-God-almyʒti.   580
  þanne shaltow come by a crofte; but come þow
    nouʒte þereinne;
That crofte hat Coueyte-nouʒte-mennes-catel-ne-her-wyues-
Ne-none-of-her-seruauntes-þat-noyen-hem-myʒte.
Loke ʒe breke no bowes þere but if it be ʒowre owne.
  Two stokkes þere stondeth, ac stynte ʒe nouʒte þere; 585
They hatte Stele-nouʒte, ne-slee-nouʒte; stryke forth by
    bothe;
And leue hem on þi left halfe and loke nouʒte þereafter;
And holde wel þyne haliday heighe til euen.
Thanne shaltow blenche at a berghe Bere-no-false-witnesse,
He is frithed in with floreines and other fees many;   590
Loke þow plukke no plante þere for peril of þi soule.

54

þanne shal ȝe se Sey-soth-so-it-be-to-done-
In-no-manere-ellis-nauȝte-for-no-mannes-biddynge.

þanne shaltow come to a courte as clere as þe sonne,
þe mote is of Mercy þe manere aboute,   595
And alle þe wallis ben of Witte to holden Wille oute,
And kerneled with Crystendome, mankynde to saue,
Boterased with Bileue-so-or-þow-beest-nouȝte-ysaued.

And alle þe houses ben hiled, halles and chambres,
With no lede, but with loue and lowe-speche-as-bretheren.
þe brugge is of bidde-wel-þe-bette-may-þow-spede;   601
Eche piler is of penaunce, of preyeres to seyntes;
Of almes-dedes ar þe hokes þat þe gates hangen on.

Grace hatte þe gateward, a gode man forsothe,
Hys man hatte Amende-ȝow, for many man him knoweth;   605
Telleth hym þis tokene, þat Treuthe wite þe sothe:
'I parfourned þe penaunce þe preest me enioyned,
And am ful sori for my synnes and so I shal euere,
Whan I þinke þereon, þeighe I were a pope.'

Biddeth Amende-ȝow meke him til his maistre ones,   610
To wayue vp þe wiket þat þe womman shette,
Tho Adam and Eue eten apples vnrosted;
        Per Euam cunctis clausa est, et per Mariam virginem
            [iterum] patefacta est;
For [s]he hath þe keye and þe cliket þouȝ þe kynge slepe.
And if Grace graunte þe to go in in þis wise,
þow shalt see in þiselue Treuthe sitte in þine herte,   615
In a cheyne of charyte, as þow a childe were,
To suffre hym and segge nouȝte aȝein þi sires wille.

Ac bewar þanne of Wrathþe þat is a wikked shrewe;
He hath enuye to hym þat in þine herte sitteth,
And pukketh forþ pruyde to prayse þiseluen.   620
þe boldnesse of þi bienfetes maketh þe blynde þanne,
And þanne worstow dryuen oute, as dew, and þe dore closed,
Kayed and cliketed to kepe þe withouten,
Happily an hundreth wyntre ar þow eft entre.
þus myght þow lesen his loue to late wel by þiselue,   625
And neuere happiliche efte entre, but grace þow haue.

55

Ac þere aren seuene sustren þat seruen Treuthe euere,
And aren porteres of þe posternes that to þe place longeth.
þat one hat Abstenence and Humilite an other;
Charite and Chastite ben his chief maydenes,   630
Pacience and Pees, moche poeple þei helpeth;
Largenesse þe lady heo let in ful manye;
Heo hath hulpe a þousande oute of þe deueles ponfolde.

    And who is sibbe to þis seuene, so me God helpe!
He is wonderliche welcome and faire vnderfongen.   635
And but if ȝe be syb to summe of þise seuene,
It is ful harde, bi myne heued,' quod Peres, 'for any of ȝow alle
To geten ingonge at any gate þere, but grace be þe more.'

    'Now, bi Cryst,' quod a cutpurs, 'I haue no kynne þere'.
'Ne I,' quod an apewarde, 'bi auȝte þat I knowe'.   640

    'Wite God,' quod a wafrestre, 'wist I þis for sothe,
Shulde I neuere ferthere a fote for no freres prechynge.'

    'Ȝus,' quod Pieres þe plowman, and pukked hem alle to
      gode:
'Mercy is a maydene þere hath myȝte ouer hem alle;
And she is syb to alle synful, and her sone also;   645
And þoruȝe þe helpe of hem two (hope þow none other),
þow myȝte gete grace þere, bi so þow go bityme.'

    'By seynt Poule,' quod a pardonere, 'perauenture I be
      nouȝte knowe þere,
I wil go fecche my box with my breuettes and a bulle with
      bisshopes lettres!'
'By Cryst,' quod a comune womman, 'þi companye wil I
      folwe,   650
þow shalt sey I am þi sustre.' I ne wot where þei bicome.

'This were a wikked way, but whoso hadde a gyde
That wolde folwen vs eche a fote,' þus þis folke hem mened.
Quod Perkyn þe plouman: 'bi seynt Peter of Rome,
I haue an half acre to erye bi þe heighe way;
Hadde I eried þis half acre and sowen it after,   5
I wolde wende with ȝow and þe way teche.'
   'þis were a longe lettynge', quod a lady in a sklayre,
'What sholde we wommen worche þerewhiles?'
   'Somme shal sowe þe sakke,' quod Piers, 'for shedyng of
      þe whete;
And ȝe louely ladyes with ȝoure longe fyngres,   10
þat ȝe han silke and sendal to sowe, whan tyme is,
Chesibles for chapelleynes' cherches to honoure.
Wyues and wydwes wolle and flex spynneth,
Maketh cloth, I conseille ȝow, and kenneth so ȝowre douȝtres;
þe nedy and þe naked, nymmeth hede how hij liggeth,   15
And casteth hem clothes, for so comaundeth Treuthe.
For I shal lene hem lyflode, but ȝif þe londe faille,
Flesshe and bred bothe to riche and to pore,
As longe as I lyue, for þe Lordes loue of heuene.
   And alle manere of men þat þorw mete and drynke lybbeth,
Helpith hym to worche wiȝtliche þat wynneth ȝowre fode.'   21
   'Bi Crist,' quod a knyȝte þo, 'he kenneth vs þe best;
Ac on þe teme trewly tauȝte was I neuere.
Ac kenne me,' quod þe knyȝte, 'and, bi Cryst, I wil assaye!'
   'Bi seynt Poule,' quod Perkyn, 'ȝe profre ȝow so faire   25
þat I shal swynke and swete and sowe for vs bothe,
And oþer laboures do for þi loue al my lyf-tyme,
In couenaunt þat þow kepe holikirke and myselue
Fro wastoures and fro wykked men þat þis worlde struyeth;
And go hunte hardiliche to hares and to foxes,   30
To bores and to brockes þat breketh adown myne hegges;
And go affaite þe faucones, wilde foules to kille:

For suche cometh to my croft and croppeth my whete.'

    Curteislich þe knyȝte þanne comsed þise wordes:

'By my power, Pieres,' quod he, 'I pliȝte þe my treuthe   35
To fulfille þis forward þowȝ I fiȝte sholde;
Als longe as I lyue I shal þe mayntene.'

    'ȝe, and ȝit a poynt,' quod Pieres, 'I preye ȝow of more:
Loke ȝe tene no tenaunt but Treuthe wil assent.
And þowgh ȝe mowe amercy hem, late mercy be taxoure   40
And mekenesse þi mayster, maugre Medes chekes;
And þowgh pore men profre ȝow presentis and ȝiftis,
Nym it nauȝte, an auenture ȝe mowe it nauȝte deserue:
For þow shalt ȝelde it aȝein at one ȝeres ende
In a ful perillous place, purgatorie it hatte.   45

    And mysbede nouȝte þi bondemen, þe better may þow
      spede;
þowgh he be þyn vnderlynge here, wel may happe in heuene
þat he worth worthier sette and with more blisse
[þan þow, bot þou do bette, and lyue as þow shulde]:
    Amice, ascende superius.
For in charnel atte chirche cherles ben yuel to knowe,   50
Or a kniȝte fram a knaue þere, knowe þis in þin herte;
And þat þow be trewe of þi tonge and tales þat þow hatie,
But if þei ben of wisdome or of witte, þi werkmen to chaste.
Holde with none harlotes ne here nouȝte her tales,
And nameliche atte mete suche men eschue: 55
For it ben þe deueles disoures, I do þe to vnderstande.'

    'I assente, bi seynt Iame,' seyde þe kniȝte þanne,
'Forto worche bi þi wordes þe while my lyf dureth.'

    'And I shal apparaille me,' quod Perkyn, 'in pilgrimes wise,
And wende with ȝow I wil til we fynde Treuthe;   60
And cast on me my clothes, yclouted and hole,
My cokeres and my coffes for colde of my nailles,
And hange myn hoper at myn hals in stede of a scrippe;
A busshel of bredcorne brynge me þerinne,
For I wil sowe it myself and sitthenes wil I wende   65
To pylgrymage as palmers don, pardoun forto haue.

    Ac who so helpeth me to erie or sowen here ar I wende,

Shal haue leue, bi owre Lorde, to lese here in heruest,
And make hem mery þeremydde, maugre whoso bigruccheth it.
And alkyn crafty men þat konne lyuen in treuthe,   70
I shal fynden hem fode þat feithfulliche libbeth,
Saue Iakke þe iogeloure and Ionet of þe stues,
And Danyel þe dys-playere and Denote þe baude,
And frere þe faytoure and folke of his ordre,
And Robyn þe rybaudoure for his rusty wordes.   75
Treuthe tolde me ones and bad me tellen it after,
Deleantur de libro viuentium; I shulde nouȝte dele with hem,
For holicherche is hote of hem no tythe to take:

    Quia cum iustis non scribantur;

They ben ascaped good auenture; now God hem amende!'
    Dame Worche-whan-tyme-is Pieres wyf hiȝte,   80
His douȝter hiȝte Do-riȝhte-so-or-þi-dame-shal-þe-bete,
His sone hiȝte Suffre-þi-souereynes-to-hauen-her-wille-
Deme-hem-nouȝte-for-if-þow-doste-þow-shalt-it-dere-
    abugge-
Late-God-yworth-with-al-for-so-his-worde-techeth;
'For now I am olde and hore and haue of myn owen,   85
To penaunce and to pilgrimage I wil passe with þise other.
Forþi I wil, or I wende, do wryte my biqueste:
In dei nomine, amen. I make it myseluen.
He shal haue my soule þat best hath yscrued it,
And fro þe fende it defende for so I bileue,   90
Til I come to his acountes, as my *credo* me telleth;
To haue a relees and a remissioun on þat rental, I leue.
    þe kirke shal haue my caroigne and kepe my bones,
For of my corne and catel he craued þe tythe.
I payed it hym prestly for peril of my soule,   95
Forthy is he holden, I hope, to haue me in his masse,
And mengen in his memorye amonge alle crystene.
    My wyf shal haue of þat I wan with treuthe, and nomore,
And dele amonge my douȝtres and my dere children,
For þowghe I deye todaye my dettes ar quitte;   100
I bare home þat I borwed ar I to bedde ȝede.
    And with þe residue and þe remenaunte, bi þe rode of Lukes!

I wil worschip þerwith Treuthe by my lyue,
And ben his pilgryme atte plow for pore mennes sake.
My plow-pote shal be my pyk-staf and picche atwo þe rotes,
And helpe my culter to kerue and clense þe forwes.'   106
   Now is Perkyn and his pilgrymes to þe plowe faren;
To erie þis halue acre holpyn hym manye.
Dikeres and delueres digged vp þe balkes;
þerewith was Perkyn apayed and preysed hem faste.   110
Other werkemen þere were þat wrouȝten ful ȝerne,
Eche man in his manere made hymself to done,
And some, to plese Perkyn, piked vp þe wedes.
   At heighe pryme Peres lete þe plowe stonde,
To ouersen hem hymself; and whoso best wrouȝte,   115
He shulde be huyred þerafter whan heruest tyme come.
   And þanne seten somme and songen atte nale,
And hulpen erie his half acre with 'how! trolli-lolli!'
   'Now, bi þe peril of my soule!', quod Pieres al in pure tene,
'But ȝe arise þe rather and rape ȝow to worche,   120
Shal no greyne þat groweth glade ȝow at nede;
And þough ȝe deye for dole, þe deuel haue þat reccheth!'
Tho were faitoures aferde and feyned hem blynde;
Somme leyde here legges aliri as suche loseles conneth,
And made her mone to Pieres and preyde hym of grace— 125
'For we haue no lymes to laboure with, lorde, ygraced be ȝe!
Ac we preye for ȝow, Pieres, and for ȝowre plow bothe,
þat God of his grace ȝowre grayne multiplye,
And ȝelde ȝow of ȝowre almesse þat ȝe ȝiue vs here:
For we may nouȝte swynke ne swete, suche sikenesse vs
      eyleth.'   130
   'If it be soth,' quod Pieres, 'þat ȝe seyne, I shal it sone
      asspye.
ȝe ben wastoures, I wote wel, and Treuthe wote þe sothe,
And I am his [h]olde hyne and hiȝte hym to warne
Which þei were in þis worlde his werkemen appeyred.
ȝe wasten þat men wynnen with trauaille and with tene.   135
Ac Treuthe shal teche ȝow his teme to dryue,
Or ȝe shal ete barly bred and of þe broke drynke.

But if he be blynde or broke-legged or bolted with yrnes,
He shal ete whete bred and drynke with myselue
Tyl God of his goodnesse amendement hym sende.   140
Ac ʒe myʒte trauaille as Treuthe wolde, and take mete and
      huyre
To kepe kyne in þe felde, þe corne fro þe bestes,
Diken or deluen or dyngen vppon sheues,
Or helpe make morter or bere mukke afelde.
    In lecherye and in losengerye ʒe lyuen, and in sleuthe, 145
And al is þorw suffrance þat veniaunce ʒow ne taketh.
    An ancres and heremytes þat eten but at nones,
And namore er morwe, myne almesse shul þei haue,
And of my catel to cope hem with þat han cloistres and
      cherches.
Ac Robert renne-aboute shal nowʒte haue of myne,   150
Ne posteles, but þey preche conne and haue powere of þe
      bisschop;
They shal haue payne and potage and make hemself at ese,
For it is an vnresonable religioun þat hath riʒte nouʒte of
      certeyne.'
    And þanne gan a wastoure to wrath hym and wolde
      haue yfouʒte,
And to Pieres þe plowman he profered his gloue;   155
A Brytonere, a braggere abosted Pieres als
And bad hym go pissen with his plow, forpynede schrewe!
'Wiltow or neltow, we wil haue owre wille,
Of þi flowre and of þi flessche fecche whan vs liketh,
And make vs myrie þermyde, maugre þi chekes!'   160
    Thanne Pieres þe plowman pleyned hym to þe knyʒte
To kepe hym, as couenaunte was, fram cursed shrewes,
And fro þis wastoures wolueskynnes þat maketh þe worlde
      dere:
'For þo waste and wynnen nouʒte; and þat ilke while
Worth neuere plente amonge þe poeple þerwhile my plow
      liggeth.'   165
Curteisly þe knyʒte þanne, as his kynde wolde,
Warned Wastoure and wissed hym bettere—

61

'Or þow shalt abugge by þe lawe, by þe ordre þat I bere!'
'I was nouȝt wont to worche,' quod Wastour, 'and now wil
I nouȝt bigynne!'
And lete liȝte of þe lawe and lasse of þe knyȝte,   170
And sette Pieres at a pees and his plow bothe,
And manaced Pieres and his men ȝif þei mette eft sone.
'Now, by þe peril of my soule!' quod Pieres, 'I shal apeyre
ȝow alle!'
And houped after Hunger þat herd hym atte first:
Awreke me of þise wastoures,' quod he, 'þat þis worlde
schendeth!'   175
Hunger in haste þo hent Wastour bi þe mawe,
And wronge hym so bi þe wombe þat bothe his eyen wattered;
He buffeted þe Britoner aboute þe chekes,
þat he loked like a lanterne al his lyf after.
He bette hem so bothe he barste nere here guttes;   180
Ne hadde Pieres with a pese-lof preyed Hunger to cesse,
They hadde ben doluen bothe, ne deme þow non other.
'Suffre hem lyue,' he seyde, 'and lete hem ete with hogges,
Or elles benes and bren ybaken togideres,
Or elles melke and mene ale': þus preyed Pieres for hem. 185
Faitoures for fere herof flowen into bernes,
And flapten on with flayles fram morwe til euen,
That Hunger was nouȝt so hardy on hem for to loke
For a potful of peses þat Peres hadde ymaked
An heep of heremites henten hem spades,   190
And ketten here copes and courtpies hem made,
And wenten as werkemen with spades and with schoueles,
And doluen and dykeden to dryue aweye Hunger.
Blynde and bedreden were botened a þousande,
þat seten to begge syluer, sone were þei heled.   195
For þat was bake for bayarde was bote for many hungry,
And many a beggere for benes buxome was to swynke,
And eche a pore man wel apayed to haue pesen for his huyre,
And what Pieres preyed hem to do, as prest as a sperhauke.
And þereof was Peres proude, and put hem to werke,   200
And ȝaf hem mete as he myȝte aforth, and mesurable huyre.

þanne hadde Peres pite and preyed Hunger to wende
Home into his owne erde and holden hym þere—
'For I am wel awroke now of wastoures, þorw þi myȝte.
Ac I preye þe, ar þow passe', quod Pieres to Hunger,　205
'Of beggeres and of bidderes, what best be to done?
For I wote wel, be þow went, þei wil worche ful ille:
For myschief it maketh þei beth so meke nouthe,
And for defaute of her fode þis folke is at my wille.
þey are my blody brethren,' quod Pieres, 'for God bouȝte vs
　　alle;　210
Treuthe tauȝte me ones to louye hem vchone,
And to helpen hem of alle þinge ay as hem nedeth.
And now wolde I witen of þe what were þe best,
And how I myȝte amaistrien hem and make hem to worche.'
　'Here now,' quod Hunger, 'and holde it for a wisdome:　215
Bolde beggeres and bigge þat mowe her bred biswynke,
With houndes bred and hors bred holde vp her hertis,
Abate hem with benes for bollyng of her wombe;
And ȝif þe gomes grucche, bidde hem go swynke,
And he shal soupe swettere whan he it hath deseruid.　220
　And if þow fynde any freke þat fortune hath appeyred,
Or any maner fals men, fonde þow suche to cnowe;
Conforte hem with þi catel for Crystes loue of heuene;
Loue hem and lene hem, so lawe of God techeth:
　　Alter alterius onera portate.
And alle maner of men þat þow myȝte asspye　225
That nedy ben, and nauȝty, helpe hem with þi godis;
Loue hem and lakke hem nouȝte—late God tak þe veniaunce;
Theigh þei done yuel, late þow God aworþe:
　　Michi vindictam, et ego retribuam.
And if þow wilt be graciouse to God, do as þe gospel techeth,
And biloue þe amonges low men, so shaltow lacche grace:
　　Facite vobis amicos de mamona iniquitatis.'
　'I wolde nouȝt greue God,' quod Piers, 'for al þe good on
　　grounde;　231
Miȝte I synnelees do as þow seist?', seyde Piers þanne.
　'Ȝe, I bihote þe,' quod Hunger, 'or ellis þe bible lieth;

63

Go to Genesis þe gyaunt, þe engendroure of vs alle:
"*In sudore* and swynke þow shalt þi mete tilye,   235
And laboure for þi lyflode"; and so owre Lorde hyȝte.
And Sapience seyth þe same, I seigh it in þe bible:
"*Piger pro frigore* no felde nolde tilye,
And þerfore he shal begge and bidde and no man bete his
        hunger."

Mathew with mannes face mouthed þise wordes,   240
þat *seruus nequam* had a nam, and for he wolde nouȝte chaf-
        fare,
He had maugre of his maistre for euermore after;
And binam hym his mnam for he ne wolde worche,
And ȝaf þat mnam to hym þat ten mnames hadde,
And with þat he seyde, þat Holicherche it herde: 245
"He þat hath shal haue and helpe þere it nedeth,
And he þat nouȝt hath, shal nouȝt haue and no man hym helpe;
And þat he weneth wel to haue I wil it hym bireue."

Kynde witt wolde þat eche a wyght wrouȝte
Or in dykynge or in deluynge or trauaillynge in preyeres, 250
Contemplatyf lyf or actyf lyf, Cryst wolde men wrouȝte.
þe sauter seyth in þe psalme of *beati omnes*,
þe freke þat fedeth hymself with his feythful laboure,
He is blessed by þe boke in body and in soule:
        Labores manuum tuarum, etc.'

'ȝet I prey ȝow,' quod Pieres, '*par charite*, and ȝe kunne   255
Eny leef of lechecraft, lere it me, my dere:
For somme of my seruauntz and myself bothe
Of al a wyke worche nouȝt, so owre wombe aketh.'

'I wote wel,' quod Hunger, 'what sykenesse ȝow eyleth;
ȝe han maunged ouermoche, and þat maketh ȝow grone. 260
Ac I hote þe,' quod Hunger, 'as þow þyne hele wilnest,
þat þow drynke no day ar þow dyne somwhat.
Ete nouȝte, I hote þe, ar hunger þe take
And sende þe of his sauce to sauoure with þi lippes;
And kepe some tyle soper-tyme and sitte nouȝt to longe; 265
Arise vp ar appetit haue eten his fulle.
Lat nouȝt sire Surfait sitten at þi borde;

64

Leue him nou3t, for he is lecherous and likerous of tonge,
And after many manere metes his maw is afyngred.

And 3if þow diete þe þus, I dar legge myn eres   270
þat Phisik shal his furred hodes for his fode selle,
And his cloke of calabre with alle þe knappes of golde
And be fayne, bi my feith, his phisik to lete,
And lerne to laboure with londe, for lyflode is swete—
For morthereres aren mony leches, Lorde hem amende!   275
þei do men deye þorw here drynkes ar destine it wolde.'

'By seynt Poule,' quod Pieres, 'þise aren profitable wordis!
Wende now, Hunger, whan þow wolt, þat wel be þow euere!
For þis is a louely lessoun, Lorde it þe for3elde!'

'Byhote God,' quod Hunger, 'hennes ne wil I wende   280
Til I haue dyned bi þis day and ydronke bothe.'

'I haue no peny,' quod Peres 'poletes forto bigge,
Ne neyther gees ne grys, but two grene cheses,
A fewe cruddes and creem and an hauer cake,
And two loues of benes and bran ybake for my fauntis.   285
And 3et I sey, by my soule, I haue no salt bacoun,
Ne no kokeney, bi Cryst, coloppes forto maken.
Ac I haue percil and porettes and many kole-plantes,
And eke a cow and a kalf and a cart-mare
To drawe afelde my donge þe while þe drought lasteth.   290
And bi þis lyflode we mot lyue til Lammasse tyme;
And bi þat I hope to haue heruest in my croft;
And þanne may I di3te þi dyner as me dere liketh.'
Alle þe pore peple þo pesecoddes fetten,
Benes and baken apples þei brou3te in her lappes,   295
Chibolles and cheruelles and ripe chiries manye,
And profred Peres þis present to plese with Hunger.

Al Hunger eet in hast and axed after more.
þanne pore folke for fere fedde Hunger 3erne   299
With grene poret and pesen; to poysoun Hunger þei þou3te.
By þat it neighed nere heruest newe corne cam to chepynge;
þanne was folke fayne and fedde Hunger with þe best,
With good ale, as Glotoun tau3te, and gerte Hunger go slepe.

And þo wolde Wastour nou3t werche, but wandren aboute,

Ne no begger ete bred þat benes inne were,   305
But of coket or clerematyn, or elles of clene whete;
Ne none halpeny ale in none wise drynke,
But of þe best and of þe brounest þat in borghe is to selle.

Laboreres þat haue no lande to lyue on but her handes,
Deyned nouȝt to dyne aday nyȝt-olde wortes.   310
May no peny-ale hem paye ne no pece of bakoun,
But if it be fresch flesch other fische fryed other bake,
And þat *chaude* or *plus chaud*, for chillyng of here mawe.

And but if he be heighlich huyred ellis wil he chyde,
And þat he was werkman wrouȝt waille þe tyme;   315
Aȝeines Catones conseille comseth he to iangle:

Paupertatis onus pacienter ferre memento.

He greueth hym aȝeines God and gruccheth aȝeines Resoun,
And þanne curseth he þe kynge and al his conseille after,
Suche lawes to loke laboreres to greue.

Ac whiles Hunger was her maister þere wolde none of hem
    chyde,   320
Ne stryue aȝeines his statut, so sterneliche he loked.

Ac I warne ȝow, werkemen, wynneth while ȝe mowe,
For Hunger hiderward hasteth hym faste.
He shal awake with water wastoures to chaste.
Ar fyue ȝere be fulfilled suche famyn shal aryse;   325
Thorwgh flodes and þourgh foule wederes frutes shul faille.
And so sayde Saturne, and sent ȝow to warne;
Whan ȝe se þe sonne amys and two monkes hedes,
And a mayde haue þe maistrie and multiplied bi eight,
þanne shal Deth withdrawe and Derthe be iustice   330
And Dawe þe dyker deye for hunger
But if God of his goodnesse graunt vs a trewe.   332

Passus septimus

Treuthe herde telle herof and to Peres he sent

To taken his teme and tulyen þe erthe,
And purchaced hym a pardoun *a pena et a culpa*
For hym and for his heires for euermore after,
And bad hym holde hym at home and eryen his leyes;   5
And alle þat halpe hym to erie, to sette or to sowe,
Or any other myster þat myȝte Pieres auaille,
Pardoun with Pieres plowman Treuthe hath ygraunted.

   Kynges and knyȝtes þat kepen holycherche
And ryȝtfullych in reumes reulen þe peple,   10
Han pardoun thourgh purgatorie to passe ful lyȝtly,
With patriarkes and prophetes in paradise to be felawes.

   Bisshopes yblessed ȝif þei ben as þei shulden,
Legistres of bothe þe lawes, þe lewed þerewith to preche,
And in as moche as þei mowe amende alle synful,   15
Aren peres with þe apostles (þis pardoun Piers sheweth),
And at þe day of dome atte heigh deyse to sytte.

   Marchauntz in þe margyne hadden many ȝeres,
Ac none *a pena et a culpa* þe pope nolde hem graunte:
For þei holde nouȝt her halidayes as holicherche techeth,   20
And for þei swere by her soule, and 'so God moste hem helpe,'
Aȝein clene conscience her catel to selle.

   Ac vnder his secret seel Treuthe sent hem a lettre,
That þey shulde bugge boldely þat hem best liked,
And sithenes selle it aȝein, and saue þe wynny[n]ge,   25
And amende *mesondieux* þeremyde and myseyse folke helpe,
And wikked wayes wiȝtlich hem amende,
And do bote to brugges þat tobroke were,
Marien maydenes or maken hem nonnes,
Pore peple and prisounes fynden hem here fode,   30
And sette scoleres to scole or to somme other craftes,
Releue religioun and renten hem bettere—
'And I shal sende ȝow myselue seynt Michel myn archangel,

þat no deuel shal ȝow dere ne fere ȝow in ȝowre deyinge,
And witen ȝow fro wanhope if ȝe wil þus worche,   35
And send ȝowre sowles in safte to my seyntes in ioye.'

þanne were marchauntz mery; many wepten for ioye,
And preyseden Pieres þe plowman þat purchaced þis bulle.

Men of lawe lest pardoun hadde þat pleteden for mede:
For þe sauter saueth hem nouȝte such as taketh ȝiftes,   40
And namelich of innocentz þat none yuel ne kunneth:
   Super innocentem munera non accipies.
Pledoures shulde peynen hem to plede for such, an helpe;
Prynces and prelates shulde paye for her trauaille:
   A regibus et pryncipibus erit merces eorum.

Ac many a iustice an iuroure wolde for Iohan do more
þan *pro dei pietate*, leue þow none other!   45
Ac he þat spendeth his speche and spekeþ for þe pore
þat is innocent and nedy and no man appeireth,
Conforteth hym in þat cas withoute coueytise of ȝiftes
And scheweth lawe for owre Lordes loue as he it hath lerned,
Shal no deuel at his ded-day deren hym a myȝte,   50
þat he ne worth sauf and his sowle; þe sauter bereth witnesse:
   Domine, quis habitabit in tabernaculo tuo, etc.

Ac to bugge water, ne wynde ne witte, ne fyre þe fierthe,
þise foure þe fader of heuene made to þis folde in comune;
þise ben Treuthes tresores, trewe folke to helpe,
þat neuere shal wax ne wanye withoute God hymselue.   55

Whan þei drawen on to deye and indulgences wolde haue,
Her pardoun is ful petit at her partyng hennes,
þat any mede of mene men for her motyng taketh.
Ȝe legistres and lawyeres, holdeth þis for treuthe,
þat ȝif þat I lye Mathew is to blame,   60
For he bad me make ȝow þis and þis prouerbe me tolde:
   Quodcumque vultis vt faciant vobis homines, facite eis.
Alle lybbyng laboreres þat lyuen with her hondes,
þat trewlich taken and trewlich wynnen
And lyuen in loue and in lawe for her lowe hertis,
Haueth þe same absolucioun þat sent was to Peres.   65

Beggeres ne bidderes ne beth nouȝte in þe bulle,

But if þe suggestioun be soth þat shapeth hem to begge.
For he þat beggeth or bit but if he haue nede,
He is fals with þe fende and defraudeth the nedy,
And also he bigileth þe gyuere ageines his wil:　　　　70
For if he wist he were nou3te nedy he wolde 3iue þat an other
þat were more nedy þan he, so þe nediest shuld be hulpe.
Catoun kenneth men þus, and þe clerke of þe stories:
Cui des, videto is Catounes techynge,
And in the stories he techeth to bistowe þyn almes:　　75
　　　Sit elemosina tua in manu tua, donec studes cui des.
Ac Gregori was a gode man and bad vs gyuen alle
þat asketh, for his loue þat vs alle leneth:
　　　Non eligas cui misererais, ne forte pretereas illum qui
　　　meretur accipere. Quia incertum est pro quo Deo magis
　　　placeas.
For wite 3e neuere who is worthi, ac God wote who hath nede;
In hym þat taketh is þe treccherye, if any tresoun wawe;
For he þat 3iueth, 3eldeth and 3arketh hym to reste,　　80
And he þat biddeth, borweth and bryngeth hymself in dette.
For beggeres borwen euermo and her borghe is God almy3ti,
To 3elden hem þat 3iueth hem and 3et vsure more:
　　　Quare non dedisti peccuniam meam ad mensam, vt ego
　　　veniens cum vsuris exegissem illam?
Forþi biddeth nou3t, 3e beggeres, but if 3e haue gret nede:
For whoso hath to buggen hym bred—þe boke bereth witnesse—
He hath ynough þat hath bred ynough þough he haue nou3t
　　elles:　　　　　　　　　　　　　　　　　　　　　　86
　　　Satis diues est, qui non indiget pane.
Late vsage be 3owre solace of seyntes lyues redynge,
þe boke banneth beggarie and blameth hem in þis manere:
　　　Iunior fui, etenim senui; et non vidi iustum derelictum,
　　　nec semen eius [querens panem].
For 3e lyue in no loue ne no lawe holde;　　　　　89
Many of 3ow ne wedde nou3t þe wommen þat 3e with delen,
But as wilde bestis with 'wehe' worthen vppe and worchen,
And bryngeth forth barnes þat bastardes men calleth.
Or þe bakke or some bone he breketh in his 3outhe,

And sitthe gon faiten with ȝoure fauntes for euermore after.
þere is moo mysshape peple amonge þise beggeres   95
þan of alle maner men þat on þis molde walketh;
And þei þat lyue þus here lyf mowe lothe þe tyme
þat euere he was man wrouȝt whan he shal hennes fare.

Ac olde men and hore þat helplees ben of strengthe,
And women with childe þat worche ne mowe,   100
Blynde and bedrede, and broken here membres,
þat taketh þis myschief mekelych, as meseles and othere,
Han as pleyne pardoun as þe plowman hymself;
For loue of her lowe hertis owre Lorde hath hem graunted
Here penaunce and her purgatorie here on þis erthe.   105

'Pieres,' quod a prest þo, 'þi pardoun most I rede,
For I wil construe eche clause and kenne it þe on Engliche.'

And Pieres at his preyere þe pardoun vnfoldeth,
And I bihynde hem bothe bihelde al þe bulle.
Al in two lynes it lay and nouȝt a leef more,   110
And was writen riȝt þus in witnesse of treuthe:

> *Et qui bona egerunt, ibunt in vitam eternam;*
> *Qui vero mala, in ignem eternum.*

'Peter!' quod þe prest þo, 'I can no pardoun fynde,
But "dowel, and haue wel and God shal haue þi sowle,
And do yuel, and haue yuel, hope þow non other
But after þi ded-day þe deuel shal haue þi sowle".'   115

And Pieres for pure tene pulled it atweyne,

> And seyde, '*si ambulauero in medio vmbre mortis, non*
> *timebo mala; quoniam tu mecum es.*

I shal cessen of my sowyng,' quod Pieres, 'and swynk nouȝt
so harde,
Ne about my bely-ioye so bisi be namore.
Of preyers and of penaunce my plow shal ben herafter,
And wepen whan I shulde slepe, þough whete-bred me faille.

þe prophete his payn ete in penaunce and in sorwe,   121
By þat þe sauter seith, so dede other manye.
þat loueth God lelly, his lyflode is ful esy:

> *Fuerunt michi lacrime mee panes die ac nocte.*

And, but if Luke lye, he lereth vs bi foules

We shulde nouȝt be to bisy aboute þe worldes blisse: 125
Ne solliciti sitis, he seyth in þe gospel,
And sheweth vs bi ensamples vs selue to wisse.
þe foules on þe felde, who fynt hem mete at wynter?
Haue þei no gernere to go to, but God fynt hem alle.'
    'What!' quod þe prest to Perkyn, 'Peter, as me þinketh,   13c
þow art lettred a litel. Who lerned þe on boke?'
    'Abstinence þe abbesse,' quod Pieres, 'myne a.b.c. me
        tauȝte,
And Conscience come afterward and kenned me moche more.'
    'Were þow a prest, Pieres,' quod he, 'þow miȝte preche
        where þow sholdest,
As deuynour in deuynyte, with *dixit insipiens* to þi teme.'   135
    'Lewed lorel!' quod Pieres, 'litel lokestow on þe bible,
On Salomones sawes selden þow biholdest—
            Eice derisores et iurgia cum eis, ne crescant, etc.'
þe prest and Perkyn apposeden eyther other,
And I þorw here wordes awoke and waited aboute,
And seighe þe sonne in þe south sitte þat tyme,   140
Metelees and monelees on Maluerne hulles,
Musyng on þis meteles, and my waye ich ȝede.
    Many tyme þis meteles hath maked me to studye
Of þat I seigh slepyng, if it so be myȝte,
And also for Peres þe plowman ful pensyf in herte,   145
And which a pardoun Peres hadde alle þe peple to conforte,
And how þe prest impugned it with two propre wordes.
Ac I haue no sauoure in songewarie, for I se it ofte faille.
Catoun and canonistres conseilleth vs to leue
To sette sadnesse in songewarie, for *sompnia ne cures.*   150
    Ac for þe boke bible bereth witnesse
How Danyel deuyned þe dremes of a kynge
þat was Nabugodonosor nempned of clerkis.
Daniel seyde, 'sire kynge, þi dremeles bitokneth
þat vnkouth knyȝtes shul come þi kyngdom to cleue;   155
Amonges lowere lordes þi londe shal be departed.'
And as Danyel deuyned, in dede it felle after:
þe kynge lese his lordship and lower men it hadde.

And Ioseph mette merueillously how þe mone and þe sonne
And þe elleuene sterres hailsed hym alle.   160
þanne Iacob iugged Iosephes sweuene:
'*Beau filtz*,' quod his fader, 'for defaute we shullen,
I myself and my sones, seche þe for nede.'
  It bifel as his fader seyde in Pharaoes tyme
þat Ioseph was iustice Egipte to loken;   165
It bifel as his fader tolde, his frendes þere hym souȝte.
  And al þis maketh me on þis meteles to þynke;
And how þe prest preued no pardoun to dowel,
And demed þat dowel indulgences passed,
Biennales and triennales and bisschopes lettres;   170
And how dowel at þe day of dome is dignelich vnderfongen,
And passeth al þe pardoun of seynt Petres cherche.
  Now hath þe pope powere pardoun to graunte þe peple
Withouten eny penaunce to passen into heuene;
þis is owre bileue, as lettered men vs techeth: 175

> *Quodcumque ligaueris super terram, erit ligatum et in
> celis, etc.*

And so I leue lelly (Lordes forbode ellis!)
þat pardoun and penaunce and preyeres don saue
Soules þat haue synned seuene sithes dedly.
Ac to trust to þise triennales, trewly me þinketh,
Is nouȝt so syker for þe soule, certis, as is dowel.   180
  Forþi I rede ȝow, renkes þat riche ben on þis erthe,
Vppon trust of ȝowre tresoure triennales to haue,
Be ȝe neuere þe balder to breke þe ten hestes;
And namelich, ȝe maistres, mayres and iugges,
þat han þe welthe of þis worlde (and for wyse men ben holden)
To purchace ȝow pardoun and þe popis bulles,   186
At þe dredeful dome whan dede shullen rise,
And comen alle bifor Cryst acountis to ȝelde,
How þow laddest þi lyf here and his lawes keptest,
And how þow dedest day bi day, þe dome wil reherce;   190
A poke ful of pardoun þere ne prouinciales lettres,
Theigh ȝe be founde in þe fraternete of alle þe foure ordres
And haue indulgences double-folde, but if dowel ȝow help,

I sette ȝowre patentes and ȝowre pardounz at one pies hele.
   Forþi I conseille alle cristene to crye God mercy, 195
And Marie his moder be owre mene bitwene,
þat God gyue vs grace ar we gone hennes
Suche werkes to werche while we ben here
þat after owre deth day Dowel reherce
At þe day of dome, we dede as he hiȝte. 200

TABLE OF VARIANTS[1]

(including select readings from A and C texts)

PROLOGUE

20 putten] W; put L; putte *A*
34 giltles] *A*; synneles L (which should perhaps be retained)
37 þei sholde] hem list *A*
39 is Luciferes hyne] W, *A*; *om.* LMC
67 myschief] mychief L *marked for correction*
74 bonched] cf. *A* bunchide *and varr*; bouched L
99 constorie]: cf. *A* ii. 139, iii. 29; consistorie WCO
140 answeres] LR; answered C
147 myd] W; with L
151 hem[2]] RCO; *om.* LW
179 it] WCRO; *om.* L
186 croupe] L; crope R
197 mannus] LR; mannes *other MSS.* (*-us* a W. Midl. form; cf. *folus* ii. 162)
215 money] monoy L
224 longe] WCO, *A*; dere L (cf. *Sir Gawain*, 92)
226 and] WRO; a L; an C

PASSUS I

37–8 þat leef . . . likam] RO; *om.* LWC *by homœoteleuton*; *v.* Donaldson, *TCA*, p. 192 n. 36
41 sueth] R; seest L; seiþ C2; seeþ WO
   seith] setth C
   it] *om.* O: *v.* n.
57 hij] he *A*
73 asked] h[a]lside *A*
81 kenne] WCRO (cf. *A*); kende L *marked for correction*
100 wolden al] aske þe *A*

---

[1] Most of the readings are chosen from Skeat's collations. They are intended to be illustrative, not inclusive or systematic: the phrase *most MSS.* sometimes refers merely to those cited by Skeat. For explanation of symbols *v.* his parallel-text edn. (1886), pp. lxiv–lxv, and xi above.

107 muryer] C; murger L
139 quod] F, subst. Sk, metri causa; quia L et al.
145 worche] CO; worcheth L (? -þ in exemplar anticipating þ[ow])
150 plante] A (plonte 'D'); plente L etc.
180 good] goed L
204 siȝte of] supplied from A

PASSUS II

8 wortheli] wondirliche A
9 finest] purest A
27 bona] C; bonus LWO
59 chaffare] most MSS.; chaffre L: cf. pr 31
83b for euere to laste A
87 borghe] CR; borgthe L
91 ne in margin bef. wolde L; wermanship L; werk- other MSS.
97 breden] most MSS.; bredun L
116 weddynges] WRO; wendynges L
118 engendred] WO; engendreth LCR (A reads [m]endiu in this l.:
      v. Kane, p. 99)
165 flaterere] WCRO; flatere L
175 deuorses] C; deuoses LR
188 hym] hem A
227 mynstralles] most MSS.; mynstalles L (and at iii. 132)

PASSUS III

6 molde]: Kane justifies A world (p. 437)
17 wil] R; wol W; om. L
58 þe] WO; om. LC
61 whiten] C; whitten L
73 ne] WCR; no L
95 thynke] thynko L
97 brenne] WCO; berne L; forbrenne A
98 þat] WCRO; om. L
107 þe¹] R; þee WO; om. L
127 WRO ins. and after popis
161 she] he RF, A
187 it] WRO, A; om. L and 'D' (A MS.)
227 Quod] WCRO; Quaþ A; Quatz L: cf. vi. 3
252 receperunt] O (cf. Vulg.); reciepebant L etc.
304 other] R; orther L
320 That] C text; Thanne L and other B MSS.

75

322 smytheth] WO; smithie R; smyteth LC
337, 338 she] WC; ʒe L

PASSUS IV

After l. 9 *A*: Of Mede and of mo oþere, what man shal hire wedde;
      C text: Of Mede and of other mo and what man shal hure
      wedde
 24 rit] RO; rydes C; ritte L
 27 for þei] WBO, hy *A*; *om.* L *marked for correction in margin*
 68 ywrouʒt] *most MSS.*, wrouʒt *A*; ywrouʒte L (cf. ypliʒte v. 202)
128 byʒende]: *v.* Donaldson, *TCA*, p. 200

PASSUS V

 13 were] W; was L etc.
 20 at] ar L; er *A* (or V); er C text
 29 Felice] RCO etc.; filice L
108 baren] C; beren W; bar L (hym / þat bar *A*)
143 han] W; *om.* L
154 suffre] *most MSS.*; soeffre L
189 Heruy] WO, *A*; Henri L: *v.* Donaldson, *TCA*, p. 193
212 paknedle] WCO, *A* (pakke-); batnedil L *and* 1 A MS. *v.* ibid.,
      p. 199
213 pynned] C; pynnede O; pyned L
224 no] *most MSS.*; na L
232 Repentedestow] W; Repentestow L
236 be¹] C; *om.* LR
253 Lentestow] W, *and varr. in other MSS.*; Lenestow L
272 tellest] WCRO; telleth L *but marked for correction*
[273] *om.* LWRO etc.; Sk *inserts from* C, *but the sense is doubtful
      and the l. may be spurious*
280 haue¹] C; hath LMR: *v. TCA*, p. 202
281 Ben] WCO; Is LR
291 *quasi*] WCOR; *om.* L
312 she] W; he L
336 aryse þei bisouʒte] arose bi þe southe L; *v. n.*
[338] *om.* LWR; *inserted from* OC
347 godly] *marked for correction but cf.* godeli C text; gothely C
357 þrumbled] cf. [þr]umblide *A*, thrumbled C text; trembled L
      marked for correction; stumbled WCO
370 wif] WO; witte L (His wif [wit]ide hym *A*)

388 to] WCO; *om.* L (? taking *fast(e)* as adv., 'readily')

434 þe] WCO; *om.* L

440 fernyere] WC; ferne ȝer O; farnere L

441 forȝete] *most MSS.*; foȝete L

446 ran] L *marked for correction*; C text ȝede (ȝarn (< OE ȝe-ærnan
'run') as at xi. 59 and C xxii. 380 (and cf. *v. ll.* at C iv. 271)
would provide the expected allitn. The form was sufficiently
rare to induce a scribe to substitute the more familiar *ran*;
v. also Kane, p. 161)

447 haue] C; haue I WO; *om.* L (Donaldson, *TCA*, p. 195 n. 38
suggests that *haue* weakened to *a* in spoken English, and
then disappeared; but he offers no 14th-c. exx.)

448 quod] R, *subst.* Sk, *metri causa*; quia L

514 *nos*] R; *om.* L

549 fourty] LR; fifty WCO

557 of hym] R; *om.* L *et al.*

[569] *om.* LWR, *A*; *inserted from* CO

586 hatte] CR; hatten O; hat L (sg.); hote *A*

590 fees] WCR; foes L; [fees] *A*

600 With] WRO; Wit L *marked for correction*

612 *cunctis*] C; *cuntis* L; *iterum* R; *om.* L *et al.*

613 cliket] C; clikat LR

623 cliketed] C; clikated L

627 aren] R; ar L

PASSUS VI

3 Quod *or* Quaþ *many MSS.*; Quatz LMR (? rationalizing
abbreviation q³: Donaldson, *TCA*, p. 199); cf. iii. 227

6 wolde] WO; wil LR

9 þe¹] WCRO; *om.* L

[49] C; *om.* LWRO: *feeble and prob. spurious*

133 holde *A*; olde L

138 or¹] WCRO; and L

206 to] WCRO; *om.* L

214 And] An L *marked for correction*

223 hem] RO; hym LW

228 aworþe] LMR; yworþ W (cf. C xi. 163: leteth hem yworthe)

229 wilt] WCO; wil L *marked for correction*

230 biloue] WCO; bilow L *marked for correction*

243 hym] WCRO; *om.* L

313 *chaude*] *chaud A and* C text
323 hiderward] WCRO; L
325 ȝere] R; ȝeer O; *om.* L (and several *A* MSS.)

PASSUS VII

16 þis] WCO; þus LR
25 wynnige L wynny*nges* R
75 *tua*[1]] CO; *om.* LR
77 *Deo*] W; *Deum* L
83 *exegissem*] Vulg. *exigissen* CR; *exigerem* L
   illam] *om.* MSS.: cf. Vulg.
88 *querens panem*] OC (cf. Vulg.); *om.* LWR
94 And] A, *marked for correction* L
   ȝoure] here *A*
115 But] WCO; þat LR
137 *Eice*] O (= *Ejice*) (cf. Vulg.); *Ecce* LWRC
187 dede] WCR; ded L

Square brackets in the text represent editorial insertions usually dependent on readings noted above; bold brackets point to a suspect reading.

For a fuller collection of variants *v.* Skeat's edition of the B text (EETS 38; 1869); those in his parallel text edition are selective.

NOTES

PROLOGUE

The opening lines offer verbal resemblances to certain passages in
Somer Soneday, a stanzaic alliterative poem in the W. Midland
dialect, which is assigned by its editors to the period 1327–50:
v. C. Brown, *Studies in English Philology* (Minneapolis 1929,
pp. 362–74, and R. H. Robbins, *English Historical Poems* (1959),
no. 38. The stanzas begin, 'Opon a somer soneday se I þe sonne';
the poet 'warp on [his] wedes' and soon 'in launde under lynde me
leste to lende'; 'So wyde I walkede', he says, 'þat I wax wery of
þe way'. There follows a visionary hunting scene, which edd. take
to allude to the death of Edward II (1327). It is not necessary to
infer that L knew this particular poem (which does *not* include a
dream proper); but the similarities of phrasing suggest that a convention for beginning such alliterative poems had been established
before his time. Two other alliterative poems datable *c.* 1350 have
similar openings:

(i) *The Parlement of the Thre Ages*, which begins:

> In the monethe of Maye when mirthes ben fele
> And the sesone of somere when softe bene the wedres
> Als I went to the wodde, my werdes to dreghe, . . .

and describes a hunt in a wood: the sun grows so warm that the
poet 'slomerede a while' and 'dremed a ful dreghe swevyn' (102).

(ii) *Wynnere and Wastoure* (ed. I. Gollancz), which after a Prologue
of 30 ll. introduces the poet as 'wandrynge myn one / Bi a bonke
of a bourne, bryghte was the sone'; he lies down, but cannot sleep,
'for dyn of the depe water and darylling of foullys':

> Bot as I laye at þe laste þan lowked myn eghne,
> And I was swythe in a sweuen sweped belyue.
> Me thoghte I was in the werlde, I ne wiste in whate ende [quarter],
> On a loueliche lande þat was ylike grene . . . (45–8)

L possibly alludes to this poem at ll. 22 and v. 24–5 below.

Of the relevant conventions that were evidently common by L's
time, the chief is that which associates a dream with a fine May

morning, trees and birds, flowers and flowing water. This is as old as the *Roman de la Rose*, and is adopted by Chaucer in the *Book of the Duchess* and the *Legend of Good Women*. In the first two of these poems the May morning and its setting are part of the dream itself; *PPl*, like *LGW* and *Parlement of the Thre Ages*, makes the May morning the *occasion* of the dream. In casting his Prologue into this form L is appealing to an audience well-read in fashionable secular literature both French and English.

The convention requires that the *persona* of the dreamer should be fictional, whether a purely passive spectator, or the protagonist. In L's *persona* the roles alternate: in the Prologue he is the spectator, in the following passus the interlocutor.

2. *shepe*. Skeat argues, and other editors assume, that the poet purports to be a shepherd; and indeed *shepherde* is the reading of at least one C MS. (HM 137). But the spelling *shepe* should indicate [ē]; *shep*, 'shepherd', [ʃep] is a different form: cf. *OED*, s.v. *shep*. The word for 'sheep' is regularly *shepe* in the Laud MS., e.g. xv. 354, though variant spellings are certainly to be found in other MSS.

In fact l. 3 indicates that the garment resembles a hermit's, not a shepherd's; and *shepe* may simply indicate that this garment is of sheep's wool, or russet; cf. viii. 1: 'Thus yrobed in russet I romed aboute'—referring to this passage; cf. also xviii. 1: 'wolleward and wete-shoed'. *The Romaunt of the Rose*, 6480–1 shows that a hermit's (woollen) dress was distinctive: 'For as thyn abit *sheweth wel* / Thou semest an hooly heremite'. There Amour is addressing Faux-Semblant, and his point is that 'l'abis ne fet pas l'ermite'; Faux-Semblant is a hypocrite, revelling in his hypocrisy. The narrator perhaps means to suggest that his dress made him resemble those hypocritical hermits who went about begging—wolves in sheep's clothing (cf. C x. 140–1, 240 ff.).

4a. *wyde in þis world* is a variant of an earlier formula found in Laȝamon, who describes himself as faring 'wide þurh þes leonde' in search of historical lore. It does not connote travel beyond one's own land.

4b. Cf. allitv. *Morte Arthur*, 2514: 'wondyrs to seke' (of Gawain).

5. *Maluerne*. The evidence connecting the poet with the Malvern district was collected by A. H. Bright in *New Light on Piers Plowman* (1928), which includes some photographs of the area.

Mr. Bright identified to his own satisfaction a field ('Longlands') on the W. side of the Herefordshire Beacon, from which L took his name; the 'burn' of l. 8 by which he slept—traditionally known as Primeswell (now a source of bottled Malvern water) and even the alehouse of vi. 117. Coupling such identifications with ostensible biographical details in the text, Mr. Bright was able to give the poet not only a local habitation but a romantic history of illegitimacy etc., his evidence for the illegitimacy being a passage in C iv. 369—an allegorical episode susceptible of a completely different interpretation. No validity attaches to Mr. Bright's biographical claims, yet some of the topographical correspondences are plausible—in particular, the dale, field, and tower of 14–17; despite the (conventional) disavowal of l. 12, the poet certainly did not take the setting for his 'sleeping' at random. The Malvern Hills do give an unsurpassed panorama, and the spacious setting prepares us for the range and scope of the ensuing visions.

6. *byfel a ferly*: a traditional alliterative phrase; cf. *S. Cuthbert* (Surtees Soc.), 1023: 'Here a ferly þat bifel', *Cursor Mundi*, 11 (Göttingen MS.): 'Of ferlijs þat his knyghtes fell', *Geste Hystoriale*, 95: 'all the ferlies þat fell' [at Troy]; other exx. in *DOST* and *MED*, s.v. *ferly*.

of fairy etc.: 'it seemed to belong to the realm of fantasy'. For the sense of *fairy* as the realm of the supernatural cf. *CT*, F 96 and Henryson, *Fables*, 1775. S. d'Ardenne's explanation of the variant *a faeyrie* is questionable: cf. E. J. Dobson, *RES*, N.S. 17 (1966), 72.

7. *wery forwandred*. The combination of adj. *wery* and what appears to be a past participle with intensive prefix *for* (or some other prefix) is frequent in ME: cf. *wery fortravailled*, allitv. *Morte Arthur*, 806; but neither the grammatical construction nor the way in which it was apprehended in the 14th c. is clear. Several scholars regard *for* in such compounds as formally a preposition governing what was originally a verbal noun similar in character to OE verbal nouns in *-aþ* (*on huntaþ* = a hunting); cf. *gon abegged*, C ix. 138, where *-ed* is historically a nominal suffix, not a p.p. suffix. It is argued that the compound was later 'metanalysed' as a p.p., the prefix (or 'preverb') *for* then being felt as an intensive; probably by the 14th c. the construction was confused with that exemplified in phrases like 'for pure ashamed' (= 'because of pure shame'). Since the combination of *wery* with such compounds seems to be formulaic, the phrase may be treated as a unit—'weary and tired out with wandering'.

For the intensive prefix *for* v. *Knight's Tale*, ed. Bennett, p. 135; *Parlement of the Thre Ages*, ed. Offord, l. 101 n.; and for discussion of current theories v. M. L. Samuels, *English Studies*, 36 (1955), 310–13, and T. F. Mustanoja, *A Middle English Syntax*, i (1960), pp. 382, 562).

⸵ The weariness of the dreamer-narrator is a common feature of vision-literature; cf. *House of Fame*, 115, *Confessio Amantis*, i. 109.

8. *banke*: in ME indicates a feature of the ground rather than the border of a stream; cf. E. V. Gordon's note on *Pearl*, 106.

12. *wildernesse*: lexically = wild, uncultivated land, in which a traveller might lose his way (as Gawain almost does in 'the wilderness of Wirral'); but allegorically the word early took on the scriptural overtones that are still present in the opening sentence of *Pilgrim's Progress*. The Old Testament archetype is the wilderness through which the children of Israel journeyed to the promised land, as the Christian pilgrim journeys through the world (cf. De Guilleville's popular *Pèlerinage de la vie humaine* (1333)—and Chaucer's *Truth*, 17–18). For the formula of 12b cf. *HF*, 128–9, and *Pearl*, 65.

13–16. The dreamer is represented as having been walking for some time. If the dream is set in the landscape of his waking life, the sun (his only guide to time and direction) would be high in the sky as he lay down. He sees in the east a tower standing sharply against the light (identified by Bright with the Herefordshire Beacon). The position of dale and dungeon is not so clearly indicated. Sk assumed that they are in the west, comparing the plan of the 'stage' in the MS. of the morality the Castell of Perseverance: v. *Macro Plays*, frontispiece, and R. Southern, *The Medieval Theatre in the Round* (1957).[1] But there the W. is the position of *mundus skaffold*, *caro skaffold* is S., and *Belyal skaffold* N.; and as the dungeon here is to be described as Satan's (i. 63 f.) we should probably think of it and the 'merke dale' (i. 1) as on the N., traditionally the abode of Satan. 'Deep dale' is used in OE verse solely with reference to hell: *Christ*, 1532, and *Genesis*, 305, 421. (*Depedale* is a Yorks. and Hants place-name.) The 'toure on a toft'

[1] See also plans of Cornish miracle plays repr. F. E. Halliday, *The Legend of the Rood* (1955), pp. 22, 27.

would perhaps suggest the representation of a turreted *mansio* as evidenced in later plays. The scriptural associations of *turris*, *mons*, *oriens* with the Deity are to be developed in P i; they are certainly as fruitful a part of this conception as the theatrical image.

17. *faire*: probably implies *level*. Malory uses it in prose dialogue ('on a fayre fylde I shall yelde him my trewage'—i.e. on a battle-field duly chosen (*Works*, ed. Vinaver, p. 48, l. 24)). 'Faʒerfelde' occurs as a place-name in Derbys., Yorks. (Charter, Magd. Oxf. Misc. 88, 90), and doubtless elsewhere.

19. *as þe worlde asketh*: a formula of alliterative verse; cf. xix. 225, *Sir Gawain*, 530, *Morte Arthur*, 2187, *Deth and Lyf*, 5; with the sense of 'as the course of life [*or* nature *or* fate] requires'; 'worlde' is not used dyslogistically as Robertson and Huppé assume.

20 ff. A 14th-c. field would not be like a modern field, shut in by hedges or fences, but a large open piece of land, probably divided by balks or ridges (cf. vi. 109 n) into acre- or half-acre strips, on which all the villagers would be found on a May morning, either working under supervision of the lord's bailiff or looking on.

21. *swonken*. *Swinke* usually denotes *honest* physical toil—as here; cf. *CT*, A 186, 188, and 531 (referring to the honest ploughman; *v.* Hussey, p. 317 and n.). The ploughman's life was certainly hard: under the two-field system 40 acres were ploughed up every year for winter corn, 40 for spring sowing; whilst 80 acres of stubble were ploughed in April and again in midsummer—taking 283 days in all; the three-field system involved only 17 days fewer.

This early introduction of the ploughman as a typically honest labourer prepares us for the later symbolism of Piers Plowman himself (v. 545 ff.); but Robertson and Huppé's reading of the lines as a reference to the spiritual labours of bishops seems premature, at least.

28. The ME *Ancrene Wisse* conveys a vivid impression of the life of enclosed anchoresses—sometimes actually walled up in their cell or *ankerhold* (cf. *holden*), as was the anchoress who once lived on the site of Mob Quad in Merton College, Oxford (and cf. *VCH London*, i. 585); a hermit, on the other hand, was left more free to wander. Richard Rolle (*ob.* 1349) displays the effectiveness of a hermit's life at its best; but often hermits lived by roads, fords, or bridges (as at Cambridge), where they received alms or tolls, and were liable to

temptations. Piers is prepared to give alms to those of either vocation who 'eten but at nones' (vi. 147) but not to those who had
no genuine calling (cf. C x. 188 ff.). See further R. M. Clay, *The
Hermits and Anchorites of England* (1914) with its supplement in
Journal of the Brit. Archaeological Assoc., 3rd ser. 16 (1953), 74;
and the *Life of St. Christina of Markyate, a Twelfth Century
Recluse*, ed. C. H. Talbot (1959).

33. *mynstralles*. The precise occupation covered by the term has
been the subject of dispute ever since the time of Percy and Ritson.
They were clearly specialized entertainers, and essentially instru-
mentalists rather than singers. R. L. Greene claims that they are
never represented as singing (and in any case only harpers or
drummers would be able to sing as they made music): in that case
it is inaccurate to speak of 'minstrels' song-books' and so forth.
L may have in mind those gleemen who were attached to noble
households or visited them regularly (cf. C x. 128 f.)[1] as distinct from
the vagabond *jongleurs* who are 'Judas children' (a phrase found
later in *Jack Upland's Rejoinder*, 348) inasmuch as they practise
deceit for money, Judas being the prototype of the 'feigner' (cf.
xvi. 155). *iangelers* (35) evidently includes tellers of 'off-colour' or
obscene stories. For similar charges and similar phrasing *v. Jacob's
Well*, p. 134.

It is noteworthy that the poet—here inserting a personal opinion
—approves (with good scholastic warrant) of 'clean' secular entertainment, as well as of the ascetic life. This balance between various
ways of life, religious and secular, is characteristic of the poem:
cf. esp. xix. 224–45.

37. *witte at wille*: 'plenty of intelligence' (and could work if they
had to), a sense confirmed by Henryson, *Fables*, 2110–11: 'Thou
art berne full bald, and wyse at will' (cf. later exx. in Whiting,
W 377).

37–9. Sk cites 2 Thess. 3 : 10: *Qui non laborat non manducet*[2] (which
an early reader has scribbled on the margin of MS. O), and interprets accordingly: '(as for such fellows) that which Paul preaches
about them I might (but will not) prove (or adduce) it here (sc.
else I might be blameworthy myself, since) he who speaks slander
is Lucifer's servant' (*diabolos* = 'slanderer'). Sk adds: 'the quota-

---

[1] Note, e.g., the payments recorded in *BPR*, iii. 317 to a *ministral* and
a *rymour*.   [2] Vulg. *si quis non vult operari nec manducet*.

PROLOGUE

tion *Qui turpiloquium* etc. is not from St. Paul'. This is true; but it may well be a casual, inexact reference to the apostle's words in Eph. 5 : 4: '[nec nominetur in vobis] aut turpitudo aut stultiloquium aut scurrilitas'; the poet has no reason to be afraid of 'proving it' since he is not slandering but speaking truth. Hence render: 'I do not wish to prove in detail that these are the sort of people that St. Paul refers to; [enough to say that] anyone who uses foul language is in the devil's service.'

42. *Fayteden* (as against *A, flite* 'contend') indicates that they were impostors; cf. vi. 123 (which describes one of their tricks), vii. 94 ff., C x. 98 ff.; *Jacob's Well*, loc. cit., and the passage from William of Nassyngton (*c.* 1375) cit. p. 205, below.

44. *roberdes knaues.* The form *roberdesmen* occurs in statutes of Edward III and Richard II; and cf. *OED*, s.v., and *PPl Crede*, 72. It was probably originally a slang term, deriving from the jingle of *Robert* and *robber*: cf. 'Secundus (sc. frater meus) dicebatur Robertus quia a re nomen habuit: spoliator enim diu fuit, et praedo' (cit. Sisam, p. 255). At v. 469 (where again robbery is associated with sloth as an occupation of men too lazy to work) *Robert* is the typical robber.

46. The pilgrim motif that is to be developed in Pv (*ad fin.*) and Pvi is here introduced in the poet's characteristically muted, unobtrusive manner. In a symmetry that can hardly be accidental the poem closes with the same image (xx. 378–9).

palmers. Pilgrims to the Holy Land wore the badge of a palm leaf or cross of palm fronds as a token. But the word is sometimes used for a 'professional' pilgrim as distinct from one making a specific pilgrimage for a specific purpose.

pliȝted. The compact might be as formal as the guild or confraternity founded in 1365 at Burgh (Lincs.) by five men who had gone to Compostela and who made a vow when in peril of shipwreck on the return journey to build an altar to St. James (*v.* H. F. Westlake, *The Parish Guilds of Medieval England* (1919), p. 33), or as loose as the 'felawshipe' described in the opening lines of the *Canterbury Tales*.

47. *seynt Iames.* The shrine of Santiago in the great cathedral of Compostela in NW. Spain was a special favourite with Englishmen, and women (witness the Wife of Bath, *CT*, A 466), being the most accessible of foreign shrines: Margery Kempe was able to reach it within a week of leaving Bristol. In the Calendar of Fine Rolls for 1377–83 this shrine is the most frequently named. The pilgrimage thither was one of the four 'greater' pilgrimages imposed as a penance for serious crimes (the other three being to Rome, Cologne, and Canterbury); hence it is likely that any band of pilgrims bound for Compostela contained a proportion of men to whom lies and 'tall stories' came easily. A lively 15th-c. poem describes the discomforts of the sea voyage (*OBMEV*, no. 236).

seyntes in Rome: i.e. the relics of saints buried in Rome—in particular those buried in the basilicas of St. Peter, St. Paul (fuori muri), Santa Maria Maggiore, etc.; v. *The Stacions of Rome*, p. xxi. In jubilee years (e.g. in 1350) the pilgrimage carried, as it still does, a plenary indulgence; the number of churches to be visited before the indulgence is obtained has varied slightly during the centuries. The Wife of Bath made this pilgrimage too (*CT*, A 465). For the phrase cf. allitv. *Morte Arthur*, 502.

48 suggests that Chaucer did not need a literary precedent for the framework of his Tales: 'a Canterbury tale' was a common expression for 'a tall story' (v. C. Spurgeon, *Chaucer Criticism and Allusion* (1925), i. 116 and *passim*).

50. *to seke seyntes*: evidently a stock alliterative phrase; applied facetiously in allitv. *Morte Arthur*, 1171.

51–2. The association of pilgrims with 'lesinges' is confirmed by Chaucer (*HF* 2122 and *CT*, I 34: 'fables and suich wrecchednesse') and by John Heywood's *Four PP*, in which a pilgrim figures as a contestant in a lying match.

53. The 'hooked stave' may be seen in the miniature from B.M. MS. Roy. 10 E iv reproduced in J. Jusserand, *Wayfaring Life in the Middle Ages* (1892 edn.), p. 139.

54. *Walsyngham*: the most famous English shrine dedicated to the B.V.M. A chapel, perhaps intended to represent the Holy House at Nazareth, was built there in 1130, and enclosed in a special building when a priory was established on the same site. A statue of Our Lady and Child came to be more reverenced than the chapel itself; and near-by wells—still existing—were credited with healing properties. Erasmus describes the shrine as visited and endowed by countless pilgrims; cf. the famous Walsingham ballad published by Pynson, the unique copy of which, in the Pepysian library, is reproduced by J. C. Dickinson, *The Shrine of Our Lady of Walsing-ham* (1956), App. 1. Deloney's ballad of the same pattern, 'As you came from the holy land / Of fair Walsingham', is echoed by Ophelia. Lollard distrust of pilgrimages to this shrine is evidenced shortly after L wrote, when references to the 'witch of Walsingham' appear. It eventually resulted, at the Reformation, in destruction of the shrine; but the ballad kept the association alive; and the devotion has been revived, in recent years, by both Catholics and Anglo-Catholics.

58. *þe foure ordres*: viz. the Carmelites (White Friars), Augustinians (Austin Friars), Dominicans (Black Friars), and Minorites (Grey Friars). For concise descriptions *v. ODCC* and for definitive accounts of their activities in England *v.* D. Knowles, *The Religious Orders in England* (1948, 1958); W. A. Hinnebusch, *The English Friars Preachers* (1951); Aubrey Gwynn, *The Austin Friars* (1940). All friars engaged in preaching, but the Dominicans were pre-eminently the *ordo prediwuntium*. They were favoured by both Edward III and Richard II; Edward II had financed the building of the noviciate house at (and so given the royal appellation to) King's Langley.

L implies that they preached sermons palatable to their rich and powerful patrons: cf. *CT*, A 254 (where 'so plesaunt was his *In principio*' refers to the friars' favourite text); *v.* ibid. for evidence that for a consideration they could be easy-going confessors. The point was repeatedly made by Wiclifites, but no less by the un-impeachable orthodox: cf. Pantin, pp. 159, 211. Their intrusions were much resented by the secular clergy (and even in modern times relations have not always been cordial): *v. Speculum*, 28 (1953), 499–513.

61. *copis* : used for any outer garment of cleric or religious (cf. e.g., *Havelok*, 429) and so here for the friar's cloak (black in the case of Dominicans); but the modern use as the name for the semi-circular vestment worn in processions, at Benediction, etc., is also found; and friars received both kinds of garments as gifts: e.g. one friar was left 'a red Irish mantell', another had 'a blue and red cope woven of cloth of gold'. Chaucer's friar has a semicope of 'double worsted': *CT*, A 262. The king's friar-confessor received 56 ells of cloth a year; cf. *BPR*, iv. 402, 466 for other such gifts; *v.* also xx. 57.

62. *maistres freris*: *A* and C om. *freris*, which may be a marginal gloss that has been absorbed into the B text. *maistres* implies that friars with some show of learning had particular success. The orders had houses of study at both universities, and their increasing preoccupation with the learning of the Schools was often held to be a dangerous departure from the ideals of St. Francis: cf. K. B. McFarlane, *John Wycliffe* (1952), p. 106.

at lykyng: though a decree of 1316 had required all friars to wear habits uniform in length, width, colour and cost.

64. *charite*: a metonymy for the friars, ironically identified with the acts of charity they were supposed to perform: cf. xv. 225–6, xx. 249 ff. For their merchandise *v. CT*, A 232–4.

The literary tradition of anti-friar satire was established by the 13th c. (*v.* R. Tuve, *Allegorical Imagery* (1966), p. 256) and partly accounts for the tone of this passage. The phrasing of 64a is reminiscent of formulas found in popular verses on 'The Twelve Abuses' (R. H. Robbins, *Historical Poems* (1959), no. 55), *inc.*: 'Befte is domesman and gyle is chapman'.

chief to shryue lordes: friars often served as chaplain-confessors to the king and to members of the nobility.

66–7. The primary reference is probably to the growing rivalry between friars and the parish clergy (for details *v.* Pantin, pp. 124 and 157–8). Claiming to have wide powers of absolution, friars forced their way into parish churches, held (public) confessions there, and flattered wealthy parishioners in the hope that their order would benefit from their wills (cf. v. 140–6, vi. 93 n.). When they built their own churches (which sometimes encroached on ancient rights of way), they enticed communicants away from the parish church.

There may well be a further reference to the mischief caused by the interposition of the friars in the general affairs of the Church; and Fr. Aubrey Gwynn (*RES*, 19 (1943), 1–24) goes so far as to suggest that L is alluding specifically to the controversy between the mendicants and Richard Fitzralph, Bishop of Armagh and Chancellor of Oxford, 1356–60. Friars play a sinister role in the final passus.

68. From the times of Jean de Meun, in France, of Dante, in Italy (*v. Paradiso*, 5. 79), and Chaucer, in England, down to Sir David Lindsay (*v. The Poor Man and the Pardoner*), the figure of the pardoner was the constant object of criticism and satire; and L's

charges can be substantiated in many contemporary documents
(*v.* J. Jusserand, 'Chaucer's Pardoner and the Pope's Pardoner' in
Essays on Chaucer, pt. v, Chaucer Soc. Pubcns. (2nd ser., 1884)).
But two points must be borne in mind:

(i) At least two 14th-c. popes (Gregory IX and Urban VI) and
many lesser churchmen spoke strongly against the abuses of the
system of *quæstores*. The University of Oxford proposed the aboli-
tion of the office of pardoner in 1414, though this was not carried
out till 150 years later.

(ii) However scandalous the traffic became, the doctrine on which
it was based was not palpably false or irrational: a pardon, or writ
of indulgence, was simply, at first, a commutation of the temporal
punishment due to sin *in this life*; a specific number of days could
be named because originally these were deductible from a period
of penance imposed by the Church. An indulgence did not secure
salvation and the pardoner was simply the authorized channel
through which the Church dispensed indulgences out of the
inexhaustible treasury of the merits of Christ, the B.V.M., and the
saints. Nor was the money given by the faithful at the time of
receiving these indulgences originally regarded as payment for
them, but as a contribution to the work of the universal church. The
system was not abused until these payments began to be regarded
as the *price* of a pardon and the pardoner began to claim power (as
in l. 70) to absolve from sins without confession or contrition; *v.*
Southern, pp. 136–42 for further discussion, and 99 n below.

L's pardoner is—as many were—a layman, or at least only in
minor orders. His bull is presumably a papal bull, i.e. a formal
statement of the indulgence carrying the seals of various bishops
stating that they had given him licence to preach the indulgence in
their diocese: he should also have had a licence from the king, bearing the royal seal (cf. *CT*, C 335–7). But L's pardoner represents
his bull as giving him powers to absolve his hearers himself, *a pena
et a culpa*, though such absolution ought to be given only by a priest,
after hearing confession; and even a priest would require a special
licence (now known as faculty papers). The Oxford petition of 1414
notes especially that 'although *not* in holy orders the shameless
pardoners preach publicly and pretend falsely that they have full
power of absolving both living and dead alike from punishment
and guilt'.

The climax of the first part of the poem (vii. 116 ff.) is to be
nothing else than a dispute over the validity of pardons.

71. *Of falshed of fastyng* (cf. *A of falseness of fasting and . . .*) could be construed as 'of breaking their vows of fasting'; *Of falshed, of fastyng* would yield slightly easier sense, if *fastyng* in that combination can mean either 'failure to fast' or '[dispense from] obligation to fast'. *vowes ybroken* covers a distinct sin: in the 14th c. Pope Boniface IX and Richard of Bury, Bishop of Durham, both say that pardoners were particularly willing to absolve the perjured and dispense with the execution of vows.

73. The scene strikingly anticipates that at the end of the Pardoner's Tale (*CT*, C 906 ff.).

74–5. *bonched* suggests that the pardoner is pushing the brevet into their very faces, but also browbeating them, whilst *blered* implies that they were almost literally dazzled by the impressive document as well as being fooled by it (the usual sense of the phr.); cf. Lydgate, *Seying of the Nightingale*, 206: 'I was beten and *benchyd* in myn owen face' (where two MSS. read *bonched*).

ragman. The first dated occurrences of the word are in a statute of 4 Edward I (1276) and in an assize roll of 1280 *Placita de ragemannis et de Quo Warranto in Comitatu Nottingham*. Such a roll recorded the answers to inquiries put by justices in eyre to witnesses in each hundred of each shire (and hence was called a hundred-roll). The seals of the witnesses questioned were attached to these long rolls by cutting the bottom edge of the parchment into strips, which thus formed a tattered fringe; and the inquisitors who carried these ragged rolls came to be known as ragmen—half derisively, since the inquiry was designed to augment the royal treasury by fines and penalties. The term became attached to the rolls themselves, and thus to any documents presenting a similar appearance—e.g. to the charter of 1291 by which the King of Scotland and his nobles recognized the suzerainty of Edward I: this carried the seals of some 42 nobles attached in a similar manner. By 1290 'rageman' had come to be used also for a kind of medieval game of 'Consequences' played with a long roll to which things were attached; and 'ragmanroll' became 'rigmarole'; *v.* M. Bemont, in *Essays Presented to T. F. Tout* (1925), and Owst in *Studies Presented to Hilary Jenkinson* (1959), p. 277. In L's time, then, a long parchment tagged with episcopal seals would be likely to evoke the same awe in a simple-minded villager as that produced by the inquisitional visits of the royal justices. We are probably to envisage it as rolled up, so that the pardoner could 'hook in' the rings and brooches. Cf. *Mum and the Sothsegger*, [M] 1565–6.

78. *yblissed*. The bishop is blessed at the consecration ceremony, cf. vii. 13 and *OED*, s.v. *bless*, v.[1] I. 1† b. *s.a.* 1154, 1420. 'If the bishop were doing his work properly, and remembered his consecration vows . . .'

worth bothe his eres: probably a colloquial equivalent to 'worth his salt' or 'on the spot', 'alert to what is going on' (G. K. Johnston (*N & Q* 204 (1959), 243) cites a similar phrase from the Towneley Plays); but possibly = 'worthy to keep his ears', i.e. not to lose them in the pillory as the accomplice of a cheat (which he is, in so far as he allows the pardoner to practise this fraud): so Fancy in Skelton's *Magnyficence* fears 'to lose myn eres twayne (349)'. Yet this particular punishment could hardly befall a bishop. *bothe* in any case is simply emphatic: cf. *CT*, D 1941.

79. *to deceyue the peple*: Wiclif uses the same phrase for the pardoner's practices.

80. *by þe bischop*: 'with the bishop's permission'. Diocesan records show that false pardoners acted in collusion with the official of a bishop (*v.* ii. 173) and so might obtain the use of his seal (giving licence merely to proclaim an indulgence) without the bishop's knowledge.

boy: the 'rogue-pardoner' (*rogue* or *fellow* being the earliest meaning of *boy*: *v.* E. J. Dobson, *MÆ*, 9 (1940), 121; 12 (1943), 71). He persuades the parish priest to allow him to preach by offering to share the takings (81). Thus the priest is more culpable than the bishop.

83. *Persones and parisch prestes*. The distinction is between the *persona*, a rector, the incumbent of the great tithe of a parish, and the unbeneficed priest hired for a small annual salary to assist or take the place of the incumbent (who in the 14th c. was quite likely to be an absentee).

84. The line describes one of the worst effects of the Black Death —the plague (probably bubonic) that overspread Europe in a few years and reached England in 1348, recurring in 1361, 1369, and later. Not only did priests and parsons (as well as monks and friars) die off in great numbers: the cost of living rose and the clergy found that the number of their parishioners was so diminished that they could no longer live on their tithes and oblations. Hence many priests abandoned their parishes—not always waiting for their

bishop's permission—to seek more lucrative duties in London.
The post most often sought there was that of chantry priest, whose
function it was to chant the office for the dead and to say or sing
mass for the souls of the dead founder of the chantry who bequeathed
a fund or property (sometimes including a dwelling) for the support
of the clerk or priest thus engaged. By the middle of the century the
merchant guilds, now growing rapidly in wealth, were endowing
such chapels for their members. They became especially common
in London, where each decade saw some thirty established, and
especially numerous at St. Paul's, where they were greatly abused—
as L evidently knew—until Bishop Braybrook reformed them in
1381. A typical instance of a chaplain who refused to change his
easy chantry post for a parish, because a pestilence (that of 1361–2)
was afflicting the East Riding district to which he had been assigned,
is noted by Thompson, p. 123 n. 1. For the evils of non-residence
v. Pantin, pp. 27, 98–9, 115. [*v.* Addenda, p. 226.]

86. *symonye.* In so far as chantries could be obtained in return for
services rendered, or even by straight purchase, they could give
rise to simony (the purchase or sale of an ecclesiastical office or
anything annexed thereto: Acts 8: 18–24); *v. Ayenbite*, p. 41,
Pantin, p. 216. The abuse was not peculiar to the Middle Ages, or
the Catholic Church. For contemporary refs. *v.* Yunck, pp. 248, 263.

87–91. *Bischopes*: i.e. the 'curial' or 'court' bishops—so called
because they received a bishopric as a reward for being reliable
servants of the Crown. Criticism of such bishops, who were likely
to treat their office as a perquisite rather than a high duty, dates
from Stephen Langton; William of Wykeham, Bishop of Winchester, is a notable example in L's day: *v.* Pantin, pp. 14, 41, etc.

The absence of bishops from their dioceses became much more
common towards the close of the 14th c. The fact that these lines
are new in B (written *c.* 1378) may show that L took note of changes
taking place between the beginning of his first recension and of his
second. They have, indeed, all the appearance of an insertion, consisting as they do of general statement, as contrasted with the
descriptive narrative of the poem so far and of the nearest equivalent
lines in A (90–1). In A this reference to bishops occurs after A's
equivalent to 210–15. It looks as if the poet's decision to treat all
the clergy together led him momentarily to forget the dream scene
that he has hitherto been building up (he has already allowed himself critical comment in ll. 78–82). And the change to the present

PROLOGUE

tense encourages him to expand his indictment, at some cost to the
unity of tone.

Both *cure* and *crounyng* may thus be quips, in L's characteristic
punning manner—*cure* being used primarily to suggest the proper
duty of spiritual oversight of these *curial* bishops; *crounyng* (a nonce-
use; but *tonsure* is not evidenced till 1387) primarily suggests the
monastic or priestly tonsure of bishops (and bachelors of divinity),
but also indicates that they should be thinking of the roles associated
with this tonsure rather than on service to an earthly *croun*.

91. London would be the usual home of curial bishops (and in any
case many bishoprics had London palaces, used by the bishop whenever business took him to court); whilst for the lesser clergy it
served as a mart for benefices (as well as the chantries just noted).
It was possible (as the career of Wiclif shows) to sell a rich benefice
for ready money and buy with the proceeds one poorer, smaller, or
easier, using the surplus for personal needs. St. Botolph Bishopgate
is an example of a London church that changed hands six times in
twenty-one years. The traffickers in benefices acquired the name
of 'choppe-churches' (cf. 'chop and change').

Lenten. The time when priests ought to be particularly busy in
their parishes, hearing the confessions of parishioners before their
yearly communion at Easter. Thompson (p. 144 n. 5) cites a
pertinent record from Doncaster: 'there are mm [2,000] howslyng
people and above within the sayd paryshe, wherof the sayd incumbent and other vij prystes, now resiaunt in the sayd churche, can
skant here the confessions of the sayd parochians from the begyn-
nyng of Lente unto Palme Sunday; and then ministre the blessed
sacrament all the sayd weke, with other requisite besines to be doon
in the sayd churche' (*Yorks. Chantry Surveys,* i. 175).

92. The employment of clergy in secular business to the neglect
of their spiritual duties was one of the evils against which Wiclif
fulminated: he denounced such clergy as Caesarian (cf. *VCH
London,* i. 211): they rendered to Caesar what was due to God.

The particular royal service referred to in this l. is that of the
medieval exchequer—a commission for the receipt of revenue and
the audit of accounts, named from the rectangular board of red and
white pieces at which the royal officers sat.[1] Already in the reign

[1] A complete account of the functions of this office is given in the
12th-c. *Dialogue De Scaccario* by Richard of Ely (tr. C. Johnson, 1950).
Cf. A. Steel, *The Receipt of the Exchequer,* 1377-1485 (1954).

of Henry II we find a bishop present at every session—besides the permanent officers; and in the decade in which this Prologue was written, a bishop of Exeter (Thomas Brantingham) was royal treasurer.

The *Chancery* (l. 93), or chancellor's court, dealt chiefly with petitions addressed to the king. It was only *c.* 1350 that it had ceased to follow the king on his progresses and became fixed in London. The chancellor was at first always in orders—indeed, he was chief of the royal chaplains; and the officers of the chancery long retained an ecclesiastical character. Whilst mainly employed in purely secular business, many of them held prebends and parish churches with cure of souls, being granted, as royal clerks, special indulgence in the matter of non-residence. Some were notable pluralists, and in 1381 the house of Commons (like a modern Select Committee on National Expenditure) proposed staff reductions, complaining that many of the king's clerks were 'too fat in body and purse alike'; similar causes of discontent perhaps lay behind the attempt that began in 1371 to replace clerics by common lawyers as 'heads of departments'.

But possibly L has especially in mind the chancellorship itself. From 1367 to 1371 the chancellor was William of Wykeham, Bishop of Winchester, whose bishopric had been a reward for his usefulness as superintendent of building works and, later, as Keeper of the Privy Seal. Serious charges had been brought successfully against Wykeham in 1376.

The chancellor of John of Gaunt's Duchy of Lancaster (a large part of England) was at this time also a bishop, and doubtless spent much time in London.

94. *wardes. OED* follows Sk in interpreting as the divisions of a city or borough, a sense it certainly has in *wardmotes*—the meetings held in each ward at which the exchequer clerks would claim the dues payable to the king. But the very occurrence of *wardmotes* suggests that *warde* has a different reference, which may be to the minors whose guardianship the king could claim (a sense of *warde* well attested at this date). As supreme feudal lord the king could claim this guardianship whenever one of his tenants-in-chief died leaving a minor as head: until the minor came of age all the revenues of the estate concerned went to the Crown, forming as a whole an important part of the revenues collected by the exchequer. [*v.* Addenda.]

weyues: an Anglo-French legal term, often used in legal documents in the collective sg., meaning lost property collectively of a manor or the right of a lord to such property. It could thus cover anything from strayed cattle to a find of wild honey and a stranded porpoise, or other objects washed up on the beach. Certain property of this kind still legally belongs to the Crown.

streyues: is often found in conjunction with *weyues*,[1] and usually interpreted as referring specifically to strayed animals, but Sk in Gl. (1886) associates it with the form *estrayeres*, a word which means the property of deceased aliens, etc. without legitimate heirs, which property becomes crown property.

95. Wiclif (or a Wiclifite) complains of religious Pharisees that 'þei geten hem worldly offis in lordis courtis, summe to ben stiwardis of halle, summe to ben kechene clerkis, summe to ben lordis anyneris [collectors of annual accounts] . . . and also to ben chamberleyns to lordes and ladies' (*Eng. Works*, ed. Mathew, p. 13). They would 'sytten and demen' in manorial or honorial courts: cf. C viii. 33–4. *BPR*, iv. 560 records the appointment of a parson to be surveyor of the underwood and the game and warren in a forest belonging to the Black Prince.

99. For the form *constorie* (= *consistorie*) *v. MED*: a consistory court is a court held by a bishop, or his official, to consider any case in which an ecclesiastic is involved. Against its verdict there was no appeal. L had little reason to think that the consistory courts of his day would ever act effectively to suppress the practices just described. He must leave it to the Day of Judgement, to the final great Consistory when Christ, enthroned, would say to those who had neglected their duties 'depart from me, ye cursed' (Matt. 25: 41). But *consistorium* was also used for the solemn council of cardinals held regularly by the pope; and it calls to mind the dictum (based on Matt. 16: 19, which is to be cited at vii. 175) 'unum est consistorium et tribunal Christi et papae in terris'.[2] It thus leads on to a discussion of cardinals and the papal power of binding and loosing committed by Christ to St. Peter and his successors—a power that is to be predicated of 'Piers' at the close of

[1] A beast might be claimed by one lord as a 'weif' and by another as 'estreif': cf. *BPR*, iv. 255.

[2] Alvarius Pelagius (*fl. c.* 1330) *De Planctu Ecclesiae* (ed. Leyden, 1617, 1 a 12).

the poem (xix. 180) and that is central to the doctrine of indulgences already glanced at. Cf. S. Bullough, *Roman Catholicism* (1963), pp. 114, 146.

102 ff. According to St. Augustine, Fortitude, Prudence, Temperance, and Justice, the four virtues of classical philosophy (which St. Ambrose was the first to describe as 'cardinal'), can only be understood as special forms of Love, the chief of the theological virtues of Faith, Hope, Love (1 Cor. 13: 13); cf. *CA*, iv. 2326–7, and *King Hart*, 764. St. Thomas formally proves Love's pre-eminence, *Summa*, II. i. Q 66, art. 2.

The double sense of *cardinal* (< *cardo*, 'hinge') prompts L to allude first to the role of the virtues (cf. 'ryth as þe harre [hinge] gouernyth þe dore, so þise . . . vertues, vsyd and hauntyd [practised] gouerne justly a manys lyf': John Drury, cit. *Speculum*, 9 (1934), 78) and then to the cardinals of the papal consistory, who are thus associated with the pope, earthly representative of St. Peter to whom Christ gave the keys of the gates of heaven.

The clue to L's thought is perhaps to be found in the Second Epistle of Peter, 1: 5–8, where the apostle enjoins the practice of particular virtues in a sequence culminating in *amorem fraternitatis* and *caritatem*.

106. *hem* must refer to the virtues themselves: those that practise them are to enjoy heaven (cf. vii. 12, 36, 46 ff.—where again the papal function is involved).

The cardinals of the curia or consistory take their name from *cardo* (hinge) and should therefore (L implies) pre-eminently exercise the 'vertues cardinales' (cf. xix. 405–11). They represent the *sacerdotium*, the priesthood that *should* be preoccupied in preparing souls for heaven: *cauȝt of* (107) has an ironical ring: as if to suggest that they have taken the name without the virtues that go with it; and in 109 they are said to have arrogated to themselves the power of making a pope—a power which, until the Third Lateran Council of 1179, in theory belonged to the whole Church.[1]

108–9. The sense of the psg. as now punctuated is: 'I don't wish to question that they really have the power of making a pope who will have the power that Peter had . . .'

The psg. probably alludes, if cryptically, to the election of an antipope in Sept. 1378. Certain French cardinals, annoyed by

[1] See Southern, pp. 152–5, and *Documents of the Christian Church* (ed. H. Bettenson, 1943), p. 140.

Urban VI's denunciation of their avarice, declared that his election (to which they themselves had agreed) was improper, and elected Clement VI instead, thus bringing about the Great Schism. The news reached England quickly and the Crown took the side of Urban, not least because of long-standing English dislike of cardinals (French cardinals in particular) who had become increasingly oligarchical and nationalistic (especially in regard to appointments to prebends) during the so-called Babylonish captivity of the popes at Avignon: cf. Gower, *Mirour de l'Omme*, 18961 ff.

110 f. The primary sense is: a pope should be elected in accordance with the principles of love and learning—i.e. scriptural and theological knowledge; implying that the cardinals who elected the antipope had neither. But 'election' also has the theological meaning of salvation; and the verses cited above from 2 Pet. 1 (5–7) are in fact followed by a reference to this *electionem* (verses 10–11): 'satagite ut per bona opera certam vestram vocationem et electionem faciatis', etc. The whole chapter is a cluster of the themes that L is adumbrating: *letterure* corresponding to *scientia* (verse 5), love to *amor fraternitatis* (verse 7); and the Petrine emphasis on *bona opera* is relevant to the interpretation of the pardon scene in Pvii below.

112 ff. From the pope, head of all earthly kingdoms, L turns to the king, head of the secular arm. Richard II had come to the throne in June 1377, at the age of ten. His government was conducted by a council of peers, so that 'knighthood' could be said actually to guide him in his minority; and 113, a succinct statement of one medieval theory of kingship, might also be read as a neat refce. to the actual presentation of the new king to his people: at the coronation ceremony in July the Archbishop of Canterbury, as was the custom, turned to the crowd, asking if they agreed to have Richard as their king; and they answered 'Yes'—'with a great cry', says one chronicler (*v.* further *MÆ*, 12 (1943), 57).

114 ff. *Kynde Witte*: literally 'natural, innate sense of knowledge'; but usually referring to the moral aspect of human actions: cf. Dunning, p. 39, and R. Quirk, *JEGP*, 52 (1954), 182–8.

clerkes, like *clergye* (116), is often ambiguous in L since in the 14th c. men of learning were usually clerks in orders. Here the primary refce. must be to the educated bishops and abbots who sat with the lords temporal ('knyȝthode') in parliament and decided conjointly with the king what resources the Commons should

NOTES

supply so that the king and his council might carry on the government. Hence *himself fynde* will mean (*pace* Sk)'provide for them'; cf. C iv. 377 ff.:

> Ac relacion rect is a ryhtful custome
> As, a kyng to cleyme the comune at his wille
> To folwe hym, to fynde hym, and fecche at hem hus consail.

The usual senses of *comune, comunes* in the early 14th c. were commonalty, commonwealth, the common people. But by L's time *comunes* had acquired more specific meanings: (i) as describing the burgesses attending parliament (as distinct from the knights of the shire) and (ii) (since both these groups deliberated together and were dismissed together) burgesses and knights of the shire conceived of as a single group, as distinct from the lords; cf. Donaldson, pp. 88 f., J. Jolliffe, *Constitutional History of Medieval England* (1937), pp. 321–8, 358 and J. G. Edwards, *The Commons in Medieval English Parliaments* (1958).

118. *of kynde witte*: ? 'in accordance with the dictates of good sense': cf. C: 'Kynde wit and the comune contreuede alle craftes.'

119. The Commons required ploughmen (by synecdoche, the labouring classes) to work honestly. There may be specific refce. to legislation passed after the Black Death regulating wages and conditions of labour. 'Profit of all the people' is a variant of the phrase *common profit* found frequently in treatises and documents (e.g. *BPR*, iii. 73) of the period. On L's political philosophy *v.* A. B. Ferguson, *The Articulate Citizen* (1965), pp. 60 and 65.

121–2. On *lewte* in the sense of *justicia*, good rule, *v.* P. M. Kean, *RES*, N.S. 15 (1964), 254–6 (Blanch, p. 147).

123–45. The ulterior purpose of this incident is to indicate how king, lords, and commons may best 'know their own', i.e. recognize their true rights, and duties (on the implications of the phrase *v.* F. Copleston, *History of Philosophy* (1950), ii. 172, and P. M. Kean, loc. cit., p. 243). There is no warrant for the fancy that the lunatic represents the poet in another *persona*, but certainly his prayer is to be taken seriously. For lunatics as prophets and apostles *v.* C x. 111–18.

128 ff. An *angelus aureus* appeared in the pageant presented to Richard II on the day before his coronation (Walsingham, *Historia Anglicana*, R.S., i. 331–2); and a similar device was used at the entry of Queen Isabella into Paris in 1380 and in another royal pageant in London in 1392 (*v.* E. Rickert, *Chaucer's World* (1948), p. 38). Owst (*MLR*, 20 (1925), 270) proposed to relate the present psg. to the sermon *pro rege et pace regni* preached by Thomas Brinton, Bishop of Rochester, on the day after the coronation (17 July 1377), on the mutual duties of lords and ecclesiastics, etc. —possibly that now printed as Sermon 44 in Brinton's *Sermons*, ed. M. A. Devlin (Camden Soc., 1954): *v.* her Introd., pp. xx, xxvii. L may well have such a sermon, and such a pageant, in mind, though the opposition between justice (*jus*) and mercy (*pietas*) is a commonplace. C gives the verses to Conscience. Latin was still the usual language of such sermons (as of political tractates). 129–30 do not (*pace* Sk) imply that 'common people ought not to be told how to justify themselves; all who could not understand Latin or French had best suffer and serve', but simply that they did not know how to present their views: they themselves speak Latin at 144. For preachers likened to angels *v.* Owst, p. 579.

The verses are not original: they are found in Lambeth MS. 61, f. 147ᵛ, where they were added by a scribe to the text of a sermon preached in 1315 by Henry Harclay, Chancellor of Oxford; for minor variants *v. N & Q*, 205 (1960), 364 and 436. A later version is found in B.N. lat. 5178, f. 69.

For the metre (*versus leoninus*, after Pope Leo the Great) *v.* E. R. Curtius, *European Literature and the Latin Middle Ages* (1953), p. 151.

Translate: '[You say] "I am a king, I am a prince"; but you may be neither hereafter. You who administer the supreme laws of Christ the king [of kings], that you may do it the better, be merciful as you are just. Naked justice needs to be clothed by you in mercy. Sow as you would reap. If justice is stripped bare [by you], may it be measured out to you in the same fashion. If mercy is sown, may you reap mercy.'

Cf. the first version of *CA*, viii. 2989–92, where Gower praises Richard II for his 'justice medled with pite'.

139. *goliardeys*: for the association with the mysterious if not mythical Golias (Goliath) *v.* J. H. Hanford, *Speculum*, 1 (1925), 35–58. The term covered any clerk who had abandoned or dishonoured his vocation; hence Owst's identification (Owst, pp. 576–88; cf. Donaldson, pp. 113–14) with the worthy Sir Peter de la Mare, Speaker of the 'Good' Parliament, is very doubtful (cf. C. Brett, *MLR*, 22 (1927), 261–3). The insistence on strict *jura* bespeaks a political theorist rather than a parliamentarian, and is consonant with the doctrine of Dominion that Wiclif had developed before Convocation in Feb. 1377; hence *goliardeys* may allude to his garrulous Lollard followers (cf. Pantin, p. 170). L apparently accepted the supposed etymological connection with *gula* (gluttony), for which *v. Neophilologus*, 51 (1967), 230 ff.

The Latin verses are a variant of a couplet:

> O rex, si rex es, rege te, vel eris sine re, rex;
> Nomen habes sine re, nisi te recteque regas, rex.

(cit. Sk from *Political Poems*, ed. T. Wright (1859), i. 278). They depend on a petrified etymology popularized by Isidore of Seville (*v. Speculum*, 3 (1928), 580). Charlemagne embodied it in his *Capitulum*, drawing the conclusion that a king who did not keep his coronation *praecepta* should be deposed: *v.* Gierke, *Political Theories of the Middle Ages* (tr. Maitland, 1900), p. 141; Bloomfield, p. 210 n. 34; and Gower, *Cronica Tripertita*, i. 4–12. The ll. were to prove prophetic of a charge brought against Richard at his deposition.

145. A metrical variant of a maxim of Roman law: *quod principi placuit legis habet vigorem*—behind which, in fact, lay the thesis that all power was ultimately derivable from the people (*v.* Gierke, p. 147); hence the caution implied in 'construe hoso wolde'. On the medieval interpretations of the maxim *v.* Fortescue, *De Laudibus Legum Angliæ*, ed. S. B. Chrimes (1942), pp. 24–7, W. Ullmann, *The Listener*, 13 July 1961, p. 54, and *Speculum*, 38 (1963), 296 ff., 39 (1964), 240.

146 ff. The fable of the Cat and the Rats was a favourite *exemplum*, used by Odo of Cheriton (*ob.* 1247), Nicholas Bozon (*fl. c.* 1320), Eustace Deschamps, John of Bromyard (in his *Summa Predicantium*; *v.* Owst, p. 583), and by Bishop Brinton in a sermon preached before convocation, 18 May 1376, during the Good Parliament (Sermon 69 in M. A. Devlin's edn.; *v.* her Introd., p. xxv). But L's version has features not found elsewhere, including the 'raton' of 158 and the 'mous' of 182; Brinton's is slighter in scale, and different in purpose, for he urges action.

The rats may stand for the lords temporal (cf. 116) or for the knights of the shire, the mice for either M.P.s in general or the burgesses, especially those representing the rising middle classes. The cat may be John of Gaunt (rather than Edward III), whose Duchy of Lancaster constituted almost a separate kingdom: the

Good Parliament had denounced his conduct of the French campaigns and insisted on his being replaced by a council. There was at least one attempt on his life. For fuller discussion *v.* Bennett, *MÆ*, 12 (1943), 55–64, and E. M. Orsten, *Medieval Studies*, 23 (1961), 216–39 (a somewhat different view); and cf. the figs. in Skelton's *Why Come Ye not to Court?*, where Wolsey is the mastiff cur chasing the mouse-like nobles (290–6).

The fable is represented on a 15th-c. misericord in Great Malvern Priory, and in the Rutland Psalter, f. 61 (pl. 10 in L. M. Randall, *Images in Margins of Gothic MSS.* (1967)).

158. The description fits Peter de la Mare (*v.* 139 n.), who is described as 'bien parlaunt et sagement rehersant les maters et purpose de ses compaignons' (*v. MÆ*, loc. cit.). 160b suggests that he is speaking from the viewpoint of Westminster.

161–2. (C: *byȝes of bryȝt gold*). In *Purity* Belshazzar promises Daniel that he will put 'þe byȝe of bryȝt gol aboute þyn nekke' (1638); *v.* R. J. Menner's edn., p. xxx. But L's later inexact refce. to Daniel (vii. 152 ff.; *v.* n.) militates against the suggestion that he knew this particular alliterative poem.

The *biȝes* and *colers* may be early allusions to the collars worn as livery by supporters of certain great lords: Gaunt kept such a posse about him in London, and his badge included a collar of S's (first represented on the tomb of Sir John Swinford at Spratton, *c.* 1371). Richard II was to use similar badges; and one of Henry IV's first acts was to refuse to allow any save his own servants to wear livery badges (cf. *Mum and the Sothsegger*, ii. 2 ff.).

176 ff. may obliquely intimate that the proposals of the Good Parliament were of little effect, or, more generally, that parliament was not yet strong enough to impose its will.

181. Cf. xvii. 246: 'Al thi laboure is loste and al thi longe trauaille.'

185 ff. As long as the King was a minor ('kitoun'), the chances were that if Gaunt were removed he would be replaced by another Protector, and the nobles ('ratones') would remain tyrannical, whilst the commons (the mice) would continue to behave selfishly.

186. *benches*: perhaps alluding to the benches on which M.P.s sat.

189. Evidently formulaic; cf. Heywood, *Dialogue* (1546): 'Many yeres sens, my mother seyd to me . . .' (2108–9).

191. Lat. *Vae tibi, terra, cujus rex puer est et cujus principes mane comedunt*: Eccles. 10: 16. A favourite medieval quotation, found in John of Salisbury, *Policraticus*, 550a; Dante, *Convivio* (Temple Classics edn., p. 311); Adam of Usk, *Chronicle, s.a.* 1382; *Political Poems* (ed. Wright), ii. 268 (and cited by Buckingham in More's *Life of Richard II*, p. 74 n.; *v.* also *Life of Wolsey*, ed. Sylvester, p. 88). For the variant cit. Bloomfield, p. 210 n. 34 *v. Speculum*, 44 (1969), 676.

193 ff. Gaunt was concerned with larger game than mere burgesses—with the rival nobles (like Edmund Mortimer), who were likely to be equally inimical to the commons' interests. For the possibility of a more literal interpretation *v. MÆ*, 12. 55–64: the supply of conies for feasts was a matter of some importance to great lords; cf. *BPR*, iv. 182, 433.

200. *wille: reik*, the reading in C as found in Bodl. 814 (cf. *reed* HM 137, *reed* under *ryot* HM 143, and Southern *Octavian*, 182), improves the allitn.; a scribe has probably replaced it by a more familiar word: *v. MÆ*, 8 (1939), 118.

203–5. C's *ne carpen* is syntactically more coherent; and one would expect pl. prons. at 205 (where alliteration fails).

206. Sk translates 'coupled and uncoupled' as 'held in or free' (cf. *Midsummer Night's Dream*, IV. i. 113); but if the animal is held in it cannot run after its prey, whereas the speaker is advising that it should be allowed to do so: 'jointly or severally' would suit the context.

210 ff. The transition to the law-courts appears less abrupt if we recall that parliament itself was still primarily a court and some of the knights of the shire were lawyers who took the opportunity of transacting their clients' business at Westminster.

210. *houues*: coifs or skull-caps tied beneath the chin, originally covering the tonsure; at this time the distinguishing mark of men of law (cf. the Ellesmere miniature of Chaucer's lawyer). On the status of serjeants-at-law *v.* G. O. Sayles, *Select Cases in the Court of King's Bench under Edward III* (1965), VI. xxx.

215a. The phrase appears in a similar context in the 15th-c. *London Lickpenny*, 28. To plead for money had once been thought dishonest—'vendre sa langue'. Cf. vii. 42 n.

216. *Barones*: possibly here = 'judges of the court of exchequer' (who were sometimes in orders) or even 'aldermen of the City of London'; cf. *MED*, s.v. 4 (b).

218. *Baxsteres and brewesteres*: the *-stere* suffix is not necessarily fem., even in OE use; but the trades of baking and brewing were often carried on by women; cf. v. 219.

For these and the other occupations referred to *v.* Lipson (index) and L. F. Salzman, *Building in England* (1952), pp. 1–26, 82, etc.; 'miners' included men employed to dig foundations, 'masons' covered master craftsmen, 'layers', 'setters', etc. For butchers *v.* E. L. Sabine, *Speculum*, 8 (1933), 335.

224. 'and pass the whole day [cf. *CT*, I 300 and *CA*, iv. 3390 for this sense of 'drive forth'] singing "Dieu vous save, Dame Emme" ' —evidently the refrain of a traditional song, perhaps about Emma wife of Canute, who was falsely accused of unchastity, and survived the ordeal of walking on red-hot ploughshares. A minstrel sang 'the deeds of Emma' at St. Swithun's Winchester in 1338: *v.* Warton's *History of English Poetry* (1871 edn.), ii. 97. The story may have been given a ribald turn by the dubious associations of the Dame Emma of xiii. 340.

225 ff. The street cries hardly varied for three centuries, as Gibbons's 'London Street Cries' and Morley's *History of Bartholomew Fair* (1857), bear witness. The *locus classicus* is *London Lickpenny* (*OBMEV*, no. 200); *v.* also *CT*, A 4346–51.

228 ff. *Osey* is usually identified with Alsace (Auxois). The sweet 'straw' wine still made there was certainly imported in some quantity; but in the 15th-c. *Libelle of English Policy* 'Osey' is listed as a commodity of Portugal; the name probably came to be applied to other wines of similar character. Gascon wines were renowned for their strength and fine ruby colour, and the French wars never entirely interrupted the traffic (for which *v.* M. K. James, *Studies in the Medieval Wine Trade* (1971), esp. pp. 21 ff.). La Rochelle was, as it still is, an export centre for Bordeaux wine (cf. *CT*, C 571); ceded to England by the Treaty of Brétigny (1360), it had been under French control since 1372; hence both red Bordeaux and white Rochelle were scarce at this time, and Rhenish (white) was always scarce and dear. For the collocation 'Rhenish and Rochelle' cf. *Sir Degrevant*, 1430 and n., and the contemporary allitv. *Morte Arthur*, 200–5.

PASSUS I

1. *this montaigne*: the toft of pr 14. L is to associate it with the scriptural *mons sanctus, mons Domini*; cf. Ps. 14 (cited at ii. 38) and Isa. 2: 2–4 (cited at iii. 306, 322).

3 ff. The 'loueli ladi' is introduced to explain the dream scene much as is Raison in the *Roman de la Rose* (and to that extent she provides another fleeting suggestion of the locutions of secular poetry):

> The lady of the highe ward
> which from hir tour lokide thiderward
> —Resoun men clepe that lady—
> Which from hir tour deliverly
> Com down to me withouten more...
> God himself that is so high
> Made hir after his image.
>
> (*Romaunt*, 3191 ff.)

Raison warns against Amors, just as Holy Church warns against worldliness, while commending Reason and *caritas* (54, 87).

The device of a dialogue in which a wise and comely lady instructs catechistically is as old as Boethius' *Consolatio*; and Holy Church appears as a spokeswoman for Reason and *caritas* in the 14th-c. *Mirror of Simple Souls*. In De Guilleville's *Pèlerinage de la vie humaine* (1333) (tr. Lydgate, 1496 ff.) Raison likewise descends from a tower and discourses.

In medieval art and drama Holy Church is regularly represented as a beautiful woman, partly because of the traditional interpretation of the Song of Songs, partly because of the consequential identification with the bride of the Lamb in Apoc. 19: 7. There she is arrayed, as Holy Church is here, in fine linen—in contrast to the Whore of Babylon, just as Holy Church is to be contrasted with the overdressed Lady Meed in P ii. L would be familiar with representations of this figure similar to those that survive in innumerable miniatures of the Crucifixion (e.g. Gorleston Psalter, f. 42); on the chapter-house doorway at Rochester Cathedral, and the S. porch of the SE. transept at Lincoln, and in glass at Canterbury and York.

5. *sone*: cf. the confessor's address to 'mi sone' (*CA*, i. 206). Holy

Church, as a superior, uses 2 sg. forms in all remarks addressed to the dreamer alone, while he uses the respectful plural (e.g. 136).

slepestow: does not necessarily imply reproach for 'spiritual torpor' (Robertson and Huppé); the same phrase is used by Mandeville in an account of a knight who appeared in a vision to a certain Changuys, saying: 'Can, slepest þow? The immortall god hath sent me', etc. (*Travels*, ed. Hamelius, p. 147, l. 2); and cf. *Guy of Warwick*, 10557 f.

6. *mase*: as the Rat fable in which this word is used (pr 196) is not found in A, its occurrence here cannot be a direct identification of the confusion of human endeavour with that symbolized in the Prologue fable. Yet 'maze' does quite clearly indicate what impression the Prologue's description of miscellaneous and undirected human activity was intended to convey: namely the restlessness of people caught in the labyrinth of the search for worldly gain. For miniature mazes which supposedly typified the labyrinth of man's life and spiritual progress in this world *v.* Jean Gimpel, *The Cathedral Builders* (1961), pp. 52, 53. To traverse these routes was a stay-at-home's substitute for a real pilgrimage to the Holy Places of Jerusalem.

7. Holy Church first draws a general lesson: most men are so occupied with gain or comfort that they never look up to the tower of Truth, i.e. of God; cf. Ps. 60: 4 (*turris alethiæ* is a stock association— *v. MÆ*, 34 (1965) 226; cf. also Chaucer, *Boece*, IV, pr vi, 239: 'the hye tour' of God's providence). God in creating man provided for all his necessities, and bade the earth bring forth everything after its kind (17–18 being an allusion to Gen. 1: 11 ff.). But these *bona naturæ* (in the scholastic phrase) are to be used in moderation.

This exordium includes three of L's basic conceptions:

(i) The creation was an act of divine goodness (cf. i. 82 and v. 488);

(ii) One should not fix one's heart on worldly pleasure (cf. vii. 125);

(iii) One should observe the mean in all things. From this last principle (common to ascetic and scholastic doctrine)[1] derives most of the criticism and satire in the poem. Thus Meed (ii. 15 ff.), the friars (pr 61–2), *Gula* (v. 346), the dreamer himself (viii ff.), all contravene it.

---

[1] For its 14th-c. associations with Aristotle *v. Mediæval and Renaissance Studies*, 4 (1958), 116.

9. Alluding to the doctrine of Luc. 6: 24.

14. Sc. *þat* ('who') after *feith*; cf. 39 (where C has *þat wolde*); a common omission of the relative.

20. A re-statement of the medieval doctrine of common use (as distinct from communism), stated by Gratian thus: 'communis usus omnium quae sunt in hoc mundo omnibus hominibus esse debuit'. This provides a partial gloss on pr 17 ff.: the ploughmen should not keep to themselves all the food they produce, nor craftsmen work merely for themselves. For *curteisye* in this context cf. 'Yet is God a curteis lord', *OBMEV*, no. 131. For the 'þree þinges' cf. Ecclus. 29: 28: *initium vitæ hominis aqua et panis et vestimentum et domus* . . . (expanded at 39: 31).

27. The story of Lot is the standard example of the abuse of things given in common: his gluttony leads to lechery and so to still direr consequences; cf. *CT*, C 481–6, again with reference to Lot. The quotation after 31 is from Genesis 19: 32, (Vulg. *inebriemus*); *v. N & Q* (1971), p. 284.

33. The Moabites and Ammonites who sprang from the incestuous union became the inveterate enemies of the Israelites; cf. Gower, *CA*, viii. 222, where the gloss describes the Moabites as *generacio prava et exasperans contra populum dei.* [*v.* Addenda.]

37b–38a. Om. L; possibly a marginal insertion in the exemplar (as in other MSS.): 'caesural homoeteleuton could have caused the error independently in a number of MSS.' (Donaldson, *TCA*, p. 192 n. 36).

41. The general sequence of ideas at this point is clear enough: the Devil (father of lies) is in league with the World and the Flesh to betray man's soul through his bodily senses. But all MSS. of the B text offer difficulties. The reading *seeth* (WO) for *seest* (L) involves the minimum of alteration and allows us to render: 'Both of them thy soul sees and tells it [i.e. gives warning] in thy heart'. In ix. 55 the heart is regarded as the home of *Anima* (the soul). Yet this appears to make the warning of l. 42 otiose; and it is noteworthy that in HM 143 of the C text that line runs:

And wisseth þe to ben ywar what wolde þe desseyue.

sueth (R: or *seweth*; cf. pr 45) and *sleth* (HM 128) would provide a plausible alternative:

This and that sueth þi soule and sleth it in þin herte

PASSUS I

'The flesh and the devil are for ever pursuing thy soul [cf. 'Synne suweth us euere', xiv. 323] and [they] slay it [thy soul] in thy heart.' *A* reads: '[And þat] shend [iþ] þi soule; set it in þin herte'.

43. Holy Church has not yet commented on the wealth that is not part of the *bona naturæ*. Hence the dreamer now asks whether money too is for common use. Any answer to this question inevitably involved the exegesis of Matt. 22: 20-2, from which Holy Church infers that one should not have more money than Reason allows. This may seem too general a precept to be of practical value; but here L is concerned only to supply a key to the Prologue and to outline a general position; detailed application will come later.

61 ff. The devil—symbolized by the donjon—embodies the very opposites of Truth (12); of love manifested in creation (14 ff.)— as opposed to destruction (66); and of measure (67), Judas's crime being presented as the result of his love of money: cf. Yunck, p. 3 etc.

The characterization of the devil derives from Joh. 8: 44: *homicida erat ab initio . . . mendax est et pater ejus.*

66. The form *Caym* is common from AS times; cf. *Beowulf*, 107 (MS.) and *Thesaurus Linguae Latinae Onomasticon.*

68. Matt. 27: 3-5, does not mention tree (and Acts 1: 18 gives a different account of Judas's end). 'Judas tree' is still a local name for the elder tree (as distinct from the Judas tree that bears purple flowers) and the elder is still associated with treachery. In the Holkham Bible (*c.* 1310) the tree is called an elder ('seur') in the A-N text but represented as a sycamore in the accompanying illustration. Mandeville (*Travels*, ed. Hamelius, p. 61, l. 31) *et al.* refer to the very elder tree on which Judas hanged himself as still extant. But in earlier tradition the tree was a fig tree. St. Leo says, 'the devil showed Judas a cord and taught him to hang himself' (*sermo iii de passione*).

73. *þe hieȝe name*: possibly used here to avoid 'in goddes name' or 'in goddes halve'—phrases which because of their casual everyday use would not express the urgency of the present request. For the *altissimum nomen* of Christ *v.* Phil. 2: 9; cf. *Ayenbite*, 103, also A. Spicq, *La Vie spirituelle*, 86. 5-18, 19-37. A treatise on 'the hygh names of criste' is in Magd. Coll. Camb. MS. F. 4. 13, f. 59ᵛ.

75-6. The dreamer is to recall this revelation at a later crisis: xi. 112 f. (cf. ix. 74-8).

77. Sc. þow from acc. þe (76). In the ME *Bestiary* the newly baptized Christian (or his sponsor) promises 'to helden with herte þe bodes of holikirke' (136). In the Sarum Rite the baptizing priest said: 'custodi baptismum tuum, serva mandata.'

81 ff. The implication here is that he should be taught what belief in Christ really involves. 84 is a version of two similar questions in the Gospels: the rich young ruler's 'What shall I do to inherit eternal life?' (Luke 18: 18) and the disciples' 'What shall we do that we might work the works of God?' (Joh. 6: 28). *treasure* (83, 85) likewise has many N.T. associations.

82. *worchen his wille*: for exx. of the phrase in OE and ME *v.* D. Bethurum, *JEGP*, 34 (1935), 562.

   to man: *v. EMEVP*, xiii. 64 n., and J. Hall, *Selections from Laȝamon*, l. 34.

86. *deus caritas*: this reference to 1 Joh. 4: 8 (and 16) must be read in the light of the whole of that epistle, in which the doctrine of the Atonement, and hence of Salvation, is linked with the necessity of truthful action in love (*v.* below).

90–1. Cf. ix. 63, where *Qui manet in caritate in deo manet* (1 Joh. 4: 16) (cit. also at v. 494) is glossed 'alle that lyuen good lyf aren like God almiȝti' (cf. 3 Joh. 11: *Qui benefacit ex deo est*). The reference to Luke (*pace* Sk) is probably to Luc. 18: 18 (cit. xi. 264–5), but L may also have in mind Luc. 6: 35, with its close bearing on the main theme of the *visio*. For the theological basis of the identification of the Christian with Christ *v.* (e.g.) *Summa*, I Q 4, art. 3, Q 93, art. 4 (and cf. Q 13, art. 19). On 'deification' *v.* M. Lot-Borodine, *Rev. hist. rel.*, 106 (1932–3), and K. W. Schmidt, *Eranos-Jahrbuch* (1947); and cf. St. Bernard, *Letters*, tr. B. Scott James (1953), 12.

92. *agrounde and aloft*: an inclusive formula: cf. xviii. 45.

94 ff. Holy Church at once relates her basic teaching to the activities of the chief orders of society as portrayed in pr 112 ff. We are now told how such men should act in the light of *deus caritas*. The clergy are to proclaim this gospel, kings and nobles are to defend it by making it possible for all Christian men to live peaceably (cf. vi. 28–9 and xix. 224).

95. *Riden*: i.e. in arms; cf. *CT*, A 45 and *OED*, *s.v.* 2.

PASSUS I

96. *transgressores*: with primary reference to the divine Law; cf. Isa. 53: 12. See *William of Palerne*, cit. s.v. *barouns, MED*.

97. 'Truth' is here conceived of as acting as a judge; cf. *Summa*, I Q 21, art. 2: 'Here [Ps. 84: 10] Truth stands for justice.' Translate: 'Till Truth has passed her final verdict.'

99. *a Fryday*: i.e. only *one* Friday. For the knightly obligation to fast *v.* M. Bloch, *Feudal Society* (1961), p. 318.

100. *wiþ him and with hir*: 'with the man and the woman'; cf. Chaucer, *Tr.*, v. 1835, *CT*, B 460.

102–5. In A lines 102–3 more appropriately follow 97, and A's equivalent to 104 is in present tense: the knight's 'profession' (vow) is 'to serve truth'.

apostata (orig. of a religious man who quitted his order after a year's novitiate; cf. Robbins, *English Hist. Poems*, no. 65, l. 170 and Skelton, *Colin Cloute*, 386) emphasizes the religious character of the order of knighthood. The term is applied to Lucifer in Henryson, *Fables*, 1897–8, and in *CA* viii. 11.

David is here conceived of as a chivalric feudal king: cf. *Parlement of the Thre Ages*, 451; he is commonly depicted with a knightly retinue in medieval art, e.g. in the Tickhill Psalter (*v.* fcsm., ed. D. D. Egbert, 1940). The specific reference is probably to 1 Chr. (Paralip.) 12: 18: *suscepit ergo eos David, et constituit principes turmæ*. The chivalric image is resumed in xviii. 12–23 (where Jesus appears as *filius David*). In the Cornish Plays David swears by his order of knighthood. Since David is also the traditional antitype of Christ, who is *rex regum*, the allusion to his knights leads naturally to mention of the archetypal pattern of order and obedience—the hierarchy of the blessed angels (cf. *SE Legendary*, ii. 408).

From the time of Philo *ten* was regarded as representing the completeness of creation. Lucifer's apostasy made the number odd (hence the number 9 is associated with his fall at 119); cf. OE *Genesis*, 237, *Towneley Play of Noah*, 10: 'Angels thou maide ful euen, all orders that is'; *Golden Legend* (ed. F. S. Ellis, 1900), i. 56.

109. *bi þe trinitee* (*A thoruȝ*.): presumably 'By means of (the example of) the Trinity God taught them to recognize what Truth was'—i.e. perfect loyalty in perfect love (none being greater or less than the other); cf., e.g., St. Bernard, *Letters*, 12: 'What else but Charity preserves that supreme and unspeakable unity in the blessed

109

Trinity . . . Charity is the divine substance itself . . . the eternal law, the creator and ruler of the universe.' But *bi* possibly has the sense 'about'—'the full Truth about the mystery of the Trinity'; angels supposedly have complete knowledge of the Trinity—which the blessed will share. Cf. Geoffrey de Vinsauf, *Poetria Nova*, 1441–4.

111. Cf. *legiones angelorum*, Matt. 26: 53. To a medieval writer the concept of 'legion' would be closely linked, as here, with knighthood and chivalry (cf. C. S. Lewis, *Allegory of Love* (1936), p. 72). Cf. also *Coventry Play of Mary Magdalene*, 366–7: 'The joye / That Lucyfer with many a legion lost for thir pryde'; and *Pearl*, 1121. *A* reads after 111: 'And was þe louelokest [of siȝt] aftir oure lord' (cf. OE *Genesis*, 254–5, 337–8). B has probably lost this line; cf. the emphasis in 113b.

112. For the more usual view of Lucifer's fall as due to pride *v.* xv. 50–1.

115. Cf. *St. Patrick's Purgatory*, 120: 'never mote in sunnebemes þikker þan þe fendes ȝede.'

117. The allusion is ultimately to Isa. 14: 13–14: '. . . sedebo in monte testamenti, in lateribus aquilonis. Ascendam super altitudinem nubium, similis ero altissimo' (cf. xv. 47–51). But L's line is closer to St. Augustine's conflation of the Old Latin text of this verse into 'Ponam sedem meam ad aquilonem, et ero similis altissimo'; cf. A. L. Kellogg , *Traditio*, 14 (1958), 386 ff. Satan's 'seat' is also referred to in OE *Genesis*, 281–2; cf. Skelton, *Colin Clout*, 335, etc. *pedem* is doubtless a genuine reading (C refers to the phrase at ii. 119, 'hus fote for to sette'). Kellogg suggests that it shows the influence of St. Augustine's gloss on Ps. 35: 12, 'Non veniat mihi *pes* superbiæ': 'Why did the psalmist call that [self-regarding love] pride? Because by becoming proud it deserted God and went from him. The psalmist declared that the foot of pride was [self-]love' (*v.* also *PQ*, 45 (1966), 712).

118b must be read in the light of the deliberate echo at 151, where it is *love* that heaven could not hold, as it reaches down to human nature. Cf. xii. 142: 'Loue shal lepe out', and R. E. Kaske, *MÆ*, 29 (1960), 22.

119. *nyne dayes*: cf. *Paradise Lost*, vi. 871; according to Hesiod (*Theog.* 722–5), it took nine days and nights for a weight to fall from heaven to earth, and another night for it to fall from earth to Tartarus.

120. *God of his goodnesse*: cf. v. 488, and *Ludus Coventriæ*, p. 35/1. *stable*: cf. *Historia Regum Britanniæ*, ed. Griscom (1929), p. 382: [the fallen angels remained] in the places and forms under which they were when God bade them cease'.

121. *stonden in quiete*. In the *Contemplacioun of Synnaris* it is said of the renewal of the universe after Doomsday: 'Then sall þe elementis be clarificate / And stande in quyete but commocioun' (STS 3rd ser., 23, p. 123); cf. note in Goodridge's *PPl*, and Boethius, *De Cons. Phil.*, III m. X.

122 ff. reflect traditional Christian belief (*v*. St. Aug., *Sunday Sermons*, i. 95), reaffirmed by Hooker: '. . . some in the air, some in the earth, some in the water, some among the minerals, dens and caves that are under the earth'. Cf. *Anticlaudianus*, iv. 271 ff., *SE Legendary*, i. 186, Robinson's note on Chaucer, *HF* 930, and C. S. Lewis, *The Discarded Image* (1964), pp. 135–6. Irish tradition preserves the belief that angels fell headlong (cf. illustrations in MS. Junius XI) but that when the 'lid' of heaven was closed those who were still falling remained suspended in the air and became the fairies (R. Flower, *The Western Islands* (1944), p. 20; cf. J. M. Synge, *The Aran Islands* (1910), p. 11).

126 ff. The apparent digression is now related to the main theme, Lucifer appearing as the prototype of those who break troth and do ill, as opposed to the 'loyal' man who works well (128–9 thus link up with 88–9). The scriptural basis of 128–30 is presumably John 5: 29 ('they that have done good shall come forth to the resurrection of life'), which is to be cited at a crucial point in P vii (l. 111). Indeed the motif of *Dowel* there emphasized is here heard for the first time.

131. *troneth*. The reference is probably to Matt. 19: 28, 'Ye also shall sit upon twelve thrones' (cf. Apoc. 20: 4). Cf. *Sawles Warde* (*EMEVP*, p. 256, l. 292). KF print *tronen*, which they apparently interpret as an infinitive.

132. *þise textis*: i.e. *reddite Cesari* (52) and *deus caritas* (86); but possibly including the contrasting *ponam pedem* (118).

136. *kynde knowing*: innate sense, natural instinct, natural understanding; cf. Dunning, p. 39.

137. 'How [knowledge of] truth is implanted in the body, and in what part of the body it has its dwelling.' (140 shows that it is in the *heart*.)

138. *doted daffe*: 'stupid dolt!' Cf. *dronken daffe*, xi. 417. In the medieval view this plain speaking would no whit diminish Holy Church's dignity; cf. the B.V.M.'s habit of speaking 'mult aire-ment' in French Legends of the Virgin, and *Pearl*, 290.

139. The dreamer is reproved for not having applied himself to study; he does not know elementary theology. The Latin line recurs at v. 448; it is found in a 14th-c. Collection of Proverbs and Riddles in Ryland Lat. MS. 394, ed. Pantin, *Bulletin of the John Rylands Library*, 14 (1930).

140. Truth and love have by now become identical: *Caritas* is to love Truth and obey God's commands—the conclusion that is rephrased in 143-4; where it is implied that this is but an interim answer to the question of 137, to be expanded later (cf. 144). Here we are concerned only with the natural instinct for God and Truth implanted in the hearts of all men: cf. *Summa*, II i. Q 94, art. 2; St. Bernard, *De diligendo deo*, viii. 23 (amor est affectio *naturalis*); and William of Saint-Thierry (cit. Kean, *RES*, n.s. 16 (1965), 360). So Gower speaks of

> thilke love which that is
> *Within a mannes herte afformed*
> And stant of charite confermed.
> (*CA*, viii. 3162)

143 ff. The teacher who is to 'teche þe better' is evidently Christ himself. God the Father showed his love in creation (148) and taught love to Moses (149) in making love the first and greatest commandment which was to be supplemented or amplified, not abrogated, by Our Lord (Mark 12: 29-31).

146. *triacle*. The figurative use is based ultimately on patristic interpretation of the serpent in the wilderness (Num. 21: 8-9). Ben H. Smith (*Traditional Imagery of Charity in Piers Plowman* (1967)) cites Hugh of Saint-Cher, *Opera*, vi. 297ᵛ:

Christus dicitur serpens: quia sicut de serpente fit venenum, et de serpente fit tyriaca in veneni remedium: ita facto de veneno serpente, i. de diabolo, voluit Dominus fieri serpens, ut de eo fieret tyriaca contra venenum diaboli . . .

i.e. venom comes from a serpent; but so does its antidote (tyriacon—triacle): so Christ offers himself (like the brazen serpent in the wilderness) as antidote to the Devil. Cf. *CT*, B 479, and Kean, art. cit. The use of 'triacle' in the description of plants with healing virtues provides a nexus with the following line.

147. *spise*. Sk's gloss 'species' [sc. of remedy] is lexically possible, but a figurative use of *spise*, i.e. the aromatic substance derived from plants, seems preferable, and is well evidenced from *Ancrene Wisse* onwards. Smith (op. cit.) compares Hugh of Saint-Cher's gloss on Cant. 1: 11, when he interprets *nardus* as charity and humility, and Honorius of Autun (Migne, *PL*, 172. 376) connects the verse directly with Christ. Cf. Bacon, *Advancement of Learning* (Book I, *ad init.*) on Charity: 'this corrective spice, the mixture whereof maketh knowledge so sovereign . . .'.

150. *plante* (v. Varr.): Love is not only the healing spice (cf. *salue* C ii. 148) or balm for man visibly (cf. *sene* 147) wounded by sin;[1] it is the plant of peace. Sense and sequence justify the interpretation of 150b as a climactic characterization of *love* (cf. pr 103) rather than as qualifying *pees*; hence C's *'and* most preciouse'. *vertues* has a special aptness; for plants have their special efficacy or virtue; cf., e.g., 'Ther is no rose of swich vertu' (*OBMEV*, no. 169).

The figure probably derives from the Messianic interpretation of Isa. 53: 2: 'Et ascendet sicut virgultum coram eo, et sicut radix de terra sitienti.' Cf. the sanative leaves of Apoc. 22: 2. Heavenly love is a plant that yearned to establish its root on earth—to eat its *fill* of earth—a vivid figure for the fact that, as St. Gregory said, 'The King of heaven has taken into himself the flesh of our earth' (*Sunday Sermons*, i. 121).

As heaven could not 'contain' the rebel angels, so it could not 'contain' love, which fell by its own weight to earth; cf. St. Aug., *Conf.* xiii. 9 (cit. Kean, *RES*, N.S. 16 (1965), 360. A variant image of similar application appears in xii. 141:

> For the heihe holigoste heuene shal tocleue
> And loue shal lepe out after into this lowe erthe
> And clennesse [the B.V.M.] shal cacchen it and clerkes [the Magi] shullen it fynde;

In the present psg. the emphasis is on the completeness of the

---

[1] The figure is found in St. Bernard, and frequently in applications of the story of the Good Samaritan (*v.* xvii below, where L adds the detail that the Samaritan *enbawmed* the wounded man (70)).

Incarnation, with the implication (152) that Christ's life on earth had an express purpose which was fully accomplished.

The figure of the rain that causes the earth to germinate, likened to God's word which 'shall not return unto me void' (Isa. 55: 11, read in Quadragesima), may have contributed to L's image.

154. The refce. is to the Ascension, Christ's 'leap' back to heaven; in *The Castell of Perseverance* the phrase is used of the soul ascending to God: 'Lo here Mankinde, Ly3ter than lef is on lynde' (3595–6); the lime-tree leaf being moved by the slightest breeze. For the image of Christ 'springing' to heaven cf. *OBMEV*, no. 185, and for the simile cf. *CT*, E 1211.

155. Smith (op. cit.) cites Hugh of Saint-Cher's extension of Chrysostom's commentary on Luc. 18: 25:

Rectus et acus, cujus prima pars subtilis est, et acutor, non perforata sed perforans, et significat Divinitatem, quae impassibilis est [cf. v. 495 n.], posterior pars grossa est, et perforata, et significat humanitatem, quae passa est:

i.e. the point and eye of a needle symbolize the dual nature of Christ (whom L sees as both light *and* heavy). But there is probably an additional allusion to Christ as the incarnate word, or *logos*: the word of God is more penetrative than a two-edged sword (Heb. 4: 12). St. Ambrose in a passage read on the Feast of the Purification (*Brev. Fasc.*, iii. 139) specifically applies that verse to Christ the incarnate word in order to express the urgency of divine *caritas*; *v.* also Kean, art. cit., 363 n. 1.

156. Alluding primarily to the Tomb and the Roman soldiery guarding it.

157. The suggestion is: 'Because love has this great penetrative power it can lead back into heaven the redeemed of mankind who had forfeited heaven by sin.'

Christ is specifically named *dux* with refce. to the resurrection in the verse cited in precisely the same context at v. 498 (q.v.). So the l. may refer primarily to Christ's redemption of those in limbo; cf. xviii. 404, and the OE *Dream of the Rood*, 151. But *leder* also suggests headship in the sense of Rom. 8: 29: . . . *ipse primogenitus in multis fratribus*.

158. The suggestion of earthly rule in the term *leder* (cf. pr 126 ff.) gives rise to the image of the mayor as intermediary—fittingly applied to Jesus the mediator of the new covenant, *testamenti novi mediatorem* (Heb. 12: 24). Cf. the use of *mene* for the second person of the Trinity in xvi. 181 ff., and iii. 76–7, where the mayor as chief magistrate is the channel by which justice flows from its fountainhead, the king (cf. G. A. Williams, *Medieval London* (1963), p. 29). The simile is new in B, and sorts with the political emphasis of B's prologue. The role as mediator or balance between 'les grauntz, les petites, et les meynes' (cf. Williams, p. 313) was to be strikingly illustrated by the events of 1381, when William Walworth, mayor of London, acted as intermediary between king and commons.

159–60. Christ delivers judgement (*lawe shapeth*) and assesses the fine on mankind: *amercement* was a payment for pardon made to the king when an offence had put the transgressor 'in mercy' (*v.* Williams, p. 28 n. 4, and Yunck, p. 234). L asserts a bold paradox by a bolder word-play: the fine that Christ imposes is no fine—it is *mercy* (he is the perfect king who clothes *nudum ius* with *pietus*; cf. pr 135); hence the choice of the form *merciment* for *amercement*.

161. 'And, so that you may recognize it [i.e. Love, *caritas*] by natural instinct, it springs up in the heart [seat of reason], by divine power.' Cf. St. Bernard: 'Fons siquidem vitae caritas est . . . quae Deus est.' Might (*potentia*) is the attribute always associated with God the Father; cf. xvi. 30 and 184.

The near repetition in 163 is suspicious; A (which has no equivalent to 161) there preserves alliteration, reading . . . *comsiþ a miȝt.* (*A*)

165–6. A concise re-statement of 1 Joh. 4: 9.

168. *mercy*: a semi-personification, and compressed construction: He sought for mercy but also beseeched 'the merciful God'. ('Father, forgive them.')

171–2. Christ is still, on the cross, not deprived of divine power; the Dual Nature is the mainspring of much of L's theology: cf. v. 496 ff. and xviii. 21 ff. His heart was pierced by the hatred of mankind but literally also by Longinus, who at xviii. 87–91 begs for '*reuth*' (according to legend his blindness was miraculously cured).

174. *mote*: 'cite, summon to court', resuming the legal metaphor of 159–60. The logic is again that of 1 John (where the love of God is

associated with love of the brethren, i.e. the *poor* of 173; *v.* esp.
1 Joh. 3: 16; 4: 11, 20).

178. The newly baptized infant is cleansed from original, and is as
yet free from *actual*, sin.

The singling out of chastity as an insufficient virtue is merely
pointing dramatically the theme of 1 Cor. 13.

180. *parteth*: should strictly be sjv., as *louen* (179) apparently is;
cf. AV *parten*.

182. *Malkyn*: a familiar derivative of Mary, the typical name of
a woman, esp. of lower classes; in later dial. use = 'slut' (Nfk.);
frequently found (doubtless from alliterative compulsion) in
apposition to *maiden*, e.g. in Durham Hallmote Rolls, 'Maud
Malkynsmaydin' (cit. G. G. Coulton, *Medieval Village* (1925),
p. 103) and in *De Clerico and Puella* (*EMEVP*, xv. 47). The suggestion evidently is not that Malkyn is unchaste (as in *CT*, B 30–1)
but that she who is so undesired that she has no hope of getting
a husband has no right to pride herself on her virginity. (Cf. F. G.
Cassidy, *MLN*, 63 (1948), 52.)

183. Kane, p. 435, questions *iugged* preferring *ioynide*, 'enjoined'.

185. 'dead as a door tree' was current in Lancs. as late as *c.* 1950.
No explanation of the phrase is forthcoming (*v.* Archer Taylor,
The Proverb (1962), p. 222). The Latin line is from Jac. 2: 26;
quoted also in *CA*, v. 1800 (mgn.).

186. *worth*: dramatic use of pr. sg. of *worthen* with ingressive force
of 'coming to be': = 'is going to be'.

187. Alluding to the parable of the foolish virgins (Matt. 25) in
which, according to Chrysostom, the oil denotes charity, alms, and
every aid rendered to the needy; the lamps denote the gift of virginity; and the virgins are called foolish because having gone
through a greater toil they lost all for the sake of the less: 'for it is
a greater toil to overcome the desires of the flesh *than of money*' (cf.
188). Cf. *Ayenbite*, p. 233: 'Maydenhod wiþoute þe love of God
is ase the lompe wiþoute oyle', and Augustine, *Sermo* xciii. 5.

192. Inadvertently repeated by a copyist from 186? A has it above
(but marked with a cross in T) and in most MSS. in line corresponding to 192.

193. *curatoures*: i.e. priests with cure of souls; cf. xx. 278–9. On the charge of 194 *v.* Dunning, p. 57.

196. Cf. 109 above; again the Trinity is put in contradistinction to Satan and hell.

197. 'And an inducement to laymen to be the less forthcoming in bestowing their goods on the poor.'

199. The quotation is from Luc. 6: 38.

After 199 the text seems to be defective and to require the two ll. found in the HM MS. of A (printed by Sk, though not admitted by Kane to *A*):

> ʒoure grace and ʒoure good happe ʒoure welthe for to wynne,
> And therwith knoweth me kyndely of that I ʒou sende.

The sense would then be: 'Give and it shall be given unto you. It is I [Christ] who gives to all of you your good fortune and the means of acquiring wealth; by means of that wealth show you recognize, as you ought ('kyndely'), its source in me'—viz. show by practising *caritas* that you realize that your wealth is merely given you in trust by God, who is Himself *caritas*. *þat* (200) has a very pregnant force, referring to the operation of *caritas*, which 'unlocks' the love of God, who pours forth divine grace on those who practise it. For a similar image in a context possibly related to the present passage *v.* v. 613–16.

202. Holy Church now summarizes the doctrine of the passus as a whole, reverting to the metaphor of 146 f. ('triacle'). For 'leche of lyf' cf. *The Prymer* (EETS 105), i. 30.

205. For the homiletic treatment of 'treasure' (? based on Ecclus. 29: 14) *v.* P. Bawcutt's n. to *King Hart* 764[1]; and for the conception of Truth as *rectitudo*—an accord between man's will and God's brought about by love—*v.* E. Vasta, *PQ*, 44 (1965), 17–29.

Worldly treasure forms the subject of the following passus.

[1] In *The Shorter Poems of Gavin Douglas*, STS 4th Ser. 3 (1967).

PASSUS II

1–2. Now that the dreamer knows what Truth is, he is better prepared to detect Falsehood (already glimpsed in the Prologue as busy in the world). The invocation of Mary (2) is a counterpart to i. 73 (cf. ii. 49). He kneels in recognition of Holy Church's claims—but also to keep her from departing before he has learnt all that he wishes to know (i.e. all that the poet proposes to explain of the allegory). Mary is, as always, linked first with mercy ('grace') and then with her son (cf. v. 518–19). *mercy*: 'please', rather than 'thank you'.

Marie: this form of the genitive derives from Lat. *Mariæ*, though in fact it is indistinguishable from the uninflected genitive as found in certain personal names (e.g. *Arthur*).

3. A variant of a formula found in *William of Palerne*, 1689, and *Awntyrs of Arthur*, 222.

5–6. *þi left half*: the dreamer is facing east (*v.* pr 13, i. 1–12), so Fals and his followers appear in the north (the Devil's quarter; cf. i. 117 n.). L is proceeding by his favourite method of antithesis.

6. *Fauel*: this OF term ('lying', from L. Lat. *fabella*) is first used to name a personification of duplicity, fraud, or intrigue in *Le Roman de Fauvel*. No English author is known to have used it thus before L; but the character appears later in Occleve (*De Regimine Principum*), Skelton (*The Bowge of Courte*, 134), and Wyatt (*Sat.*, ii. 67). The name Favel appears as early as the 12th c. as a Lincs. personal name (Hugo Candidus, *Chronicle*, p. 133).

10. The comparison is found in the OF romance *Jehan et Blonde*, where it is said of the clasp of Blonde's chaplet that 'li rois nul plus rice avoit' (4730); but there the effect is rhetorical, whereas L's audience might infer from the present line that the king had actually bestowed the crown on the lady. Cf. also *Mum and the Sothsegger*, i. 33 ff.

The rhetorician Geoffrey de Vinsauf considered that jewels had a place in the description of a beautiful woman (*Nova Poetria*, 607–9). But L deliberately concentrates on Meed's rich array to enforce the contrast with Holy Church's lovely face and pure linen (i. 3, 10). Cf. Dunbar's emphasis on the pleasure of a widow at being dressed 'In gownys of engraynit claith and gret goldin chenyeis / In ringis ryally set with riche rubye stonis'—all bought by her merchant-husband to gain her favours (*The Twa Mariit Wemen and the Wedo*, 366–7); *v.* also the description of 'Richesse' in *Roman de la Rose*, 1053–108 (*Romaunt*, 1071–120), and *Parlement of the Thre Ages*, 118–28.

11. *fretted*: apparently here used of the gold rings as interspersed among others. For the richness of medieval rings and jewellery *v. Guide to Medieval Antiquities* (British Museum, 1928), p. 138; for the 14th-c. fashion for precious stones *v. BPR*, iv. 141, 301, 403, and *Pearl*, 201–21.

12b. *as red as any glede*: cf. *CT*, A 1997.

13. *double manere safferes*: the two kinds are the 'light' and the 'dark' (known in the Middle Ages as male and female); *v.* J. Evans and M. Serjeantson, *English Medieval Lapidaries* (1933), p. 101.

14. *Orientales*: pearls of richness and brilliancy; cf. *Pearl*, 1–4, *LGW*, F 221. *ewages*: 'water' sapphires (described by Lydgate as 'blew'). These particular stones are not usually credited in the lapidaries with prophylactic powers (for those of the sapphire and diamond *v.* Evans and Serjeantson, op. cit., pp. 83, 101): 14b must be taken as a general refce. to the virtues of stones—virtues sometimes thought to reside in the texts, prayers, or figures of saints inscribed on them. In *Roman de la Rose* Richesse wears the stone that preserved from 'venim' (in the lapidaries this is a distinctive virtue of the diamond) and another that cured palsy and toothache (*Romaunt*, 1084–98). Such beliefs (of Greek origin) explain why knights were often required to swear, before tournaments, that they were not using charmed rings; cf. *Sir Gawain*, 2027; *v.* also *EMEVP*, p. 115, ll. 65 ff.

16. *red golde*: medieval gold was alloyed with copper, which gave it a reddish tinge. The emphasis on the colour red in ll. 12–16 suggests a sensual quality in the dress; cf. *Reason and Sensuality*, 1557–68, and Bennett, *Parlement of Foules* (1957), p. 93 n. 2.

18. *whas wyf she were* (new in B). As a description of Meed appears already in A, Sk hesitated to use this phrase as evidence that L was alluding throughout the passage to Alice Perrers, Edward III's mistress; but if we accept the view that the A text may not have been finished before 1369 (*v. PMLA*, 58 (1943), 566; cf. ibid. 54. 37), chronological difficulties disappear, as Alice's connection with the King goes back to 1365, at least. In 1373 she was given the

NOTES

late Queen Philippa's jewels; at the Good Parliament of 1376 she was charged with using magic rings; and she is said to have stripped the rings off Edward's fingers when he died. Extravagant dresses set with gems were a feature of the period (cf. E. Rickert, *Chaucer's World* (1948), p. 36, and *Awntyrs of Arthur*, 14–26); but Alice's (which included some made of cloth-of-gold tissue) cost the inordinate amount of £469. 18s. 8d. in the years 1375–7 alone (*Issue Rolls of Exchequer*, ed. F. Devon, pp. 193, 209).

The robe and the rubies are perhaps intended to recall the scarlet woman of Babylon, Apoc. 17: she too is seen in a dream in the wilderness, arrayed in purple and scarlet decked with gold and precious stones. Moralists and preachers of the time doubtless drew, or suggested, the parallel in criticizing Edward III's unlawful attachment; just as John of Bridlington alludes to the liaison by means of the David and Bathsheba story (*Prophecies*, R.S., 14. 169). In 1376 Alice married (though without Edward's knowledge) William of Windsor, the king's deputy in Ireland; this may be hinted at in the present line.

Effective as these topical allusions are, L is primarily intent on illustrating in Meed (and in Alice Perrers in so far as she is identifiable with her) the vice of cupidity which has beset so many of the folk in the field. P i has concluded with a description of true, heavenly *amor*. Cupidity, the perversion of this love, is now to be shown associated with falseness and the devil. The further association of Cupidity with Guile and Lying may be found in the early-15th-c. *Dives and Pauper*, a dialogue the theme of which may be gathered from Pauper's comment that 'From the least to the most all they follow avarice and false covetise, from the prophet to the priest all they make *lyings* and do guile and falsehood [Jerem. 8: 10] . . . All they love gifts and follow meed' (cit. Coulton, *Medieval Village*, p. 327). We must allow something for homiletic heightening; but Dante speaks of this sin of cupidity just as strongly (cf. Gilson, *Dante*, 3rd edn., 1953, p. 176). Chaucer's introduction of Meed into *PF* 228 is worth noting: *v.* op. cit. 16 n. above, p. 89. The vice assumed new forms and dimensions—all to be noted in the poem—as the merchant classes came to have more opportunities of amassing wealth.

20. Meed is technically a maiden—a virgin; but unlike Holy Church is never described as a lady. Her literary antecedents include the *Munera* of *Speculum Stultorum*: *v.* Yunck, *passim*.

PASSUS II

21. *Lewte*: momentarily fem. (22) under the influence of French grammatical gender; C corrects to *hym*. The word (< Lat. *legalitas*) still preserved some of its original force of 'fair dealing', righteousness, justice. The implication is that Righteousness is a divine attribute, loved and taught by Holy Church but seen by Meed as deserving punishment from those very men whose duty it is to maintain justice (cf. i. 96).

23. *þe popis paleys*. For most of the 14th c. the papal residence was located at Avignon (and 'paleys' was used specifically of the residence there). In the latter half of the century it increased in splendour, as the curia increased in venality; but complaints of papal corruption go back at least to the Goliardic satirist who wrote: 'Cum ad papam veneris, habe pro constanti / Non est locus pauperi, soli favet danti' (*v.* Tawney, p. 42 and notes). Cf. Wright, *Political Songs* (1839), p. 324.

24. *a bastarde*. L, who elsewhere voices strong views on heredity, and repeatedly uses images of relationship, in order to indicate that Meed is illegitimate in the broader sense lays much stress on her lineage. But Fals can hardly be her father (25) since in 40 he is the bridegroom (though the possibility of incestuous union, with its moral implications, cannot be ignored; cf. i. 28 ff.); C gives the name as *Fauel*, A as *Wrong*. Wrong has already been named as 'Fader of falshed' (i. 64); 26 clearly refers to his (i.e. Satan's) appearance on earth in the form of a serpent (Gen. 3: 1–4).

27. Lat. *Qualis pater, talis filius*: proverbial (Whiting, F 80); *bona arbor etc.*: Matt. 7: 17.

28. Holy Church, almost pettishly, indicates that she is far higher in lineage and so ought to be more honoured.

30. *O God withoute gynnynge*: a credal affirmation, dating from the time of the Arian heresy: cf. *unus æternus* in the *Quicunque vult*.

31. *to marye with myself*: (strictly) 'to marry myself with', i.e. mercy is a dowry given by God with Holy Church; the man who is willing to take this dowry is to have her. But the alternative interpretation of Mercy as the bridegroom is defensible.

33. *leef*: 'portion'; perhaps with refce. to Matt. 5: 7 ('Blessed are the merciful for they shall obtain mercy').

34. *taketh Mede*: (1) accepts Meed in marriage; (2) receives bribes: a neat *double entendre*. One would expect an adversative copulative (instead of *And*), the contrast being between the man who marries Mercy (or Holy Church) and the man who marries Meed. The marriage-figure, thus almost casually introduced, is to provide the main action of this passus.

35. *hir loue*: obj. gen., 'love of her'.

a lappe of caritatis: *OED* (s.v. *lap* sb.²) treats as 'a lick, smack, taste', but cites no other example before 1820; more probably fig., 'a [portion of] the skirt of a robe', etc. (*lap* sb.¹). The man who 'falls' for Meed will never touch the skirts of *true* love. A plausible emendation would be 'lippe': cf. v. 250 and 'a lippe of godes grace' (C xii. 226) and 'a lippe of oure byleyue' (C xviii. 253).

36. *construeth*: lit. 'interprets'; but contextually 'answers the question of Ps. 14: 1'.

Dauid þe kynge (cf. OE 'Ælfred se cyning'): the type of Christ and of the ideal earthly king (cf. i. 103–5) whom, it is implied, English kings should follow. The intended reference is to the *last* verses of Ps. 14 (the first being quoted, as often, merely as a direction to the whole psalm): 'Qui pecuniam suam non dedit ad usuram et munera [= meed] super innocentem non accepit'. The same psalm is quoted in the description of 'þe ryȝtwys man' in *Pearl*, 676–87; *þat meynteneth treuthe* (37b) is evidently a gloss on 'Qui operatur justitiam' (verse 2). For a similar refce. to this psalm (with similar preface) *v.* vii. 50–1 and xiii. 126.

39. *worth*: 'is to be', 'shall be' (relic of OE pr. for fut.). In fact the marriage never takes place.

mansed: probably 'accursed' in the strict sense of 'excommunicated', since the words are used by Holy Church herself.

40. *Fals Fikel-tonge* is the Devil's offspring since, as seen above, the Devil is 'the father of lies'; the name possibly alludes to *linguis suis dolose agebant* (Ps. 5: 11, cit. Rom. 3: 13).

41. *þis folke*: i.e. the folk of the field (pr 17). C's 'hath Mede foule enchantid' runs more easily with 42 and is consonant with the view developed later that Meed is not *naturally* evil inasmuch as reward for service is in itself legitimate; the alliteration in 42 is defective; but *A*'s 'þat hy ligen togederis' does not sort with the facts.

43 ff. *Tomorwe*: there is no other indication of the passage of time, except that the dreamer seems to begin a new dream at 52. We may regard 1–50 as an interchapter closing with a benediction (49: cf. i. 207).

46–8. Behind these lines lies the view that even in condemnation and censure there is an order, a differentiation of function. It is for *Lewte* (Justitia) to punish, i.e. for just and upright rulers (cf. i. 94). The individual may 'put forth his reason', i.e. bring a charge against the wicked—in due time; but it is not for him to lay hands on them: cf. pr 187 and vi. 227–8.

lat hem worth: a 'calque' on OF *laisser ester* (where *ester* orig. = *stare*), *worth* being subst. for *be(n)*: v. J. Orr, *Words and Sounds in English and French* (1953), p. 37; apparently a common W. Mid. idiom (found in Laȝamon, etc.); cf. vi. 84.

50. *conscience*: here evidently = 'guilty conscience': following Meed will cause one to be burdened by a guilty conscience. But 'acombre/encombre neuere thy conscience' (C text) is attractive, and supported by a 15th-c. parallel: 'Whos conscience is combred and stondith noȝt clene, / Of another manis dedis the wursse woll he deme' (*Reliquiæ Antiquæ* (1845), i. 205).

52b. One of several 'floating' clauses that look before and after, and require a double rendering in translation. Cf. vi. 148–9 and *Sir Gawain*, 866 ff.

54–5. *The Oxf. Dict. Eng. Proverbs* (3rd edn., 1970, p. 503) curiously quotes these ll. as the first ex. of the proverb 'It is meet that a man be at his own bridal'; but they are purely descriptive. 55, echoing pr 18, suggests that the wedding will offer a microcosm of the world (or part of it) described in the Prologue, and this is borne out by 57–61. But the poet or an editor perhaps felt the verbal repetition to be infelicitous, and C alters the line.

58. *sysours*: the jurors who made up the assize. Originally they had simply given sworn testimony. By the 14th c. they were beginning to take on the functions of modern jurors, but as they were not required to judge on evidence they were very liable to corruption by bribes; hence their presence here, and the reference in xx. 160: 'a sysour that never swore treuthe / One Thomas Two-tonge, ateynte at uch a queste' (i.e. challenged as dishonest). Cf. *Jacob's Well*, 131: 'false sysouris gon vpon qwestys, and puttyn a man fro his riȝt thrugh a fals verdyȝte.' Such corrupt jurors would be fitting guests at Fals's marriage with Meed.

NOTES

sompnours: the officers (apparitors) who summoned defendants to an ecclesiastical court, which had jurisdiction over cases of immorality, drunkenness, etc. The *locus classicus* is *CT*, A 623–68. They are regularly associated with blackmail in medieval literature, i.e. with Meed in another of its manifestations; but we must allow something for satirical exaggeration. In fact few indications of irregularity are found in (e.g.) the Act book of Canterbury.

59. *Bedelles*. The *bedell* summoned tenants to the manorial court, told them when they were required to gather their lord's corn, and impounded stray cattle. Bedells were occasionally accused of neglect or oppression. But here the refce. is probably to a tipstaff or under-bailiff. In 'A Song of the Husbandman' (Robbins, *Historical Poems*, No. 2) the bedell delivers demands from the exchequer (ll. 37 ff.). The term survives in this spelling at Oxford and Cambridge.

60. *Forgoeres*: purveyors, probably especially those pre-empting for the king; the abuses of the practice are indicated by an act of 1362 to the effect that the heinous name of *purveyor* be changed to *achatour* (*v. History of the King's Works*, HMSO (1963), i. 170–1). Purveyance included the impressing of labour and materials for the king's building operations.

vitaillers: sometimes used specifically of an army, but probably here of the victualling trades in general. They would include millers, bakers, and brewers, hatred of whom was 'deeply engrained in the hearts of medieval burgesses' (Lipson, p. 294, q.v.).

vokates of þe Arches: the proctors or advocates engaged in the archbishop of Canterbury's provincial court, which from the end of the 13th c. sat in the church of St. Mary de Arcubus (Bow Church—so called from the arches supporting its steeple), presided over by the archbishop's official, who was sometimes also 'dean of the Arches'. Both sides in a case at this court could call witnesses and employ these lawyers; they were sometimes chantry priests, sometimes beneficed clergy; in either case they charged fees. Cf. I. J. Churchill, *Canterbury Administration* (1933), i. 450–2, B. L. Woodcock, *Medieval Ecclesiastical Courts in the Diocese of Canterbury* (1952), pp. 40–5, and F. M. Powicke, *The Thirteenth Century*, (2nd edn., 1962), p. 492 n.

61. The suggestion is of disorder as well as of multitude; hence the frequent description of hell as 'without number' (cf. 115 n.).

62. *Symonye: v.* pr 86 n. The sin is vaguely personified in an early-14th-c. poem: cit. *OED*, s.v. 1†b, and Mandeville says, 'Now is Simonye king'. But L evidently conceives of him as a canon lawyer (*v.* the rest of the line), hence his title 'Sir' (113); cf. *Colkelby's Sow*, 105. He reappears in xx, when the poet turns back to consider the condition of England after having followed the path of *individual* perfection to its close.

64. *boure:* generally in ME a private room as distinct from a hall. But here and at iii. 14 specifically a 'lady's private room'; cf. A.S. Chron., *s.a.* 755 (Parker MS.).

65. *brokoure:* here = 'matchmaker, who arranges marriages on behalf of interested families' (as formerly in Russia, and still in some Jewish communities). L contrasts such 'mariages de convenance' unfavourably with love-matches in xiv. 264–70. The ll. suggest that Meed was cajoled into agreeing to the match, and to that extent support the view that she was led astray rather than intrinsically evil.

66. *beire:* a late relic of OE gen. pl. *beg(r)a*; it also occurs in C xxi. 36, where B has *botheres* (the form in C iii. 67); B presumably employs it here to avoid repetition (*v.* 67).

68. *chartre:* here apparently a deed of gift, or conveyance; cf. *CT*, E 1698. Guile appears to be bestowing various gifts on the pair (*togidere*, 69); he does not appear in A, and C alters slightly.

Antecedents for an allegorical marriage are found in Grosseteste's AN poem on the marriage of the Devil's nine daughters (ed. P. Meyer, *Romania*, 29 (1900), 54–72): he marries Simony to Holy Church, Hypocrisy to Religion, Rapine to Knighthood, Usury to 'burgeys', Tricherie to merchants, Sacrilege to 'faus loys', Fauce servyce to 'provostes' and 'faus baillyſs', and so on. A similar allegory appears in *Le Roman de Fauvel*, Book II of which tells of Fauvels proposed marriage to Fortune. R. D. Cornelius (*PMLA* 47 (1932) 363–7) argues that L knew this work. Gower was to present the marriage of Sin's daughters with almost equal vividness in his *Mirour de l'Omme*, 840–1000 (*v.* Macaulay's edition). Owst, p. 96, suggests possible sermon sources.

The device of an allegorical marriage charter would develop naturally in this genre. The closest parallel appears to be 'la chartre au diable fait as coveitons' in the AN *La lumiere as lais: v.* Ch. V.

NOTES

Langlois, *La Vie spirituelle au Moyen Âge* (1928), and cf. the 14th-c. Harlech MS. of Geoffrey of Monmouth

Vers son [prince] e vers nostre seingnur.
(*Historia Regum Britanniæ*, ed. Griscom (1929), p. 35.)

A more remote parallel is the early-14th-c. AN verse-letter of 'Sir Orguylle ly empereur' addressed from the Court of Rome (ed. Vising in *Deux Poèmes de N. Bozon*, 1919), and the *Epistola Luciferi* (1352) of which a ME version is printed in *Medieval Literature and Civilisation*, ed. D. A. Pearsall and R. A. Waldron (1969), p. 233. For this type of satire *v.* P. Lehmann, *Die Parodie im Mittelalter* (Munich 1922), pp. 85–101, and G. Zippel, *Bulletino dell'Istituto Storico Italiano per il Medio Ævo*, 70 (1958), 125. In Heywood's *Four PP* a passport begins 'To all the devils, greeting . . .' and ends 'Given in the forneys of our paleys / In our heye court of the master of malys'.

73 ff. *Sciant presentes et futuri.* The prescribed formula for the opening of a charter; cf. the allegorical Charter of Christ, *c.* 1350, cit. Hussey, p. 57; similar formulas at 101, 103–4, 107. The feoffs consisting of the capital sins are largely new in B (though A has 'the ile of usurie' not found here) and obscure the strict legal pattern of the charter of land in fee simple since they dissolve into a list of sins and vices. Thus from the phrase in which Pride (properly placed *first*) occurs (79) we expect it to be an allegorical principality, but in fact it is at once linked to a series of miscellaneous sins.

83. *wratthe*: C's *yre* improves the alliteration. The sin is not mentioned at this point in A under either name. For the figure cf. 'the erl Auarous', viii. 88.

87. *bargaines*: business 'deals': cf. *CA*, v. 4414: 'Yit wolde thei have a pound again, / As doth Usure in his bargain.'

92. *Glotonye*: linked with 'grete othes' since both, like the jangling, etc. of 94, are sins of the mouth; cf. x. 50, xiii. 400, and *CT*, C 471 ff.

95. *ar ful tyme were*: C 'by-for noon'; cf. v. 496. Only one proper meal is permitted on a fast-day, and it is not to be taken before 'nones' (orig. *c.* 3.0 p.m. but by 14th c. = midday).

97. *burgh swyn*: pigs living on the rubbish of a town street would be well fed.

99. *wanhope*: *v.* v. 449 n.

hym: i.e. a typical sinner (cf. *his* 98). The ll. have nothing to do with the charter proper; the poet is carried away by his detestation of gluttony.

104. A parody of the common legal formula *reddendo annuatim*: they are giving up their soul, after a brief period of sensual delight, to the Devil for ever.

107a. Formulaic: cf. (e.g.) 'Into witnesse of the which . . . my seele I have put to' (*Reg. Oseney Abbey* (EETS, o.s. 133) i. 120).

108. *Paulynes doctrine* (A *doctor*; C *queste*). Sk saw here a reference to the crutched friars, sometimes called Paulines; *quest* was used (as still in Ireland) for 'the collection of alms or donations by friars'. But friars were not usually pardoners, and the later reference (177) is evidently to a class or order different from either. There may be an allusion to St. Paul's or its neighbourhood, the haunt of priests and clerks. In the 13th c. the name *Paulyne* was at least once applied to a priest.

110. The reeve looked after buying and selling on the manor; as he had charge of the manorial accounts he was in a position to conceal things from his lord and tyrannize over 'bailiff, hierde, and hyne' (cf. *CT*, A 593–612, Bennett, pp. 166–175).

Pace certain critics, there is no evidence that the refces. to particular districts here and at 109 (where C has *Banneburies sokne*) display the poet's personal spite. That Buckingham was *at this time* 'celebrated for thieves' (Sk) seems doubtful.

111. *Munde þe mellere.* Mund is evidently a stock name for a miller (? < OE *mund*, cogn. with OFris. *mund* 'strength'): cf. x. 44, which suggests that proverbially millers were as ignorant as they were dishonest (*v. CT*, A 562–3). A M. Scots rhyme runs: 'Tak a wobster that is leill / And a myllar that will not steill' (Maitland Folio MS., STS, 1919, p. 412).

112. Skelton uses the expression 'the devil's date' at least five times, e.g. *Speke, Parrot* (*Works*, ed. Dyce, ii. 22): 'The date of ower Lord / And the date of the Devyll doth shrewdlye accord.' The ME *Ep. Luc.* (*v.* 68 n.) concludes: 'datum at the centre of the erthe yn our tenebrous palace yn presence of ynfynyte legions'.

114 ff. Theology (who appropriately enough takes over in part the role of Holy Church and is likewise of divine origin: 127) is of course opposed to the marriage, though not hostile to Meed in itself, since Scripture sanctions reward for services rendered (122). This aspect of Meed is allegorized by treating her (118) as *moylere*, < OF *mulierée*, Lat. *mulierata*, 'of legitimate birth' (cf. H. Bradley, *MLR*, 2 (1907), 163). The curious reading *Iuweler* (AV), in which Huppé saw an oblique allusion to Alice Perrers (*perré* = a jewel), is probably due to a scribe's misreading of a large M.

That Meed, daughter of Fals, should here be said to be 'engendred' of Amends is not necessarily a contradiction; this verb could be used of either parent. Amends may be thought of as an honest woman deceived into making an alliance with Fals: canon law admitted many children to be *mulieratus* who were not born in lawful wedlock but after a putative marriage in which one parent (here, Amends) had acted in good faith not knowing of any impediment (such as, e.g., a previous alliance between Fals and another woman). The allegorical point is that Meed is good in so far as it involves the concept of proper payment and of making amends for sin by disposing of temporal goods rightly; she is bound by pre-contract (*A grauntide*) to Truth—i.e. God has sanctioned the giving of fair rewards in return for honest work.

In C (iii. 129) Theology is still more closely identified with scriptural teaching ('Ich Theologie the tixt knowe'), which in B is later identified with Treuthe (iii. 339). The Church claimed marriage, divorce, and indeed sexual morality in general (cf. 124b) as under its jurisdiction—as well as simony (125) and perjury (including breach of promise: ? cf. 124a). Thus the passage represents the adverse judgement of an (ideal) ecclesiastical court on such a marriage as Favel is here attempting to engineer, one which *Civil* Law on the other hand is willing to connive at. Significantly, there is no mention at any point of a church ceremony (there are no banns); and, properly speaking, a woman could not be endowed except at the church door.

126*: *v.* Addenda.

131. *of gode*: i.e. of good family, rather than 'wealth' (*MED*); cf. *Sir Gawain*, 38.

132. *cosyn*: i.e. 'kynswomman' (C). If she acted rightly she could marry into the royal family, i.e. there would be a place for Meed in the Christian economy.

133. *bi wisdome and bi witt*: 'according to traditional teaching and natural moral intelligence'.

134. *Londoun*: the courts of law being by this time generally held at Westminster; hence Civil (Law) assents (141) *v*. Owst, p. 347.

137b. Cf. *witig god, Beowulf*, 1056: God sees and knows all.

145 ff. The change from indirect to direct speech is common: cf. *lat* 170. As *faille* is pr., 145–7 appear to represent direct speech; but Sk regards 147 only as quotation.

154. *with a gode wille*: 'gladly'; cf. Douglas, *Eneydos*, prol. xiii *ad fin*.

156. *in ioye*: AH *to be ioyned*; cf. 136.

161 ff. This striking psg. represents an extension of traditional imagery of the Vices. But Covetyse rides a horse in a satirical poem *temp*. Edw. II (*Pol. Songs*, ed. T. Wright (1839), p. 326 which anticipates L in other details.

163. *a schyreue*. For an example of a sheriff's obedience to 'Meed' *v. BPR*, iii. 321 (1358): a complaint from the men of Englefield that the sheriff's under-bailiffs 'do grievously destroy and burden the prince's tenants, levying divers gifts and aids four times a year and more'. In C the sheriff carries Meed 'fram syse to syse', i.e. on the progresses twice-yearly throughout the shire, when he could levy fines at the assizes of bread and ale.

170. *prouisoures*: clerics nominated to benefices by the pope. Such 'provisions' were regularly obtained by gifts to officials or cardinals —simoniacally, on a strict definition. The universities of Paris and Oxford regularly submitted, for provisions, lists of graduates deserving advancement. Hostility to the practice was expressed in the 14th-c. Statutes of Provisors and elsewhere; but it partly emanated from those who wished to keep control of benefices in their own hands: *v*. Southern, pp. 159–68.

172. *suddenes*: rural deans, parish priests chosen to assist the bishop in enforcing discipline as regards local testamentary, moral, and (originally) matrimonial matters; in certain territories they filled the office of archdeacon.

172 ff. The grammatical construction is not entirely clear, but the sense appears to be: 'Deans and subdeans, draw together. Have archdeacons [etc.] saddled [lit. 'cause to be saddled'] with your silver—i.e. buy them with your money—so that they will connive at our sin[ful practices].' The possible emendation *ʒowre* (174) would involve imputing to deans and subdeans the sins of 175, which the officers of an ecclesiastical court are prepared to wink at for a consideration. 176 returns to the image of 174 but strictly speaking has nothing to do with the journey to London.

173. *Erchdekenes* (in large sees there might be as many as five or eight) are mentioned here because they were primarily ecclesiastical judges (often dealing with matrimonial questions); usually men of birth or ability, they were trained in the law (sometimes at such universities as Bologna). Their two duties were parochial visitation and the imposition of fines for moral or ecclesiastical offences. 'Purs is the ercedekenes helle', says Chaucer's summoner (*CT*, A 658), who as an officer of the Archdeacon's court had good reason to know, and envy, his takings. Coulton (*Medieval Panorama* (1938), p. 135) collects unfavourable comments on their avarice and corruptibility: they could be bribed not to summon culprits and even to forgo visitations: *v.* Thompson, pp. 60 ff. and the will there cited of an archdeacon of Lancaster (*ob.* 1361) who prays God's forgiveness for his exactions but states that he merely followed the example of his brethren. Cf. Pantin, p. 207.

officiales. The official was the bishop's permanent delegate and *alter ego* in judicial affairs; he had full powers in the consistory court, and there was no appeal from him to the bishop. He was also the archdeacon's business officer—usually a beneficed incumbent in the archdeaconry whose function was to see that procurations were collected and drinkers fined. When (as often) the archdeacon held a chancery post or some other office in Westminster, his official performed all his archidiaconal duties for him; the office was sometimes combined with that of vicar-general. For an example of an official's 'oppressions and extortions . . . under colour of correction of souls' *v. BPR*, ii. 9; *v.* also Yunck, p. 229.

regystreres (1st ex. *OED*). The bishop's registrar, a notary public, was about as important as his official or his vicar-general: *v.* D. M. Knowles in *Medieval England* (ed. Poole, 1958), p. 414. Weak allitn. renders the line suspect and it is not found in A.

176. *visytynge*: the bishop's inspection of his diocese, in theory repeated triennially after his enthronement. Episcopal manor-houses were established for his convenience on such progresses (*v.* R. A. L. Smith, *Collected Papers* (1947), p. 96), but sometimes became centres for lavish hospitality, the cost of which ultimately fell on parishioners (Thompson, p. 46).

177. *Paulynus pryues* (*A peple*): *v.* 108 above. ? In allusion to the legal sense of *prive*—anyone who has an interest in an action or contract (*OED*, s.v. *privy*, B. I. 2). They are evidently to do Civil's dirty work (? so that the guilty escape and Civil lawyers profit). For *consistorie v.* pr 99 n. The jurisdiction of the court was in practice often committed to the bishop's commissary (*v.* 179), and in the diocese of Canterbury it is still known as the Commissary Court and the judge as the Commissary-General.

178. The speakers are Simony and Civil at 168, though by 171 Simony is referred to in the third person. A gives the whole speech to Civil; who in C names Simony as 'my felawe', which makes for clarity. Yet it is hard to see what Civil Law is doing in this context at all; the courts and officers concerned are those of Canon Law.

179. The poet appears to be adapting the motif of allegorical beasts drawing carts, found (e.g.) in Bozon's *Le Char d'Orgueil*, an anti-feminist poem in which Superbia's chariot, built out of various vices, is drawn by four horses, one being Envy. A. Katzenellenbogen (*Allegories of the Virtues and Vices in Medieval Art* (1939), fig. 60) has found patristic sources for the motif; cf. also Bloomfield (op. cit., p. 155) p. 403, and *Faerie Queene*, 1. iv. 18 f. Here the animal imagery has the function of establishing a nexus with the Prologue (since it recalls the Cat and Rats fable); and behind it is St. Bernard's conception of man, though created upright, deformed by cupidity: 'Magna prorsus dissimilitudo de paradiso ad infernum, de angelo ad *jumentum* ['carthorse'].

180. Since no priest is present to marry Meed and Fals, the ceremony would have made them *fornicators*, technically speaking. The point is that they will live off the fat of the land by taking bribes to overlook fornication.

181. Two A MSS. om. *of*; Liar is elsewhere (68 etc.) a person, and to make a cart *for* him would seem more appropriate. The (four-wheeled) *longa caretta* figures as the vehicle in which Luxuria rides in the allegorical tradition beginning with Prudentius and Origen's interpretation of Exod. 15. 1–14 (*v.* Kellogg, *Traditio*, 14 (1958), 393 ff.); it was used for military transport, and so evidently specified here as capable of holding a large number of passengers. Even the different types of horses here named (C adds *hakeneyes*) apparently derive from the same tradition.

188 ff. *Sothenesse*: not a synonym for 'Truth' but signifying specifically accuracy, exactness, almost 'clear-sightedness': thus he can detect Guile afar off and under any disguise. *Conscience* is perhaps conceived of as the chancellor, the officer of the court closest to the king, who was in fact originally, in technical phrase, 'the keeper of the king's conscience' and who addresses him as familiarly as Conscience speaks to man.

For a case of a similar kind (a girl being imposed on by men acting as her guardians) which was brought to the King on private information, *v.* J. F. Baldwin, *The King's Council* (1913), p. 269 (the men were commanded to appear and to bring the girl before the council).

196. If a man was arrested he was usually 'replevied' (*repligiatus*) or *mainprised* (*manucaptus*)—i.e. he was set free as soon as sureties (*plegii*) undertook (*manuceperunt*), or became bond for, his appearance in court. As imprisonment prior to trial was costly to the sheriff, he preferred to hand a man over to his friends in this way. But this was illegal if a prisoner was taken at the special command of the king (as here).

198. *a constable* (AV *þe*; but all texts have *a* at iv. 85). The Lord High Constable was responsible for the punishment of all offences in or near the King's Court; '*a* constable' would refer to one of his subordinates.

199. *A, for any tresour.*

205. *Drede*: Timor has a not dissimilar role in one of the Parabolæ ascribed to St. Bernard, in which his function is to disperse evil passions; and at this point at least the allegory is to be interpreted morally as well as politically.

dome (cf. *A*, *doom*) may seem inappropriate, as no sentence has been pronounced; several MSS. of all three versions read *dyne* ('noise') or variants: cf. R. W. Chambers, *MLR*, 31 (1926), 31–4 and Kane, p. 437. The reference in *dyne* might be to the custom of crying the name(s) of the parties summoned at the door of the royal council chamber (Baldwin, *The King's Council*, p. 294).

210 ff. The depiction of Falseness's unchivalric and cowardly behaviour allows the poet to remind us of the dubious activities of those who 'choose chaffer' (pr 31) as well as of pardoners (pr 68), friars (58 ff.), etc.

213. We are perhaps to think of him as displaying shoddy wares in shop windows. For detailed descriptions of London shops of the period *v.* documents printed by L. F. Salzman, *Building in England* (1952), pp. 441, 446; for shop windows *v. BPR*, iii. 329.

216. Cf. *CT*, G 658.

220. The lanes of 14th-c. London were notoriously dirty: cf. *Speculum*, 12 (1937), 19.

cloutes: the context suggests the sense 'a child's small clothes'; though we need not rule out a possible allusion to the old rags that sometimes did duty as spurious relics (e.g. as 'Our Lady's Veil', carried by Chaucer's pardoner). But L is chiefly concerned to indicate that in duplicity Lyer is a mere babe-in-arms compared with pardoners.

221. *seles*: *v.* pr 69 n.

222. Sc. *he* before *gaf*; with (common) omission of a nom. pron. that has occurred in an oblique case in the previous clause.

poundmel aboute: 'a pound's worth here, another pound's worth there'. The phrase gains in force from its juxtaposition with *gaf*. For the sin of selling pardons *v.* pr 75 n.; *pens* would be silver coins.

223–4. *leches*: the suggestion is that physicians gave untruthful diagnoses (based on inspection of patients' urine) in order to reap fat fees (cf. vi. 272 n.).

227. *messageres*: the running of messages counted as one of the duties some inferior tenants owed to their lord. Like itinerant minstrels they would be prone to spread false rumours. In Chaucer's House of Rumour there are 'Currours and eke messagers / With boistes crammed ful of lyes' (*HF* 2128–9). 'Messagerye' is associated with Meed in *PF* 228.

228. Six months and eleven days was exactly the length of Edward III's French campaign, 1359–60: he landed on 28 October, and the Treaty of Brétigny was signed on 8 May (for details *v.* Bennett, *PMLA*, 58 (1943), 566–72). If we accept the allusion (found also in A) as intentional, the line thus provides a *terminus ante quem* for the A version. For undoubted references to the campaign *v.* iv. 184 ff. and n. It would certainly be a period when rumour was rampant.

A's variant *wykes* may reflect popular use of 'eleven weeks' for an indefinite period; cf. Dunbar, *This Nycht*, 26.

230. *comeres*: the term replaces OE *cuma*, but survives only in 'all-comers'. The friars, familiar with all tricks of importance, dress him up to prevent his being recognized: perhaps an allusion to the wicked or unscrupulous men who, along with men less blameworthy, at the end of their life 'Dying put on the weeds of Dominick/ Or in Franciscan think to pass disguised'.

233. C adds 6 ll. which account, though clumsily, for the disappearance of Simony and Civil. It is doubtful whether the lines ever occurred in B, which evidently covers their disappearance under '*alle* fledden for fere'.

234. If Mede ran away the action might be held up indefinitely. But the allegorical point is surely that since she relies on her power to bribe she is prepared to stand her ground. She herself has not been denounced: the reference at 204 is scrupulously neutral—the king merely asks for her to be summoned. But her weeping and wailing may suggest a guilty conscience—and conscience will figure prominently in the next passus.

236. *wronge* (*A, wrang*): this absolute use of 'wring' is found elsewhere, notably in *CT*, E 1212: 'lat hym care and wepe and wrynge and waille'; but several A MSS. have 'wrong here/hire hondes'.

PASSUS III

1–8. Meed is treated by the king like a ward in chancery who has got into bad company but is still an honest woman. He acts in the first instance as an ideal king, a divine deputy (cf. 8a). If details of the following scenes are indistinct, it is partly because the various aspects of the king's legal authority were not always clear-cut, and his council might turn itself into a court of chancery according to the case before it. L was at least following early jurists in indicating that Conscience, Truth, and Reason were the basis of equitable jurisdiction, superior even to statute and precedent; and several details bespeak first-hand knowledge. Thus the 'clerk' (3) represents the permanent salaried secretary of the King's Council, and the scene of 10–14 suggests the chamber built in 1340 for meetings of the Council. The moral significance of the scenes is discussed by A. L. Hench, *The Allegorical Motif of Conscience and Reason, Counsellors*, Univ. of Virginia Studies, 4 (1951), 193–201.

10. Alliteration is defective here and in A: ? read *boure* for *chaumbre* as in 14 and in C iv. 11. C here inserts *myldeliche*.

12. By the 14th c. the courts of Common Pleas, of Chancery, and of the King's Bench were all established in the Great Hall of Westminster—the first near the entrance to the Exchequer, the other two on the dais at the S. end.

14. *boure* and *birde* is a favourite alliterative collocation.

16. Justices can be bribed to give the king false advice. One of the charges brought against Alice Perrers was that she tampered with the course of justice.

28. *laste*: 'live'; but the point is that they will stick to her for just so long as the money lasts.

35. Cf. Chaucer's friar (*CT*, A 221 ff.), who was 'famulier' with women.

39. *fyfty*: *A, fiftene*. In any case the suggestion is that age cannot wither Meed's appeal.

48. The friars' churches, like parish churches, often bore witness to gifts or endowments made by parishioners in return for prayers

135

said for their souls (cf. vii. 191 n.). Windows bearing the names or figures of donors begin to appear by the late 13th c. (in Merton College Chapel the name and figure of the donor appears 15 times). For a gable window thus paid for *v.* D. Rock, *Church of Our Fathers* (1905 edn.), ii. 304, and for one in the friars' church at Chelmsford paid for by the Black Prince *v. BPR*, iv. 394.

62–3. i.e., pay for the windows to be filled with stained glass with portraits of donors inserted, and be enrolled in the friars' letters of fraternity (? or regarded as a lay sister).

65. A further didactic intrusion. The objection is not to the adornment of the church but to the glorification of benefactors who think, like Meed, that heaven can be won by cash payment.

67 f. 'God perceives your inward thought, your real motive and disposition [*or* what you spend], and your greed, and knows to whom the money spent rightly belongs' (viz., the poor; cf. Owst, p. 163 n.).

71. *greden*: 'cry aloud to attract the notice of men of God'; alluding to Matt. 6: 1–4.

72. Cf. Matt. 5: 12: 'merces vestra copiosa est in cælis' (and Matt. 6: 1); cf. *CT*, E 1647, and contrast vii. 104–5.

Nesciat sinistra etc. is a further allusion to the theme of ostentatious good works in Matt. 6: 'Te autem faciente eleemosynam, nesciat sinistra tua quid faciat dextera tua.' (vs. 3).

76–86. In all three versions this psg. is not clearly related to its context, and it fails to account for the presence of the mayor at l. 88. It must represent an officious scribe's intrusion or a fragment of a larger episodic discourse that was missing from, or never completed in, the *Ur*-text. C extends the psg.

76a probably represents a scribal reminiscence of the collocation *maire and macere*, as in *St. Erkenwald*, 143: 'the maire with mani maȝti men and maceres befor hym'.

maceres: mace-bearers were merely attendants, with no right to punish. *maistres* 'magistrates' (cf. iii. 245) as in several A MSS. would be an attractive reading (*pace* Kane, p. 438).

78. Pillories were ordained by a statute of Henry III as punishment for forestallers and regraters (*v.* iv. 56 n. and 83 below), users of deceitful weights, fraudulent millers and bakers, etc.: Lipson, pp. 268, 348. Pining—later 'cuck'—stools were chairs in which women offenders (usually) were carried about the town, often with a symbol of their crime hung about their necks: *v.* J. W. Spargo, *Cucking Stools and Judicial Folklore* (Durham, N.C. 1944), p. 72, *BPR*, iv. 269, and *Place Names of Oxfordshire*, i. 23.

79. Cf. the satire ptd. *OBMEV*, no. 62: 'ye bakers with your loves smale . . . ye pincheth on the right weight ayens Goddes law / To the faire pillory ich rede ye take hede.'

81. *parcel-mele*: it is easy to give short weight or measure on small portions, and as the poor can only buy thus, they chiefly suffer.

83. *regraterye* (*v.* Gl.) becomes almost a synonym for profiteering, including participation in combinations or price rings. Wiclif criticizes merchants, grocers, and victuallers who 'conspiren wickidly togidre that noon of hem shal bie over a certeyn prys', etc. (cit. Tawney, p. 259); cf. *Eng. Gilds* (EETS, o.s. 40), p. 381.

85. 'If they dealt honestly they would not have the money to build such fine houses.'

87. *þe maire.* In the 14th c. the mayor's chief role was as a magistrate responsible for fair trade practices: *v.* Lipson, pp. 329–30.

89. i.e. bribes in the form of silver objects (cf. 'a piece of plate'; prob. spec. sense of *pièce*, Med. Lat. *pecia*). As no actual money passed, no one could be accused of bribery.

92. *somdele*: 'just a little'—'don't be too strait-laced'.

93–9. Further authorial comment. The text is in fact from Job 15:34, but Solomon was traditionally regarded as the repository of such wisdom. It is also cited by John of Salisbury, *Policraticus*, ed. C. C. I. Webb, i. 175.

99. *ȝeresȝyues* (not in *OED*): 'gifts', i.e. tolls or bribes taken by royal officers on entering office and repeated annually; cf. *N & Q* (1869), p. 560 (cit. Sk).

100–12. Apparently the king has a private interview with Meed and receives her (suspiciously prompt) submission. Her willingness may indicate her appetencies for good, or mere moral indifference.

109. *biȝunde* (SW. dial. form: cf. Donaldson, *TCA*, p. 200). Later references associate the knight with the French wars.

114. The change of scene is not clearly marked; the 'clerks' here would presumably be the lords spiritual.

126. *ȝowre fadre*: AV, *Vr fader Adam*. At the presumed date of A (*c.* 1370) the father of the reigning king would have been Edward II, whose death at Berkeley Castle was contrived by Queen Isabella and Mortimer. But no tradition associating it with bribery or greed of gold survives. Yet V's reading is no easier: Meed cannot be said to have played a part in the Fall.

127. At least two popes were rumoured to have died by poison: John XIV (984) and Benedict XI (1306). But the main reference must be to the legend associated with the Donation of Constantine: 'An angel men herde an heigh at Rome crye: "*dos ecclesie* this day hath ydronke venym"' (xv. 521–2); cf. *Inferno*, 19. 115 and other refces. in Dante (*v. ODCC* and Toynbee, *Dante Dictionary* (1968 edn.), p. 234).

131a. The first record of a popular phrase. To Whitings's exx. (C 64) add Gower, *Balade*, 43. 14 'si es comun plus qe la halte voie' and 2 *Henry IV*, II. ii. 165. For Meed's pliability *v.* Yunck, p. 295.

133. Cf. the summoner in *Ludus Coventriæ*, 'Bot ȝit sum mede and ȝe me take / I wyl withdraw my gret rough toth' (p. 128, l. 125).

141. Meed's clients disdain the possibility of being excommunicated (for bribery or usury?) by the consistory court presided over by the bishop's commissary.

145. *ȝowre secret seel*: the king's personal seal, with which he would seal his *congé d'eslire* for an election—to a chapter (for an abbacy or bishopric) or to a bishop (for a living); but before it came to hand a provisor had interposed with his bull (simoniacally purchased at Rome, 147). For protest and legislation against provisions at this time *v.* Pantin, pp. 82–95.

146–50. The suggestion is that a provisor would simoniacally buy the preferment at the papal curia; Meed secures the consecration of imperfect bishops (cf. pr 78 n.), provides prebends for parsons, and abets immoral priests.

154. Cf. Huppé, *PMLA*, 54 (1939), 51, n. 26.

157. *louedayes*: sessions of the manorial court, ostensibly to compose differences: *v.* J. W. Bennett, *Speculum*, 33 (1958), 351–70, and Wiclif, *Eng. Works*, p. 234. Bribery evidently played a part.

158. *lawe*: justice. But the different suggestion in 160 ('the majesty of the law') argues in favour of C's *leaute*.

159. *hir*: awkward as obj. of *mote*; om. *A*. Some MSS. read *here*, i.e. in the king's courts.

That appeals were costly is indicated by a complaint that cases from distant parts were often adjourned to Westminster, to the appellants' 'great toil and expense, often to little purpose because of the delays they encountered' (*BPR*, iii. 6 (1351)).

161. *she*: *A*, *he*. The refce. is evidently to 'a mene man'.

176. Cf. 'Mede may spede' (rather than truth): Whiting, M 49 (cf. iv. 25 n.).

180. *half*: C, *hals*: cf. AVH *nekke*.
elleuene: indef. = 'many'.

181. *gyue*: p.p. (cf. ARH² etc., ȝiuen) or inf. The point appears to be that a conscientious man disposes of money lawfully earned to charity.

183. 'I can still honour you, as I used to be able to . . . and support your dignity better than you realize.'

188 ff. Conscience now becomes identified with the failure of a campaign in Normandy, Meed representing herself as preserving the king's life and his troops' morale at that time. The allusions are evidently to the hardship of the 1359 campaign, culminating in the terrifying hailstorm of Black Monday (14 April 1360), when 'il sembla proprement que le siècle dût finir'; Froissart suggests that this decided Edward to make peace; 206 refers to the meagre rewards of the Treaty of Brétigny; for documentation *v.* 228 n., and Chaplais, *Some Documents* . . . (Camden Soc., 3rd Ser. 80, 1952).

But 194–202 appear to refer to events of a different period and perhaps represent an insertion made when the poet was revising the *Ur*-text (? *c.* 1370). If we identify Meed with Alice Perrers, the A version of 197 ('Maade him murthe ful muche, mournynge to lete') may allude to her shameless attempts to console Edward III for the death of Queen Philippa in 1369, when he was again campaigning in Normandy, and when John of Gaunt brought much plunder to Calais.

Meed in any case is *advocatus diaboli*: imperialistic conquest is utterly alien to L's thought.

194–5. Presumably English plunderers carried off brass (i.e. copper) utensils as the only handy objects of value in the Norman villages, and sold them at Calais, the chief commercial centre (being the staple for wool and cloth).

NOTES

206. At Brétigny, in return for the cession of Aquitaine and some neighbouring territories, and a ransom of 3,000,000 écus for the French king, Edward renounced his claim to the French throne; cf. *Camden Miscellany*, XIV, p. xxiv.

208 ff. Meed heaps up instances of 'meed' in the sense of customary reward for services rendered or expected; and indeed the chain of such benefits was 'the universal law of medieval life' (Southern, p. 112).

210. *alienes*: ? mercenaries, or ? messengers or merchants from abroad.

213. *A* reads *to* [ʒerne]: cf. Varr. v. 446, and C (HM 143): *Thorough ʒiftes han ʒeman to ʒerne and to ryde*; ʒemen = yeomen, attendants: cf. *OED*, s.v. I. i and the quotation from allitv. *Morte Arthur*, 2628.

218. 'Beggars in return for their prayers ask for a reward.' Kane, p. 438, compares. vi. 128.

220. A general refce. to royal revenues.

221a. *A*, [*kenne*] *clerkes*.

222. *A* and C rightly take *asken mede* at the head of 223.
A penny or part of a penny was the usual offering to a priest for a mass said for friends or relations; cf. *Eng. Gilds*, pp. 35, 122.

224. i.e. they require premiums.

229–30. As a true knight, Conscience follows decorum.

233 ff. Ps. 14: 1, 2, 5.

242 ff. Cf. Luc. 6: 35 (*benefacite, et mutuum date, erit merces vestra multa*, etc.) and i. 90–1 n.

244. *at a grete nede*: viz., at the hour of death; cf. Good Deeds in *Everyman*: 'at thi most nede be bi thi side'.

245. The concept of 'mesurelees mede' involves a tacit allusion to Luc. 6: 38, recognizable once the earlier refce. (242) is detected: 'Date et dabitur vobis; mensuram bonam . . . et supereffluentem.' The good receive reward beyond their strict due: the bad seek for immoderate gain.

247. Lat. Ps. 25: 10; vv. 6–12 constitute the *Lavabo* prayer of the Mass.

252. A weak, defective line; *A*, 'Shal haue mede in þis molde'.

257. [*libro*] *Regum*: 1 and 2 Samuel ('otherwise called the first and second books of Kings', A.V.); *v.* 1 Sam. 15 and cf. Exod. 17: 8.

268. 'Nunc ergo vade, et percute Amalec et demolire universa ejus': 1 Reg. 15: 3 (with no mention of burning; and it is not there stated that Saul would *die* for his son).

276. *A* om. *Saul*, which is metrically awkward.

278–9. Cf. pr 111, 209. The application of the lesson of Saul's covetousness to either Edward II or Richard II would have been hazardous. (*A, me* for *men*.)

282 f. 'I, Conscience [here almost = Practical Knowledge, *applicatio scientiæ ad actum*, St. Thomas] perceive—for Natural Understanding has shown me—that the moral faculty of Reason will one day rule . . .'.

The nexus of 284–6 is based on the events of 1 Reg. 15–16. After Samuel had hewed Agag in pieces the Lord sent him to anoint David as the future king of Israel. 286–7 allude to David as the ideal earthly king, and type of Christ, and so aptly preface the prophecy of millennial righteousness. Thus Samuel will represent the spiritual authority of the Church, Saul the temporal power that must be chastened if necessary. The well-known psg. at x. 326 ff. has a similar millennial application.

291. *taketh*: 'takes money (meed)'.

293–4. *cloke*: C's alliterating *paueylon* ('coif') is attractive. A's 'Ne no ray robe with riche pelure' alludes to the *raye mancé*, distinctive dress of serjeants-at-law. Lawyers will not grow rich on fees because they will not be needed at all.

295–6. 'Meed makes lords of many misdoers [*pace* Sk], and sets at naught the law as the lords establish it.' Variants in A and C suggest that the ll. are corrupt.

299–349. Not in A. Sk read the psg. as reflecting the momentary enthusiasm caused by Edward III's jubilee (1377). But L can hardly have had much faith in that debauched and decrepit monarch. The quotation at 307 indicates that he is thinking rather of Isa. 2: 2–5 (read at matins in the first week of Advent) as glossed by St. Augustine *et al.*

303. *baslarde*: a sword worn by private persons. A carol on the weapon (*OBMEV*, no. 197) says (with probable *double entendre*) that it has 'a sheath of red and a clean locket [neat band] of lead'.

309. *Placebo Domino in regione vivorum* is the antiphon to the first psalm in the vespers for the dead (Ps. 114:9). The primary suggestion is that priests will concern themselves with their duties instead of hunting (cf. v. 424 and xv. 120): a 14th-c. archbishop of York is said to have hunted with 200 horsemen; cf. *CT*, A 166. But there is also a punning hint that they will please the Lord better by saying their office properly. For a slightly different punning application of *placebo v. Ayenbite*, p. 60.

310. Cf. 'I donke upon David til my tonge talmes': *OBMEV*, p. 186.

312a. 'the benefice that he boasts of'.

318–19. The Court of the King's Bench was the chief criminal court, as distinct from the Court of Common Pleas. *chapitele*: a cathedral or monastic chapter in its disciplinary aspect. *baroun*: the barons of the exchequer were also justices.

320. Cf. Tom Tell-truth, *Oxf. Dict. Eng. Proverbs*, s.v.

323–7. Obscure prophecies (e.g. those of 'John of Bridlington' and others found in MS. Harl. 559) are not uncommon at this period and gave rise to burlesques of the type 'when mice mow corn with waving of their tails'; but burlesque is no part of Conscience's intention; and L shows a penchant for riddling astronomical allusion again at vi. 327 and xiii. 152.

The appearance of several supposed suns was always a dire portent; 'weak credulous men think they see two or three suns when they see none but meteors' (Donne). Such signs were given apocalyptic meaning in the light of Actus Apost. 2: 19–20 (which cites Joel 2: 30) and Apoc. 6: 12—where the blackening of the sun is associated with the opening of the *sixth* seal; the opening of the seventh (ibid. 8. 9) brings the destruction of *ships*.

H. Bradley (*MLR*, 5 (1910), 342) interpreted *schippe* as 'X', corresponding to the outline of a medieval ship; a sheaf of arrows usually contained 24 arrows; and some such numerical clue to date may be hidden in C's version of vi. 328 ff. (q.v.). Another possible allusion may be to Habacuc 3: 11: *sol et luna steterunt in habitaculo suo, in luce sagittarum tuarum*. See also Bloomfield, p. 87 (and pp. 211–12). For a similar riddle cf. *Fasciculus J. W. Clark dicatus* (1909), p. 11, n. 1.

325–6. The crucifixion (and, it was thought, the creation) took place in the middle of the Paschal month; and when it was first publicly preached at Pentecost St. Peter quoted Joel 2 (*v. supra*) and spoke of 'the times of the restitution of all things' (Actus Apost. 3: 21). The suggestion seems to be that as Jews were converted at Pentecost, which marked the beginning of the Christian dispensation, so they will be saved (as Peter the Venerable, St. Bernard, and others maintained) at the end of that dispensation, which will likewise take place in the middle of the Paschal month. *þat siȝte* might appear to refer to the Paschal full moon (hardly, as Sk thought, to the conversion of the Jews). But the quotation from Prov. 22: 1, which rounds off the whole psg. (327), suggests that the 'sight' is of Christians living virtuously in peace and charity.

326. The Saracens will accept the doctrine of the Incarnation heralded by the angelic song at the Nativity (Luc. 2: 14). C substitutes *credo in spiritum sanctum*, indicating the doctrine of the Trinity; cf. xv. 594 ff.

327. Mahomet is often named as a dependant of Satan; L devotes attention to him as an apostate Christian at xv. 389 ff., associating him with clerks' Covetise. *diuicie* is to be glossed 'meed', as Meed's own angry rejoinder testifies.

328a. Formulaic; cf. *Sir Gawain*, 319, *Mum and the Sothsegger*, iii. 153, and *N & Q* (1924), p. 44.

329 ff. Meed's mock-modest disavowal of learning is at once ironically confirmed: she does not realize that *melius est bonum nomen*, etc. is from the same book that she now cites. The inaccuracy she shows in citing *Liber Sapientiæ* (which to be sure was generally attributed to Solomon) is wholly in character. The verse she has in mind is *Victoriam et honorem acquiret qui dat munera* (Prov. 22: 9). Conscience, on the other hand, not only recognizes the psg. and applies the remainder of the text (346): he glosses the whole of the verse (348–9).

334–9. Lat.: 1 Thess. 5: 21. The 'fele wordis' include the following verse: *Ab omni specie mala abstinete vos*.

349. 'The soul that receives the present is to that extent under an obligation' (Sk) glossing the text cit. 346, the sense of which is uncertain.

PASSUS IV

3. *Kisse hir*: in reconciliation; cf. the 'kisse of saghtling', *Cursor Mundi*, Göttingen MS. 17198.

5. Conscience (whether in relation to the individual will or to the temporal power represented by the king) cannot act—as the king, well-intentioned as he is, at once recognizes—without the direction of Reason; 12 ff. indicate their intimate connection: Conscience gives Reason the knowledge on which to act.

The position assigned to Reason, and the tone of his utterances, suggest that he is a person of dignity: in P v he will be given clerical status. He here acts with the dignity of a bishop-chancellor, who would be assisted in council by other bishops and by doctors of the Civil law.

16. The household servants represent (i) elementary learning (Cato = the popular *disticha Catonis*: *v.* vi. 316 n.); (ii) honest speech as opposed to slander and scandalmongering. The horse represents Patience in the sense of biding one's time, its girth Good Counsel (Witty words): patience and prudence go together.

Similar names consisting of phrasal compounds are found in French allegory and in Skelton's *Magnyficence* (e.g. Frantyke Fansy Service).

25. 'Mede is strong' was evidently proverbial: cf. *CA*, iii. 4846, and *v.* Whiting, M 490–4.

26. The appearance of Wisdom and Witty so soon after the figure of 20 is suspicious; in any event Wisdom here must stand for no more than 'worldly' wisdom, the faculty of judging in practical matters; and Witty need be no more than natural intelligence. They are perhaps momentarily conceived of as legal officials of, or defendants at, the courts, who have acted illegally. Chancery considered grievances relating to fraud or violence, refusal of access *to* courts or of remedy *by* courts. By the time of Richard II petitions to this court exceeded all others in numbers.

35–6 Lat. Ps. 13: 3.

41. *knoweth*: 'acknowledges, has to do with': perhaps alluding to Matt. 7: 23 (*nunquam novi vos*).

PASSUS IV

44–7. Refce. to the king's son (cf. *A*) would be natural enough at any time before the death of the Black Prince in 1376; and it would be difficult, and unnecessary, to alter the line after that date: the emphasis is on the place of honour given to Reason. The king still presided at his 'parlement' or council of earls, barons, etc. sitting as a court and listening to the 'bills' (petitions, complaints) of private persons; and it is the king who pronounces judgement (83). This Court of the King's Bench (*v.* 45) was by now completely laicized and sat usually at Westminster (*v.* Sayles, op. cit. pr 210 n., Introd.). Various ordinances laid it down that petitions of the poorest suitors should be considered first (Baldwin, *The King's Council*, p. 277). Most conciliar cases involved petitions arising out of excessive or violent exactions of sheriffs or escheators in circuit areas in which the ordinary legal authorities were likely to be corrupted or intimidated. Peace is here presented as a peaceable private citizen who wants only his rights; Wrong is in accord with the characterization in ii. 88, etc., but is now identified with purveying. Purveyors originally preceded the king's court on its travels, requisitioning provisions for which they fixed their own prices, paying by tallies (*v. Archæologia*, 62 (1911), 367–80) which in theory were good for a sum to be set off against the victims' taxes. Several 14th-c. statutes attempted to correct abuses of the system, insisting that purveying should be for the king and queen's personal needs only and that cash should be paid—but without much effect.

54. 'And paid not a farthing in cash, no matter what legal claim I made.'

56. *Forstalleth*: the term covers various acts in restraint of trade, especially the buying of merchandise before it comes into the market, so establishing a monopoly. Evidently Wrong not only commandeers goods for royal use but uses his position to seize other goods, which he sells at his own price for his own profit: *v.* Lipson, p. 300 (a forestaller sends up the price of wheat from 3*s.* 6*d.* to 5*s.* per 4 bushels), and *Eng. Gilds*, p. 343.

feyres differed from *chepynges* (*v.* F. E. Harmer in *The Early Cultures of North-West Europe* (1950), pp. 350 ff.) in that they lasted for at least three days and were centres for wares from outside the district; they were generally annual institutions. The Statute of Northampton (1328) forbade men to ride armed to fairs and market; but there is at least one reference to armed attacks on a fair *temp.* Ric. II.

NOTES

57. Cf. complaints against a Sir John Danvers that he took off horses, broke the doors of granges, and threshed crops not his: *BPR*, iii. 59 (1359).

58. Cf. Wiclif, *Sel. Eng. Writings*, ed. Winn: 'Lordis . . . taken pore mennus goodis, and paien not þerfore bot white stickis' (102). A tally was a split stick marked with notches, the number, length, and position of which indicated the amount received. It was so split that debtor and creditor each had a portion with identical markings: *v.* H. Jenkinson, *Archæologia*, 74 (1925), 289–351, and *Chaucer Life Records* (1966), p. 136.

65. An overweighted line (as in *A*): possibly a scribe has expanded original þe king (cf. AV)/*lorde* into the fuller formula.

66. *his powere*: ? 'his armed supporters': cf. *A, hem* 66b; perhaps ironical, but they could hardly be said to 'pleyne'. Possibly *powere* = the jurisdiction (hence the authorities) of a town (cf. *OED*, s.v., 4 †c), who would have charge of markets, etc.

72. 'Unless Meed make it up (put things right) your ruin is imminent.'

75. The suggestion is that Wrong passed money behind his back to Wisdom as in the game of this name (possibly alluded to in *Sir Gawain*, 67).

76–7. Meed is (*a*) money wrongfully paid out (cf. *catel* 82) and (*b*) Lady Meed, who has been standing by and is now brought back into the action as likely to prevail with the king; for the perversion of justice and Wit and Wisdom cf. xx. 120–32. Meanwhile Peace proceeds with his complaint, pointing to his broken head as evidence and calling on Conscience and 'the common man' as witnesses.

86 f. *seuene ȝere*: a common formula for an indefinite period—? 'at his majesty's pleasure'. Wrong's feet would be hidden by the stocks (108). The king's oath (83) emphasizes his determination (cf. 104 and *v.* xvii. 298 ff.). But worldly Wisdom is quick to make the cunning suggestion that it would be better to let him have bail and 'square' Peace by paying handsome compensation: in a suit before the King's Council the injured party usually asked not for damages, as at common law, but for 'recovery' and 'restitution' (including all attendant losses and expenses: Baldwin, op. cit., p. 278). 90b may envisage a fine that would go into the royal coffers. *Meynprise* is momentarily personified: 'Let Bail take charge of him and go security for him as regards wrongdoing and buy him compensation and so patch up the trouble to everyone's benefit.'

90. G. Russell (Hussey, p. 41) sees this line as a scribe's variant of A's sparer *'Amende þat mysdede'*.

92–3. Wit wittily extends the word-play on *bote* (reparation/profit) and *bale* (injury/offence): 'Better that compensation reduce the wrong done than that the offender be beaten and no one benefit.'

98 f. Peace in his character as a peaceable citizen would accept compensation and withdraw his charge.

113–33. This long discourse is not obviously relevant, but anticipates Reason's sermon at v. 26 f.; hence the suggestion that it represents a scribe's attempt to adapt that sermon when he had accidentally turned over two leaves of his exemplar. Its pattern owes something to the *topos* of *impossibilia*, for which *v.* Curtius, *European Literature and the Latin Middle Ages* (1953), pp. 95–8.

115. *al*: ? read *alle* (n. pl., as in C); cf. 114b.

116. *Pernelle*: < Petronilla, St. Peter's supposititious daughter. Possibly because priests sometimes passed off concubines as daughters, citing this pseudo-apostolic precedent, the name became a generic term (cf. v. 63–7); but both English and Latin forms are found frequently in respectable, indeed aristocratic, use (cf. *CA*, i. 3396) and amongst nuns (cf. v. 160 n.); here it simply represents women of fashion.

117–18. *chastyng*: A's *chastised* yields easier sense: the spoiling of children will be properly punished, and superficial holiness (cf. pr 2) be given its true value (lit. 'treated as a servant').

119. *and to fede*: probably a scribal extension, or relic of a lost line equivalent to C's 'Here pelure and here palfrayes poure menne lyflode'.

120. *religious romares*: members of religious orders who leave their cloisters without due cause; cf. x. 306 (and *CT*, A 165). *recordare*: probably a punning suggestion (cf. *placebo* iii. 309) that they should 'remember' their monastic duties, and sing their offices. Sk refers to a mass prescribed by Clement V (*ob.* 1313), beginning *Recordare, domine, testamenti tui*; but several offertories in the Sarum Missal also begin with *Recordare*.

121–2. St. Benedict instituted the monastic life, St. Bernard of Clairvaux the Cistercian reforms, St. Francis the Friars Minor. There seems no authority for the suggestion that St. Francis urged religious to stay in their monasteries; the line must be interpreted as a general hint that *all* orders of monks and friars should observe their respective rule: *prechoures* being specifically the Dominicans; cf. *OED*, s.v. †2.

126. See pr 47 n.; but C's variant suggests an allusion to the definition of 'pure religion' in James 1: 27.

127. *That* (cf. *A*; but AV *And*): ? 'so that' (? sc. after *And* 126); ? implying that a man should make but one pilgrimage, at the end of his life, *or* that he follow St. James spiritually.

128 f. *Rome-renneres*: priests or monks journeying to the papal court to have elections confirmed, papal procurators, etc. Wiclif criticizes priests 'who can faste renne to Rome and bere gold out of þe lond and paie it for deed leed and a litil wrytinge' (*Eng. Works*, p. 245; cf. pp. 22, 26). For the phrase cf. *Paston Letters*, ed. N. Davis (1958), no. 72.

robberes of byȝende: (C *in Fraunce*): armed freebooters prowled about France, even in times of truce or peace: cf. *Papal Registers*, ed. W. H. Bliss (1894), iv. 103; but there may be a covert allusion to the 'robbers' of the papal curia, so described in Latin satires (*Carmina Burana*, ed. Hulka–Schumann (1930), no. 42; T. Wright, *Pol. Songs* (1839), p. 27; H. Waddell, *Med. Latin Lyrics* (1929), p. 192/3).

129 ff. Acts of 1355 and later years forbade the export of sterling and required pilgrims to pass through Dover, to ensure that they were not carrying gold: *v.* Lipson, p. 461. No acts exempted the travellers mentioned in 132–3, and conceivably 133 is misplaced, and should follow 128; but it would accord with L's general reasonableness that only the venal 'Rome-runners' should be prevented from taking money with them; he presumably would not object (e.g.) to a bishop travelling to Rome or Avignon for his investiture. A satirical interpretation would not be in character here.

133. A *prouysoure* would go to receive benefices or offices already given. Apparently priests had to obtain special licences to go to the Curia. *Cal. Pat. Rolls*, 1367, p. 52, gives a special licence granted to a chaplain travelling to the Roman Curia (with a letter of credit): *v.* Rickert, *Chaucer's World*, p. 283, item 6. That papal provisions involved export of treasure was a common complaint: *v.* Pantin, pp. 52 ff. For a similar complaint against an abbot of Chester who 'has caused great sums of gold and silver to be taken out of the realm' *v. BPR*, i. 111. For the searching of a pilgrim *v.* Rickert, p. 285.

134. *And ʒet*: the nexus, such as it is, is with 126–7.

143: alluding to the dictum of Innocent III: 'Ipse est iudex iustus . . . qui nullum malum præterit impunitum, nullum bonum irremuneratum' (*De Contemptu Mundi*, iii. 15). It is cited also in the *Meditationes* of the Monk of Farne (*Studia Anselmiana*, xli), and doubtless had a wide currency. It is quoted again at xvii. 304.

154 ff. Worldly wisdom cannot resist Meed's tacit invitation; drunk with money, he staggers, and loses the power of speaking in support of Reason (or, like a reasonable man), but Wit (natural intelligence) follows Reason, in accordance with scholastic theory.

159. *þe moste peple* (cf. 166): present partly as witnesses (cf. 80), partly as spectators.

þe grete: presumably the lords judging the case.

163–4. Cf. ii. 75. Whoever weds Meed will be cuckolded, since she is always willing to sell her favours. The strong language indicates that Meed is antithetical to Love.

167 ff. Meed is free to leave, as she has been neither formally charged nor convicted. She realizes that she is in disfavour and that her occupation has gone. Yet she hardly reaches the door before officials who are (by implication) deaf to Reason, Love, and Truth (Lewte) are after her. 173 suggests that she is still within sight, if not hearing (cf. 180) of the king.

A sheriff's clerk would serve writs—or avoid doing so, for a consideration: cf. Baldwin, *The King's Council*, p. 268.

175. The primary suggestion apparently is that Meed bribes lawyers to quash trials for crimes of treason or felony or to produce supposititious heirs, so that the property in question does not revert to the Crown (for the office of escheats *v.* H. M. Chew, *EHR*, 58 (1943), 219). The moral application would be that those who submit to Cupidity do not give Truth its due; the anagogical, that they do not give God his due.

177. Sk: 'an obvious allusion to the very recent accession of Richard II' (1377). But a young and healthy king would qualify his assertions thus only in the sense of *deo volente*. The passage may well have been written when the aged Edward III was still alive.

182–4. A gives this speech to the king (reading *my* for *ȝowre* 184). It is hardly appropriate for Conscience unless it is considered especially proper for him to suggest that the co-operation of the Commons is necessary for good government.

186–7. Reason will rule if Obedience supports him—i.e. if both king and Commons obey Reason.

188–9. 'I will make formal obeisance to Reason when my full council is assembled' (i.e. lords spiritual and temporal, *in pleno parliamento*).

[C inserts at the beginning of the next passus the ostensibly biographical passage reproduced, e.g., in Sisam VIIIB; cued in neatly enough except that it makes the dreamer on the Malverns wake in Cornhill, and involves a distinct break with the earlier vision.]

PASSUS V

1. *his knightes*: i.e. those of the royal household. The union of Reason, Conscience, and the king, and the king's presence at the service of 'Holy Church' form an appropriate end to the first dream. It had begun with the sun already high in the (summer) sky (pr 13); but dreams do not observe ordinary time; and in any case 'matins' is probably used (as elsewhere when combined with 'mass') to refer to the whole of the public service preceding the mass, which might be at any hour up to noon.

The scene prompts the awakened dreamer to say the creed ('bileue') himself (with the possible implication that he is too far from any church to get to mass himself?); the probable suggestion is that he is now in a more devout frame of mind than at the beginning of the poem. As a devout man he carried what elsewhere (cf. xv. 119) he calls 'A peyre bedes' (i.e. '[of] bedes')—a rosary, or *paternoster*, on which he would now say a series of *Pater Nosters* and *Ave Marias*, as lay folk were enjoined to do after mass. The custom was introduced by the friars, and followed by Chaucer's prioress (*CT*, A 159); a portrait of Chaucer is the earliest evidence for their use by lay folk. The suggestion of the hypnotic effect of the 'babeling' (cf. Dunbar's 'patteris on beidis') producing slumber (cf. pr 10) leads naturally to another dream, and a dream-church.

11–12. Reason (who has already spoken as if with priestly authority, iv. 113 ff.) is a more appropriate preacher than Conscience, the knight, to whom A assigns the sermon following.[1] He is presented as a bishop carrying his crozier; the references in l. 42 would come most fittingly from an *arch*bishop, who could most appropriately address his remarks to [representatives of] the whole realm (10), bishops (42), and even to the pope (51); but the custom of Dominican friars preaching at an open-air cross, or even in the fields, may have suggested the setting of the sermon.

His language is that of a typical medieval bishop (e.g. Brinton of Rochester) who conceives of his duty as moral reformation among clergy and people; but the closest, at least the most accessible, analogue to this *sermo ad status* is Gower's *Vox Clamantis*: cf.

[1] 'Dame Reason' mounts a pulpit and preaches in De Guilleville's *Pèlerinage de la vie humaine*, tr. Lydgate, 2383 ff.

151

M. Wickert, *Studien zu John Gower* (1953), *passim*. Pride (15) is traditionally attacked first as the root of all evils; but here with special appropriateness as both Wrong and Meed have been associated with Pride in i–iii; so too l. 26 links with iv. 116 (cf. ii. 9), which is in turn linked with the confession of Superbia (63 below).

13. *þise pestilences*: the primary reference would be to the great plague of 1349; but those of 1361, 1369, 1375 would give point to B's plural. Bromyard, writing his *Summa Predicantium* about this time, attributes the mortality of the period to 'a general and public vengence taken by God for the vices of mankind'. Cf. Brinton, *Sermons*, ed. cit., p. 216.

14. *þe southwest wynde*: the tempest of St. Maurus's day, 15 Jan. 1361/2, described in several contemporary chronicles (cf. *PMLA*, 58 (1943), 572, n. 14) including the Anonimalle Chronicle, which specifies that it occurred on a Saturday 'et a terre abatist en pluseurs esglises et clochers, mesons et mures, molyns, pountes et arbres en boys et en orchardes a graunt plente' (ed. V. H. Galbraith, Manchester, 1927, p. 50); cf. the 14th-c. Chronicle of Greyfriars at Lynn (cit. *EHR*, 72 (1957), 275, s.a. 1361). The storm and the pestilence are strikingly linked in a contemporary inscription in Ashwell church, Hants.: *v.* V. Pritchard, *English Medieval Graffiti* (1967), p. 183 (where B. Dickins notes that the wind must have been force 11 on the Beaufort scale). For further evidence of its widespread effects *v. BPR*, ii. 189, iv. 426, 432, 464, and R. L. Greene, *English Carols* (1962), no. 73.

15. *pure*: not in A or C, and otiose.

17. *ʒe segges*: as it stands in B, the l. appears to be a phrase from the sermon; but *hem* (20) requires a reading here close to 'segges' (*A*).

18. Beeches and oaks are specified as the most firmly rooted of trees.

20. *at*: Sk's emendation; but *ar* (*v.* Varr.) is defensible.

21. For the deliberate restraint cf. pr 111 etc.

24–5. 'Waster' is to recover by hard labour what he has squandered. The phrasing recalls the title of *Wynnere and Wastoure*, which has a setting similar to the opening of *PPl*, but the collocation may have been traditional.

PASSUS V

26. *purfyle*: 'ornamental border', i.e. finery such as Meed had worn; cf. ii. 9.

28. *Thomme Stowue*: probably a common name, equivalent to a modern 'John Smith' and chosen for alliteration (cf. *Watt* etc. below): Tom is to keep his wife in order *himself*; the whole passage being concerned with family discipline. The *staves*, *pace* Sk, are probably to beat his wife with, *two* (if not purely alliterative) suggesting that he would need more than one. A model husband like the Menagier de Paris would hardly treat, or need to treat, his wife thus; but a medieval Petruchio would not have regarded the punishment as brutal if it kept his wife from the 'pyne' of the ducking-stool in which a shrew or chatterbox was 'ponded'. The Dominican Nicolas Byard (*fl. c.* 1300) (cit. Coulton, *Medieval Panorama*, p. 615) was typical of the time in approving the beating of a wife by her husband for her correction.

30. Wat's wife was blameworthy in that her headdress cost 6s. 8d., then as much as a skilful workman could earn in a fortnight; the reference is presumably to substantial 'coverchiefs' of the kind worn by the Wife of Bath rather than the trellised ornaments as shown on Queen Philippa's tomb at Westminster.

31. For an illustration of a groat of the period *v. Ashmolean Mus. Report*, 1969, pl. xii.

32. *Bette* is found as a masc. name: cf. 'Bette the Bocher', below; but *Botoun* (? fem.) (33) is unusual (*Bethune*, V, R).

34. Like the *nouveaux riches* at all times, the rising merchant-classes would be especially liable to spoil their children (and pander to them—35).

40. The verse (Prov. 13: 24) was regularly appealed to in the Middle Ages as the basis for discipline in the home; cf., e.g., Turgot, *Life of Saint Margaret* (of Scotland), para. 11 (tr. W. Forbes-Leith, 1884).

46. *religioun*: i.e. members of religious orders; they are to obey their *regula* lest the king stint them of provisions (sc. by appropriating their endowments); the hint is enlarged in a well-known passage in x. 292–329; cf. Pantin, p. 126.

49–50. *It*: viz. the 'comune' (as explicitly in C vi. 182): the love of one's subjects is the surest wealth and safeguard or sovereign help (*triacle*) in all dangers; cf. pr 125–6 and i. 132–4. The force of 'if tresoun ne were' is uncertain: perhaps = though there is no defence against treason. The original possibly had 'trewe tresore', simply, as in one MS., 'tresore' being then written twice and the second occurrence emended and expanded to make some sort of sense.

51b. This strong expression perhaps = 'deal gently with'; Urban VI, pope at the presumed date of B's composition, was in fact, though high-minded, somewhat harsh and dogmatic. .

52. *grace*: 'forgiveness' (as often with *give*). The specific sense 'indulgence' (cf. the *gratiæ generales* of a jubilee year) does not seem to be evidenced in English.

55–6. The allusion is to the parable of Matt. 25: 1–12, as indicated by the following quotation from the Vulgate: those who act like the foolish virgins are, in Christ's own words, shut out from the kingdom of heaven; but we should expect, rather, a reference to some such text as Matt. 7: 23 or 25: 41, or Luc. 13: 27.

57. Recalls pr 44 ff., where such pilgrims are identified with lying.

57–8. The preacher's words are remembered, and applied, after the confessions that now follow: cf. 519. That 'seynt Treuthe' is the Holy Spirit (cf. Joh. 14: 17 and 16: 13) is evident from the way in which the sermon closes by naming the other two persons of the Trinity in the doxology (*qui . . . vivit et regnat per omnia sæcula sæculorum amen*).

59. *þat . . . bifalle*: 'May God's blessing be on those who . . .': cf. French *que* with sjv. and adjurative *as* (*v. EMEVP*, vi. 326 n.), and *OED* that 4te. Alternatively, *þat* = 'so that'.) .

61. *reherced his* (KF etc. *this*) *teme*: 'repeated Reason's theme' (Sk) is justifiable, but *reherce* need not mean 'repeat': the word was still current in the sense 'say' in 19th-c. Scots. Repentance may be envisaged as a priest-confessor; in any case the suggestion is that the listeners were at once moved to repentance. (For 'ran' cf. *Speculum Sacerdotale*, p. 64, l. 37: advice to a penitent: 'renne to the preste'.) *kirke-ward* (305) is the only indication that the confessions were made in church; the vagueness is doubtless intentional: at the end of the passus we are to return to the panoramic setting of the opening. .

62. *Wille* may be (1) a momentarily personified abstraction of the human will—referring to the wilful offenders about to express contrition: or (2) a personal name (in two MSS. of A the form is *William*; H₂ has *Wylcoc*): in which case it is either an everyday name for a typical auditor *or* the dreamer (usually referred to as 'I'; but at xv. 148 as Longe Wille) *or* the author as distinct from the *persona* of the dreamer. A *Wille* evidently intended to represent a person (perhaps the poet) is introduced at A viii. 42-4 (but not in B); and at A ix. 118 (= B viii. 124) the poet indirectly but unmistakably indicates that his own name is 'Wille', as at B xv. 148. But the only strictly textual authority for *Will(e)* as the name of the author is A xii. 99 (I MS.)—a conclusion probably added by one John Butt, *perhaps* from first-hand knowledge, perhaps as a deduction from the present and similar ll., perhaps from the colophon at the end of A viii, C x in some MSS. For occurrences in C *v.* Kane, *Evidence for Authorship*, p. 63.

The long series of confessions that follows has long attracted attention, not only because of their vividness but also because the presentation differs considerably in each recension (though details of formal confession are found in each). The 219 ll. extant in A are extended to 457 in B and 596 in C, which cancels some of B's matter but adds much that is new—mainly from B xiii where one Haukyn the actyf man appears with his coat of Christendom (i.e. his white robe of baptismal innocence fouled with the capital sins). The omission of *Wrath* in A and the supposedly inappropriate confession that he makes in B were seized on some sixty years ago by certain critics as evidence in favour of 'multiple authorship'; J. M. Manly further claimed that the treatment of the confessions as a whole was intentionally different from A where they are 'sudden outcries from hearts wrought to repentance', significant of A's crypto-protestant views; but he exaggerated the differences. The subsequent discussions may be followed in *The PPl Controversy* (EETS, o.s. 139, extra issue, 1910).

The theme of the seven capital sins in medieval literature has been exhaustively treated by M. W. Bloomfield (*The Seven Deadly Sins*, Michigan 1952); *v.* also R. Tuve, *Allegorical Imagery* (1966), p. 90 etc., and S. Wenzel, *Speculum*, 43 (1968), 1-22. It is clear that L was indebted to a tradition far more than to a particular source— though the appearance of the sins in earlier (or even later) Latin and vernacular texts may well throw light on his manipulation of the theme. Thus it is worth noting that the Sins are given seven 'pageants' in the Beverley *Paternoster Play* (1469), as in a play performed at Tours in 1390 (E. K. Chambers, *The Medieval Stage*, ii. 154), and the York *Paternoster Play* (apparently well-established by 1378) evidently included representation of Accidia and the other sins (H. Craig, *English Religious Drama of the Middle Ages* (1955), p. 338); cf. also *The Castell of Perseverance*, 830 ff. (in *Macro Plays*). The influence of priests' manuals touching on confession is plausibly suggested by Pantin, p. 226; the poet's emphasis on the circumstances of the sin is certainly found in such manuals. Archbishop Thoresby's 'Catechism' (EETS 118) or summary of instruction on the seven sins, virtues, etc., had been put into English verse before 1356 (Pantin, p. 212); and the *Speculum Christiani* (1360–80) includes English quatrains in which the sins speak in the order: Superbia, Invidia, Ira, Avaritia, Accidia, Gula, Luxuria, somewhat unrepentantly.

Bloomfield shows that from patristic times the capital sins were usually enumerated in one of two orders—the Gregorian (as above) or Cassian's, which begins with Gluttony. L follows Gregory inasmuch as he begins with *Superbia*, but no special significance can be attached to his ordering, which varies elsewhere in the poem (and considerably in the other texts). Pride comes first as the first sin denounced in the sermon; the sin of inward pride ('heiȝe herte') is emphasized, but the delight in ostentatious display typical of Lady Meed and touched on at 26 is also adverted to (66). As a sin lacking the 'degrees' of other sins it cannot be easily described in concrete terms; C extends the confession to 58 lines, but only by introducing allied vices; in any case Pride has already been embodied to some extent in Meed. It is perhaps for this reason that this sin (alone) is presented as a woman; though it also figures as a woman (that is to say as feminine) in (e.g.) the A-N 'Marriage of the Daughters of the Devil' (*v.* ii. 68 n.) and in De Guilleville's *Pèlerinage* (tr. Lydgate, 14826 ff.).

For the iconography of the sins *v.* Tuve, op. cit., *passim*, and A. Caiger Smith, *English Medieval Mural Paintings* (1964). Some of the sins are illustrated in Cambridge MS. Gg. 4. 27 (*CT*), others on bench ends at Blythburgh, Suffolk.

63. For the prone posture cf. Dunbar's *Tabill of Confessioun*, 7–8 ('Falling on face full law before thy feit, I cry the marcy . . .').

66. *vnsowen*: suggests that she is to affix the hair shirt as a lining. The use of the name Pernel (Parnell) recalls the association with fine clothes at 26 above and at iv. 116. Her sin evidently lay partly in love of fashion—frequently attributed to pride, as in the (unedited) poem on Pride and Fashion (Brown–Robbins, Index No. 3705); cf. *King Hart* (ed. cit., p. 117 n. 1), 947 n.

67. *fierce*: often combined with a synonymous use of 'proud' (e.g. *Tr*, i. 225). For the construction with a gerundive cf. 'ferse to fight' (*York Mystery Plays*, ed. L. T. Smith (1885), p. 380/131).

68. The nom. ['I'] is to be understood from *me* in the preceding clause.

71. *al þis*: (acts of) humility (whereas in A she asks pardon of 'all those that I have envied', and in C 'for all the things I have hated'). Cf. the *Confiteor*: . . . *quia peccavi nimis cogitatione, verbo, et opere.*

The doctrine of penance has from the time of St. Gregory involved: (1) *contritio*; (2) *conversio mentis*; (3) *satisfacio operis*; and each of L's penitents acts accordingly, in some degree.

72. *Luxuria* has no more than five lines in any recension. The lecher puts himself at once under the protection of the B.V.M. (example and patroness of chastity), vowing to honour by regular abstinence the day of her votive mass; cf. *Handlyng Synne*, 845 ff. and *Winnere and Wastoure*, 310–11. Not (*pace* Sk) that there was a special danger of getting drunk on that day but that it was especially fitting to observe then the temperance in food and drink which was associated (e.g. by Mirk, Shoreham, and Chaucer's Parson) with chastity (cf. the account of Lot in i. 27 ff. and xiv. 249 ff.). St. Bernadino remarked that the 'devotees of the B.V.M. are wont to fast on Saturday out of reverence for her, because on the Saturday after our Lord's passion the whole faith of the mysteries of Christ remained in her' (cf. Kennedy, *Passion of Christ*, 1344: STS 3rd ser. 23 (1949), p. 50.

76. *Inuidia* here, as often, connotes ill will and its various effects; the objects of Envy here, as distinct from those in (e.g.) *Ancrene Wisse*—temporal goods and success.

In some earlier representations Envy figures as a woman (e.g. De Guilleville, *Pèlerinage*, tr. Lydgate, 14826 ff., where she is daughter to Pride, and *Romaunt of the Rose*, 248 ff.). It is invariably characterized as 'sory of oother mennes wele, and glad of his sorwe and his unhele' (*CT*, C 114–17, and Parsons Tale (I), § 484) and of unpleasing appearance (cf. *RR*, 291–2: 'she ne lokede but awry Or overthwart, all baggyngly').

77. *mea culpa, mea culpa, mea maxima culpa* is the conclusion of the first sentence of the *Confiteor* (for variants *v. Lay Folks' Mass Book*, p. 186); *shewe* refers elliptically to the revelations of his sins in the following recital.

78a. The point of the simile is uncertain: *pelet* may be either a stone ball (used as a missile) or the pelt or skin of a sheep.

81. *forsleues*: presumably referring to half-sleeves covering the forearm, and certainly intended to suggest that envy was a characteristic of the friars.

82. *A* reads *pat* after *leke*.

84 ff. The nexus of faults probably derives ultimately from 2 Cor. 12: 20: 'Let there not be any debates [cf. 98] envyings, wraths [cf. 83], strifes, backbitings, whisperings, swellings [cf. 84], tumults', etc. (cf. also Rom. 1: 29–30 [... *detractiones, susurrationes, inflationes, seditiones*, Vulg.]).

L was doubtless conversant with homiletic material based on glosses of the verse—and also with St. Bernard's conception of the disfiguring effects of such sins on man's nature.

86. Cf. the trans. of the *Confiteor* in *Lay Folks' Mass Book*, p. 8: 'in worde and werke I am to wite'.

87. The formula (cf. ON *varpa orði*) is found outside alliterative verse, e.g. *Owl and Nightingale*, 45. The adder 'of attri onde' (*Ancrene Wisse*), one of the traditional symbols of the capital sins (Bloomfield, op. cit., App. I), is associated with backbiting (*v.* 89) in *Handlyng Synne* and Dunbar's *Dance of the Seven Sins*, 50.

89. *bakbitynge* (cf. OE *heawan æfter*): figures as a 'species' of envy in (e.g.) *CA*, ii. 1605.

93b. A 'wey' was 3 cwt. in Essex as against 2 elsewhere. The reference (new in B) suggests that the writer had lived in a district where Essex cheeses (made of ewes' milk) would be known; i.e. in the SE. Mid. or SE. (including London, where they would be marketed); they were noted for their massiveness and thickness: cf. *Elynour Rummyng*, 429, and note in R. S. Kinsman's *Skelton* (1969), p. 156.

95. *lordes*: the pl. can hardly be pressed. Presumably he is falsely accused at the manorial court and so fined.

98a. The original reading may have been 'a man and his menye', which is perhaps partly preserved in *A*'s *hym and his menye*.

105–6. Those who left money for masses stated that the priest should offer prayers for them, 'their relatives, and all other souls' either at the 'Lavabo', or the *ne nos inducas* of the P.N. For the prayers at the *præparatio missæ v. Lay Folks' Mass Book*, pp. 2–3 (and notes):

> To god thu pray on this manere,
> As next thu fyndest wryten here.
> Nu lord god, for thi godenesse,
> At the begynnynge of this messe,
> Thu graunt to alle that hit schal here
> That in concience they may be clere . . .
> And alle that hit hereth to here soules helthe
> Thu help them with thi grace and thi welthe.

I have not found any text of the Mass which includes specific reference to pilgrims and palmers.

107. *knees*: for kneeling on both knees—indicative of reverence—*v. LFMB*, p. 163.

107–8. *hem*, etc.: the snappers-up of unconsidered trifles such as the sheets Autolycus found hanging on hedges to dry. Instead of praying, Envy broods over the petty losses he has suffered. Cf. xiii. 384–7. Kane's renderings (p. 441) of *bolle* as 'bull' and *my broke schete* as 'fouled my brook' are questionable: *broke* is evidenced as a p.p. form in *PPl*.

110. *Eleyne*: dramatically more appropriate than *A*'s alliterating *Heyne* (masc.); but it involves a man being envious of a woman's garment. A Blythburgh bench end shows a man looking round as he prays.

111b: 'and the whole piece from which it was cut, as well'.

114. He self-righteously condemns them for making dishonest gains.

120. *myʒte*: 'have not been able to'. The observation is based on sound psychology and physiology.

122–3. Sugar, scarce and costly in the Middle Ages, was esteemed as a drug and imported from Sicily or Andalusia (where it had been introduced by the Arabs, and is still grown).

diapenidion: twisted sticks of (barley) sugar, used as an expectorant.

125. ჳus: regularly used to express strong affirmation (as distinct from the ჳe of mere assent) after an actual or implied negative: 'It can be done, and quickly'; cf. 643.

127. 'Sorry? Why, I'm never happy'. Envy misapplies Repentance's phrase 'sorwe of synne' (contrition for sin); cf. Covetise's misunderstanding at 232–3. For the association of leanness with melancholy cf. Burton, *Anatomy of Melancholy*, *passim*.

130. 'I made backbiting my agent . . .': by means of disparaging talk he devalued other men's merchandise. If he had made direct charges or opprobrious statements he might have been brought before the piepowder court (*v.* Lipson, p. 252).

133. The supplementary confession (lacking in A) ends abruptly; but C does not attempt to expand it.

134 ff. The characterization of Wrath (lacking in A, as in A's version of Meed's marriage charter) has been criticized as that of a 'mere counsellor of evil, a mere cause that the sin is in other men', (Manly), rather than that of an angry man. But in fact all his offences are recognized branches of *Ira* as described (e.g.) in the Parson's Tale.

134. *whyte eyen*: turned aside so that the whites are conspicuous.

136 ff. Wrath is the only sinner to announce himself, like a morality character (cf. *Macro Plays*, *Mankind*, 115, *Wisdom*, 1–4). He could hardly have been a friar and a gardener at the same time: the latter was a lay office, the chief duty being to keep the convent's kitchen (cf. 155) supplied with herbs and vegetables.

138. *limitour*: a friar (like Chaucer's Hubert) licensed to beg in defined districts. *CT*, A 252bc suggest that such a friar-mendicant paid a fixed sum to the convent, was protected from competition, and kept any surplus over his 'ferme'.

listres: us. = lectors (a minor clerical office) but here evidently = 'lecturers', i.e. preaching friars (pre-eminently Dominicans).

139–42. The friars' flattery and supposed unwillingness to scourge sins or exact rigorous penance recommended them as confessors in great houses; cf. pr 64, *CT*, A 218, and *Roman de la Rose*, 7677 ff., where Faus Semblant, coped as a friar, is speaking—a passage that helped to fix a satirical stereotype. On criticism of religious in general *v.* D. Knowles, *The Religious Orders in England*, ii, (1955), ch. vii.

144. *possessioneres*: here prob. = 'beneficed clergy', though often used of monks (*v.* D. Knowles, op. cit., p. 65). Either sense would suit at *CT*, D 1722 where a limitour urges hearers to give gifts for building 'holy houses', and not to possessioners, who have plenty.

148–9. *spiritualte*: a play on the two concrete senses: (i) ecclesiastical properties or dues, (ii) endowments (sc. 'that I, Wrath, provide'): they compete *angrily* with each other. There is the further suggestion that Wrath is far from spiritual. When the mendicants receive as offerings goods that would have gone to pay tithes to the parish priest, the priest in turn has to preach begging sermons (aimed at the friars).

150. *Or elles*: from an alternative point of view (that of the result), both friar and priest grow rich enough to buy horses and travel about.

152. *grace*: C (which improves the psg. by reducing 150–2 to two ll.) reads *fortune*. There is a quibble on this and other senses of 'grace'.

153: 'I have an aunt who is a nun, indeed an abbess' (? read: *to aunte a nonne*; cf. 'we have Abraham to our father' (A.V.)).

154. Cf. *CT*, A 148. Chaucer's prioress would weep at sight of any pain, L's if she experienced any (? with reference to bodily penance). But the detail is not strictly relevant to an account of Wrath.

155. Friars were prohibited from entering nunneries without apostolic licence (Franciscan Rule, cit. *Eng. Works of Wiclif*, p. 44)—just as Wrath should not have been allowed to enter.

158. In de Guilleville's *Pèlerinage* (tr. Lydgate, 15348 ff.) Detraction as governess of Envy's kitchen makes 'mortrews and colys' for her, and 'straunge mes with farsyd erys full of poysouns / Put on a spyte by Traysoun', etc.

160. *Peronelle.* The name (for which *v.* iv. 116 n.) is found in conventual records; e.g., a dame Petronilla was a cellarer of Grace Dieu, Leics., *temp.* Ric. II: Gasquet, *English Monastic Life* (1904), pp. 158 ff. The evidence that some priests had concubines is not confined to the Miller's Tale; for the charge that the concubines were sometimes nuns *v.* Coulton, *Five Centuries of Religion* (1928), ii. 182. For quarrels in convents *v.* E. Power, *Medieval English Nunneries's* (1922), pp. 66, 82, 299, and Note E.

worth: 'will be', suggests that the line is part of the implied direct speech of the prec. ll.

161. The chapter of the convent would know about it because she would be 'convened' in chapter before being brought before the ecclesiastical courts that tried ecclesiastical offences, of which incontinence was one (*v.* Bennett, p. 246).

166 ff. Authorial comment; *were prest*: i.e. be authorized to hear confession; the half-l. 'floats' between 167b and 168b.

ordeigned: Crowley (1550 edn.) *provided*.

166. Gregory IX, pope from 1227 to 1241 and friend of St. Francis, commissioned Raymond of Penaforte to collect the papal decretals here referred to. The psg. in question runs:

Nova quædam nostris auribus intimata quod Abbatissæ moniales proprias benedicunt; ipsarum quoque confessiones in criminibus audiunt . . .: cum igitur id absonum fit et pariter absurdum, mandamus quatenus ne id de cætero fiat cunctis firmiter inhibere [because the keys of heaven were committed to the Apostles, not to the B.V.M.]. (*Decretals*, ed. Friedeberg, ii. 887.)

168. *infamis*: apparently a rare technical use; cf. Paulus, *Sentences*, cit. Lewis and Short, s.v.: 'quo facto (maledicto) condemnatus infamis efficitur'. The refce. must be to the betrayal of the secrets of the confessional. The feminine weakness alluded to is humorously given a pious turn at xix. 157.

169–74. It is not that monks are immune to Wrath but that, owing to their better discipline, it is found among them less often. A prior could hold chapter as often as he wished. Wrath's tale-telling (172) would be an infringement of the rule of monastic silence and be noted as such by the superior and the guardians of the cloister. Public chastisement with the rod, administered in the chapter-house directly after the accusation, was a common penance, and penances of all kinds were generally performed on Fridays.

175. A Norman font at Southrop (Glos.) shows *Patencia* scourging *Ira* in this position: *v.* R. E. Kaske in *JWCI*, 31 (1968), 162.

186. *Esto sobrius*: alluding to *Sobrii estote*, 1 Pet. 5: 8. The prons. *me* are probably *lapsus calami* (corr. in C).

189. *Heruy* was a not uncommon name; it was borne by a scullion of the Black Prince (*BPR*, ii. 198); but *sire* implies rank, or priest's orders. Skelton has a Hervy Hafter in *The Bowge of Court* who could 'wel pick a male' (43; cf. 234 below), and in *Why Come Ye not to Court?* M. E. Richardson's suggestion that the name refers to a Norwich wool-weigher (*TLS*, 13 Jan. 1940) is supererogatory.

194. C's *bondemenne bacon . . . yshaue* presents a different picture of a few hairs remaining here and there. For the association of bacon and labourers cf. vi. 286; Hazelton Spencer (*MLN*, 58 (1943), 48) sees an allusion to the serf's meagre slice of bacon. For the sense of *bondemen v.* Furnivall and Hales, *The Percy Folio MS.* (1868), ii, p. xxxiii.

199. *welche*: the connotations are apparently those of flannel in later times. In 1395 a Bristol burgess left material described as *pannus Walliæ* to clothe 13 needy folk, and in 1436 a London testator ordered that gowns and hoods 'of the best Welsh grey russet were to be distributed amongst the poor'. For the jumping lice cf. *Castell of Perseverance* (*Macro Plays*), 806–7.

200 ff. The prominence given to mercantile fraud reflects the scholastic emphasis on it as a sin against society; cf. *Summa*, II ii. Q 77; *v.* also *Castell of Perseverance*, 852 ff. Chaffering that involves false weights, measures, and descriptions is treated as the eighth daughter of Avarice in *Ayenbite*, pp. 44 f. Apprenticeship was a feature of the (luxury and) mercantile crafts; cf. Williams, *Medieval London*, p. 181.

201. *Symme-atte-stile*: for the use of *at* (*the*) (cf. William atte lake, *Reg. Godstow Nunnery*, ii. 565) as part of a name *v.* *OED*, s.v. *John-a-stiles*. It survives in Lancs. dial. ('Jack at Lumblaithe').

205. The refces. suggest a London rather than West Country standpoint: there was a trade route from London to Winchester. Weyhill (*Wy*) lies on the high road from Andover to Devizes. The fairground (described in *The Mayor of Casterbridge*) lies a little to the W. of the village. The fair was originally held from 28 to 30 Sept., later 8–14 Oct.; sheep, horses, and cheese were the chief merchandise: *v.* *VCH Hants*, iv. 206, and Lipson, p. 231.

Winchester was a staple for wool, and its fair was important as a centre of traffic between France and S. England. The stalls of St. Swithun's convent were famed for their wines and spices.

207. *þe grace of gyle*: Guile being Avarice's god.

209. *donet*: the 4th-c. grammar of Ælius Donatus (tr. W. J. Chase, Madison 1928) was a popular school book. In the 14th c. only the abridged text was used, under the name of Donatus minor (A. L. Gabriel, *Garlandia* (1970), p. 104). Here = 'rudiments' (cf. the title of Bp. Pecock's *Donet*). Sometimes an indenture actually made provision for schooling in grammar and writing (Lipson, p. 309 and n. 4). For London drapers (who were largely importers) *v.* Williams, p. 136.

212–13. The exact process is not clear, but it evidently involved a frame for stretching cloth, of the kind later forbidden by law: *Statutes*, iv. i. 139 (1532). For such 'racking straining or tenturing' *v.* also *Eng. Gilds*, p. 351 n.

215. Cf. the Wife of Bath, *CT*, A 447–8, and Williams, loc. cit.

216. If the yarn was loosely spun it would go further in the loom and lend itself to a stretching process. But the webster cheats the spinners (probably also women) as well as the customer: by using heavy weights she pays for a pound but gets 1¼lb.

For punishments for fraudulent weaving *v.* Lipson, pp. 274, 329. Ordinances against 'deceits' in cloth-making are found in the Patent Ordinances, 1364–7.

219. 'Barly malt maketh better Ale than other malt or any other corn doth; it doth ingendre gross humours; but it maketh a man strong' (A. Boorde, *Regyment* (1557), f. Gii). At this period brewing was carried on, and ale was sold, by most city housewives of any position (for a male brewer *v.* xix. 394 f.). The best ale sold at 1½*d.* a gallon, inferior ale at 1*d.* (but prices varied according to the season). The dishonest alewife figures prominently in contemporary records; cf. Lipson, pp. 295–6, and *Chester Plays*, xvii. 269 ('Of cannes I kepte no trewe mesure', etc.). A misericord at Ludlow shows a wife being carried off to hell with her measure. Cf. *Ayenbite*, p. 44.

220. Cf. xix. 397–8: 'drawe it at on hole, / Thikke ale and thinne ale'—i.e. from the same barrel. Pudding ale was evidently 'thick'— the dregs (still used within living memory in a form of suet pudding and in the curing of hams); *A pilewhey* (? whey ? perry).

221–5. *hymselue* (Crowley *itselue*): 'lay' can hardly refer to 'low folk'; the barrel from which they were served stood apart from the

rest. *hemselue* (C) would imply that there were two barrels, one supposedly containing thin ale, the other thick. The best ale was kept
in the parlour or bedroom, and one paid twice the usual price for
it, as something special ('þereafter'). Moreover ('And ȝit') she sold
it by the cup, and could thus give short measure (especially if it
was dented or had a false bottom).

226. Regraters (*v.* iii. 83 n.) bought up commodities in the open
market (whereas forestallers bought up goods on the way thither)
and sold them advantageously: *v.* Lipson, p. 301.

228. *so the Ik*: a N. and E. Mid. variant of S. *so theech*; cf. *CT*,
A 3864 (Norfolk reeve *loq.*).

The vow of pilgrimage (made by no other penitent) comes before
confession and repentance are complete; thus suggesting that
Avarice is typical of the pilgrims referred to in pr 46 ff.

231. Bromholm was (near) the site of the Priory of St. Andrew,
Norfolk, founded 1113 and originally subordinate to the Cluniac
house of Castle Acre. Its possession of a patriarchal cross made
from the true Cross and brought from Constantinople in 1223 or
earlier made it famous even beyond England, and many miracles
were attributed to it; cf. *CT*, A 4286. For a 14th-c. Latin prayer
probably meant for recitation at the foot of the cross (. . . *me
defendas de peccato Et de facto desperato*) *v. VCH Norfolk*, ii. 362,
and M. R. James, *Cat. of Fitzwilliam MSS.* (1895), pp. 138–9.
Pilgrims to Walsingham would be likely to visit Bromholm, only
a few miles away; but a chapman would in any case know of it from
the annual fair held there on the Feast of the Exaltation of the Cross
(14 Sept.) and the day before and after it.

oute of dette: i.e. save him from the *debita* of the Dominical
Prayer. A concludes the confession at this point, but in B the promise of such a prayer is not sufficient to satisfy Repentance, whose
searching question is the occasion for a self-portrait of Avarice in
a new character—that of broker and money-lender.

234. *yrifled*: the *y*-prefix is found only in L (where a marginal
cross marks it for correction) and R. Cf. *yspilte*, v. 380, and ? *i-
made*, 5. 162. For a possible explanation *v. TCA*, p. 202 n. 61.

Bracton (*de Legibus*, f. 235) refers to things that merchants must
do by day and not by night 'on account of the snares and attacks of
robbers'.

236. 'You would more properly have been hanged for this.'
L *haddest better worthy*, where *worthy* is apparently adverbial (cf.
Sir Gawain, 1477, and *Raif Coilȝear*, 360): a comparatively rare
use, evidently not understood by some scribes, as most MSS. read
be (þe) better—perhaps, as Donaldson suggests (*TCA*, p. 197),
because of the common comparative form *better worþy* (cf. Chaucer,
LGW, F 317). *haddest* should strictly be a sjv. of unreal condition
(*hadde*).

238. *on boke.* Cf. *Havelok*, 2327: 'romanz reding on þe boke'.
A survival of early ME use of *on = in*: *OED*, *in*, 5.

239. i.e. he speaks no French at all. Thus Walter Map describes
'Marlborough French'—supposedly spoken by those who tasted
a certain spring at Marlborough—as bad French (*De Nugis Curi-
alium*, tr. M. R. James (1923), p. 271). 'Norfolk French' appears
to have been used for the Norfolk dialect (E. Partridge, *Slang*, p. 38);
and the dialect of N. Norfolk still has a distinctive character. Here
there may be a special allusion to the reputation for cheating and
dishonesty enjoyed by the *baratores de Norfolchia*: *v. The Chronicles
of Jocelin of Brakelond*, ed. and tr. H. E. Butler (1949), pp. 12, 42,
and cf. 'pedlar's French', used of canting terms unintelligible to
the uninitiated.

240 ff. In asking these detailed questions Repentance is, so to
speak, following the instructions regularly given in penitentials and
synodal statutes: *v.*, e.g., *Thesaurus novus Anecdotorum* (ed. 1717),
iv. 696 ff.: '. . . the priest is to make enquiry as to rapine, usury,
pledges made by deceit of usury, barratry, false and lying sales,
unjust weights and measures, lying, perjury and craft.' For further
refces. *v.* Tawney, c. 1, nn. 68–72.

The sections on Penance in *Cursor Mundi*, Pt. V, *Speculum
Sacerdotale*, Chaucer's *Parson's Tale*, *The Ayenbite of Inwit*, Mirk's
Instructions for Parish Priests, *Pupilla Oculi*, etc. should also be
studied.

Repentance's refces. to his catechism at 240, 253 ff. also follow
regular penitential practice; cf. *Castell of Perseverance*, 843 ff.,
where Covetise tells mankind that he should destroy his neighbours,
give nothing to beggars, and use subtle sleight in merchandise. In
the catechism of Abp. Andrew (1552) those who 'may keip thair
nychbour fra povertie and myschance and dois it nocht' are dealt
with under the seventh commandment (*v.* Tawney, p. 266).

PASSUS V

saue in my ʒouthe suggests that he has naïvely, or sniggeringly, misunderstood 'usurie' (Fr.) as 'lechery'. For the phrase *use marchaundyse* cf. *Castell of Perseverance*, 851.

242–3. The Lombards replaced the Jews as money-lenders when the latter were expelled in 1290; they incurred particular odium in the period 1359–79: *v.* A. Beardwood, *Alien Merchants in England* 1350–77 (1931), pp. 11 f., 23, 57.

This is one of several refces. (cf. *BPR*, iv. 202 (a Wm. Ysaake figures as attorney of a Lombard merchant) and *Rot. Parl.* ii (1376), 332a, 350: the Commons complain that Lombard merchants were harbouring Jews) suggesting that some Jews returned to England in the 14th c. and practised money-lending and coin-clipping. They resorted to the latter as they were forbidden to make profit out of their capital: the clippings were melted into bullion. The offence (for which Lombards in London were prosecuted in 1364) was not only fraudulent but treasonable, since it involved tampering with the royal image and superscription, which was regarded as tantamount to an attack on the king's person; cf. *Chronicles of Old London*, ed. H. T. Riley (1863), p. 239, *CA*, ii. 2100–27, and *Medieval England* (ed. A. L. Poole, 1958), p. 283.

244. *it* (om. C): the clipped coin, which was passed as current? 'I learned to lend [coin] out of love for the cross' [on the reverse of the coin, not for the Cross on which Christ showed his *charitas*]. Cf. 'bothe riche and religious that rode thei honoure / That in grotes is ygraue and in golde nobles' (xv. 506–7). Wiclif sarcastically refers to friars who will take gold but 'wilen not touchen an halpeny or ferþing wiþ the coyn and armes of the cros and of the kyng, and þis semeth for dispit of þe cros or of þe kyng' (*Eng. Works*, p. 49). Cf. also *Carmina Burana*, no. 42, st. 9, and Yunck, p. 177.

The remainder of the line is elliptical (C reads: '. . . for loue of the wed, the whiche ich let beter'): '[for the borrower] to deposit a pledge and lose it'—i.e. because he cannot redeem it from Avarice; the bond ('dede') was so drawn that there was no escape clause, and the lender showed none of the mercy enjoined by Ps. 111:5 (Vulg.).

The activities of 244 fall under the medieval definition of usury: 'quidquid sorti accedit, subaudi per pactum vel exactionem, usura est' (*Summa Decretalium*, cit. Tawney, p. 54); cf. Tawney's quotation from Wiclif: 'the usurer would not loan men these goods but if he hoped winning, that he loves more than charity. Many other

167

NOTES

sins be more than this usury, but for this men curse and hate it more than other sin' (p. 51).

247–8. To conceal the charging of interest, the loan was made in the form of goods, which the lender would then buy back at a low valuation. This was known as 'false chevisance'; cf. 249. For exx. *v.* M. Postan, *Econ. Hist. Rev.* 1 (1927), 245.

249. *Eschaunges*: the precise sense is unclear; in the *Liber Albus* (cit. *Oxf. Mag.*, 4 (1887), 46) exchange of money signifies the conversion of old money to new-minted coins (or bullion?).

250. 'And lend to folk who are willing to lose a fraction of every coin they borrow.'

251. *Lumbardes lettres*: the bills of exchange used by Lombard bankers (usually merchants of Lucca) in forwarding money to the papal camera; cf. Gower, *CA*, pr 207–10, and W. E. Lunt, *Papal Revenues in the Middle Ages* (1934), i. 53.

252. 'To take by tally' usually (cf. *CT*, A 570) = 'to buy on credit'; but here there is perhaps a refce. to some manipulation of bills of exchange by the local collector of papal dues: at Rome he fraudulently paid in (*tolde* = 'counted') less than he had received. See Bennett, *MLR*, 40 (1945), 309–10, and Lunt, op. cit., i. 302, 313, ii. 53; and cf. Thomas Gascoigne's later complaint: 'thousands of pounds are paid here in England to Lombards for exchange, to the impoverishment of the realm' (*Loci e Libro Veritatum*, ed. J. E. T. Rogers (1862), p. 52). The merchants of iv. 132 must belong to a different category. (Cotgrave (1660) has a different definition of *lettres Lombardes*.)

253. *mayntenaunce*: here, *pace OED* (s.v., 5), perhaps = the support of their followers (who wore their livery) without regard to the merits of a (legal) case (cf. *Mum and the Sothsegger*, iii. 312–16), i.e. the lender in effect purchased the support of a lord or of his followers, so that justice was overcome. [? Or simply 'dignity, rank', as in later 'cap of maintenance'.]

255. The lords had to forfeit silks and cloths rightfully theirs or sell back at a cheap rate those bought by the feigned sale alluded to above.

256. *peire gloues* (an earlier ex. of the phrase than those in *OED*): evidently given as a present or pledge when apprentices were indentured. For analogous use *v. OED* and *DOST*, s.v. *glove.*

259. Cat fur was one of the furs that commoners were allowed to wear by a sumptuary law of 1383.

260. *manlyche*: charitable, 'humane'.

261. i.e. he is utterly unneighbourly. Cf. OF proverb: 'chiens en cuisine son per n'i désire', and EME: 'Wil de hund gnagth bon, ifere nel he non': *v.* Whiting, H 596. There is an ironic allusion to the formula 'as hende as hawk in halle' (*Pearl*, 184, Whiting, H 195).

The p.p. *holden* survives in formulas.

265–6. *haue, bisett*: infins. dependent on *leue* (263)—like *be* (267, where there is a slight change of construction).

bisett: 'bestow': sc. on chantry masses sung by a (chantry) priest for his soul (and regularly provided for in medieval wills); or ? in alms that would do his soul good (cf. *Peterborough Chron., s.a.* 1137). Here Repentance is insisting on sorrow of heart as a condition of forgiveness. Cf. *Castell of Perseverance*, 1384 ff.

267. '[May God grant that] your wrongful gains are not squandered by wicked men.'

268. *For* seems illogical. The sense evidently is: no *honest* friars would take such tainted money to buy copes or repair their church, even if offered an illuminated Psalter (? or missal, etc.) of the finest quality; religious houses ought to make minute inquiry lest they risk profiting by such funds.

271. *brent golde*: strictly = gold burnt (refined) by fire; but there is possibly confusion with *burned* (< OF *burnir*) 'burnished'; cf. *CT*, VII 2864). The refce. is to the gold grounds (polished to increase their brilliance) usually found in fine illuminated MSS. The library of the Austin Priors at Gorleston provides an example of friars' riches in this kind: *v.* S. C. Cockerell, *The Gorleston Psalter* (1907), Introd., p. 6.

272. Suggests, however awkwardly, that it was incumbent on such houses to ensure that they did not receive tainted money.

274–5. The Latin verses are in the tone, though not the metre, of the *Disticha Catonis*, and doubtless come from a similar source.

276. *vnkynde*: usury being contrary to natural law—'a breed for barren metal'—as well as to divine; cf. 'covetyse kendeles' in the allitv. jingle cit., Bloomfield, *The Seven Deadly Sins*, p. 168, and (in a confessional context) *Lay Folks' Mass Book*, p. 134, l. 233.

277. *rekne with*: 'pay the reckoning [you owe] to *each* man'.

278 ff. For the role of reason cf. the anagogical development of this theme by the Samaritan at xvii. 299 ff., where the psg. here cited recurs.

279. 'Si enim res aliena, propter quam peccatum est, cum reddi possit, non redditur, non agitur pœnitentia, sed fingitur; si autem veraciter agitur, non remittetur [v.l. remittitur] peccatum, nisi restituatur ablatum': St. Augustine, *Epistolæ*, cliii, sect. 20. The whole section had an important influence on later views of usury, and this passage is cited in (e.g.) Gregory's *Decretals*, Peter Lombard's *Sentences*, and *Speculum Christiani* (which reads *numquam dimittitur peccatum*: EETS, o.s. 182, p. 33).

280. *hath* LR, other MSS. *haue, han*. Donaldson, *TCA*, p. 202 n. 58 interprets *hath* as a miswriting of *haveth*: though it may be a rare instance of an analogical plural formed from the 3rd sing.

281. *Is* LMRF, *Ben* other MSS. For sing. form cf., e.g., v. 99, and *v*. E. Maetzner, *An English Grammar* (1874), ii. 139–40.

282. *þis*: the doctrine of restitution.

283. 'I refer to the verse in the psalm that mentions Truth', i.e., Ps. 50:8: 'Ecce enim veritatem dilexisti: incerta et occulta sapientiæ tuæ manifestasti mihi.' The *Glossa Ordinaria* sums up patristic comment:

Sic misericordias dat ut servet veritatem: ut nec peccata sint impunita eius cui ignoxit. Ignoscit enim se ipsum punienti [cf. St. Augustine: impunita peccata eorum quibus ignoxis non reliquisti] *veritatem dilexisti*: i.e. sic misericordiam prerogasti ut servares et veritatem.

284. *werkman*: probably used merely for alliterative convenience (unless it alludes to the parable of the vineyard). Possibly 'no one at all, not even a single labourer'. Or the allusion may be to the doctrine that 'hevene is yeven to them that wol labouren' (*Parson's Tale*: *CT*, I 715). Tainted money can do no good to anyone. The quotation from Ps. 17: 26–7 is incomplete, omitting, as often, the relevant clause: *et cum perverso perverteris* ('with the froward thou wilt show thyself froward').

286. *wanhope*: cf. ii. 99 n.; for despair leading to self-murder *v*. *Handlyng Synne*, 12290 ff.

288. 'Fix your attention on the divine mercy'. Cf. *CT*, I 1020: 'Thou most eek shewe thy synne by thyn owene propre mouth' for the insistence on oral confession.

289. An effective if arbitrary interpretation of Ps. 144: 9: 'Suavis Dominus universis; et miserationes eius super omnia opera eius': *super* being rendered as 'more than' rather than 'on, extended over'. Cf. 'The mercy of God is evere redy to every penitent and is aboven alle his werkes' (*CT*, I 696). St. Augustine (cit. *Glossa Ordinaria*) offers an explanation no less arbitrary: 'Si enim tollas opera tua mala, et non in te remaneant nisi opera eius, non te dimittet miseratio eius.'

291. The figure is based on the simile *sicut scintilla in medio maris*, cited in *Castell of Perseverance*, 3599. A similar quotation (but reading *omnis impietas viri*) is derived from St. Augustine in *The Pricke of Conscience*, 1615–19 (cit. Sk), apparently on the basis of his commentary on Ps. 143: 2.

292. *marchandise* = merchantry in the abstract (Lat. *mercatura*); cf. 'Mercatura raro aut numquam ab aliquo diu sine crimine exerceri potuit' (*Vita S. Gudonis*, cit. Tawney, p. 33 n.). Tawney (p. 50) also quotes a Cologne merchant's will in which the testator offered what atonement he could by directing his sons to make restitution and follow an occupation less dangerous [to the soul].

With the seemingly otiose repetition of 288a cf. vii. 164, 166.

293. *grounde*: ? 'claim'—to enough money to buy a cake of fine bread—the smallest luxury; though the context would lead one to expect 'a crust'. *no good on grounde* ('no money of thine own anywhere') is a tempting emendation.

294. *tonge*: viz. by begging.

296. *perwith*: 'by this ill-gotten wealth'. The general sense is Covetise cannot be allowed to continue in business because everything he has is already forfeit as the product of an original capital that was dishonestly acquired. But the relation of this to the context has been thought unsatisfactory.

297 ff. Tawney (p. 60 n.) fully documents the teaching that if for practical reasons restitution is impossible and if the injured party cannot be found the money is to be spent, under the guidance of bishop or priest, on pious works, and especially on the poor. Cf.

also *Golden Legend* (ed. F. S. Ellis), i. 286: '. . . if he know not [to whom restitution is due] let him do by the counsel of holychurch'.

302. 'Put your trust in his lenten teaching'—the corrective instruction of lenten sermons preparatory to Easter communion. A pun on *lene* is perhaps too obvious to be intentional; cf. xviii. 5.

The metaphor of borrowing and lending is here given a spiritual turn: the bishop lends *spiritual* wealth without interest; but he must render an account of his stewardship at Doomsday, the great Consistory of pr 99. There is an oblique allusion to the parable of the talents, Matt. 25: 15. The tone here is of a manual of confession rather than the confessional itself.

304 ff. The account of Glotoun is notable for the complete absence of any preliminary description; but there is ample compensation in the dramatic presentation of his activities for several days (in C they begin on Friday (C vii. 352) and in B they end on Sunday (367–8)). In both A and B the section begins with a reference to formal confession in church and ends with a somewhat inconsequential vow (in B made to Repentance as confessor). *Kirkeward* (305) indicates that the sinner's intentions are good (and he is prepared to say the *Confiteor*)—but he is easily diverted; and the dangers of putting off shrift ('to longe abiden') are continuously emphasized in the manuals: e.g. *Ancrene Wisse*, CCCC text, p. 108.

305. *kaires*: a Northern 3 sg. form found also in some other MSS.; cf. pr 140, xviii. 365. *A*, *ca[iriþ]* (LN *kaireth*).

coupe: the *mea culpa* of the *Confiteor*.

310. *gossib* already carried the suggestion of 'crony', and possibly of 'drinking companion', as in the later carol 'Good gossips mine' (R. L. Greene, *English Carols* (1962), no. 86), and Skelton, *Elynour Rummyng*, 204.

311–13. He feels the need of something to nibble (? as a remedy against flatulence) whilst still half inclined to observe the fast (mandatory on Friday). Fennel seed was 'of much use to expell wind' (J. Parkinson's *Paradisus*, 1629). Peony seed was drunk with wine as a cure for palsy. Glutton knows that an alewife would be likely to have them on hand for use in brewing: cf. *Roman de la Rose*, 10896–8 (*Romaunt*, 6025–8). Spices were added to wines to mitigate their acidity, producing the mixture called *piment*, used much like a modern liqueur: cf. *Meals and Manners* (EETS), p. 87. Does Bet tempt Glutton in by suggesting that these seeds will 'keep him going' without really infringing his fast?

314. *Grete Othes*: momentarily personified as a companion to Gula, being likewise a sin of the mouth; cf. 375, ii. 92, and the description of Haukin's coat xiii. 400. He 'follows after', in that where gluttony is, swearing is never far behind. In a 14th-c. tract 'Grete othes' figures among the sins who hold a merry meeting in a tavern (Owst, pp. 434–41). Gluttony is associated with the tavern in the *Ayenbite* (p. 56): at church God does his miracles, making the crooked straight and the blind to see, etc.; in the tavern the devil does his: a man enters upright but when he comes out has no foot to sustain him, etc.

315. For similar lists of Christian names with alliterating occupational surnames cf. those of the jurors summoned for the trial of Joseph and Mary in *Ludus Coventriæ* (p. 123): Tom Tinker, Piers Potter, Wat-at-the-Well, Paul Pewterer, Bette the Baker, Pernel Prane—as well as John Jurdon, Malkyn Milkduck, etc.

319. *Cokkeslane*: probably the place where game-cocks were kept, running between Snow Hill and Pie Corner (Ekwall, *Street Names of the City of London* (1954), p. 105). Though respectable persons held property there, it was known from at least *c*. 1300 for its houses of ill-fame.[1] Clarice was doubtless a common woman. The references to a priest take point from the fact that the Church of the Holy Sepulchre was close by. Lechery 'is annexed unto glotonye': *CT*, C 481 ff.

clerke of þe cherche. The phrase is not usually used of the parish priest or parson: it might refer to a parish clerk (like Chaucer's Absolon, who frequented 'gaylard tappesteres': *CT*, A 3336), but A's lack of a line equivalent to 320 suggests that the clerke is Sire Piers, whose title shows that he was in major orders. We must perhaps infer that Parnel was his concubine. Some of the Flemings killed in the rising of 1381 (cf. *CT*, B 4586) were bawds, and even in the 16th c. (according to Stow) prostitutes were chiefly Flemish.

321. *Pridie*: alluding to *Qui pridie quam pateretur* in the canon of the mass: a psg. in Mirk's *Instructions for Parish Priests*, cit.

[1] *v.* Riley's *Memorials of London*, p. 535 (cit. Sk); the verses in Trin. Coll. Camb. MS. O. 9. 38 (also cit. Sk), which juxtapose *cheppstupha* (brothel) and *coklana*, were ed. by A. G. Rigg, *Anglia*, 85 (1967), 27–37.

R. Oliphant, *N & Q*, 205 (1960), 168, indicates that a priest who found he had forgotten to bring the bread and wine was obliged to recommence at this point: hence the name indicates that Sir Piers was incompetent.

322. *ribibour*: a performer (here a professional?) on the small rubible (rybybe, rubibe) a stringed instrument played at the shoulder. A 14th-c. example is shown in F. W. Galpin, *Old English Instruments of Music* (1911), p. 82.

ratonere: sanitary regulations introduced after the Black Death would give this officer some standing. There are several 14th-c. refces. to a 'Rats' Alley' in the City.

rakyer: rakers gathered and disposed of the filth and rubbish in streets and lanes and were paid quarterly for doing so by the wards of the City: *v.* Sabine, *Speculum*, 12 (1937), 23, 42. Cheap was one of the 26 wards.

323. *ropere*: an early allusion to the craft of rope-making, and perhaps the first to its existence in London.

redyngkyng: obscure. The word occurs elsewhere only at C iii. 112. The suggestion that it stands for 'riding king' (though supported by the reading of one MS.) and that it would therefore have the same meaning as late OE *rādcniht*, 'tenant holding land on condition of performing certain services on horseback' is unsatisfactory.

324. *Garlekehithe*: probably the landing-place of that name on the Thames, though it was also an alternative name for Garlickhill or Cordwainer Street, in the present Upper Thames Street, Cannon Street, area (so Ekwall, op. cit., p. 178). For a similar name indicating a similar purpose cf. the late medieval 'Sedgehithe' near Magdalene Bridge, Cambridge, where sedge for strewing on floors, etc. was landed. The church of St. James Garlickhythe had its own guild (*Eng. Gilds*, p. 3).

Gryfin: a typical Welsh name (probably < *griffith*: cf. one MS. *Gruffith*); the suggestion that it alludes to the heraldic 'griffin' on the ancient shield of the principality of Wales is far-fetched.

328. *new faire.* Evidently two contestants proposed articles for exchange and nominated agents (the chapmen of 331) to value the goods and assess the compensation to be paid with the inferior article: i.e. if one man puts down a hood and the other a cloak and the cloak is judged the better article, the contestant who takes the hood gets some compensation. If they disagreed over the amount of this compensation an umpire was appointed (337). It looks as though onlookers took sides (e.g. Bette takes Hickes's side). Here Hickes gets the cloak in exchange for his hood and Clement stands him a drink (or stands a round of drinks?, 344). If either wished to get his own garment back (342) he had to pay a gallon of ale—in accordance with the usual mercantile practice: a buyer who changed his mind had to pay a fine (v. Lipson, p. 231). Readers of *The Return of the Native* will recall the chapman's raffle of a gown (Book III). Refces. in the Grocers' Records suggest that the practice was of ill repute. For the phr. 'God's grace is worth a new fair' v. Mirk, *Festial*, 86/20.

329. *hakeneyman*: here (cf. 339) a stabler or ostler (of habits and reputation similar to those indicated in *1 Henry IV*, II. i). The term is found as a 14th-c. surname in the records of the consistory court of Canterbury (Woodcock, op. cit. ii. 60 n., p. 27 n.); cf. P. H. Reaney, *Surnames* (1956), s.n. Palfreyman.

330. *Bette* (< 'Bertelmew' (Bartholomew), or Bertram) is found as a surname from 1197 (Hone, *Ancient Mysteries* (1823), p. 58, and v. Reaney, s.n.).

333. *Two*: *A, þo* ('they'): v. Kane, p. 443.

336b. v. Varr.: a notorious crux, discussed by R. W. Chambers, *MLR*, 26 (1931), 129–51. It is obviously a corruption of the phrase in C: *ryse thei bysouhte* (*A, was red to arisen*).

344. Cf. *CA*, vi. 60: 'baillez ça the cuppe'.

346–7. The amount does not seem extraordinary, but it was perhaps the final gill that brought him down; the beer was probably stronger than the modern tipple. Kaske (*JWCI*, 31, 161) notes that a choir-stall in Little Malvern Priory church shows two pigs guzzling in a single pot: the allusion may be to the noise made by such grunting contestants.

353. Possibly a performing dog rather than (Sk) a blind fiddler's guide-dog, which has the sagacity to see straight (v. illustration in Jusserand, *Wayfaring Life in the Middle Ages*, p. 275). Itinerant fiddlers were often blind (like the Irish Blind Raftery). In E. Anglian dial. 'drunk as a fiddler's bitch', *bitch* means a trull.

355. i.e. criss-cross.

357. *þrumbled*: *stumbled* WCO evidently represents a scribal variant of *thrumbled* (*v.* Varr.) 'staggered' or 'jostled'; not otherwise found before the 16th c.) and there is no justification (*pace* KF) for preserving it.

364. G. V. Smithers (*Leeds Medieval Studies*, N.S. 1 (1958), 216; cf. *Kyng Alisaunder*, ii. 75) maintains that *with* in such phrases has the force of 'despite'.

369. A nice point: he still thinks he is in the tavern.

371. The intention apparently is to show that his wife's words brought him to a mood of repentance. A and C have a different transitional psg.

376. For the association of swearing and gluttony cf. 314 n., and Bloomfield, op. cit., pp. 163, 168, 425 and n.
   and halidom: some MSS. omit, perhaps rightly; but the full phrase is evidenced elsewhere: *v. Sir Gawain*, 2123, and edd. n. C HM 143 has 'godes soule and his sydes', the type of oath alluded to in *CT*, C 472-5.

381 ff. A breach of the obligation of fasting and a double sin of gluttony: (1) his food is over-dainty, (2) he stops so long at table that he falls asleep with food actually in his mouth.

383. 'I dined in taverns, where I could hear tales, in order to satisfy my thirst more easily.'

390. *aunte*: a weak personification in a weak line. Cf. vii. 132. The point evidently is that he will not eat till late on Fridays, and then only fish, as Church law required.

392. Sloth comes appropriately after Gluttony (in the description of which it is already seen operating) but in the normal order of the Seven Sins it comes before *gula*: *v.* Bloomfield, op. cit., pp. 72 ff. For a full discussion of the broadening connotations of *Accidia v.* S. Wenzel, *The Sin of Sloth* (1967).
   B expands and particularizes the somewhat abstract presentation of Sloth in A, suggesting that he goes to sleep in the very act of beginning his confession (*v.* 398-9). At Blythburgh Sloth sits up in bed.

397. *benedicite*: the penitent begins his confession with the formula: 'Bless me, father, for I have sinned.'

400. *bi þis day*: apparently a mere assertion, though C's order suggests 'today'.

PASSUS V

401. Here and elsewhere *Accidia* connotes laziness in duties to God, especially as regards church attendance; cf. Bloomfield, p. 96. The paternoster should have been said before making confession; a lost York play on Accidie was played by the guild of the Paternoster (*v.* R. M. Wilson, *The Lost Literature of Medieval England*, edn. of 1970, p. 223); cf. the refces. to accidie in a similar context in the fragment of an early primer, cit. *Horæ Eboracenses* (Surtees Soc., 1920), p. 151.

402. The first reference to Robin Hood is found in a Pipe Roll of 1230, where he figures as *fugitivus* and as sought by the sheriff of Yorkshire. The name occurs in the Court Rolls of Edward II for 1320, associated with Wakefield. For other refces. *v.* E. K. Chambers, *English Literature at the Close of the Middle Ages* (1945), p. 130 (an implausible suggestion); F. M. Powicke, *Henry III and the Lord Edward* (1947), ii. 530 n.; R. H. Hilton, *Past and Present*, 14 (1965), 30–44.

In the 14th-c. *Speculum Vitæ* (ed. *Englische Studien*, 7 (1884), 469) the paternoster is similarly juxtaposed to the romances of Bevis of Hampton and Guy of Warwick (ll. 43–5); cf. *Dives & Pauper* (early 15th c.; edn. in progress), which speaks of those who prefer to 'heryn a tale or a song of robyn hode or of sum ribaudry than to here masse or matyns'; the Tudor *Godmanys Primer*: 'it is a shame to se so many prentyses so well learned in Robyn hode and naughty trifels and so fewe that knowe the commaundementes of God, their belefe, nor their P.N.'; and Chaloner, *Praise of Folie*, p. 53: '. . . praise a rime of Robyn Hode for as excellent a makyng as Troilus of Chaucer'.

Randolf. It is doubtful which earl of Chester was thus commemorated: probably the third of this name, Ralph de Blundeville (1172–1232), who became a popular hero by (sometimes) resisting unjust taxation. For a full discussion *v.* G. H. Barraclough, *Trans. Hist. Soc. of Lancashire and Cheshire*, 103 (1952), 29.

405. 'Of accidie cometh first that a man is anoyed and encombred for to doon any goodnesse . . . now comth Slouthe that wol nat suffre non hardnesse *ne no penaunce*': *CT*, I 685. Sloth here compounds his sin by disobeying priestly injunction; cf. Southern, p. 219.

412. The first two of the corporal works of mercy—feeding the hungry, giving drink to the thirsty, clothing the naked, receiving strangers, and burying the dead being the other five. They are appropriately mentioned here since they are based on Matt. 25: 35–6 (the burial of the dead was added from Tobit 1: 19, 20 to make up the mystic number 7): v. *Summa*, II, ii. Q 32, art. 2. We are to suppose that Accidie equally rejects all of these.

The works of mercy were a common theme of late medieval art: v., e.g., G. N. McN. Rushforth, *Archæological Journal*, 2nd Ser. 25 (1918), 47–68; C. Woodforde, *Stained Glass in Somerset* (1946), p. 170; A. Caiger Smith, *English Medieval Mural Paintings* (1963), pp. 53–5 and Index.

413. *somer-game*: usually equated with midsummer sports in general. But the mention of shoemakers rather suggests some special entertainment pertaining to that craft—possibly a guild performance of a play or a mumming, or a game (? football, as at Chester) played at a fair in which shoemakers had stalls (for the prominence of such stalls v. Dunbar, *Poems*, STS edn., iii. 207; and for depreciatory refces. to soutars v. Dunbar's *Turnament*).

415. i.e. the lessons (readings from the Epistles and Gospels) for the day. Cf. *Winnere and Wastoure*, 310–14, where Waster wishes that Winner and Wanhope

> And eke ymbryne dayes and evenes of sayntes,
> The Fridaye and his fere one the ferrene syde [i.e. Saturday, day
>   of Our Lady's Mass]
> Were drownede in the depe see there never droghte come.

417 ff. Accidie displays almost all the other sins—ira (407, 436), luxuria (417), gula (410, 461), avaricia (464), invidia ('wikked wille', 435), thus giving the impression that the writer has in mind the pattern of a penitential; cf., e.g., Dunbar's *Tabill of Confessioun* and the prefixed *Confiteor* in *Register of Godstow Nunnery* (EETS, 1905), p. 8.

418. He does not go to his parish church, which was strictly his duty; cf. vi. 93 n. Coming into church at *missa est*, he would hear only the last prayer, blessing, and Gospel; contrast the emphasis at xix. 2–3 ('to here *holy* the masse . . .'); cf. xix. 384–8, and *Handlyng Synne*, 820 ff.

421. *two ȝere*: C's *ten* is more attractive: annual confession was obligatory for all after 1216.

422 ff. present a new aspect of this composite character, which can hardly be reconciled in realistic terms with the immediately preceding ll. But L has carefully refrained from giving Sloth (as distinct from the other sins) any other occupation.

423. The charge indirectly made is an old one. Stephen Langton described some of the clergy as dumb dogs, perhaps even unable to read the Canon of the Mass; a curate in 1222 knew nothing of reading or singing (*Registrum S. Osmundi*, R.S., i. 304 ff.).

seyntes lyues: viz. in the *Legenda Sanctorum* (*v. ODCC*, and cf. vii. 87, where it is recommended for reading or similar compilations (e.g. the vernacular verse *South English Legendary*).

424. *in a fourlonge*: in the balks between the ploughed furlongs, which were often overgrown with 'brakes and brambles', and in the adjacent 'headlands': *v.* vi. 109 and F. Seebohm, *The English Village Community* (1896 edn.), pp. 18, 9.

425. *beatus vir* (Ps. 1 or 111), *beati omnes* (Ps. 127): both should have taught him to rectify his own conduct.

427. *louedayes*: meetings of the manorial court, which would involve him in secular affairs (cf. pr 96). For an example of a priest presiding over a loveday ('for the whiche . . . we spendid of the churches money yt. tyme iiijd') *v. Speculum*, 33 (cit. iii. 157 n.). Cf. also *CT*, A 258 and the warning 'ȝe þat have made lovedayes beware þat it be not Iudas loveday, þat spake fayre to Crist' (*Middle English Sermons*, ed. Ross, p. 132).

Priests who acted as manorial stewards would have to check the reeve's accounts.

428. *canoun*: probably Canon Law rather than the Canon of the Mass: the decretals of Gratian, etc. being the works that, with the commentaries thereon, constitute Canon Law (*v.* A. J. Carlyle, *Medieval Political Theory in the West* (1928), c. IX). For the use of *canoun* in this sense cf. *Legends of the Saints* (STS 1895–6), p. 28: 'In duble science tacht was he; in canone and divinite', and *Cambridge Middle English Lyrics* (ed. H. A. Person, 1953), p. 45. But a Wiclifite (nonce) use of *canon* as 'the canonical books of scripture' (cit. *OED*, s.v., 4) should also be noted.

429. Contrast Piers's statement of Christian practice, vi. 100 f.

433. To neglect payment of wages may certainly be regarded as an effect of Sloth; but in *Ancrene Wisse* it falls under Avarice: 'Edhalden oðres hure ouer his rihte terme, nis hit strong reaflac—hwa se gelden hit mei—þe is under ȝisceunge?' (CCCC text, p. 108, l. 7); *The Lay Folks' Catechism* constantly links Sloth and Covetise (pp. 352 ff.); and Avarice is in fact suggested at 439. It is a further indication that this is the confession of a man in whom Sloth is the chief of several sins.

439. A falconer's lure is either a dead pigeon or a bunch of feathers with a piece of meat tied to it. When the hawk has learnt to take the lure she is induced to leave the lure for the hand (thumb).

442. 'He has both abstained from expressing gratitude, and made spiteful remarks that gratitude should have forbidden.'

446 suggests that he was a *clericus vagans*.

448. See. i. 139 n.

449 ff. Wanhope is represented as the final stage of Accidia in *Ayenbite*, pp. 33–4 (cf. xvii. 305, xx. 159), and is appropriately indicated by the extreme stage of physical collapse.

Pace Sk *et al.*, the refce. is probably to Matt. 26: 41: *Vigilate et orate* [. . . *spiritus quidam promptus est, caro autem infirma*]. Bloomfield (op. cit., p. 163) quotes a sermon on the Sins based on this text, and a 15th-c. poem on the Sins states that 'the double power of *vigilate* and *orate* is effective against Sloth'. The sense intended is that watching, prayer, and tears of contrition ('water at his eyȝen') will save him: cf. xv. 186 f., xx. 366 f., and Dunbar, *Passion of Christ*, 99–100: 'And for contritioun, baithit in teiris, / My visage all in watter dround'. The KF translation of A *veil* as 'nun' is risible.

454. *hym*: A *God*.

455. *here*: ? on earth.

459–60. He will go to early mass (which in a church or minster would in summer be *c.* 6 a.m., following matins at daybreak), as regularly, and as devoutly, as a monk.

Evensong (462) would be *c.* 3 p.m. C (x. 229) includes it among the services that every man ought to hear.

467. *þe rode of Chestre* stood on Rood Eye—a piece of land between the city walls and the Dee. Legend said that a wooden image floated downstream from Hawarden and the place where it was buried was marked by this cross.

468. Resumes the theme of pr 47 ff. by emphasizing that the search for divine truth is to be carried out in daily life rather than in pilgrimages, and so prepares us for the quest of P vi and the related discussion of worldly duties.

469 ff. This passage has been much disputed. Manly *et al.* argued that it shows ignorance inasmuch as robbery seems to be treated as a 'branch' of Sloth, whereas it belongs properly to Covetise. Two possibilities suggest themselves: (1) Robert is a new character, representing an eighth sin, eight capital sins being found in some medieval lists: (2) Robert-the-robber is merely a generic name for a slothful waster (cf. *roberdes knaues*, pr 44–5, and ? 'Jakke þe iogeloure', vi. 72) and the whole psg. is thus a continuation of Sloth the wastrel's confession. A waster will prove ready to rob in vi. 158–9. 469 is a dramatic way of indicating that he remembered the text *Reddite ergo omnibus debita* (Rom. 13: 7) and applied it; St. Augustine cites it in a similar context (*Epist.* cliii).

470. *nouʒte wherof*: he had nothing wherewith to make restitution; cf. 475b.

471. *to hymselue*: in private prayer.

473. *Dismas.* The penitent thief bears this name in the Martyrology for 25 March: *hoc enim nomine S. Dismæ latronis nonnulla sacella ei erecta reperiuntur*; it was doubtless popularized by its occurrence in the apocryphal gospel of Nicodemus. He is the classical argument against despair, since he was saved at the eleventh hour by his plea *Domine, memento mei, cum veneris in regnum tuum* (Luc. 23: 42). But Robert seems to plead his precedent here chiefly because he was his brother in wickedness (475); and he is cited at x. 414 simply as a great sinner saved by penitence.

475. *haue*: A, *hauiþ*: 'In the same way have pity on me, a robber who has no means to make amends' (alluding to *non habentibus illis unde redderent*, Luc. 7: 42, the parable of the two debtors).

476. *owe*: glossed in L *debeo*, to distinguish from *owe* = 'have'; 'and never expect to earn by handicraft the money I owe'.

477. *mitigacioun*: relaxation of the rigours of a law or penalty; the only earlier ex. is from *Rot. Parl.* 1348 ('mitigacioun faite de sa dite femme'). The only other ex. in a religious context cited in *OED* is in the Wiclifite trans. of Ecclus. 17: 28: *et propitiatio illius convertentibus ad se*.

482. He is to do penance, i.e. be cleansed by *satisfactio operis*, 'made in diverse maneres: in praying, in goyng on pilgrimage, in herborwinge, in almes dede, in wakyng, in fastyng' (*Speculum Sacerdotale*, pp. 73, l. 6 ff.). These are precisely the stages through which we are now to follow the penitents—or Piers, who is shortly to be associated with them.

484. *Latro*: ? with reference to his association with Dismas, the *latro* of Luc. 23; for *aunte* some A MSS. read *hyne* (J, *lemman*).

487 ff. The development of this striking climax owes something to the liturgy, and in particular the services for Holy Week. It thus follows naturally upon the confessions, which may be associated with Lent, the season when confession is enjoined on all, and upon Dismas's petition, which is used on Easter Eve. Repentance bids the penitents adopt the proper penitential attitude, that enjoined by *flectamus genua* in the mass for Good Friday. Thus his role now alters from that of a confessor to that of officiating priest; and 486–7 may be regarded as a reflection or equivalent of *Misereatur vestri omnipotens Deus, etc.*, said before the celebrant goes up to the altar; and the refces. to the Creation recall Gen. 1 (cf. 488 with *vidit Deus quod esset bonum*), which is read on Holy Saturday.

489a. A formulaic description: cf. e.g., 'god all thyng of nowth that made', *Ludus Coventriæ*, 51, l. 127, and A. L. Kellogg, *Traditio*, 12 (1956), 406–7.

491. The doctrine of the Fortunate Fall (fortunate in that it led to the Incarnation) is embodied in the canticle sung on Easter Eve as part of the blessing of the Paschal Candle:

> Exsultet jam angelica turba cælorum: exsultent divina mysteria . . .
> O certe necessarium Adæ peccatum, quod Christi morte deletum est!
> O felix culpa, quæ talem ac tantum meruit habere Redemptorem.

These expressions are probably as old as the 5th c. and appear in a 7th-c. Gallican sacramentary. They can be justified from such authorities as St. Ambrose ('Felix ruina, quae reparatur in melius . . .', *PL*, 14. 1065), St. Gregory (*PL*, 79. 222; cited by Gower *CA*, v. 1752–80), and St. Augustine (*PL*, 40. 276). But they were sometimes (cf. 491b) regarded as dangerous: Udalricus, an 11th-c. monk of Cluny says that his abbot (St. Hugh?) had done exceeding well in having the passage beginning *O certe necessarium Adæ* struck out of *Exsultet* and forbidding it to be said (*PL*, 149. 663: it is missing from many German and French MSS. before and after his time). The implicit paradox of the doctrine seems to have been

generally accepted in L's day; cf. *Sel. Eng. Works of Wiclif* (ed.
T. Arnold, 1869): 'bi this [synne] the world is beterid' (i. 320–1),
and *Castell of Perseverance*, 3340: 'Si pro peccato vetus Adam non
cecidisset Mater pro nato numquam gravidata fuisset.'

þe boke: for the collective sense (= 'the authorities') cf. 'As clerkes
finden writen in here boke' in *Adam lay ybounden* (*OBMEV*,
no. 191).

B. Strang (*N & Q*, 208 (1963), 292 suggests that the inversions
in 491–2 indicate a concealed quotation from a lost lyrical version
of *O felix culpa*.

493 ff. The virginity of Mary is emphasized as indicating the
restorative nature of the work of Christ as the second Adam; cf.
Neckam, *De Rerum Natura* (R.S., p. 233):

Anima nobilis est creatura, facta ad imaginem Dei in naturalibus et ad
similitudinem in gratuitis. Corpus vero protoplasti [viz. the first man]
est ex terra formatum virginea, non corrupta, non maledicta, in typum
secundi Adæ, cujus corpus ex virgine incorrupta sumptum est, [. . .]

A similar mystical interpretation of Gen. 1: 26 is implicit in the
following ll. *Faciamus hominem* . . . is given the sense 'Let us restore
man . . .', with allusion to 'the new Man' Christ Jesus (Eph. 2:
15–16, 4: 13, 24; 2 Cor. 5: 17); cf. xvi. 215, and the liturgy for
Holy Saturday: *hic natura ad imaginem tuam condita ad honorem
sui reformata principii*; and the hymn sung at matins from Low
Sunday to Ascension Day: 'Rex sempiterne cœlitum / Rerum
creator omnium / . . . Nascente qui mundo faber / Imaginem vultus
tui / Tradens Adamo . . .'; *v.* also *ODCC*, s.v. *Imago Dei*; and *v.*
Hussey, pp. 151–61.

qui manet in caritate, etc. (1 Joh. 4: 16), recurs at ix. 63 (with
a 'gloss'). The hymn *Ubi caritas et amor Deus est*, derived from the
same chapter of St. John's epistle, is sung on Maundy Thursday.
The application intended is primarily to Christ as Caritas, only
secondarily to the Christian (cf. Eph. 4: 15). C. substitutes: *Ego in
patre, et pater in me est* (Joh. 14: 11).

495 ff. constitute strikingly concise allusions to the doctrines of
Divine Sovereignty, Divine Impassibility, and the Incarnation
(and, in particular, to the dual nature of Christ). L emphasizes that
Christ suffered in his human nature (*sute* is a doublet of *secte* 498)
but not in his divine nature, and that the Father did not, as the Mon-
archians had asserted, suffer with the Son. This latter possibility

was regarded as incompatible with divine blessedness: *v.* St. Leo, *Sunday Sermons*, i. 237; St. Anselm, *Cur Deus Homo*, 1. 8; St. Thomas, *Summa*, III, Q. 14. 4, etc.; St. Thomas held that Christ's soul was passible, as connected with a passible body. Later discussion (e.g. by Colet and Erasmus) revolved round the Agony in the Garden, which to Donne (*Litanie*, xix) was 'still the agony of pious wits'.

C's reading—

> And madest thiselue with thy sone oure soule and our body lyche
> And sitthe in oure secte as hit semed thow deydest
> On a Fryday in forme of man feledest oure sorwe—

is not necessarily dissonant; *semed* emphasizes that the Deity did not die, and *feledest* perhaps alludes to Heb. 4: 15. Similarly, the account of the crucifixion at xviii. 59 ff. describes the death of Christ's mortal nature—indicated there, as in early Byzantine art, by the closing of his eyes; cf. also xiv. 256, xvi. 215.

In *sute* the primary reference is to the apparel of human flesh (cf., e.g., Chrysostom, *Sermo in Diem Nat.*: 'Let that handiwork be forever glorified, which became the cloak of its own Creator ... this corruptible body could not be glorified, until it had first become the garment of its Maker'). But there is doubtless a further allusion (1) to the sense 'action-at-law, cause', and possibly (2) to the sense 'suite of followers, witnesses': (1) is suggested by 'for mannes sake' (496), (2) by 498 (*v.* note).

496. *ful tyme of þe daye*: the darkness at noon, lasting till the ninth hour, when the death occurred; *nona hora* (Synoptic Gospels) having changed its application from '*c.* 3 p.m.' to 'noon', the hour of the death came to be thought of as midday: cf., e.g., Kennedy, *Passion of Christ*, 974 (in *Devotional Pieces in Verse and Prose*, STS 1949). But there is perhaps also an allusion to the *plenitudo temporis* of Gal. 4: 4, where the whole pattern of Redemption is conceived of as pre-ordained.

498. *it* = 'owre secte', i.e. human nature, which had been captive to Satan. The quotation from Eph. 4: 8 (cf. Ps. 67: 7 and 19: *Qui educit vinctos in fortitudine ... cepisti captivitatem*, etc.) implies also a reference to Eph. 4: 9 (*... descendit primum in inferiores partes terræ*): Christ led sorrowing mankind from limbo to heaven (cf. i. 157). But 498a conceivably also embraces the sorrowful witnesses of the crucifixion.

499. *sy3te* (C *lyght*: cf. xviii. 243): medieval representations of the sun at the crucifixion show it with eyes: the figure is synecdochical for the grief of all creation; cf. OE *Dream of the Rood*, 55: 'weop eal gesceaft' and Kennedy, *Passion*, 934 ff. A patristic source is found in *Sunday Sermons*, ii. 192.

500–1. *meletyme of seintes* is cryptic; 501 probably represents a development suggested by the phrase rather than a mere variation upon it. The heavenly figure of food is frequently associated with the crucifixion, e.g. Rolle, *Ego Dormio*, 232: 'he es demed to þe dede and nayled on þe rode tre, þe bryght aungels brede' (evidently an adaptation of the *panis Angelorum* of the liturgy); cf. Dunbar, *Passion of Christ*, 54: 'his face, the fude of angellis fre'. In *The Pilgrimage of the Life of Man* the angels, speaking for redeemed mankind at the resurrection, sing of 'þe dyner of þis noble day' (Songs xii and xiii). The blood was sometimes conceived of as literally flowing from the Cross down into Limbo: cf. Hone, *Ancient Mysteries* (1823), p. 123; and the image of Christ as the life-rendering pelican 'repasting' its young encouraged such associations. The *seintes*, then, will be primarily the virtuous in Limbo, whom Adam addresses as 'ʒe saintes alle' in the verse *Harrowing of Hell* (1499), but will include those who rose from the dead at the death of Christ (*multa corpora sanctorum*: Matt. 27: 52—a verse which may have prompted L's use of *seintes* here; cf. Kennedy's *Passion*, 1632–3).

Inasmuch as the crucifixion was prefigured in the Eucharist instituted at the Last Supper, the present line may point to the sacrifice of the Mass: cf. the conception of *Ecclesia* illustrated in a 10th-c. MS. from Fulda, where *Ecclesia* is shown receiving the blood of the Lamb in a chalice, with the notation: *Ecclesia ecce cernua quippe suscipit agni digna cruorem* (A. Boeckler, *Deutsche Buchmälerei* (n.d.), i, pl. 21). *Ecclesia*'s role in this representation was later transferred to Adam: *v.* L. Réau, *L'Art chrétien* (1955), ii. 488–90.

501 Lat. The verse is from Isaiah 9 (2), the O.T. lesson for the Monday of the fourth week of Advent and for Vespers at the Nativity. The association with the descent into Limbo is patristic: cf. *Sunday Sermons*, ii. 191. In the Gospel of Nicodemus, popularized by the *Legenda Aurea* and the *Speculum* of Vincent of Beauvais, Christ descends in a bright light; cf. York Play on the Harrowing of Hell, 41 ff. (where the passage from Isaiah is cited) and *Political*,

Religious and Love Poems, p. 231: 'Wat is he þat comet so brith?'
L draws largely on material from the Gospel of Nicodemus in
P xviii, where he gives symbolic meaning to the light that is with-
drawn from earth, and blinds Lucifer (134–40). The association of
the Son with light derives from Joh. 1: cf. xviii. 324.

503. *blewe*: strict syntax requires the action to be predicated of
Lucifer; if of Christ, the expected verb would be *drewe*: cf. xvii.
117, and the Antiphon for the Vigil of the Nativity: *veni et educ
vinctum de domo carceris, sedentem in tenebris et umbra mortis*; the
subject of the verb would then be 'understood' from *þe* (502). The
recurrence of *blew* with *beati* ('blessed') at 515 possibly suggests
scribal anticipation; C reads *broughte*. On the other hand, it is
Christ's *breath* that breaks hell-gate at xviii. 319.

505. *A synful Marie*: (the repentant) Mary Magdalene, according
to Marc. 16: 9, Joh. 20: 14 ('the other Mary' is mentioned along
with her in Matt. 28).

506 Lat. The quotation is from Luc. 5: 32.

507–8. Elliptical: 'All that the Gospel-makers wrote about thy
boldest exploits related to thy deeds done in the armour of our
human flesh.' Cf. xviii. 22: 'Jesus of his gentrice wole juste in Piers
armes / In his helme and in his haberjoun *humana natura*'; and
v. Religious Lyrics of the XIV c., ed. C. Brown, nos. 25 and 63,
the York *Harrowing of Hell*, 129–31, and *Ludus Coventriæ*, p. 147.
45, for similar imagery. The doctrinal implications are discussed by
R. Woolfe, *MÆ*, 27 (1958), 144 f. (and cf. *RES*, N.S. 13 (1962), 1–16)

511. *owre brother*: in the flesh; cf. xi. 194–202 and xviii. 374, and
Ayenbite, 102. The double relationship (511a) produces a variant
in hymns to the Virgin; cf., e.g., *Virgo gaude speciosa*: 'Noster ergo
factus frater / Per te, Virgo, facta mater'. Cf. *Religious Lyrics of the
XIVth c.*, ed. C. Brown, nos. 16 and 132, and *MÆ*, 34 (1965), 233.
The friars made much of the brotherhood of Christ in their
hymns.

514. *deus tu conuersus*, etc.: the priest's prayer following the
Confiteor in the *Ordo Missæ*. The figure of the horn may have been
suggested by 'pro tanti regis victoria tuba insonet salutaris' in the
Easter *Exsultet*, the first line of which—*Exsultet jam angelica turba*—

describes rejoicing similar to that in 516. Cf. the pipe of Peace and the trump of Truth, xviii. 405, 422 (again on Easter morning).

515. *Beati quorum*, etc.: Ps. 31, the second of the Penitential Psalms.

516 Lat. *Homines et iumenta*, etc.: Ps. 35: 7–8.

519b. *A* reads, 'god leue þat hy moten' (or *varr.*), which suggests a distinct break at this point, and A actually begins a new passus with the following line. In each version, to be sure, the following section is somewhat different in theme, and even in style, from the preceding; and it is notable for the introduction of the figure of the Plowman.

521. *bankes*: 'hills' rather than 'river banks', and so tautologous. *baches* (*A*, C), 'valleys', probably preserves the original: it was evidently a purely W. or W. Mid. word (cf. A. H. Smith, *Place-Name Elements* (1956), i. 23, and exx. in Laȝamon and Osency Records), and hence liable to be miscopied.

523–4. *as a paynym*: 'like a heathen', 'outlandishly': care for externals should not characterize a Christian pilgrim. A *burdoun* was two sticks bound together by a strip of cloth like a withy—i.e. spirally.

527. *ampulles* were especially the sign of the Canterbury pilgrimage: they were (miniature) lead or tin bottles carrying medicinal water, usually from St. Thomas's shrine: *v.* Dean Stanley, *Memorials of Canterbury* (1854), pp. 210, 227, and (for illustrations) *B.M. Guide to Medieval Antiquities*, pp. 20–6, 271. A meticulous pilgrim would collect one such flask every time he went abroad, or returned, via Canterbury and Dover. One found recently (prob. from Walsingham) still contained the original liquid.

528. *Synay*. The convent of St. Katharine there was a resort of pilgrims. The repetition at 533 evidently made this reading awkward in the eyes of one scribe, since C here alters to 'Syse'—i.e. Assisi; in the chapel of S. Maria degli Angeli near that town St. Francis had the vision that is now commemorated on 2 Aug.; Honorius III issued an indulgence to commemorate it, and pilgrims still visit the chapel in large numbers on that day.

Galice: several great pilgrim routes converged on Compostela, in Galicia: *v.* pr 47 n. The signs took the form of shells on account of a supposed miracle of St. James; they were at first natural shells, but probably at this time—like images of the saint, for which there was a ready market—were made out of the famous Galician jet; cf. *B.M. Guide*, cit. *supra*, p. 134. As late as 1787 Goethe could meet pilgrims journeying to Santiago and Rome wearing the traditional wide cape, round hat, and scallop shell.

529. A *cruche* would signify a pilgrimage to the Holy Land (as did a design of the Holy Sepulchre), crossed *keyes* (the papal arms) a pilgrimage to the 'seyntes in Rome' mentioned pr. 47.

530. The *vernicle* was another sign of the journey to Rome, the Vernicle (< 'veronica', interpreted as 'vera icon': *v. ODCC*) being preserved at St. Peter's. According to a late legend, Veronica offered her headcloth to Christ on the way to Calvary; he returned it imprinted with his features. Capgrave's *Solace of Pilgrims* (1450) states that a visit to the 'altar of the vernicle' earned an indulgence *totiens quotiens* of eight years: when the Vernicle was shown it carried 12,000 years' indulgence to pilgrims who had crossed the sea (ed. Mills, p. 63). The following item in the will of John Nevill (*ob.* 1386) is evidence for the devotion in England in L's day: 'Domino Archiepiscopo Ebor. fratri meo i. vestamentum rubeum de velvet cum le veronike, in granis rosarum desuper brondata' (cit. H. J. Todd, *Illustrations of Chaucer and Gower* (1808), p. 388).

534. *Bethleem*. The centre of pilgrimage was (and is) the Church of the Nativity, originally built by Constantine in 330 on the supposed site of the Holy Birth.

Babiloyne: near Cairo—not 'Babylon the Great'. 'At babyloyne þere is a faire churche of oure lady where she dwelled vii ჳeer whan she fleghe out of the lond of Iudee for drede of kyng heroud. And þere lyþ the body of seynt Barbre the virgine and martyr and þere duelled Josephe whan he was sold of his bretheren' (Mandeville's *Travels*, ed. Hamelius, p. 21).

535. *Ermonye*: Armenia. Mandeville (op. cit., p. 98) indicates that Mt. Ararat, the resting-place of the Ark, was a place of pilgrimage: 'Sum men seyn þat þei han seen and touched the schipp and put here fyngres in þe parties where the feend went out whan þat Noe seyde *benedicite*: but þei þat seyn suche woordes seyn here wylle: for a man may not gon vp the montayne for gret plentee of snowe þat is allweys on þat montayne'.

Alisaundre: Alexandria, the place where according to tradition

St. Katherine was beheaded and St. Mark martyred and buried (op. cit., p. 36).

542. As notorious liars, palmers would know nothing of Truth; it will soon appear (615) that truth is not to be found by foreign pilgrimage. The implicit criticism of pilgrimages has good patristic precedent in St. Augustine (*Epist.* 88 (*PL*, 33. 268–9), *Contra Faustum Manicheum*, 21 (*PL*, 42. 384–5)) and Gregory of Nyssa (*Epist.* 2, *PG*, 46. 1009).

544. As some C MSS. note, *hic primo comparet petrus plowman.* We learn his name from the pilgrims (563) who may well be applying the traditional name for a ploughman (cf. Jack the Joiner, etc.). The expletive 'Peter!' was used by others besides those whose name-saint was Peter; whether any significance should be attached to such usage remains doubtful, despite the suggestions offered in *Speculum*, 44 (1969), 402–20.

We must envisage Piers as poking his head through a hedge: as his half-acre lies along the highway (vi. 4), he could easily overhear the talk with the palmer.

Both his name and calling are significant—the former because in a Christian context it suggests the Apostle and first pope (who sometimes signifies the Active Life, as St. John signifies the Contemplative), the latter since he will represent (*inter alia*) the honest, hard-working Christian (as in *CT*, A 529–40). 'If you wish to *hear* Christ', said Peter Comestor, 'you should go to ecclesiastics of good living (cf. *CT*, A 528); but if you wish to *find* Christ you should go to peasants of good life.'

For the economic status of the ploughman *v.* Bennett, p. 183. It was sometimes superior to that of the ordinary labourer. [*v.* Addenda.]

545–6a. Cf. i. 140 and iii. 282.

549. *fourty wyntre*: i.e. 'many a long year', 'all my life'. A. H. Bright, accepting 1362/3 as the date of A, saw in the *fiftene* of two A MSS. (*v.* Kane) a proof that the author was the William of Colewall who was ordained in 1348; but the variants are probably merely scribal.

552–3. The ploughman was the handyman of the manor; he was expected to know how to handle his team without striking or hurting them, and to dig, thresh, make enclosures, trench land for draining, etc.: *v.* '*Seneschaucy*' in *Walter of Henley*, ed. D. Oschinsky (1971), p. 283, and *OBMEV*, no. 243; 554–5 indicate that here he is the

exemplar of all honest workmen. For the allitv. combinations in
552a *v. MED*, s.v. *dike*; *Cambridge Lyrics*, ed. Person, p. 46, l. 92;
St. Patrick's Purgatory, 1708.

556. Possibly an allusion to the *Euge, serve bone et fidelis* of Matt.
25: 23.

557-9 allude to the parable of the vineyard (Matt. 20: 1–16 in the
gospel for Septuagesima Sunday); cf. *Pearl*, 497 ff.; some words
and phrases in that passage echo similar expressions in *PPl*, e.g.
heste (*Pearl*, 633: cf. *hoteth*, 552), *hyne* (505: cf. vi. 133); *swange and
swat for long ʒore*, 586: cf. vi. 26–7); and cf. 557 with *Pearl*, 523,
605 (and 556 with *Pearl*, 1200 ff.). There is a reference to the
parable at x. 474.

565-6. Piers's answer shows an awareness of the 'two manere of
Mede' distinguished at iii. 230 ff. He has his 'reasonable hire' (557):
cf. *Pearl*, 523; to receive payment as a guide to pilgrims professedly
seeking their souls' welfare would be a simoniacal act endangering
his salvation.

566. Miracles recorded at Thomas Becket's tomb had long since
made it a popular shrine. For its position and its wealth *v.* Stanley,
Memorials of Canterbury, notes F and G.

570 ff. Piers's allegorization of the Commandments is apt enough,
inasmuch as 'the [old] law was our schoolmaster to bring us to
Christ' (Gal. 3: 24), or in St. Thomas's words, *intentio legis est ut
homines ad virtutem indicantur*. In fact, neither A, B, nor C gives
a complete résumé of the Ten Commandments: 572–4 represent
the Gospel epitome (Matt. 22: 37). The theme of the 'old law'
fulfilled, not destroyed, by Christ (cf. xv. 572) is to become important in the Vita de Dowel.

A pious labourer would be expected to know the Decalogue along
with the Paternoster and Creed—sufficient guides to salvation
(*v.* x. 459–67, and *Ayenbite*, p. 104).

The psg. has been described as pedestrian; but it can be defended
as the surest means of emphasizing the basic importance of 'the
Law'; and it compares favourably with similar imagery in De
Guilleville. Blake used a series of figures strikingly similar in
Jerusalem, chap. I, § 12. 30.

571. *wite*: '. . . that God may know the truth', i.e. 'till God who
knows the conscience [inmost thought] sees that you do indeed
love Him'.

573. Elliptical: 'do not harm your neighbour nor act toward him . . .': *apeyre* may have replaced a more neutral word.

576. For the association of the Commandments with the water of Baptism cf. i. 76 ff. *forth* is a late variant of OE *ford*, found in a few other 14th-c. texts, and in unstressed position in pl. nn.: *v.* A. H. Smith, *Pl-N. Elts.*, s.v. *ford*.

579–80. *but-if-it-be-for-nede*, etc.: cf. *CT*, I 591–4: 'If so be that the lawe compelle yow to swere . . . [or] whan thou art constreyned by thy domesman to witnessen the trouthe' (based on Jer. 4: 2). 580 is elliptical: 'and, especially, do not invoke carelessly . . .; cf. *CT*, C 314: 'Tak not my nam in ydel or amis'.

581. As a direction, this is surprising, but the import is clear: cf. 585–7, where logically the direction should be to *attend* to these prohibitions; cf. the intent of 595.

583b. *þat*–: apparently neut. sg. pron., emphatic.

584. *bowes*: sc. from the enclosing hedge.

587. *left halfe*: the direction associated with evil: cf. ii. 5.

588. A conflation of 'keep to the high road', and 'keep all the holy days'; the third commandment was applied to all holidays of the church: cf. *Handlyng Synne*, 801–2: 'The þrid commaundement yn oure lay / Ys: holde weyl þyn halyday.' Practices to be followed or avoided then are listed in *Handlyng Synne*, where sports, drinking, etc. are forbidden, 'Specyaly before the noun / Whan goddys servyse owyþ to be doun' (1045–6).

590. *He*: *þat* some A MSS.; *frithed*: 'fenced' rather than 'hemmed in with trees' (Sk): the first ex. (in the sense required) of a verb confined to allitv. verse. It is possibly related to *frith*, 'fence of wattle'. *floreines* and *fees* point to the perils of bribery (cf. iv. 156), which might well lead to perjury (592 f.).

592–3. *Non loqueris contra proximum tuum falsum testimonium*: Exod. 20: 16; cf. 23: 1. Cf. *CT*, C 636: 'Thou shalt swere sooth', etc.

594. *a courte*: a castle (cf. 'þe proude court of Paradis', *Sir Orfeo*, 376; desc. as *castel*, 377). The stone-work of a medieval castle was often brightly painted—hence *clere* suggests 'bright, gleaming'. The heavenly Jerusalem of Apoc. 21: 11, the light of which was 'like unto a stone most precious', is sometimes pictured as such a castle (e.g. by Sassetta in *The Charity of St. Francis* in the National Gallery).

The image as developed in the following passage partly resembles the description of *Chasteau d'Amour* in the poem of that name ascribed to Grossetete, and translated into ME (ed. R. F. Weymouth, 1864, and K. Sajavaara, Helsinki, 1967). That *château* is 'a wel comeliche castel, depe idiched al abouten' (with the Virgin's patient poverty); it has small towers (her virginity, chastity, and espousals) 'to witen [guard] the heiȝe tour withouten', baillies (the four cardinal virtues), seven barbicans symbolizing defences against the seven sins, and a well of Grace. Without the chief tower is a throne of ivory [a traditional image of the Virgin: cf. Cant. 7: 4; 'Nevere so feir chayȝere / Nedde kyng ne emperere'].

It is probable that L knew the *Chasteau d'Amour*; but other sources may have suggested his architectural figure; the basic image of the spiritual house derives from St. Augustine (*sermo xx in verb. Sap.*), who describes Faith as the foundation, Charity as the roof, etc.: cf. *ME Sermons*, p. 137. It is adapted in *The Abbey of the Holy Ghost* (late 14th c.), but L shares no details with that work. The iconography of the image has not been fully explored: some illustrations from a Casanetensis MS. were published by Saxl, *JWCI*, 5 (1942): *v.* Pl. opp. p. 104, where Humility (cf. 617 below) is seen addressing the aggressors. The relation to the secular depictions of the Castle of Love is obvious (*v. JWCI*, 11 (1948), 114 and nn.). For the theme in general *v.* R. D. Cornelius, *The Figurative Castle* (Bryn Mawr, 1930).

595. Mercy is the first feature of the castle: the moat represents the meeting-place rather than the boundary between the Old Law and the New, for mercy is shown to those who keep God's commandments (cf. Exod. 20: 6). In Frère Laurent's *La Somme le Roi* the moat represents Charity and Humility: *v. MÆ*, 36 (1967), 135.

595. *Witte* (= Reason, Wisdom) is traditionally opposed to *wille* (wilfulness) in medieval allegory: cf. *Sawles Warde* (*EMEVP*, XIX, *ad init.*), and 'The Conflict of Wit and Will', ed. B. Dickins (Leeds 1938).

598. An allusion to the opening words of the Athanasian Creed—from which the words of Piers's pardon are to be taken (vii. 112). On a strict view, it follows that Piers would know that creed and recognize the source of that pardon. Lay folk were expected to know only the Apostles' Creed (the 'lore' taught by Chaucer's Parson, *CT*, A 527, to his parishioners); the 'mass creed' is the Nicene. *beest* retains the consuetudinal signification of OE *bist*.

600. *A* reads: '. . . loue and lou3nesse, as breþeren of o wombe'.

601. A has no 'brugge', but a tower of Truth, and a notable image of the daystar (*v.* N. Coghill in *English and Mediaeval Studies presented to J. R. R. Tolkien*, 1962).

602. *piler*: presumably each 'pile' of the bridge across the Moat of Mercy; unless the allusion is to a drawbridge hung on, or supported by, pillars.

604. As porter, Grace signifies the passage from the Old Law of Observances—which takes one no further than to the gate of the castle—to the New Law of Love; but Grace is unavailing without amendment of life (605).

605. *for* (om. C text) is difficult, if not incoherent, even if we read *he* (*A*) for *him*. It is conceivably an anticipation of *for* found in 606 in one text: *v.* below. The double repetition of *man* is suspicious.

606b. *þat*: A, V reads *for*. *A* reads: 'treuþe wot þe soþe', treating the half-line as the beginning of *oratio recta*. B can be construed as meaning that Truth, Lord of the Castle, requires a sign or password showing that the pilgrim comes in good faith: he must produce a token of *Satisfactio* and *Contricio* 'so that Truth may know [*wite*, sjv.]' (that he is truly penitent). The porter sends in a messenger bearing such a token, who kneels before his lord (610) and humbly begs him to allow the gate to be opened: *wiket* (611) perhaps suggests that one must humbly stoop to enter—'strait is the gate'. The figure in general may owe something to Prov. 8: 34–5 (the lesson for the feast of the Rosary of the B.V.M.): 'Beatus homo qui . . . vigilat ad fores meas quotidie et observat ad postes ostii mei. Qui me invenerit inveniet vitam.'

612. *apples vnrosted*: i.e. in their primeval form. In the state of innocence Adam and Eve ate the fruit of the garden without having the labour of cooking—'No fear lest dinner cool'. *Per contra* 'when Adam of thilke appel bot / His swete morscel was to hot' (*CA*, vi. 5–6).

The nature of the 'fructus in quo Adam peccavit' was much discussed in the later Middle Ages: *v. Neuphil. Mitteil.* 59 (1958), 23–4: it was not generally identified as an apple before the 14th c.

The Latin text is from an Antiphon in the Commemoration of Our Lady said at Lauds from the Monday of the week within the Octave of Easter until the Vigil of the Ascension: *Inc*: *Paradisi portam per Evam* (with reference to Gen. 3: 23–4, and the anagram EVA / AVE [MARIA]).

The symbolism of Mary as the 'gate of Paradise' (based ultimately on the *porta clausa* of Ezech. 44: 2) is a commonplace: cf., e.g., the hymn *O gloriosa femina* and the ME version thereof (ed. C. Brown, *Religious Lyrics of the XIVth c.*, p. 48); *Political, Religious and Love Poems* (EETS, o.s. 15), p. 255; *Sunday Sermons*, i. 115–16. The phrase 'Thou art wiket of the hiȝ king' occurs in a translation in *The Lay Folks' Prayer Book* (*Prymer*), p. 12.

613. C's fuller reading is clearer: 'A ful leel lady vnleek hure of grace; / Hue hath a keye', etc. The explanation lies in one of the 'Great O's' of the Advent Liturgy: 'O clavis David et sceptrum domus Israel, qui aperis et nemo claudit, claudis et nemo aperit' (< Isa. 22: 22, 23: 'Et dabo clavem domus David super humerum ejus, etc.': Eliacim being treated as a type of Christ). Cf. Ezech. loc. cit.: '. . . Dominus, Deus Israel, ingressus est per eam, eritque clausa. Principi. Princeps ipse sedebit in ea'; a passage that was associated with Ps. 117: 20: 'hæc porta domini: justus intrabit per eam'.[1]

All these verses were applied to the inviolate virginity of Mary: she held the key to man's redemption inasmuch as the King of heaven 'slept' in her womb (Honorious interprets *Princeps* as *rex regum*; cf. also Hoveden, *Poems* (Surtees Soc.), p. 103 and n.). *slepe* is a felicitous reference to the immaculate conception.

For the figure of the key cf. i. 200 (A 176–8) and *Purgatorio*, x. 42: 'quella / che ad aprir l'alto amor volse la chiave'.

If B's *he* is treated as masc. (and not as a rare ex. of *he* < orig. W. Mid. *ho* 'she') the reference will be to 'Treuthe'—God the Father. Doctrinally a masc. form makes for slightly easier sense.

615 f. There are probably oblique allusions here to Joh. 14: 17 ff.

---

[1] Cf. 'Ista porta est beata virgo: quem in sanctuario castitatis et sanctitatis posita semper per virginitatis sequelem mente et corpore fuit clausa. Dominus solus ingressus est per eam per carnis assumpcionem.' (Berthorinus of Poitiers.)

('. . . mansionem apud eum faciemus') and Matt. 18: 3 ('nisi . . . efficiamini sicut parvuli non intrabitis in regnum cælorum'). Cf. *Pearl*, 721–2: 'his ryche no wyӡ miӡt wynne / Bot he com þyder ryӡt as a chylde'. Divine Truth dwelling in the heart (cf. i. 159–62) will produce the loving obedience of a child; cf. xv. 210: 'charyte is goddis champioun and as a good chylde hende'.

cheyne (616) is possibly a reminiscence of the blessing given with the kiss of peace in the Sarum Rite (ed. J. Wickham Legg (1916), p. 226): 'Habete vinculum caritatis et pacis ut apta sitis sacrosanctis mysteriis' (cf. Col. 3: 14: 'caritatem habete, quod est vinculum perfectionis'.[1] Yet *sitte* (615) may seem to call for the emendation *cheire*: cf. *Chasteau d'Amour*, 745, cit. *supra*—though there the 'feir chayӡere' is not allegorized. The thought is, as often, remarkably compressed: Truth sits in the heart, ruling it with love (if *cheyne* is kept it may figure as a chain of office): the penitent obeys as he would obey an earthly father. The moral teaching of the allegory is repeated in similar terms by Wyatt:

> Then seek no more out of thyself to find
> The thing that thou hast sought so long before,
> For thou shalt feel it sitting in thy mind.
> (*Poems*, ed. Muir, p. 190, ll. 97–99.)

617 has no equivalent in A or C, and makes little sense in the context.

621. 'Presuming on [the value of] your own virtuous actions'.

624. *an hundreth wyntre*: in purgatory.

627 ff. The seven virtues now take their place against the seven sins that are the concern of the earlier part of the passus and are briefly alluded to here (*v.* Tuve, *Allegorical Imagery*, ch. I, *passim*).

640. *upewarde*: a nonce-word for a 'japer' with a performing monkey; 'apes' were often associated with hell or the devil, and 'ledyng berys and apys' was classified as 'harlotrye': *Jacob's Well*, p. 134.

641. *Wite God*: 'May God know [it]' (as distinct from 'God wot')

---

[1] *cheyne* may reflect the popularity of the figure of the chain of love as used in secular and philosophical contexts (e.g. Chaucer, *Rom.* 3178, Boethius, *De Cons. Phil.*, ii m. 8; cf. *CT*, A 2991, *Tr.*, iii. 1765 (*v.* Root's note on that passage), *Kingis Quair*, 1278.

NOTES

= 'I declare to God'. Cf. C. T. Onions in *RES*, 4 (1928), 334;
5 (1929), 330; and N.S. 3 (1951), 108.

wafrestre: 'confectioners' of both sexes were traditionally pan-
ders or otherwise of ill repute (*v*. Coulton, *Life in the M. Ages*,
iii. 4). Chaucer's Pardoner names them after bawds: *CT*, C 479–80.[1]
Not even the most stirring sermon by a friar would turn such people
to repentance since they could not claim acquaintance with a single
virtue.

644–5. The teaching about divine mercy proffered at 288 is here
resumed, but with a new emphasis on the B.V.M., *mater miseri-
cordiæ*.

648–51. B's addition of these lines has been criticized as 'out of
place' (Dunning) and they would certainly be less unexpected after
642; C substitutes, ineffectively, a paraphrase of Luc. 14: 18 ff.
Yet the appearance of the pardoner helps to strengthen our recol-
lection of the wayfaring figures of the Prologue, already suggested
by 639 ff.; and 648–9 raise the question of the validity of pardons,
which is to bulk large in vii.

The implications are that the woman relies on paper pardons
rather than the practice of the virtues—and that she is the pardoner's concubine. For the euphemism of 'sister' cf. the ballad
Judas, *OBMEV*, no. 30.

651b. 'I know not where they went': cf. 'nuste ich under Criste
whaer hi bicumeon weren' (Laȝamon) and *Amadas*, 834 (Auch.
MS.). A signal that these characters are now 'out of the story'.

Sinful would-be pilgrims who have 'misgon' and 'hire journey
had forsake' figure in *The Pilgrimage of the Soul*: *v*. Hussey,
pp. 61, 62.

[1] *v*. also *CT*, A 3378–80.

PASSUS VI

The conclusion of Passus V leads one to expect a kind of Pilgrim's Progress, with Piers as guide. But he has been presented not only as a guide to Truth but as a working farmer (v. 548 ff.) on Truth's manor; i.e. he lives partly in the 'real' world of the penitents who have been shown as sinning in or against society. It would be contrary to the view of the common weal already outlined and later developed, that a Christian ploughman (i.e. any 'active' Christian) should ignore his social obligations, even when about to make a pious pilgrimage. Hence Piers now puts his duty of sowing first (63 f.); he is thus associated in the beneficent activities of pr 20 f. and 119 f. and contrasted, by implication, with the landless labourers roaming the country after the Black Death, careless of their duty to provide for the commune. Before long the conception of a literal pilgrimage fades away, but the pilgrim motif serves as a bridge joining the external activities of these opening passus to the mental and spiritual concerns of the next vision. Meanwhile Piers' half-acre serves as a microcosm of the world of the Prologue. The pilgrimage, in fact, is at no point conceived of in wholly literal terms. It is a quest in search of Truth; and it is as such that penitential pilgrimages will be commended in the last passus of the poem (xix. 373), when the images of diking and delving are to be given a wholly spiritual force.

In the earlier passus L has dwelt on the duties (and shortcomings) of the higher orders—king, knights, clergy. Now he begins with a résumé of their role in the common weal, before concentrating on the functions of the labouring classes. Piers himself is presented as a husbandman or overseer, with some sense of authority and responsibility. In his old age he has earned the right and the means to go on pilgrimage; and Chaucer's Prologue indicates that it was not unusual for a ploughman to make such journeys (unless, indeed, Chaucer's inclusion of a ploughman was suggested by this very passus). But Piers early promises that he will labour in the fields all his life (27); he is soon to say (it is a neat touch) that he will put his hopper round his neck instead of a pilgrim's scrip (63). At 116 he suggests that he and his company will not move from the field till the seed he has sown grows to wheat; and the climax of the action is to be a divine injunction that he stick to his plough (vii. 5). Whatever else he represents, he is firmly associated with the provision of the necessities of life, and (for example) his directions to the pilgrim-penitents are to be read as so many suggestions that they too should consider first their social obligations.

3. *seynt Peter.* Piers swears by his name-saint; the specifying of 'Rome' may be a deliberate indication of orthodoxy, but *A* has *seint poule þe apostel.*

4. *half acre.* Open fields were regularly divided into half-acre strips separated by turf balks—the amount that could be sown in about half a day. That Piers's half-acre was alongside the high road could be deduced from v. 544.

7. *sklayre*: probably worn over the fashionable 'horns' (cf. the only other ex. in *OED*), i.e. part of the dress of a lady of rank. The veil would not cover the whole face.

8 ff. set forth the proper role of women in the Christian community (in contrast to the behaviour of the wanton at the end of Passus v, and to that of Lady Meed). They are to be responsible for one of the necessities of life—clothing, as Piers is to be for the other—food (cf. i. 24). Their works are to be of charity and devotion.

11. *þat 3e han*: the imperative construction noted above at v. 59 n. Cf. vi. 52; *Owl and Nightingale* (Cotton MS.), 440, *Book of the Duchess*, 206 (*v.* Robinson's textual n.), Malory (ed. Vinaver (1947), i. 381/1, 394/1, *Sir Amadas*, 493 (Ireland MS.). But *A* has: *þat han silk & sendel, sewiþ it.*

silke. In a contemporary petition the Commons pleaded that only knights and ladies and those with an income of over £40 should be allowed to wear silk (*Rot. Parl.* iii. 66*b*). L implies that it should be confined to ecclesiastical use: copes of silk or cendal are mentioned as early as the 9th c.: *v.* Bishop, *Liturgica Historica* (1918), p. 272.

12. *Chesibles*: by synecdoche for church vestments and adornments in general. The rich embroidery of such work made *opus anglicanum* famous throughout Europe, and exx. of it can still be found on the Continent: *v.* A. G. I. Christie, *English Medieval Embroidery* (1938). The occupation was associated largely with high-born ladies from

PASSUS VI

OE times, but also with nuns and anchoresses: cf. *Ancrene Wisse*, CCCC, p. 215 bott. (and Marvell, *Appleton House*, ll. 123–4).

13. Spinning is a symbol of *activa vita* in (e.g.) the windows of Chartres.

16. Alluding to clothing the poor as one of the corporal works of mercy enjoined by Our Lord (Matt. 25 : 35). But *cast*, when used of clothes, should imply 'remove'.

19b. 'for love of [obj. gen.] the Lord of heaven'. For similar constructions *v.* Sisam, p. 206.

24 ff. In *A* the knight says 'I wille [conne] eren' ('I am willing to learn to plough'), suggesting that he is in danger of taking unfamiliar doctrine too literally. Piers here indicates that the knight's function is to protect society (at a time when knights were in danger of becoming a *rentier* class): 'tueri ecclesiam, perfidiam impugnare, sacerdotum venerari, pauperum propulsare iniurias, pacare provinciam, pro fratribus fundere sanguinem', as John of Salisbury had put it (*Policraticus*, ed. Webb, VI. viii; cf. *MÆ*, 26 (1957), 100 f.) Knighthood is presented here as involving duties rather than privileges (in 1353 it had been made obligatory on all holders of land to the value of £15 or over). But it is no ordinary knight who addresses a ploughman *curteislich* (34)—and no ordinary ploughman who bids a knight deal justly with his inferiors, and cites the Vulgate (49); true, his dress (61) is that of a typical labourer; but it is also to be that of 'Iesu Crist of Hevene' (xi. 180).

30 f. The beasts named are harmful to crops or livestock; some of them were 'beasts of the warren'—i.e. only manorial lords who had a royal grant of 'free warren' were permitted to hunt them (Bennett, p. 5). The hare 'oft gooth to the wortis' (*Kingis Quair*, 1092); the fox carries off fowl; wild boar and deer (*A* and C read *bukkes, bockes* for *brockes* 'badgers') damage both crops and fences.

32. *affaite þe* (*A fecche the hom*). Hawks are taken wild, and 'passage hawks' (mature birds caught whilst migrating) are preferred to eyases (young birds taken from the nest and brought up in captivity).

34. *comsed* is suspicious in itself as introducing so brief a comment as 35–6; and Kane amply justifies *A*'s *conseyuede* 'grasped, apprehended', cf. viii. 57; *þise* words = ll. 25–33.

NOTES

38. 'Good, and I ask you for one thing further'.

39. A lord could oppress his tenants by levying forced payments such as (i) tallage (rent fixed at the lord's will); (ii) heriot (a claim on the best beast, etc. at a tenant's death); (iii) 'amerciaments' (discretionary fines): *v.* Bennett, pp. 138 ff., 218. The *Memoriale Presbiterorum* instructs parish priests hearing confessions: 'You ought to enquire of a Knight if he is proud [cf. 41] . . . if he has oppressed his tenants and especially his poor villeins [*rusticos*] with undue tallages and exactions' (cit. Pantin, p. 206; cf. *Parson's Tale*, I 750, and Tawney, p. 38).

44. *at one ȝeres ende*: 'at the end of one year or another'—'sooner or later'.

46. *bondemen*: some labourers were still bound to the land. Manumission was an act of piety (Tawney, p. 67); Chaucer's Parson (loc. cit.) regards thraldom as a fruit of sin (Gen. 5) but emphasizes that 'thise lordshipes doon wrong, that bireven hir bondefolk thinges that they nevere yave hem . . . extorcions and despit of youre underlinges is dampnable.'

48 ff. allude, as the Latin indicates, to the parable of the wedding guests, Luc. 14: 8–11: 'non discumbas in primo loco, ne forte honoratior te sit invitatus ab illo' [etc.].

50. The charnel-house being the place (usually beneath the church) where bones disturbed when dug up to make room for new burials were deposited indiscriminately. For surviving charnel-houses *v.* G. H. Cook, *The English Parish Church* (1954), pp. 129–30. Cf. 'Erles miȝt and lordes stat / As cherles shal yn erþe be put': *Handlyng Synne*, 8697–8.

56. *it ben*: 'they are'; the pl. verb refers to the prec. or follg. pl: *v.* Sisam, Gl., s.v. *hit*.

57. *seynt Iame*. The name is not part of the alliteration, so is presumably introduced as appropriate for a knight (St. James's role in Spanish legend) and a potential pilgrim (*v.* pr 47 n.).

59. *pilgrimes wise*: does not necessarily imply distinctive garments (cf. 62). Staff, scrip, and hat were the conventional marks of a pilgrim (cf. v. 525 ff., to which the present passage stands in sharp contrast), and so appear in depictions of Christ as *peregrinus* on the Emmaus road—alluded to at xi. 228 in terms ('pore paraille and

PASSUS VI

pylgrymes wedes') that are evidently meant to recall the present
characterization of Piers as something more than an honest
ploughman.

64. A bushel was the regular allowance of seed for half an acre;
three times what was sown was thought a good yield.

67 ff. When crops were sown in the common fields they were per-
force sown by all, and work on the lord of the manor's fields was
probably also done in a body (Bennett, pp. 44 f; cf. xiii 373–4. It
is probable that ploughing of the common fields was likewise done
communally. The right of gleaning (68) was not always granted by
the lord of the manor unconditionally.

69. Perhaps with specific reference to the traditional festivities of
Largesse Spending or harvest frolic: *v.* G. E. Evans, *Ask the
Fellows who cut the Hay* (1956), ch. 12.

72 ff. The juggler or buffoon, gamester and immoral woman came
automatically under the Church's ban. Cf. Towneley *Judgement
Play*, 350: 'ye Ianettys of the stewys / And lychoures on lofte'.

77 ff. *Deleantur de libro viventium et cum justis non scribantur,*
Ps. 68: 29.

79. Presumably referring to v. 648–51, where the pardoner and
common woman represent the occupations here censured.

80 ff. Piers's wife and children bear names appropriate to them as
humble members of the industrious commonalty. But they also
indicate the virtues that he himself strives for or embodies, and 82
foreshadows the equation 'Dowel = to suffer' (i.e. bear with
patience: xi. 402). All the names (like those at v. 575 ff.) embody
scriptural allusions. With 82 cf. the mouse's advice in the C version
of the Cat and Rats fable: 'soffren and sigge nouht' (C i. 210).

84. It is hard to accommodate this line except as a part of the son's
name. But the whole name-passage is perhaps suspect as an inorganic
insertion (extended in C), and 99 indicates that Piers has more than
one son and daughter. Possibly *sone* (82) is an error for *sones* (at
99 *A* reads *frendis* for *dou3tres*).

Late-God-yworth: v. ii. 47 n. and vi. 228 n., and Kane's n. on
A vii. 74.

87. To make a will was a normal preliminary to a pilgrimage: cf.
e.g., the will of Henry Rumworth, 1420: 'In d.n.a. Ego H.R. sanus

et jocundus, intendens partes extraneas visitare condo testamentum meum in hunc modum' (cit. A. B. Emden, *An Oxford Hall in Medieval Times* (1927), p. 282). To die intestate was to die improperly (because unconfessed) according to the Church, and to risk being buried in unconsecrated ground: cf. *The Chronicle of Jocelin of Brakelond* (tr. Butler, pp. 91–2 and n.).

The ploughman, being illiterate, must have his will written for him (*do* is causative), just as he must have his pardon read (vii. 106 ff.); but he insists that he is making his own dispositions (88)—with the implication that he will not let others (e.g. friars) do it for him. Again Piers is the devout and dutiful Christian concerned primarily with the welfare of his soul, and with that of his dependants.

In its language, order, and disposition the bequest follows the usual pattern of extant wills of the l. 14th c., by which time they were being made in English; the opening formula is a relic of 13th-c. use of Latin in wills. (For contemporary exx. *v.* E. Rickert, *Chaucer's World*, pp. 394–5, 401–7.)

89 represents the common formula *In primis lego animam meam Deo* [*creatori meo*].

90. Probably with specific reference to the devil's attempt to seize the soul at the moment of death, a popular theme in contemporary illustrated Books of Hours. Cf. vii. 115.

91. Gower uses a similar figure: *CA*, v. 1918–20.

92 echoes legal formulas; cf. e.g., *BPR*, iv. 211, bott.

93 implies that he is to be buried in the parish churchyard—as distinct from that of the friars, who might combine a promise of burial with the suggestion that the will be made in their favour: a 15th-c. excommunication formula is directed against 'alle men of religion that makith or ledith any man be fayre wordis or behestis to behote or to swere to be biried among hem, from his parissh church' (*Reg. Godstow Nunnery*, p. 1).

94. *he*: viz. the parson (*persona ecclesiæ*). Neither church nor parson receives any legacy, though 'mortuary' bequests to them (often consisting of one of the best chattels of the testator) were common at this period: cf., e.g., *Balliol Deeds* (ed. Salter), pp. 48, 55, 59, 198. But Piers is not in the class of men who had much to spare after paying tithes.

All craftsmen and almost all field-workers (including ploughmen)
were liable for tithe of two kinds to the parish church: (i) 'great'
(*prædial*)—paid in kind on the fruits of the earth (here corn);
(ii) 'small', paid on (*a*) things nourished by the earth (sheep, pigs,
cattle, and their products—'mixed' tithe), and (*b*) profits of trade
and industry, including wages; hence Chaucer says of his ploughman: 'His tithes payede he ful fayre and wel / *Both* of his propre
swink *and* his catel' (*CT*, A 540). 'Corn and catull' (*v.* Gl.) occurs
in a similar context in Dunbar, *Testament of Mr. Andro Kennedy*, 77.

96–7. The refce. is to the *Commemoratio pro defunctis* in the Canon
of the Mass. As late as the 16th c. names were sometimes read out
at the place *N. et N.* R. Mannyng of Brunne states that the third
part of the Host is offered 'to have memory for soules that are yn
purgatory' (*Handlyng Synne*, 7957). The lines seem to exclude the
'month's mind', masses offered up throughout the month following
the death of a friend or relative.

98 ff. The law forbade men to leave land to others than their heirs
—indeed the very notion was repugnant to medieval conceptions.
But one third of personal property ('the dead's part'—cf. 94 n.)
could be disposed of after all debts were paid (cf. 100) to pay over-
due tithes or for commemorative masses, or a chantry. Of the other
two-thirds, one went to the widow, the other to the children. Here
Piers' wife is to have her due portion ('of' has partitive force) and
to share the next third among his children. The 'residue' (102) is
thus equivalent to 'the dead's part', which he is free to dispose of.
Cf. *Test. Ebor* (1885), pp. 10, 31, etc. A pious Christian might leave
such goods to the poor at death, or even to pay for a vicarious
pilgrimage. Piers, not being *in articulo mortis*, indentifies his share
with his tools and his skills, which he devotes to God and poor men
(103 ff.)—perhaps in deliberate contrast to Covetise (v. 265 ff.).

100. The making of a will, like a pilgrimage, involved the payment
of debts. Margery Kempe had it announced from the pulpit that
she would settle all debts before setting out (*The Book of Margery
Kempe*, c. 26).

101. *ar I to bedde ȝede*: presumably a reference to Deut. 24: 12 f.:
'non pernoctabit apud te pignus, sed statim reddes ei [viz. to the
owner] ante solis occasum.' Piers's care in this matter contrasts
with the casualness of Accidie (v. 429) and of Wrong (iv. 53).

102. *the rode of Lukes.* The allusion to this object of pilgrimage is apt, if ironical. 'Il volto santo di Lucca' is a wooden image of a richly clothed Christ, crowned, on a cross encircled by a large band, still to be seen in the cathedral of Lucca. It was attributed to St. Nicodemus (its actual date is probably 8th c.) and said to have come from Palestine after an adventurous voyage.

104. With this reference to the poor, the pattern of the will, arising as it does out of the notion of a literal pilgrimage, begins to fade. As the pilgrim-way 'dissolves' into Piers's furrow, so the traditional bequest to the poor is transmuted into his labours for them—labours by which he will benefit his soul as much as he would by leaving money for masses.

105. *plow-pote* A, *-fote* L. The 'foot' (*pes*) of a plough might cut through roots, but cannot be envisaged as a staff. Kane notes that a 'pusher' (much like a modern walking-stick, but with forked end) is shown in the Holkham Bible, f. 6. Other variants are: *plow-bat/ -staf*—a long-handled spade used to clear the coulter and mould-board; in the *SE Legendary* (470/186) the 'aker staf' is the typical 'weapon' of the ploughman. Piers's pikestaff (in contrast to the palmer's 'burdoun', v. 524) is to be his plain and homely tool. For a labelled medieval sketch of a plough *v. Bodleian Picture Book*, no. 14, p. 7, and for traditional methods of ploughing *v.* G. Evans, op. cit., p. 69 n., App.

106. Kane (p. 447) argues for *A*'s *close* as against *clense*: 'to help the coulter is to make sure that the sods fall true, and thus close the furrows.'

107. The plough would generally be drawn by oxen—probably four in number as in the familiar illustration from the Luttrell Psalter (*c.* 1340), f. 170. Cf. xix. 257, *CT*, A 887, and Seebohm, *The English Village Community*, pp. 74, 461.

109. *balkes*: unploughed strips dividing groups of furrows (a fur[row] long in width), under the open field system, generally over-grown with grass and bushes; also applied to smaller ridges acci-dentally left unploughed; still in Shrops. and other dialects. The system involved a large amount of communal tillage; the chief weekly services—including ploughing—owed to the lord of the manor were also performed co-operatively. Thus Piers's ploughing is an apt symbol for the life of man in society; and his labourers work at the tasks suitable for them, exactly as indicated in pr 118.

PASSUS VI

114. *at heighe prime* = 'à haute prime': *c.* 9 a.m. (*prime* = sunrise). Cartularies show that 'a day's work' as demanded of villeins often meant work only till 9 a.m. or noon (Bennett, p. 105).

Piers's assumption of authority is consonant with his role earlier: he is in fact acting like a faithful steward, or reeve; and Grace is to give him this title at xix. 253 ff. ('I make Pieres the Plowman my procuratour and my reve'). Here he embodies the precept of Truth as he himself had expounded it at v. 555 ff. and the Biblical text that the labourer is worthy of his hire (*v.* 153 n.).

þerafter (116) = 'accordingly', i.e. paid accordingly [in kind] 'when harvest time *should* come' (pret. sjv. dep. on obl. fut.).

118. Cf. Skelton, *Magnyficence*, 1251: 'He daunsys so long "hey-troly loly"'; *Complaint of Scotland*, 245, *Colkelby's Sow*, 302. One MS. alters to 'dus a dammeme', evidently a corruption of the refrain in pr 224.

119. This should prepare us for Piers's display of anger at vii. 116. But his words here are precisely in the spirit of the Commons' petition in 1376 that vagrant beggars should be imprisoned unless they promised to return home to work and that it should be forbidden to give alms to persons able to labour.

122b. The phrase recurs in *Siege of Jerusalem*, 782 and *Parlement of the Thre Ages*, 447 (*v.* Miss Offord's note thereon).

124. *aliri*: for vv. ll. and possible etymologies *v.* E. J. Dobson, *English and Gmc. Studies*, 1 (1947–8), 56, and E. Colledge, *MÆ*, 27 (1958), 111; neither accounts satisfactorily for the final *i*; it may be a 'cant' word used by 'loseles' themselves, possibly preserved in the counting rhyme 'one two three, aleery' (followed by a hop): cf. Opie, *The Lore and Language of Schoolchildren* (1959), pp. 114–15. They *pretend* (*pace* Sk) to be maimed, by tying or twisting the calf against the back of the thigh, so that it appears to be cut off; cf. C. Brett, *MLR*, 22 (1927), 261, and the detail from P. Brueghel's *Fight between Carnival and Lent* reproduced by Colledge. William of Nassyngton criticizes 'faytoures' for similar reasons:

> For lyþer wyles can þei fynde
> To make þaim seme crokede and blynde
> Or seke or mysays to mennes syght.
> So canne þai þair limes dyght
> For men suld þaim mysays deme.

A variant posture is shown in a misericord at Christchurch, Hants.

126b. *lorde, ygraced be ʒe!* The 2 pl. pron. suggests that the phrase is flatteringly addressed to Piers: cf. the change of tone and pronoun at 158 ff. This is not flagrantly inconsistent with 133, where Piers describes himself as the trusty servant (*holde* in *A* = 'bound, pledged') of Truth his overlord—in relation to whom all Christians are 'homly hyne' (*Pearl*, 1211). The moral sense of Truth as personal rectitude must be kept in mind throughout this passage; but that Truth is also the Lord of heaven is hinted at in 134, etc.

129. *here* indicates that the reward is to be heavenly: cf. Matt. 6: 4 etc.

132. On fines for or complaints about work done idly or grudgingly for the lord of the manor *v.* Bennett, p. 112. Sickness was generally considered a sufficient cause for absence.

137. *barly bred.* For the connotations cf. *CT*, D 145. It is clearly inferior to the wheaten bread of 139, which Palsgrave (1530) glosses as *pain bourgeois.*

138. *he* here must be understood as indefinite: anyone who is really blind or needing support for his legs.

141 ff. A concise description of the duties a serf regularly had to perform for his lord: cf. Bennett, p. 108 and C vi. 13–19.

143. Cf. *CT*, A 537: 'He [sc. the ploughman] wolde threshe and therto dyke and delve'.

145*: *v.* Addenda.

146. 'It is entirely owing to divine forbearance that vengeance does not fall on you.'

147 ff. Piers momentarily steps outside his role as overseer, to reinforce a point made at the outset (pr 25 ff.). By eating at noon only, the anchorites and hermits would be treating each day as a fast day.

149. *þat*: 'those who' [sc. ? religious].

150. *Robert renne-aboute*: ? a wandering hermit such as the poet feigns to be in pr 3. The context hardly allows the sense 'fugitive serf' (for which *v.* Bennett, p. 308).

151. *posteles*: *OED < apostle*: 'one who in any way imitates or may be said to resemble the Apostles'. ? influenced by *postillator*: Richard Rolle describes himself as *probatus postillator* (i.e. equipped to preach or comment on scripture); cf. *Revised Medieval Latin Word-List*, s.v., and B. Smalley, *Camb. History of the Bible* (1969), ii. 204.

powere: licence: *v.* Owst, *Preaching in Medieval England* (1926), p. 114 n.

152–3. *religioun*: ? religious order. There is an evident allusion to the appointment of the Seventy: 'in eadem autem domo manete, edentes et bibentes quæ apud illos sunt; dignus est enim operarius mercede sua' (Luc. 10: 7; cf. Matt. 10: 10 and 1 Tim. 5: 18).

156. Bretons had a reputation for bragging (as Normans did later): cf. Barbour's characterization of John Breton as 'wount to speke hely' (*Bruce*, iii. 461) and allitv. *Morte Arthur*, 1348: 'Evere ware þes Bretouns braggers of olde'; hence Bretoner had probably become a synonym for 'boaster'. It is found only once outside *PPl*, in the phrase 'Baskones [a Basque or Gascon], Chavers [?] and Bretoners' (*Commodities of England*, 1451). *MED* glosses the *PPl* exx. as 'minstrel, juggler' (perhaps with reference to Breton minstrelsy), but the context suggests rather the ne'er-do-wells of pr. 35. For the alliterative conjunction cf. *bosters and bragers*, *Townley Plays*, p. 102, l. 55, Dunbar's *Dance of the Seven Sins*, 34, etc.

163. Cf. *A*: 'From wastours þat waite wynneres to shende'. The description of the contemporary economic problem in these terms recalls the allitv. poem *Wynnere and Wastoure* (*c.* 1352).

163b. 'make [the cost of] living high' (or ? make the condition of things difficult).

165b. *liggeth*: 'lies idle'—i.e. whilst agriculture is neglected.

171. *at a pees*: at the worth of a pea. For variants *v.* Whiting, P 93, 95–101 (but he overlooks this ex.).

174. *atte firste*. Famine was never far away in the Middle Ages, least of all in the period of the Black Death.

181. *pese-lof*: like bean bread (*v.* 184), it remained the food of the poor till the 17th c.

182. 'They would both have been dead and buried, make no mistake.'

184. For the connotations cf. 'Off metys that ben of lytel prys / As off benys or browne bred' (*Pilgrimage of the Life of Man*, 12869–72) and Usk, *Testament of Love*, II. ii. 56. Beans and bran were constituents of bread fed to hounds and horses (cf. 217) and cost one-third the price of a white loaf (*Eng. Gilds*, p. 366).

185. *melke*: presumably as fed to hogs, i.e. 'three times skimmed sky blue', in Richard Bloomfield's phrase.

201. Piers acts in accordance with the dictates of Holy Church (cf. i. 20 and n.) and of Conscience (cf. iii. 254). The statement of his problem at 206–14 should be read in the light of Lipson's comment that 'there was much suffering and misery in the Middle Ages, but to all appearances the labour market was not overstocked, and there was generally employment to be found for those able and willing to work'; there had been a noticeable rise in wages after the Black Death.

210. 'They are my blood relations, for Christ redeemed us all' [by his blood]: cf. v. 511 and xi. 192 ff. (and xviii. 392–3).

216. Medieval teaching on mendicancy was much influenced by St. Augustine's *De opere monachorum*, on which Guillaume de St. Amour, and hence Jean de Meun (*v. Roman de la Rose*, 11425–88) drew liberally. But L's knowledge of this work has not been proved. At least one medieval text (cit. B. Tierney, *The Medieval Poor Law* (1959), p. 58) laid down that relief should not be given to able-bodied beggars. H. Moe, *PMLA*, 75 (1959), 40, attempts to prove that the present passage influenced the framers of the Elizabethan Poor Law. Tierney remarks that what was really needed after the Black Death was 'a kind of scholastic critique of employability in able-bodied vagrants'.

218. *Abate*: A [*a*]*baue* (= ?; the sense 'discomfit' (Kane) seems unsuitable); Donaldson, p. 131 n., substitutes *abane* (cf. KF *bane with bones*), translating it not as 'poison' (Sk) but as 'fortify'; he compares *Purity*, 620, where Abraham offers the angels 'a morsel of bred to banne your hertte' (= Vulg. *Confortate cor vestrum*, Gen. 18. 5). But *banne* is a different morpheme from *bane*. A sense 'lower' might accord with 218b: 'to prevent their bodies swelling up with wind' (in famine).

220 ff. (Cf. vii. 78 ff. and xiii. 142.) The sense and wording of this passage differ in A and C: *v.* N. Coghill, *RES*, 6 (1932), 303, and M. Day, ibid., 445. Each perhaps represents a different gloss of the difficult text cited at 230; but they agree in accepting the usual medieval view that relief of the needy was a primary obligation on those with the means to do so; to withhold alms when there is evident and urgent necessity is mortal sin—a doctrine piercingly expressed in The Lykewake Dirge: cf. Tawney, p. 233, Dunning, pp. 33, 56, and nn., and B. Tierney, op. cit., *passim*. Giving from one's superfluities was a mere act of justice owed to the poor, but to give from one's necessities was an act of mercy. But all giving had to be prompted by a right attitude to God and one's neighbour: cf. *Traditio*, 2 (1944), 97.

The *Disticha*, 86. c 9 (*v.* Tierney) distinguishes between the deserving and undeserving poor; old and sick, and those fallen from riches into want (especially if through no fault of their own) are to be helped first. Alms, according to one modification of this view, should be denied when *known* to be harmful, but day-to-day cases were not to be examined minutely.

Such was the doctrine. That it did not always issue in counsel such as Piers's may be inferred from a couplet in *Handlyng Synne*: 'þyne even cristyn þow awyst to lene / 3if þou mayst spare hit, þat I mene' (2401 2).

224b. Cf. 'Alter alterius onera portate, et sic adimplebitis *legem Christi*' (Gal. 6: 2).

226 f. Weak alliteration. The line probably represents editorial conflation: cf. *A* vii. 212–13: þat nedy ben or nakid and nou3t han to spende / Wiþ mete or [wiþ] mone let make hem [fare þe betere]. Cf. Hussey, p. 42.

Pace Coghill, it is unlikely that *nau3ty* was ambiguous at this date: cf. 'nedful and nawthi, naked and nawt' in *Somer Soneday*, l. 115. The doctrine of indiscriminate charity is based ultimately on Luc. 6: 27–38.

228b. Donaldson, *TCA*, p. 200, explains LMR *aworþe* as showing reduction of *y-* in *yworthe* (W) to *a-*, a form 'still current in the SW': *v. OED*, s.v. *a*, particle. *yworþe* possibly shows the 'infection' of the idiom *late God worthe* (*n* ii. 47 n.) by the impers. sense of OE *geweorðan* ('come to terms'): so W = ? 'let God settle it' rather than 'leave it to God'.

228 Lat. The reading *vindictam* for Vulg. *vindicta* (Rom. 12: 19) is found elsewhere, e.g. *Ancrene Wisse*, CCCC, pp. 96, 148.

230. *biloue* (WCO) is preferable to L's *bilow* (= ? 'humble thyself'; but marked for correction) as glossing the following text (Luc.

16: 9). For the word-play between -*love* and *low* cf. vii. 64. For the sentiments cf. vii. 78 ff., xiii. 142 f.

232. Piers is evidently still in doubt about Hunger's primary advice (216–20) that able-bodied vagrants are to be given only the barest necessities—unless Hunger is deliberately misunderstanding his question.

234. Genesis is the 'giant' since it is the largest work of the Pentateuch and (save for the Psalms) of the whole Bible. It is our 'engenderer' in that it tells of the origin of the human race.

236 f. 'Propter frigus piger arare noluit: mendicabit igitur æstate et non dabitur illi': Prov. 20: 4, not 'Sapience' (the Book of Wisdom).

240. In the 4th c. Matthew was symbolized by a man (and so by a man's face), Mark by a lion, etc., according to an interpretation of Ezech. 1: 5–12 and Apoc. 4: 7. A label in the Hours of Katherine of Cleves runs: 'Forma viri data matheo quia scripsit sic de deo sicut descendit ab eo quem [*sic*] formavit hominem.' (ed. J. Plummer fig. 113).

241. *nam* (gl. *besaunt* in L), Lat. *mnam* (acc.) < Gk. μνᾶ. Both *mna*[*m*] and *serv*[*e*] *nequam* occur in the version of the parable of the talents in Luc. 19: 16 ff. (the Wiclifite version of which uses *besaunt*), whereas Matt. 25 has in fact *talentum* and *serve male et piger*; but the conjunction of the reference to Matthew with the phrase from Prov. 20 suggests that it was Matthew's version that the poet originally had in mind.

His interpretation of the parable, which eliminates any reference to the failure of the steward to put out his talent at interest, is found also in the 12th-c. *Bestiaire* of Guillaume le Clerc: 'the other has no will to work, but all his life idly waits' (3846). Implicit approval of usury would offer difficulties for a medieval exegete, and in particular for the writer who has condemned Meed. *Wynnere and Wastour*, 286, perhaps refers to the same parable.

245. *herde* (pa. sjv.): 'might hear'; *A*: *his seruaunt*[*s*] *it herde*.

246. *helpe*: prob. inf. dep. on *shal* (cf. *Anglia*, 7 (1959), 137) rather than a jussive sjv. or a sb.

251. *Activa Vita* and *Contemplativa Vita* are not necessarily to be identified with the two kinds of occupation mentioned in 250: *A.V.* represents here the life of Christian charity which all who strive for perfection must lead, *C.V.* the life of inward devotion, which yet depends on *A.V.* and has its own 'activity'. Both are blessed by Christ: what natural good sense suggests is in accord with Divine purpose. For 14th-c. uses of the terms *v.* Hussey, pp. 214 ff. The doctrine implicit in 253–4 has good eremitic warrant: St. Basil insisted that labour was more important than fasting.

252. *Beati omnes qui timent Dominum . . . Labores manuum tuarum quia manducabis: beatus es, et bene tibi erit*: Ps. 127: 1, 2; 'in body' and 'in soule' (254) are perhaps glosses on these last two phrases.

258. *Of al a wyke*: 'for a whole week'; *of* represents the OE gen. of indef. time.

259 ff. must be regarded as addressed to Piers's 'servants' rather than to Piers.

268. On the relation of gluttony to lechery cf. i. 27 and xiv. 250.

272. Physicians were regularly rewarded by gifts of cloaks or other garments rather than by money payments. Arderne's *Liber de Fistula* indicates that a proper fee for a full cure of 'a worthy man and a great' would be 100 marks or £40 with robes. Arderne enjoins that, in clothing, physicians should 'show the manner of clerks', but Chaucer and Henryson indicate that they sometimes dressed more richly: *CT*, A 439–40, *Testament of Cresseid*, 250. *Ludus Coventriæ* refers to collars 'furryd with ermyn, calabere or satan' (p. 228, l. 105).

278b. 'Good luck go with you', a farewell formula. For the construction cf. 11 n.

280. *Byhote God*: for the omission of the first p. pron. (present in AC) cf. Shakespearian 'beseech you', 'prithee', and mod. 'thank you'.

281. *bi þis day*: perhaps an asseveration (cf. 'by this light'), otherwise 'on [*or* for] this day'.

282. This passage is often quoted as illustrating the hard life of a medieval peasant. Yet the poet is emphasizing not Piers' poverty but his patience in bearing it, his willingness to 'make do' till harvest-time when he will live well on wheaten bread (cf. 139). All this is preliminary to the lesson of Patience in spiritual matters that will be taught later in the poem.

283. '. . . [but have only enough money to buy] unripe cheeses'— he cannot afford to keep them until they mature.

NOTES

286. According to Andrew Boorde (*Regyment*, f. K iii b), bacon is good for 'Carters and plowmen, the which be ever labouryng in the earth or dunge': collops and eggs (287), on the other hand, are 'as holsome for them as a talowe candell is good for a horse mouth'.

288. *percil* (in soups, etc.): perhaps a different kind of parsley from that now used in sauces and possibly resembling modern 'cow-parsley' or 'Hamburg passley', the root of which is dressed.

289. The mare reappears in Chaucer's picture of the ploughman (*CT*, A 541).

290. 'To lead the manure' (in the north-country phrase preserved by Mrs. Gaskell in *Sylvia's Lovers*) was an essential part of the ploughman's duties; cf. *CT*, A 530; the dung must be spread before the dry weather of March breaks: cf. Walter of Henley's *Husbandry*, ed. D. Oschinsky (1971), pp. 20, 177.

291. *Lammasse*: 1 Aug., when the first wheat was harvested and a loaf made from it offered at mass; cf. *Pearl*, st. 1.

296. The importance of cherries in the medieval diet (being one of the first fruits gathered) is indicated by the numerous 'cherry fairs' (one is still held in Olney, Bucks.); beans were also an early crop (according to Tupper they could be sown in Feb.). For 'peascod time' cf. *2 Henry IV*, II. iv. 420. Parkinson's *Paradisus* says that the boiled roots of chervil eaten with oil and vinegar make 'an excellent sallet'.

300. *poysoun* (*A* [*peysen*] 'appease', v.l. *plesen*): perhaps intentionally different from *plese* 297 and a synonym for 'kill': eating over-eagerly, they think that they can stifle their (own) hunger permanently. But more probably a scribe has tried to improve the jingle of *pesen* and *peysen*.

301 ff. Unless *neighed nere* is a litotes, the reference must be to a breakdown of a 'corner' in wheat: merchants tried to keep the price up as long as possible, but had to release stores when a fresh harvest was ready, to avoid a glut, and to free space in barns. Cf. '[þou] a ȝere or two holdyst þy corne þat þou myȝt selle hit riȝt dere' (*Handlyng Synne*, 5378–79).

303. The good ale would be that brewed from barley newly harvested.

304. Cf. Gower, *Vox Clamantis*, V. chaps. 9–14.

PASSUS VI

305. *v.* 184 n.

306. *elles* = other kinds of pure wheat: ordinarily labourers did not eat wheaten bread except when provided by the lord of the manor as a 'boon' in return for their labour. Sk cites a MS. of Jesus College, Oxford (I Arch. i. 29, f. 268) that lists *panis de coket* as slightly inferior to *wastel* bread (*v.* v. 293).

309. A regular description of crofters or 'undermanni' whose holdings were insufficient to keep them or of poor town-workmen who had no land at all. Gower remarks that such men grumble unless they have good roast meat, etc.: *Vox Clamantis*, V. 641.

316. The reference is to *Catonis Disticha*, 1. xxi (the first l., 'Infantem nudum quum te Natura crearit', is perhaps alluded to in 315 and 317). The present l. is also quoted in MS. Digby 160, f. 60.

The Distichs were a collection of prose maxims (the *parvus Cato*) and sententious couplets (the *magnus Cato*) dating back perhaps to the 4th c. A.D. They formed a standard beginner's manual in the medieval grammar school, being studied after the *Ars minor* of Donatus (*v.* v. 209 n.), and were translated into various languages: *v.* A. L. Gabriel, *Garlandia* (1970), p. 106 and nn., Curtius, *European Literature and the Latin Middle Ages* (1953), A. Brusendorff in *Studies in honor of Frederick Klaeber* (1929), p. 320, and Robinson's note on *CT*, A 3227. The work was still used as a school book in Milton's time.

318. From 1362 onwards the King's Council promulgated the Statute(s) of Labourers, attempting to regulate wages. The unrest referred to was to issue in the 'Peasants'' revolt of 1381. That it had become noticeable by 1377 is clear from the Court Rolls cited in Lipson (p. 126): at Coleshill, Berks., one tenant refused to perform his services, another disturbed labourers at their work, a third was gone from the land, a fourth neglected his carriage duties and left hay spoiled on the ground. Cf. *Statutes*, ii. 2 (1377): 'Villeins . . . affirm them to be quite and utterly discharged of all manner servage and . . . gather themselves together in great routs and agree by such confederacy that every one shall aid other to resist their lords with a strong hand' (cit. ibid.).

321. *statut* (here used figuratively) is the strongest word that could be applied to a bill approved by Parliament (as distinct from an ordinance). The emphatic *his* points the contrast with the ineffective Statutes of Labourers.

324 ff. Like iii. 323 ff., this riddling prophecy (*pace* Sk) must be taken seriously. According to *Anima* at xv. 350 ff. to have 'no bilieue to the lifte' is the sign of a perverse generation; and at xix. 230 ff. 'astronomers' are endowed by the Holy Ghost (perhaps because, like the 'prophecyings' there mentioned, wonders in heaven were associated with the speaking with tongues which signalized the descent of the Spirit at Pentecost: cf. Actus Apost. 2: 4, 18–19).

The reference to Saturn (327) is straightforward enough. Saturn is a most malignant planet 'ennemye to all thinges that growe and bere life of nature' (*Compost of Ptolemæus*): hence he brings famine, murrain, and pestilence, cf. *CT*, A 2469, *PPl*, C ix. 350, and Neckam, *De Naturis Rerum*, i. vii (p. 40). Neckam, ibid., says: 'Saturnus igitur existente in Aquario, *inundationes* fiunt aquarum' (cf. 326). Saturn also rules over 'viscous and congealed diseases' such as those described in xx. 80 ff. (where Kind Conscience does in fact fulfil the present prophecy in an apocalyptic context). In all these respects Saturn is associated with winter: cf. Douglas, *Eneydos*, Prol. vii. 29 ff. Chaucer associates the planet not only with pestilence and 'maladyes olde' but also with 'cherles rebellyng' (? the Peasants' Revolt; but *v. MLN*, 69 (1954), 393). For a representation of such a revolt taking place under the sign of Saturn (1524) *v. Cristianisme e Ragion di Stato, Atti del II Congresso Internazionale di Studi Umanistici*, a cura di Enrico Castelli, 1952 (pl. 2).

Lines 328–9 are peculiar to B. The phenomena of 328 are presumably those of (1) an eclipse (a total eclipse occurred in 1377) and (2) curious shapes in the sky such as have been reported in later times (*v.*, e.g., *The Listener*, 18 June 1953). They would be given significance because of their likeness to the prognostication of Matt. 24: 29–30. There is no reason to doubt the reading of 328b (? a covert allusion to certain religious—or to apparitions); but we may note that Dunbar associates 'two monis sene up in the lift' with the 'irth of Antichrist ('Lucina Shining', 49). In *The Golden Legend* three suns appear in the east before the birth of Christ (ed. Ellis, i. 26).

329 is to be interpreted primarily (though perhaps not solely) as a reference to the continuing play of Meed (who is a 'maid' in

ii and iii and has 'þe maistrie' in iv. 25); but in this apocalyptic context Meed herself might be identified with the Scarlet Woman of Apoc. 17.

The construction of 329b is obscure. Donaldson construes *multiplied* (LMRF; v. l. *multiplie*) as a pp. form modifying all the preceding conditions of the prophecy. As *maistrie* sometimes has the technical sense of 'the secret of the transmutation of metals into gold' (a sense not inapposite for the operations of Lady Meed) it is possible that *multiplie* is likewise used with an alchemical reference, as the term for 'increasing' the original 'starter' metal: cf. *CT*, T 848 ff.: 'For bothe two, by my savacioun, / Concluden in multiplacioun . . .'. C increases the obscurity by adding: 'Thre shupes and a shaft [v.l. schaefe] with an vm. folwyng / Shal brynge bane and bataile on bothe half the mone' (351–2); cf. Dunbar, loc. cit., where the 'feigned friar' flies above the moon and, 'under Saturnis fierie regioun', meets Simon Magus, Mahoun, and Merlin (the first and last being associated with fallacious arts, including alchemy). Bradley (*MLR*, 5 (1910), 342) interpreted 'three ships and a shaft with vm' as a numerical rebus: xxx (30); 50 ['shaft'] = l]; 8 [= viii (vm)], viz. [13]88; if we read *schaefe*, the numerical equivalent would presumably be [13]62 (cf. iii. 324 n.)—though 'shaft' may again allude to Saturn; in Henryson's *Testament of Cresseid* Saturn has 'ane flasche [sheaf] of felloun flanis [arrows, shafts] / Fedderit with Ice and heidit with hailstanis' (167–8). No convincing reason for an allusion to the year 1388 (or 1362) suggests itself, and C was probably written after that date.

Such prophecies are a feature of the later 14th c. A simple example, which L may have been following, is *Wynnere and Wastoure* 290 ff.:

> . . . firste the faylynge of fode and then the fire after
> To brenne the alle at a birre for thy bale dedis:
> The more colde is to come, als me a clerke tolde

where Gollancz saw an allusion to the hard winter of 1352–3 as well as to the *fames* of Apoc. 18: 8. A more complex Scots prophecy in Camb. Univ. MS. Kk. 1. 5 (IV), f. 326 involves 'tre CCC in Aprille', 'an 1 as the lyne askis, Tuis X and ane R'.

The passage also shows the influence of contemporary prophecies about the coming of Antichrist, described by Bloomfield (pp. 91–4, 212).

PASSUS VII

1. *herof*: KF relate this to the warning issued by Saturn in the lines immediately preceding in A; in which case they may be read as referring to the hope of a 'truce of God' (vi. 332). But the said warning is not strictly part of the action of the poem; *herof* more probably refers to Piers's *caritas* and well-doing as they have been demonstrated throughout vi. Truth is 'the father of faith' (i. 14); hence any pardon he obtains must be true. Indeed, strictly he alone (because of Christ's payment on Calvary) can absolve *a pena et a culpa*: *Summa*, III Q48, art. 2. The implication here is that he may do this without papal intermediacy (cf. 104–5 below); but *A* reads: 'Part in þat pardoun þe pope haþ hem graunted'.[1]

3. *purchaced*: (*purchase*, the reading of many A MSS., would be more consistent with 38) at this date (*pace* Coghill, who sees a reference to the redemptive work of Calvary) need mean no more than 'obtain'; *a pena et a culpa* is a formula regularly found in indulgences—especially false ones. Strictly speaking, an indulgence could not remit the guilt of sin, but this phrase had evidently come to imply the fullest absolution that the pope could give: cf. Dunning, p. 142; Thurston, *Dublin Review*, Jan. 1900; Owst, *Preaching in Medieval England*, p. 358. For the usual connotation of these phrases cf. allitv. *Morte Arthur*, 3496–9:

> Bot I wille passe in pilgremage þis pas vnto Rome,
> To purchase me pardone of the pape selfen
> And of paynes of purgatorie be plenerly assoyllede.

Cf. also xix. 180 ff. (which provides an anagogical reading of PP vi and vii).

4. *For hym and for his heires*: a legal formula; cf., e.g., a charter cited in Round, *Geoffrey de Mandeville*, pp. 52–3: *ipse et heredes sui post eum jure hereditario* (and cf. Malory, ed. Vinaver, i. 245/27). It thus confirms the impression that a document of some kind is to be envisaged—though as no papal pardon presumed to extend its benefits to a man's children, it is evident that this pardon is of no

[1] Mirk, writing of the full remission of a Jubilee pardon (cf. pr 47n.) speaks of Christ as the Pope of heaven who grants full pardon at death (*Festial*, p. 74.)

216

ordinary kind. Similarly l. 6 recalls formulas used in papal documents regarding those who (e.g.) contribute to the support of a
church. Everyone associated with Piers benefits from the pardon;
and the mention of the knights (9) who behave as their exemplar
had agreed to do (vi. 35) gives the poet an easy opportunity to
extend its application to the whole commonwealth, bishops now
being substituted for the contemplatives and postillers of vi. 147 ff.

9. *kepen holycherche*: viz. defend her, as enjoined at vi. 28 f.

14. *bothe þe lawes*: ? canon and civil (rather than the 'Old and New
Laws' of OT and NT). The bishop's function was primarily thought
of as one of moral reformation among the clergy and people subject
to his jurisdiction, 'planting virtues and plucking and rooting out
vices with the hoe of his ordinary power of correction' (Thompson,
pp. 40–1).

16. The apostles come in order immediately after patriarchs and
prophets: cf. *Sawles Warde* (*EMEVP*, xix), 286. Inasmuch as a
formal pardon would hardly include such statements, the l. further
prepares us for a symbolic interpretation.

18. *in þe margyne*: i.e. in the form of an appendix or codicil. Merchants are to have but a partial indulgence, remitting only so many
years of purgatory (strictly, and originally, of canonical penance in
this life). The whole passage strikingly illustrates the view that
trade was dangerous for the soul and justifiable only if carried on
for the public benefit, with superfluous profits being devoted to
pious uses: cf. Tawney, pp. 45, 47 and Langlois, *La Vie spirituelle*,
p. 121.

The poet continues to develop the *figure* of a formal pardon:
hence he allows himself (19) to attribute it to the pope. An ideal
pope would, to be sure, act as here suggested, and in conformity
with Truth. C, reasonably, substitutes *Treuthe* for *þe pope*.

20. Cf. v. 588.

23. *secret seel*: in this context must be the seal impressed with the
pope's personal signet (the Ring of the Fisherman, with a figure of
St. Peter drawing a net) appended to a private letter or brief, as
distinct from a formal Bull, which bore a different *bulla*. The device
is still used to indicate the persons not named in an official bull if
(e.g.) it is desirable that the names should not be made public.
Thus the poet is implying that in practice some trade may be

legitimate and some traders pious but the Church cannot bless trade as such. For the royal *secretum sigillum* v. H. C. Maxwell Lyte, *The Great Seal* (1926), pp. 101 ff., and *B.M. Guide to Med. Antiquities*, p. 170, and for a figurative use cf. C x. 138. For Miss Woolf (Hussey, p. 55) the whole allegory suggests the analogy of a royal rather than a papal pardon.

24. Cf. *Havelok*, 53: 'And baldelike beye and sellen'. This conforms to the scholastic doctrine of the Just Price, viz. that a fair price was most likely to be reached under freedom of contract, a bargain not being struck unless both parties were satisfied. Cf. the quotations from Buridanus and Ægidius Lessinus, Tawney, pp. 52 and 53.

26. *mesondieux.* The Fr. term is appropriate as L is associating hospitals with the practice of piety: the hôpital at Beaune still reminds us that parts of France excelled in providing care for the sick: cf. *Speculum*, 3 (1928), 194, and the refces. there to J. H. Wylie, *The Reign of Henry V*.

27. *Males voies amender*, along with *prisoners relever, poverez susteigner*, is an injunction found in many bequests, e.g. that of the Countess of Salisbury, printed in *Register of Henry Chichele* (ed. E. F. Jacob, 1938), ii. 18; cf. ibid. 230, 520, 521, 551. Doubtless the original motive for repairing roads and bridges was to assist churchgoers and pilgrims, 'thaim that brigges and stretes makes and amendes' (*Lay Folks' Mass Book*, p. 65) (hence it was often undertaken by hermits, as at 'Small Bridges', Cambridge). Tablets in churches show that up to the 17th c. this was regarded as a pious work.

28. *do bote to*: an awkward expression, perhaps due to replacement of the original technical phrase 'and bynde' (= reinforce) *A*: v. Kane, p. 160.

29–32. Merchant or social guilds often undertook works of this kind, some of which carried special indulgences; cf., e.g., *Eng. Gilds*, p. 194 (help to be given to a good girl to marry or go into a religious house if her father's means are inadequate). L apparently does not object to monastic (as distinct from friars') endowments in themselves. The support of 'poor scholars' at the university was the prime motive behind the early endowments of colleges; cf. Pantin, p. 112.

33. As the angel of death, St. Michael was invoked by the faithful at the last hour with the prayer 'O Michael, militiæ cœlestis signifer in adjutorium nostrum veni, princeps et propugnator'. He is often represented in MSS. and murals as the weigher of souls holding the balance whilst the devil pulls down the scale bearing the reprobate soul.

39. i.e. they had most years in purgatory.

40–61. A long intervention by the author, characteristic of this passus.

43. Recalls pr 213. That in certain circumstances a poor client should have 'free legal aid' is asserted by St. Thomas, *Summa*, II. ii. Q 71; Dunning (p. 144), compares *Pricke of Conscience*, pp. 160–1:

> And men of laghe alswa to travayle
> And to counsaile tham that askes counsayle;
> Frely for goddes luf and for noght elles.

44. *Iohan*: a generic name for a common fellow (cf. the proverbial 'Jack's as good as his master'). OF Jehan sometimes denoted a sot or cuckold, and perhaps John had a similar pejorative use in English.

51 Lat. Ps. 14: 1. The verse in fact alluded to is 'Qui facit hæc, non movebitur in eternum' (verse 5, quoted in two MSS. of A).

52 ff. Grammatically incoherent in B, as in *A*, which names only 'water, wind, wit' and continues: 'Ne wolde neuere holy writ'.

The insertion of 'wit' may be due to the frequent association of the five wits with the four elements, as at i. 15 ff. (where A and C state that it is the elements which help man); 'wind' is often named as an element: e.g. at ix. 4, 5, and in the tag 'ffyre water wynde and lond'; in the present passage it must be thought of as providing the breath which enables lawyers to speak in court.

57–8. *Her pardoun . . . þat*: 'the pardon of those who . . .'.

59–60. Alliteration defective. *A [ȝe] wyten ȝif I leie*, with no equivalent to 60b, 61.

66. i.e. are not covered by it; the phrasing suggests a 'broad' interpretation of the bull.

67. It is implied that they are adept at the *suggestio falsi*.

73. *Clerke of þe stories*: Peter Comestor (*ob.* 1198), author of the *Historia Scholastica*, an enlarged bible. Sk identified the source as

Historia Libri Tobie, where Comoster is abridging Tobit 4: 7–11; cf. below. For L's use of Comoster at i. 27 *v. N & Q* (1971), p. 284.

74. *Cui des, videto*: from the sententiæ prefixed to the *Disticha Catonis*.

75. *he*: deictic, referring to the 'clerke'.

76. *Gregori*: in fact St. Jerome, Commentary on Eccles. 11: 6 (*PL*, 23. 1103). The full quotation, as glossed by Cornelius a Lapide, throws light on 80 ff.:

> Ne eligas cui benefacias, sed cum beneficeris nunquam a bono opere desistas. Matutinam justiciam vesper inveniat; et vesperi misericordiam solis ortus accumulet. Incertum est enim quod opus magis placeat Deo et ex quo tibi fructus justitiae præparetur. Potest autem accidere, ut non unum sed utrumque placeat Deo [*C. a Lap.*: Denique utriusque merces tibi certa parata est apud deum].

Eccles. 11: 6: *mane semina semen tuum*, would be specially appropriate for Piers and may have led L to seek beyond the *Glossa Ordinaria* (which offers little commentary on it).

79. *wawe*: 'move restlessly'; several MSS. read *walke*, which seems preferable; cf. 'where no reason is walking' (Trevisa) and later quotations in *OED*, s.v. *walk*.

81. God's book-keeping is by double-entry.

83. 'Fœneratur Domino qui miseretur pauperis; et vicissitudinem suam reddet ei': Prov. 19: 17.

83 Lat.: Luc. 19: 23. The application of the parable appears to rest on the interpretation of *mensa* as the table from which charity is dispensed, and is hardly congruous with that of vi. 240 ff.

85 f. 'whoever has the wherewithal to buy bread for himself . . .'; the authority cited after 86 is St. Jerome, who adds: 'Nimium potens est qui servire non cogitur' (*Epist.* cxxv, *PL*, 23. 1085); but L may also have had in mind 1 Tim. 6: 8: 'habentes autem alimenta . . . his contenti sumus'.

87. The collective experience of the saints (to be learned from reading their Lives) will provide moral support; referring primarily to the *Legenda Sanctorum* (cf. *ODCC* and xi. 155, 214), or such redactions as the *SE Legendary*. At xv. 264–90 the *Legenda SS* is cited for details of the desert fathers who lived without begging. The implication of the following quotation from Ps. 36: 25 is that the righteous who give away their substance will not need to beg: cf. xi. 269 (where the text is applied differently).

89–90 represent an attempt to return to the original theme from which 71–88 (new in B) are a digression. The digression has involved the use of the 2nd person, which is retained up to 94, though the original 3rd person forms are kept in 93, where *he* has consequently to be treated as indef.—'one of you'.

91. Cf. *CT*, A 4064–6, for the 'wehe' of a horse running after mares.

93. *thei breken of here children* (C) leaves no doubt that the parents deliberately incapacitated their offspring to evoke the pity of those from whom they begged. Sk cfs. Barclay, *Ship of Fools*, ed. Jamieson, i. 304. For the sham disabilities of 94–5 *v.* vi. 124 n.

101. The blind and bed-ridden are frequently specified in wills, e.g. 'lego ad distribuendum . . . cecis, claudis et pauperibus in lecto languentibus, 10*s*', *Testamenta Eboracenses*, p. 325, and other exx. cit. Rock, *Church of Our Fathers*, iii. 27 n. 30, which mentions the custom of alms being bestowed on poor folk who lay at a low window marked by a linen cloth and a pair of beads 'to show that there lay a bedrid body, unable but to pray only'.

C's *broken in here membres* is preferable. An absolute construction would not be impossible, but is unparalleled in *PPl* (but *v.* B xii. 256 L).

104–5. No precise scriptural warrant suggests itself (beyond the parable of Dives and Lazarus) but the idea is common; cf. *The Pilgrimage of the Soul*: 'So hath he had on erþe his purgatorye' (Poem 22), and the prayer in the Abergavenny MS. of the Jesus Psalter: 'Ihesu send me here my purgatory'. At x. 460–4 poor men are said to pass direct to heaven.

106. *þo*: with vague reference to Piers's receipt of the pardon. The priest may be regarded as one of the throng of penitents who had set out to seek Truth, but ineffectually (cf. v. 518–21).

The following ll. do not necessarily imply that Piers himself has not yet read his pardon: l. 16 (if not anticipatory) suggests that he is already aware of its purport. But the priest assumes that he could neither read nor understand it; hence he offers a gloss rather than a literal translation; cf. Patience's exposition of a Latin text at xiv. 276 ff. In judging the scene one must bear in mind that L does not elsewhere show any animus against priests *as such* (note Conscience's explicit approval of 'persoun or parissh prest' at xx. 317) and that the priest's action would be entirely natural in 14th-c. England.

109. The dreamer here momentarily enters his own dream in a way that he has not hitherto done; but cf. xix. 9.

110. *leef*: *A*'s *o lettre* is clearly the better reading. The brevity of the bull is not irreconcilable with the account of it given so far, which may be regarded as giving by anticipation the genuine 'gloss', the indications of what 'dowel' was in Truth's eyes.

111 Lat. The pardon, consisting of cl. 40 of the Athanasian Creed (recited at Prime in the Sarum Rite), looks literal enough at this point. But Meed's marriage feoff should have prepared us to treat such documents as texts with more than literal significance: cf. the charter of Christ at xviii. 180 (where the dominant themes of the present passage—poverty and 'parfit bileue', viz. the Creed—recur). The Latin ll. are rubricated in L: Indulgencia Petri.

The clause cited is the only passage in the Creed that bears on the conception of 'pardon': it is paraphrased in a discussion of pardon at xix. 192–3. But it can hardly be, or be meant to be, dissociated from the rest of the Creed; cf. the use of the same clause in *ME Sermons*, p. 29, where in fact it introduces a reference to another clause, which is considered to answer the question as to how Divine wrath may be suffered at Doomsday. Cf. also *Castell of Perseverance, ad fin.*

'Dowel' is again associated with the Creed at x. 230 ff., where Clergye defines it as 'a comune lyf, on holycherche to bileue / With alle the artikles of the feithe' (and where 'borel clerkes' are rebuked: 286 ff.).

That the priest is denying that the lines constitute a pardon as he understands the term is clear from 168 below; *but* (113) = 'but only', rather than 'except'. However, for the dreamer, and for us, it constitutes a reaffirmation of Holy Church's original teaching (cf. i. 126–31). Piers's anger with the priest is wholly in character (cf. vi. 119) and prompts him to pull the charter forcibly out of the priest's hands. But he would not deliberately destroy a document sent by Truth, his lord: the tearing merely dramatizes his disagreement with the priest's comment. (For other views *v.* R. W. Frank, *Piers Plowman and the Scheme of Salvation* (1957), pp. 28–9.)

113. 'Do well and have well' is a proverb found in the collection of proverbs in MS. Douce 52 (c. 1450). For a variant in Barbour's *Bruce* (c. 1375) v. Whiting, D 278. A Scots form is recorded in Ferguson, *Scottish Proverbs* (STS). John Ball writes, 'Do wel and bettre and fleth synne' in his letter of 1381 (Sisam, XIV D).

117. Ps. 22: 4. *non timebo mala* provides a comment on *qui vero mala*, as well as expressing confidence in God. The remainder of this verse is quoted at A x. 86.

118. *bely-ioye*: elsewhere only in Skelton (*Speke, Parrot*, 492), who evidently read *PPl*; it sorts with 125. Most A MSS. read *lyflode* (found in a similar context at xiv. 33). Kane substitutes *belyue* (M) ('sustenance'); cf. xix. 230.

119. Piers recognizes that penance and prayers (which he has already affirmed to be part of the Christian life, cf. vi. 250) are the *bona opera* of the pardon: cf. Dunning in Hussey, pp. 213–14. R. W. Chambers (*London Medieval Studies*, i (1937), 27–39 interprets the psg. in the light of the *Glossa Ordinaria* (cf. xii. 292).

120b. 'even though I have to go without food as a result': the sense of *whete-bred* (v. vi. 306 n.) should not be pressed.

121. *þe prophete*: David: v. Ps. 41: 4, cited after 123.

122. *Multæ* [*sunt*] *tribulaciones iustorum*: Ps. 33: 20.

123. Cf. Luc. 12: 22; but the quotation at 126 is from Matt. 6: 25. A comment on the passage, much in line with L's thought, by John Baconthorpe, a 14th-c. Oxford scholar, is printed by B. Smalley in *Medieval and Renaissance Studies*, 4 (1958), 115.

132–3. Elementary instruction began with the alphabet, usually learnt from a hornbook that included the Lord's Prayer. [*v. Addenda.*]

134b. *?* 'if thou wert obliged'. *A*'s *wh*[*an*] *þe liki*[*de*] is preferable.

135 ff. *Dixit insipiens in corde suo: Non est Deus*: Ps. 13: 1 (and 52: 1). But the allusion is possibly to current applications of the following verse: 'Corrupti sunt, et abominabiles facti sunt in studiis suis . . .'. A contemporary illustration of Ps. 52 is of some interest: it shows a fool seated in front of a Dominican friar to whom he says: '*Non est deus*'. The friar replies: '*Tu mentiris aperte*'. On a scroll issuing from the mouth of God is written '*ecce dicit insipiens*' (Bodl. Rawl. G 185, f. 43ᵛ, repr. *Camb. Hist. of the Bible*

(1969), ii, pl. 39). Piers counters the priest's insinuation that he is an ignorant fool by showing his acquaintance with the wisdom of Solomon, citing Prov. 22: 10 (inexactly).

138. A priest and a ploughman are set in opposition in *The Scale of Perfection*, i. 61.

140. *south*: so it is almost noon (*sitte* = 'stand', not, *pace* Frank, 'set'), and he has been dreaming all morning.

142. *A*, C *a myle wey* is attractive (cf. v. 5); it requires a period at *tyme* (140).

143–200 constitute an epilogue. But besides putting arguments *pro* and *con* about the value of dreams (cf. *HF*, Proem), it introduces new topics, if in a markedly tentative way. The last incident in the dream has not shaken the narrator's belief in the validity of genuine pardons, but he believes that the individual Christian should trust rather to well-doing: indeed Doomsday (the consistory associated at the outset (pr 99–101) with the papal power of binding and loosing) will show that pardons are useless without good works.

149–50. Cf. *Disticha Catonis*, ii. 31:

> Somnia ne cures, nam mens humana quod optans
> Dum vigilat sperat, per somnum cernit ad ipsum.

Cf. *CT*, B² 4130–1, and edd. notes. The ll. would be too familiar to educated readers to need quoting in full. The reason given for scepticism is that dreams are fulfilments of waking desires. Yet this cannot apply to the biblical dreams next cited.

153. There is apparently confusion here between Nabugodonosor (a spelling of Nabuchodonosor found in *St. Juliene*, *CT*, *CA*, etc.) and his reputed son and successor Baltassar/Belshazzar (cf. *CT*, B² 3373). 155 ff. represent Daniel's interpretation of the writing on the wall of Belshazzar's palace, Dan. 5: 28. C *om. kyng* before Nab., and attempts to correct by adding a reference to his sons (*sic*). It omits the interpretation, possibly because of implications for Richard II that might have been read into it. The dream of Nabugodonosor (A.V. Nebuchadnezzar), which Daniel (*cujus nomen Baltassar*) also interpreted, is described in Dan. 4.

154b. *A*'s *þi sweuene is to mene* improves the alliteration.

159 ff. See Gen. 37: 9, 10, though no similar interpretation is there given. Cf. *CT*, B² 4320.

165. *iustice*: cf. Gen. 41 : 41. Medieval miniatures (e.g. in the Velis-lav Bible) show Joseph carrying Pharaoh's sceptre.

167. The scriptural stories incline the dreamer to impute significance to his own dream, though it was scarcely open to prophetic interpretation.

169. Sc. *I* before *demed*. The reference (cf. 171) is to the *qui bona egerunt* of the pardon. The affirmation of the Creed is a firmer basis for hope than the priest's assumptions about the unconditional efficacy of pardons.

170. *Biennales and triennales*: masses said for two/three years after the death of the beneficiary. *bisschopes lettres*: licensing the preaching of indulgences: *v.* pr 80. The whole passage constitutes a return to the opening scene of the first vision, sharpening the contrast made there between the honest ploughmen and bogus pilgrims and pardoner: hence 172 may allude specifically to the indulgence attached to visiting the basilica of St. Peter (cf. pr 47).

173–4. In *A* and C *þe peple* stands (rightly) at the head of the following l.; but A, Ch agrees with L. Kane treats the ll. as interrogative.

175 Lat. Matt. 16: 19; cf. pr 99 n. and xix. 184.

176 ff. summarize and co-ordinate the two strands of thought in the preceding passage: salvation can be won both by prayers and penance and by a genuine papal pardon (*don* 177 is causative rather than emphatic); but formal pardons, however costly, will not cancel failure to live well. The reference to riches (181 ff.) calls to mind the emphasis on charity in i. 173 ff., and implies that for the rich 'dowel' involves sharing their riches with the poor. L's view of indulgences is orthodox enough, and not unlike Dante's: cf. *Par.*, 27. 53, 29. 94–126; *v.* also Dunning, p. 156, and Owst, *Preaching*, p. 353. Wiclif, on the other hand, while likewise insisting on charity, in effect denies the pope's power of absolution, and bids men 'leave this lead' (the *bulla*) (*Sel. Eng. Works*, iii. 362).[1]

191–2 refer to 'letters of fraternity' granted to lay folk by religious, admitting them to the provincial suffrages of the order; all such letters had the seal of the provincial minister attached. 'Confraters'

[1] Here and elsewhere I refer to these texts as Wiclif's, though aware that the ascription is questionable.

had their names inscribed in the *Liber vitæ* of a monastery, and they were read out at the conventual mass, the *Liber* being laid on the altar during the Canon. The community also prayed for confraters at death. Often whole families of a benefactor were enrolled together and received at a ceremony in the chapter-house. The custom was revived in the 19th c. in modified form and survives in at least one English Benedictine house.

That the letters were popularly thought to be a passport to heaven is indicated by references in *Pol. Poems* (ed. Wright), i. 256, ii. 21. For the text of a Franciscan letter *v.* A. G. Little, *Proc. Brit. Academy*, 27 (1941), and for English exx. of letters obtained from more than one source, Little, *Bodleian Lib. Record*, 5 (1954), 13; *v.* further E. Bishop, *Liturgica Historica* (1918), c. xvi; H. E. Cowdrey, *Journal of Eccl. History*, 16 (1965), 152–62; *Ampleforth Journal* (1970), p. 437; *Archaeologia* (1926), 19–60.

199–200. Dowel is now firmly personified, and its commands identified with those of Christ himself.

ADDENDA

pr 84. On chantries *v.* Rosalind Hill in *The Reign of Richard II: Essays in Honour of May McKisack* (1971), pp. 242–5.

pr 94n. *v.* J. A. Tuck, ibid., pp. 1–20; on the biennial wardmotes *v.* D. W. Robertson, *Chaucer's London* (1970), pp. 169–71.

i. 33. For the contemporary connotation of *churl* as brutish and surly *v.* B. White in *The Reign of Richard II*, p. 73.

ii. 126. *v.* C. R. Cheney, *Notaries public in England in the xiii and xiv c* (1972). In drawing up documents notaries marked them with the distinctive signs referred to in A iii. 82.

v. 544. A ploughman represents the ideal Christian in a Welsh poem by Iolo Goch (*c.* 1400): *Medieval Welsh Lyrics*, ed. J. P. Clancy (1965), p. 138.

vi. 145. The line lends support to J. R. R. Tolkien's view that in English *losengeour* was associated with *losel: Essais de Philologie moderne* (1951), pp. 63–76.

vii. 132. Nunneries sometimes acted as 'dame-schools' for young boys: *v.* E. Power, *Medieval English Nunneries* (1922), p. 263.

A NOTE ON METRE[1]

1. Each half-line contains two or more strong syllables, two being the original and normal number. More than two are often found in the first half-line, but less frequently in the second.

2. The initial-letters which are common to two or more of these strong syllables being called the *rhyme-letters*, each line should have two *rhyme-letters* in the first, and one in the second half. The two former are called *sub-letters*, the latter the *chief-letter*.

3. The chief-letter should begin the *former* of the two strong syllables in the second half-line. If the line contain only two rhyme-letters, it is because one of the sub-letters is dispensed with.

4. If the chief-letter be a consonant, the sub-letters should be the same consonant, or a consonant expressing the same sound. If a vowel, it is sufficient that the sub-letters be also vowels; they need not be the same, and in practice are generally different. If the chief-letter be a combination of consonants, such as *sp*, *ch*, *str*, and the like, the sub-letters frequently present the same combination, although the recurrence of the first letter only would be sufficient.

These rules are easily exemplified by the opening lines of the prologue. (The secondary, or slighter accents, are not marked.)

> In a *só*mer *sé*son whan *só*ft was the *só*nnë
> I *sh*ópe me in *sh*róudës as I a *sh*épe wérë,
> In *h*ábite as an *h*éremite vn*h*óly of wórkës,
> Went *w*ýde in þis *w*órld *w*óndres to hérë.
> Ac on a *M*áy *m*órnynge on *M*áluerne húllës
> Me by*f*él a *f*érly, of *f*áiry, me thóuȝtë;
> I was *w*éry forwándred and *w*ént me to réstë
> Vnder a *b*róde *b*ánkë bi a *b*órnës sídë,
> And ás I *l*áy and *l*éned and *l*óked in þe wáteres,
> I *sl*ómbred in a *sl*épyng, it swéyued so mérye.

[1] These remarks are reproduced, with slight changes, from Skeat's pages on the subject. The point dividing the half-lines in most MSS. (but 'not infrequently misplaced') is omitted in this edition, following the example of the Athlone edition. In the Notes the first half-line is denoted by 'a', the second by 'b'.

A NOTE ON METRE

A few variations may be noticed:

(*a*) The chief-letter may begin the *second* strong syllable of the second half-line: e.g. i. 190:

> Vn*k*ýnde to her *k*ýn and to állë *c*rístene.

(*b*) Sometimes (but rarely) there are two rhyme-letters in the second half-line, and one in the first: e.g. *A* ii. 107:

> Týle he had *s*ýluer for his *s*áwes and his *s*élynge.

(*c*) The chief-letter is sometimes omitted; e.g. pr 34 (L: *v.* varr.).

(*d*) By a bold licence, the rhyme-letter is sometimes found at the beginning of weak or subordinate syllables, as in the words *for*, *whil*, in the lines:

> þanne I *f*ráinëd hir *f*áirë *f*or hým þat hir mádë. (i. 58)
> And *w*ith hím to *w*ónye *w*ith *w*ó *w*hil gód is in héuene. (ii. 106)

(*e*) *k* seems to have been sounded before *n*; hence *kn* is alliterated with *k*, as in v. 1. Also, *w* seems to have been sounded before *r*, so that *wr* is alliterated with *w*; see iii. 182.

———

[For more recent studies see 1954 reprint of Skeat's edition of 1886, pp. ci–cii, and Kane, pp. 141–2, 157–8. An adequate discussion must await the publication of the Athlone edition of the B text.]

GLOSSARY

The abbreviations used are intended to be self-explanatory. In general, grammatical forms are identified only when there is possible ambiguity or uncertainty. The sign ~ represents the head-word of the entry. *i/y* are treated as forms of the same letter. Etymologies are not usually given; those in Skeat's 3-text edition should be checked by the *Oxford English Dictionary* and the *Middle English Dictionary* (in progress).

a (weakened form of **on**) in *or* on 3, 48, 202

a(n) one, a single 1. 99, 106, 6. 38

abate *imp. sg.* reduce, keep under 6. 218

abc [æbsi], the alphabet, elementary instruction 7. 132

abie pay the penalty, atone for 3. 249

abiggen, abugge pay the penalty, atone for 2. 127 etc.; cf. **abie**

abosted defied 6. 156

about *adv.* = busy 4. 81

abouten *prep.* about 1. 6

ac but pr 5, etc.

accidie sloth, a fit of sluggishness 5. 366

acomptes accounts 5. 434

acombre encumber, overwhelm 2. 50; *p.p.* ~d 1. 32 etc.

acorde(n) agree 5. 335, account, grant 3. 317; *pa.* t. ~d 4. 91

acorse *pr. sjv.* curse, excommunicate pr 99

acountes day of audits 6. 91

aday in the daytime, on the morrow 6. 310

adoun, adown down 4. 92, 5. 7

afelde to the field 4. 147, 6. 144

afer(e)d(e) *p.p.* frightened 1. 10 etc.

affaite(n) tame 5. 67; (for thyself) 6. 32

afor before 5. 12

aforth afford 6. 201

after depending (on this) pr 201; along with it 5. 111

afyngred *p.p.* very hungry 6. 269

agast *p.p.* terrified, in fear 2. 211

agrounde in this world 1. 90

aȝein *adv.* again 7. 25, 6. 44

aȝein(es), ayein *prep.* against 3. 92, etc.; in the way of 3. 155; in return for 5. 437; [come] ~ to meet 4. 44

al *adj.* the whole of 6. 258 [138

al *adv.* entirely pr 26, 194, 6.

aliri *see* 6. 124 n.

alkin of every kind pr 222, 6. 70; *g. sg.* ~nes 3. 224

alle everyone (d.) 7. 76

almes(se) alms 3. 75, 7. 75

aloft on high 1. 90 [195

als(o) also 3. 72; as 3. 328, 4.

alswythe immediately 3. 101

amaistrie(n) teach, instruct, govern 2. 147, 6. 214; *p.p.* ~d 2. 153 (surv. in Shropshire)

amende *v.* heal 1. 166; correct, reform 3. 94; cure 5. 487

amendes *n.* compensation 2. 118, 5. 332

amercy amerce, fine 6. 40

amonges amongst 5. 209, 7. 156

ampulles phials 5. 527

an (i) and pr 216 7. 44; (ii) if 2. 132; (iii) on pr 13; (4) in 3. 72, 5. 580

ancres anchorites pr 28, 6. 147

and if 2. 192 etc.

angreth makes angry 5. 117

apayed *p.p.* content 6. 110, 198

ap(p)ertly manifestly, evidently 1. 98, 3. 256

229

GLOSSARY

apewarde a keeper of apes 5. 640

apeyre, appayre injure 6. 173;
2 pl. sjv. 5. 573, *3 pl. sjv*, diminish 5. 47; *pr. sg.* ~**th** 7. 47; *pa.
pl.* ~**d** despoiled 6. 134; *p.p.* ~**d**
6. 221

apoysounde *p.p.* poisoned 3. 127

apparaille array 2. 170, 6. 59;
pa. pl. ~**d** pr 23; *p.p.* ~**d** 5.
523

appendeth is proper 1. 45

appiere appear 3. 113

appose question 3. 5; *pa. sg.* ~**d**
1. 47; *pl.* ~**den** disputed (? in
scholastic fashion) against 7. 138

ar, or ere, before 1. 73 etc.

aredy ready 4. 192

ar(en), arne are pr 164, 1. 21,
6. 100 etc.

arest at rest 5. 234

armes (coat of) arms 5. 508

armure armour 1. 156

arraye *n.* dress 2. 17

arraye(n) *v.* (refl.) prepare 4. 15;
vest 5. 11

arrere backwards 5. 354

arst first, soonest 4. 105, 5. 468

artow art thou 5. 260

arwes arrows 3. 324

ascapen escape 2. 202; *p.p.* ~**d**
6. 79

askep asks, requires pr 19 etc.

as(s)pye spy out 5. 170; see 6.
131, 225

assaye examine 3. 5, sample 5.
310; endeavour 6. 24

assele *1 pr. sg.* seal 2. 112

assente agreement: **be of myne** ~
agree to act with me 4. 187

assoil(l)e(n) absolve 3. 40 etc.;
pa. sg. ~**d** 3. 47, 5. 186; *p.p.*
3. 143; *pr. sg.* ~**th** solves,
answers 3. 236

asswage soothe, subdue 5. 122

at of 3. 25; in 7. 128 from 2. 180
at ones together 5. 163

atte at the 1. 24 etc.; ~ **firste** at
once 6. 174

atweyne in twain, apart 7. 116

atwo in two 6. 105

auarousere more avaricious 1. 189

auaunced *p.p.* promoted 1. 189,
3. 33

auncere steelyard 5. 218

auȝte *n.* something 5. 439; everything 5. 489; at all 5. 311, 540

auȝte *v. 1 pa. sg.* ought 2. 28: see
owe

auoutrie adultery 2. 175

auowe *n.* vow 5. 457

auowe *v.* assert, avouch 3. 255;
pa. sg. ~**d** made a vow 5. 388

auter altar 5. 109

auenture chance: **good** ~ by
good luck 6. 79; **an (on)** ~ in
case 3. 72 etc.

aworpe 6. 228: var. of **yworp(e)**:
see **yworth**

awreke *imp. sg.* take vengeance on
6. 175; *p.p.* **awroke** avenged
6. 204

axe(n) ask 4. 103, 5. 543; *pr. pl.
sjv.* 5. 430; *pr. sg.* ~**th** 2. 27;
pa. sg. ~**d** 1. 49 etc.

babeled *1 pa. sg.* babbled (over)
5. 8

baberlipped with thick lips 5. 190

bachelers graduates pr 87

bailliues bailiffs 2. 59, 3. 2

bakbite *v.* slander 2. 80; ~**ynge**
5. 89

balder bolder 4. 107, 7. 183

bale injury, wrong 4. 89, 92

baleised *p.p.* beaten 5. 175

balkes ridges of greensward left
between plots in ploughing a
common field 6. 109

banke slope, hillside pr 8

banne curse 1. 62; *pr. sg.* ~**th** forbids 7. 88

bar see **bere**

bargaines haggling 2. 87

barne childe 2. 3; *pl.* ~**s** 3. 151,
7. 92

baroun baron 3. 319

barste *pa. sg.* burst 6. 180

baslarde, dagger hung from girdle
3. 303

batailles battles 3. 321

batered *1 pa. sg.* clapped 3. 198

baudy dirty 5. 197

230

baxsteres, bakesteres bakers pr 218, 3. 79

bayard(e) (popular n. for a) (bay) horse 4. 53, 6. 196; *pl.* ~s 4. 124

be be pr 79 etc.; *1 pr. pl.* **beth** 3. 27; *2 pr. pl.* **ben** 6. 132; *3 pr. pl.* **ben** 6. 79; **ar(en)** pr 164 etc.; Fut. sense: **beest** 5. 598, **beth** 7. 66; *imp. 1 pl.* **be we** pr 188, *2 pl.* **be 3e** 7. 183, **beth** 2. 137; *2 pr. sg. sjv.* 6. 207; *3 pr. sg. sjv.* **be** 4. 189; *pa. sg. sjv.* **were** pr 165; *p.p.* **be** 5. 129, 155; **it ben** they are 6. 56

be *prep.* see **bi**

beau filtz fair son 7. 162

beches beech trees 5. 18

bedden *3 pr. pl.* (refl.) = go to bed 2. 97

bedel under-bailiff or apparitor 2. 109; *pl.* ~**les**, ~**lus** 2. 59, 3. 2

bedeman messenger, servant 3. 41, 46

bed(e)rede(n) *p.p.* bed-ridden 6, 194, 7. 101

behote, bihote *1 pr. sg.* promise, vow 5. 462, etc.; *pa. sg.*

bei3, bihighte 329 ring or collar for neck or arm pr 165, 176; *pl.* **bi3es** pr 161

beire *g. pl.* of both 2. 66

bely-ioye appetite, pleasure in food 7. 118

belye lie against, slander 5. 414

bemeneth, bymeneth means, signifies pr 208, 1. 1

benefys benefice, eccl. living 3. 312

benfait benefit, kind deed 5. 436; *pl.* **bienfetes** 5. 621

bere carry 6. 144; *3 pr. sg.* ~**th** 4. 57; *imp. sg.* 3. 268; *2 pa. sg.* **bere** 3. 195; *3 pa. sg.* **bar(e)** 2. 3 etc.; *pa .pl.* **baren** 5. 108, 365; *pa. pl. sjv.* **bere** 5(139.

berghe hill 5. 589

bernes barns 6. 186; *g. sg.* **bernes** 4. 57

bete beat 5. 33; **bet** (contr.) beats 4. 59; *pa. sg.* **bette** 6. 180

bete satisfy 6. 239

Beto(u)n Betty (dim. of *Bette*, Sk) 5. 33

bette better 5. 601, 6. 49

Bette Bat, Bartholomew 5. 330

bi, by, be by 4. 134; in accordance with 4. 70, etc. with ref. to 4. 71, 5. 180; ~ **my-self** for my part 4. 137; ~ **so** provided that 5. 647; ~ **my power** to the extent of my power 6. 35; ~ **pat** by that time 6. 292, 301; ~ **pat** according to that which 7. 122

bicche bitch 5. 353, see n.

bicome *pa. pl.* (with *where* =) have gone 5. 651

bicometh *impers.* becomes, is proper 3. 208

bidde pray 5. 231, beg, 'cadge' 6. 239; *1 pr. sg.* pray 5. 407; *3 pr. sg.* ~**th** begs 7. 81, **bit** (contr.) begs 7. 68, bids, commands 3. 75; *pr. pl.* **bidden** beg, solicit 3. 218; *imp. sg.* **bidde** pray 5. 454; *imp. pl.* ~**th** 5. 610, 7. 84; *pa. sg.* **bad** commanded 2. 159, 7. 5; *pa. pl.* **beden** 327, *p.p.* **boden** invited 2. 54 (confusion of OE *bēodan* and **biddan**)

bidder(e)s beggars pr 40 etc.

biddynge prayers 3. 218

bidraueled *p.p.* covered with grease 5. 194

biennales the saying of masses for a departed soul for two years 7. 170 (sole ex.)

biernes men 3. 265

bifalleth belongs (as of right) 1. 52 *pr. sjv.* **bifalle** it may turn out (well with them) 5. 59 *pa. sg.* **bifel** happened 5. 479, 7. 164

bifor(n) before pr 183, 7. 188

bigge strong 6. 216

bigge(n) buy 4. 89, 6. 282; *1 pr. sg.* **bigge** 5. 429; *pa.* **bou3te** 2. 3 etc.

bigileth beguiles, cheats 7. 70

bigruccheth murmurs at 6. 69

bi3ete offspring 2. 40

231

biȝunde, byȝende lands beyond the sea 3. 109, 4. 128

biheste promise 3. 126

bihote, bihight, see behote

bihoueth needs, requires 5. 38

bihynde in the rear 3. 34; in arrears 5. 433

bikenne *1 pr. sg.* commit 2. 49

biknowen acknowledge, confess pr 204; *1 pr. sg.* biknowe 5. 200; *p.p.* ~n welcomed 3. 33

bileue creed 5. 7, 7. 175

bille petition 4. 47

biloue (refl.) *imp. sg.* make (thyself) beloved 6. 230; *p.p.* ~d beloved 3. 211

bilowen *p.p.* told lies about 2. 22

binam *pa. sg.* took away from 6. 243, see bynome

birde girl 3. 14

bireue take away by force 6. 248

bisette bestow 5. 264, 299

bishetten *pa. pl.* shut up 2. 213

bisi, bisy occupied 7. 118, 125

bisitte lie heavy on 2. 140

bislabered *p.p.* besmeared 5. 392

bismer calumny 5. 89

bisouȝte *pa. pl.* begged 5. 336

biswynke earn by labour 6. 216

bit see bidde

bitelbrowed with beetling (sharp) brows 5. 190

bitter (*adj.* as *n.*) bitterness 5. 119

bittere bitterly 3. 249

bitwixen amongst 5. 338

bityme betimes, soon 5. 647

blenche turn aside 5. 589

blent *p.p.* blinded 5. 502

blered *pa. sg.* deceived, dazzled pr 74; *p.p.* as *adj.* bleared, inflamed 5. 191

blesseth consecrates 3. 148; see (y)blissed

blisful blessed 2. 3

blisse joy(s) 7. 135

blissed *p.p.* as *n.* happy ones, the beatified 5. 503.

blo livid 3. 97

blody related by blood, akin 6. 210

blosmed *pa. pl.* blossomed, spread 5. 140

blustreden *pa. pl.* wandered blindly about 5. 521 (cf. *Purity*, 886)

boden see bidde(n)

boke book, writings 7. 85, 88; epistle(s) 1. 183; Bible 3. 249, 7. 88

bolded *1 pa. sg.* emboldened 3. 198

boldnesse presumption 5. 621

bolke belch 5. 397

bolle bowl, platter 5. 108 etc.

bollyng swelling; for ~ of her wombe to prevent their bellies from swelling 6. 218

bolneth swells 5. 119

bolted *p.p.* supported (by iron bands) 6. 138

bonched *pa. sg.* banged, beat pr 74

bondman labourer who held his land by rent, customary work, or gifts 5. 194; *pl.* bondemen pr 216, 6. 46

bores boars 6. 31

borghe (i) borough, town 2. 87, 6. 308

borghe, borwgh (ii) pledge, security, bail 7. 82, 4. 89; *pl.* borwes 1. 77

bornes *g. sg.* (of a) brook, bourn, pr 8

borwe borrow 5. 257; *1 pr. sg.* I promise to pay 5. 429; *3 pr. sg.* ~th 7. 81; *pr. pl.* ~n 7. 82; *1 pa. sg.* ~d 6. 101; *3 pa. sg.* ~d 4. 53; *3 pr. sg. sjv.* borwe go surety for 4. 109

bote remedy, relief, amendment 4. 89 etc.; repairs 7. 28

bote *pa. t.* bit 5. 84

botened *p.p.* restored, bettered d 6. 194

boterased *p.p.* buttressed 5. 598

boure, bowre bower, lady's chamber, 2. 64 etc.

bow bough, branch 5. 32; *pl.* ~es (enclosure, hedge) 5. 584

boweth (forth) *imp. pl.* turn, proceed 5. 575

bown ready 2. 159

GLOSSARY

boxome see **buxome**

buy rogue, fellow pr 80

bras brass, copper, 3. 195

bredcorne (inferior) (seed) corn for bread 6. 64. (Sk notes Lincs. dial. use)

brede breadth 3. 202

breden breed 2. 97

breke break 7. 183; *3 pr. pl.* **~th** 6. 31; *2 pr. pl. sjv.* **breke** 5. 584; *3 pa. pl. sjv.* **breke** should fail to keep 5. 245

bren bran 6. 184, 285

brenne burn 3. 97; *imp. sg.* 3. 265; *p.p.* **brent** (= burnished) 5. 271

breuet letter of indulgence pr 74; *pl.* **~tes** 5. 649

brewestere female brewer 5. 306; *pl.* **~s** pr 218, 3. 79

bridale, bruydale wedding (feast) 2. 43, 54   [156, 178

Britoner, Brytonere Breton 6.

broche piece together 5. 212

broches jewels pr 75

brocour, brokour broker, procurer, matchmaker 2. 65 etc.

brokages marriage arrangements 2. 87

broke *n.* brook 5. 575, 6. 137

broke *p.p.* torn 5. 108

brouzle put 3 pa. pl. 5. 365, pp. 5. 395

brolle child, brat 3. 204

brugge (draw)bridge 5. 601; *pl.* **~s** 7. 28

bugge(n) buy pr 168 etc.; *pr. pl.* **buggen** 3. 81

bulle papal bull pr 69, 7. 109; *pl.* **~s** 3. 147, 7. 186

bummed *pa. sg.* tasted 5. 223 (? echoic)

burdoun staff 5. 524

burgages tenements 3. 86

burgeis(es) burgesses pr 216 etc.

burgh-swin town pigs 2. 97

busked hem (refl.) prepared thsvs., went 3. 14

but except 3. 112 etc.; only 6. 147
~ if except 3. 305, 5. 420, etc.

buxome, boxome, buxum

obedient, willing 1. 110 etc.; gentle 5. 575

buxomnes, buxumnesse obedience 1. 112, 4. 187

byfel happened to pr 6; see **bifalle**

bynome *p.p.* taken away 3. 312 ('shall be taken from him')

byschrewed *pa. sg.* cursed 4. 168

bytwene between the two pr 17

[For other forms in **by-** see **be-, bi-**]

cacche catch pr 206, 2. 192; *pa. pl.* **cauȝt (of)** took, obtained pr 107

caityue wretch 5. 200

cake (cake) loaf 6. 284

calabre Calabrian (grey) fur 6. 272

Caleys Calais 3. 195

can *1 pr. sg.* I know (how to) 3. 3 etc. am able to pr 111; *3 pr. sg.* pr 199; *pl.* **conne(th)** pr 33 etc.

canonistres experts in canon law 7. 149

canoun canon law 5. 428

caple horse 4. 23; *pl.* **~us** 2. 161

cardinales (Fr.) *pl. adj.* cardinal, fundamental pr 107

care sorrow 1. 61; anxiety 2. 150

cared *pa. pl.* were worried about 2. 161

careful anxious, troubled 1. 201

carefullich anxiously, sorrowfully 5. 77

caroigne, caroyne carcass, body 6. 93, pr 193

carped said, told 2. 191

carpyng talking, discussion pr 203

cartesadel *imp. sg.* harness 2. 179 (a *cartesadel* was a small saddle used on draught-horses: cf. *OBMEV* p. 422)

cas mishap, misfortune 7. 48

caste contrivance, device 3. 19

casten *pa. pl.* planned, determined pr. 117; *imp. pl.* **~th** give 6. 16

catel wealth, goods, property pr 204 etc.

caudel mess 5. 362

caurimaury coarse material 5. 79 (cf. Skelton, *Elynour Rummyng*, 150)

certis certainly, assuredly 2. 151, 7. 180

Cesse Cicely 5. 315

cesse(n) desist 2. 151, etc.; *imp. pl.* ~th 4. 1

chaffare *n.* trade, commerce, pr 31 etc.

chaffare *v.* bargain 6. 241

chalangynge fault-finding 5. 88

chalengen *pr. pl.* make a claim for pr 93; *p.p.* chalanged charged with offences 5. 174

chapel(l)eynes chaplains 1. 188, 6. 12

chapitel(e) chapter (of monks etc.) 3. 318; ~hous chapter-house 5. 174

chapitere chapter (of a nunnery) 5. 161

chapman merchant, huckster, tradesman pr 64; *pl.* chapmen 5. 34 etc.

charnel bonehole (us. in crypt, where bones from cemetery were deposited) 6. 50

chartre conveyance 2. 68 [etc.

chaste(n) chastise, correct 5. 34

chastelet little castle 2. 84

chastyng chastisement 4. 117

chateryng idle talking 2. 84

chaud(e) (plus) hot(ter) 6. 313

cheker exchequer pr 93, 4. 28

chekes, maugre here (and varr.) 4. 50 etc. (*see* maugre 'despite all she could do': cf. maugre (his) tethe 18. 81

chele coldness, chilliness 1. 23

Chepe Cheap(side), London 5. 322 (cf. next)

chepynge market 4. 56 (see n.), 6. 301

cherissyng indulging 4. 117

chervelles chervil (a pot-herb) 6. 296

chesibles chasubles, mass-garments 6. 12

chest dissension 2. 84

chetes escheats, reversions of property 4. 175

cheuen *pr. pl.* succeed, thrive pr 31

cheuesaunces money-lenders' contracts 5. 249

chewen *pr. pl.* devour 2. 191

chibolles stone-leeks 6. 296

chief foremost, pre-eminent pr 64

chide(n) complain 4. 52; *pr. pl.* cry 1. 191; chide *3 sg.* complain 6. 314

childryn *g. pl.* of children 4. 117

chiries cherries 6. 296

chirytime cherry season 5. 161

chiueled trembled 5. 193

clamep *pr. pl.* demand (the knowledge) 1. 93

Clarice Clarissa 5. 159, 319

clene pure 3. 21

clense trim 6. 106

clere bright 5. 594; ~matyn fine white bread 6. 306

clergealy in formal style pr 124

clergye learned men pr 116, 3. 164; *g. sg.* clergise (*psf.*) 3. 15

clerke a man of learning 3. 3, 7. 73; *pl.* ~s pr 114, 7. 153; *g. pl.* ~n 4. 119; parish clerk 5. 319

cleve cleave, divide 7. 155

cliket latch(key) 5. 613

cliketed *p.p.* fastened with a latch 5. 623 (Shrops. dial.: Sk)

cloches claws pr 154

clokke hobble, lag 3. 34

clowe *v.* claw pr 154

coffes mittens 6. 62

cofre chest 5. 27

cokeres leggings 6. 62

coket fine white bread 6. 306

Cokkeslane Cock Lane (Smithfield) 5. 319

coloppes fried ham and eggs 6. 287

comen come 7. 188; *pa. sg.* come pr 112 etc.; *pa. sg.* cam pr 114; *pa. pl.* comen 2. 150; *p.p.* comen 4. 189; *pa. sg. sjv.* come should come 6. 116

comeres chance comers 2. 230

GLOSSARY

comissarie bishop's officer 2. 179,
3. 142
comseth begins 1. 161 etc.; *pa.
sg.* ~d 3. 103 etc.
commune *n.* commonalty pr 115
etc.; *pl.* ~s pr 113 (allowance of)
provisions(cf. Oxford 'commons')
5. 47; in ~ for the use of all 1. 20
comune *adj.* general; ~ profit,
profyte general good pr 148,
4. 123
conforte *n.* help 4. 151
conforte *v.* strengthen, relieve
1. 201; *imp. sg.* 6. 223
congey(e) bid goodbye, dismiss 3.
173; *imp. sg.* 4. 4
conscience guilty conscience 2.
50; inner thought 3. 67; uninfl.
g. sg. 3. 19
conseille council pr 148, 3. 114;
confidential matter 5. 183; of
owre ~ one of our advisers
4. 193; bi my ~ = if you take
my advice pr 202
con[si]storie consistory, bishop's
spiritual court pr 99 (fig.) etc.
construe explain pr 144 etc.
co(u)ntenaunce outward show,
display pr 24; favour 5. 183
contrarieth acts or speaks against
5. 55
contreued devised pr 118
conynges conies, rabbits pr 193
cope provide a (friar's) cope for
5. 269; *pr. sg.* ~th 3. 142; *pa. pl.*
~d 2. 230; *p.p.* ~d 3. 35
copes (-is) hooded cloaks pr 56
etc.
coppis cups 3. 22
corps body 1. 137
corseint saint 5. 539
coste expenditure 3. 68
costed *pa. sg.* cost, put out of
pocket pr 203; *p.p.* pr 204
costes regions 2. 85
cosyn kinswoman 2. 132
coteth provides with a coat 3.
142
couenaunt condition 6. 28
couent religious house 5. 155; *g.
sg.* ~es 5. 137

coueteise avarice pr 61 etc.
counte county 2. 85
countenaunce see contenaunce
coupe fault, sin 5. 305
coupes goblets, bowls 3. 22
coupleth links, fastens 3. 164; *pa.
pl.* coupled (refl.) joined themselves 4. 149; *p.p.* pr 206
courbed bent 1. 79, 2. 1
course (of kynde) (natural) disposition 3. 56
courte (1) ? courtyard 5. 594, see
n.; (2) the Roman Curia pr 107
courteby, kourteby short coat
(sts. particoloured: cf. *BPR*, i.
14) 5. 80; *pl.* courtpies 6. 191
couth *1 pr. sg.* make known 5. 181
(< OE *cȳðan*)
couthe *pa. sg.* knew pr 182, 5. 520;
could 1. 115; ~ of was skilled in
2. 226; *2 pa. pl.* couthe 3. 340; *2
pa. pl. sjv.* pr 200.(< OE *cunnan*)
cracche, cracchy scratch pr 184,
186
craft(e) faculty 1. 137; craft 2. 4,
3. 19; handicraft 5. 554; occupation *pl.* ~es pr 221, 7. 31
crafty skilful, cunning pr 162;
skilled 3. 224, 6. 70
craued demanded 6. 94
credo the Creed 6. 91
croft(e) small enclosed field 5. 581,
6. 33
crope *2 pa. sg.* didst creep 3. 190;
1 pa. pl. sjv. croupe (v.l.
crope) pr 186
croppeth bite heads off 6. 33
crounyng tonsure pr 88
cruche (mark of a) cross 5. 529
cruddes curds 6. 284
crystendome baptism 5. 597
culled see kullen
culorum conclusion 3. 278 (<
saeculorum, at end of the *Gloria
Patri*: cf. *lorum*, Henryson,
Fables, 2831)
culter, kulter coulter, iron blade
in front of ploughshare 3. 306,
6. 106
cupmel cupfuls 5. 225; cf.
parcelmele

235

curatoures priests with cure of souls 1. 193

cure cure (care) of souls pr 88

curteise courteous 4. 16

curteisye courtesy, kindness 5. 437; grace 1. 20 (cf. xii. 79)

curteisliche courteously 3. 103 etc.

cutpurs cutpurse, thief 5. 639

Cyuile (practitioner of) civil law (as pr n.) 2. 62

dafte dolt 1. 138

dampne damn, condemn 5. 478; *p.p.* **~d** 2. 102

dar *1 pr. sg.* dare pr 209, 6. 270; *1 pa. sg.* **durst** 3. 201; *3 pa. sg.* **dorst** pr 178

daunten tame, subdue 3. 286

Dawe David, Davy 5. 320, 6. 331

debate strife, dissension 5. 98, 337

ded death 3. 265 (cf. forms of OE *deað* in compounds like *dædliche*)

dede *pl. adj.* the dead 7. 187

dede *v.*, see **do**

dedes *pl. n.* tasks, jobs pr 223

defaute lack; **for ~** for want, need 5. 6 etc.; **in ~** in fault 2. 139, 5. 145

defendeth forbids 3. 64

defien, defye digest pr 229; be digested 5. 389; *ger.* (= for the digestion) 5. 121

dele *n.* part: **some ~** partly 5. 438

dele(n) *v.* (i) divide, share, distribute 6. 99; give away 1. 197; *2 pr. pl.* **~n** 3. 71; (ii) have dealings 6. 77; *2 pr. pl.* **~n** 7. 90

delicatly indulgently 5. 184

delitable delectable, pleasant 1. 34

deluen dig 6. 143; *1 pr. sg.* **delue** 5. 552

deiueres diggers pr 223, 6. 209

deme decide, think, judge 1. 86, 4. 178; *1 pr. sg.* **deme** 5. 114; *2 pr. sg.* **~st** sayest 3. 187; *3 pr. pl.* **~n** pronounce judgement, arbitrate pr. 96; *1 pa. sg.* **~d** 7. 169; *p.p.* condemned 4. 181; *imp. sg.* **deme** 6. 83, 182

Denote pr. n. 6. 73

departed *p.p.* divided 7. 156

depraue revile 3. 178; *3 pr. pl.* 5. 144

deɪe *adj.* (i) great, glorious 1. 87; (ii) loved 5. 459

dere *adv.* dearly; **as me ~ liketh** as pleases me best 6. 293.

dere(n) *v.* injure, harm 7. 34, 50

derne secret 2. 175

derrest most dear, valuable 2. 13

derworth precious 1. 87

descryue, discreue describe 5. 188, 79

despended *p.p.* spent 5. 267

despiseth holds in despite 5. 148

destruye destroy pr 197; *2 pr. sjv.* 3. 269; *3 pr. pl.* **~th** pr 22

Deth the Black Death 6. 330

deuine (ȝe) *imp. pl.* interpret pr 209; *pa. sg.* **deuyned** 7. 152

deuynyte theology 7. 135

deuynour expositor, teacher 7. 135

dew due; **as ~** deservedly 5. 622

dey(e) die 1. 142 etc.; *2 pr. sjv. pl.* 6. 122; *2 pa. sg.* **deydest** 5. 472

deyinge (time of) dying 7. 34

deyse (heigh) judgement seat 7. 17

diademed crowned 3. 286

diamantz diamonds 2. 13

diapenidion expectorant 5. 123 (see n.): < Gk. *dia* = consisting of (> 'medicine (containing)') + *penidion* little thread

diete (refl.) *2 pr. sjv.* diet thyself 6. 270

dignelich worthily, honourably 7. 171

diȝte make ready 6. 293

diken make ditches 6. 143; *1 pr. sg.* **dyke** 5. 552; *pa. pl.* **~ den** 6. 193

disgised *p.p.* tricked out pr 24

disoures tellers of tales 6. 56

dissheres maker or seller of dishes 5. 323 (? *leg.* **disshere** (*A*): one MS. of B has **dyssheres douȝter**)

do do, cause 6. 87; *2 pr. sg.* **doste** 6. 83; *2 pr. pl.* **done** 1. 53; *3 pr. pl.* **don** 6. 66; *p.p.* **do** ended 5. 418; causative+inf. w. passive force 3. 60, 62, 6. 87, 7. 177; +inf. w. active force 5. 95 etc.; *ger.* **to done** to transact business

GLOSSARY

4. 27 (cf. a(f)faire, ado), to work 6. 112, to be done 6. 206; **doth him to go** prepares to go off. 2.211; **do me** make my way 5. 459; *imp. pl.* **doth** 5. 44; *2 pa. sg.* **dedest** 7. 190; *3 pa. sg.* **dede** 3. 140; *pl.* **dede(n)** 5. 547, 7. 122; **did** caused 5. 245; **do it on** appeal to 1. 86, 3. 187; **dede bi** dealt with 1. 28

doel, dole mourning, grief 5. 386, 6, 122

doke duck 5. 75

dome sentence, decree 2. 205; judgement 3. 316 etc.

domesday judgement day 5. 20,478

donet see 5. 209 n.

dongeo(u)n castle-keep, prison pr. 15 1. 59

dore-tree side-post *or* bar of door 1. 185

doted simple, foolish 1. 138

doute fear pr 152

draddest *2 pa. sg.* didst fear 3. 192

drawe bring 5. 44; *3 pr. pl.* ~**n on** draw near 7. 56

dredes terrors pr 152

dremeles dream 7. 154

drewery (object of) affection, darling 1. 87

drowe *1 pa. sg.* (refl.) betook myself, went 5. 209; *3 pa. sg.* **drowgh** drew near 5. 356

dryest *2 pr. sg.* art thirsty 1. 25

dryuen (forth) *3 pr. pl.* pass pr 224 (cf. 'drive the night along', Dr. Johnson *Letters*, ed. Chapman, no. 954)

dureth endures, lasts 1. 78, 6. 58

dwelled was lodged 3. 14

dyches moats pr 16

dyker(e) ditcher 5. 320, 6. 331; *pl.* ~(e)s pr 223, 6. 109

dym dark 3. 192

dyne eat 5. 75 etc.; *? pr. sjv.* **dyne** 6. 262

dyngen thresh 6. 143; keep pounding away at 3. 310

dys-playere dice-player 6. 73

eche a every 3. 310, 6. 249

edwite reproach 5. 370

eet eat 5. 120; *pr. pl.* **eten** 6. 147; *pa. sg.* **eet** 6. 298, **ete** 7. 121; *p.p.* **eten** 5. 381, 6. 266

eft again 3. 344, 5. 624 (OE *eft*).

efte afterwards, again 4. 107, 5. 626 (OE *æftan*)

eftsone(s) soon afterwards, again 5. 481, 6. 172

egged incited 1. 65

eighen, eyen *pl.* eyes 5. 62 etc.

ek(e) moreover 2. 236; besides 2. 92

elde old age 5. 193

eldres forefathers 3. 261

Eleyne Helen 5. 110

eller elder-tree 1. 68 (cf. *eller-* cpds. *Pl.-N. Elements* (Pl-NS) and *Pl. N. Ox.*, ii. 442)

elles, ellis else, otherwise, pr 91 etc.; **?** other kinds of 6. 306; ~**where** in various places pr 164

elyng miserable, wretched pr 190

ende region 5. 239; **to þe** finally 1. 97

enfourmeth instructs, 3. 240.

engreyned *p.p.* dyed in grain, 'fast' 2. 15

enioyned *pa. sg.* appointed, imposed 5. 607; *p.p.* **enioigned** united in marriage 2. 65

ennuyed *p.p.* troubled, annoyed 5. 94

ensa(u)mple example, warning 5. 17; *pl.* ~**s** 1. 170, 4. 136

enuenymes poisons 2. 14

eny any 2. 203; ~ **kynnes** of any kind 2. 200

er (= **ar**) until 5. 352

erde dwelling, native place 6. 203

ere formerly 1. 129

erie(n) plough 6. 4 etc.; *p.p.* ~**d** 6. 5

eschaunges exchanges 5. 249, see n.

eschue shun, avoid 6. 55

esy easy (to procure) 7. 123

euene-cristene fellow-Christian(s) 2. 94, 5. 440

euermo perpetually, continually 7. 82

ewages beryls, aquamarines 2. 14

eyleth *pr. sg.* troubles, ails 6. 130, 259

eyre air pr 128, 1. 123

eyres heirs 2. 101, 3. 277

eyther . . . other each . . . the other 5. 148 etc.

fader, fadre father 1. 14, 3. 126

fail(l)e *pr. sjv.* be lacking 4. 194, 7. 120

faire, feire plainly 1. 2; kindly, graciously 1. 4, 6. 25; prosperously, well 5. 59

fairy (place of) enchantment pr 6

faite deed, action 1. 184

faiten beg under false pretences 7. 94

faitour(e)s malingerers 2. 182 etc.

falle *1 pr. sg.* fall (amongst), light (upon) 4. 156; *3 pr. sg.* ~**th** appertains 1. 164; **falle** *3 pr. sjv.* come to pass 3. 323; *p.p.* ~**n** come to pass pr 65

Fals the false one 2. 25, 123; *pl.* false men 3. 138

falshed(e) falsehood pr 71 etc.

famed *p.p.* slandered 3. 185

fange take, receive 5. 566

fantasies outlandish tricks pr 36

fare go, depart 7. 98; *pr. pl.* ~**th** travel, fare 2. 183; *2 pa. pl.* **ferde** fared 3. 340; *p.p.* ~**n** gone 5. 5

faste heartily 6. 110

faucones falcons 6. 32

Fauel Fraud 2. 6

fauntes -is children 6. 285, 7. 94

fayne glad 4. 12, 6. 273

faytreden *pa. pl.* shammed pr 42

feble see **fieble**

fecche(n) take 2. 180, 5. 29; *pr. pl.* ~**th** steal 4. 51

fee money 4. 131

feffe retain by fees 2. 146; *pr. sg.* ~**th** endows with property 2. 78

feffement deed of gift 2. 72

feire see **faire**

felawes companions 2. 209, 7. 12

felaws(c)hip society, fellowship 1. 113; alliance 3. 118; crew 2. 207

fel skin 1. 15

fele many 3. 338

felle shrewd 5. 170

felle *pa. sg.* happened 7. 157; *pa. pl.* ~**n** fell 1. 119

felled *pa. sg.* felled, caused to fall 3. 126

fende fiend 1. 40; ~**s** 2. 40

fenel-seed seed of the fennel (used to spice drinks) 5. 313

ferde see **fare**

fere *n.* comrade 4. 26; *pl.* ~**s** 2. 6, 5. 170

fere *v.* frighten, terrify 7. 34

ferly marvel pr. 6; *pl.* ~**is** pr 65 [OE *feorlic* remote, strange; ? modelled on ON *ferligr*: see S. d'Ardenne, *S. Juliene*, Gl.]

fernyere formerly 5. 440

ferthynge farthing 4. 54, 5. 566; ~**worth** farthing's worth, small quantity 5. 313

fest *p.p.* fastened 2. 123

fet (contr. from *fedeth*) *pr. sg.* feeds pr 194

fetislich handsomely 2. 11, 165

fette *pa. sg.* fetched, produced 2. 162, 5. 450; *pa. pl.* ~**n** 2. 229, 6. 294

fettren fetter 2. 207; *imp. pl.* ~**ereth** 2. 200

feynen (refl.) *pr. pl.* invent pr 36; *pa. pl.* ~**d** pretended to be 6. 123

feyntise faintness 5. 5

feyres (market) fairs 4. 56; cf. **faire** 5. 205, 328

f(i)eble sick, weak pr 180 etc.

fierce eager, prone 5. 67

fierthe fourth 7. 52

fikel treacherous 2. 129, 3. 121

file concubine 5. 160

flapten *pa. pl.* laid on 6. 187

flatte *pa. sg.* dashed 5. 451

Flaundres Flanders 5. 321

flayles flails (for threshing corn) 6. 187

flei3 *pa. sg.* fled, flew 2. 210; *pa. pl.* **flowen** 2. 233, 6. 186

flex flax 6. 13

floreines florins, coins, money 2. 143 etc. (the rare Eng. coin of this name was minted only in 1344; for Italian and Flemish florins see *Speculum* 36 (1961) 283)

fluxe discharge 5. 179

folde earth 7. 53

foles fools pr 26

folus *pl.* foals 2. 162

folwar follower 5. 549

folwen accompany 6. 2

fonde *imp. sg.* endeavour 6. 222

fonde *pa. sg.*: see **fynde**

foon foes 5. 96

for (i) *conj.* because, for the reason that 2. 166 etc.; (ii) *prep.* (as a preventive) against 1. 24 etc.; despite 2. 199 etc.; in the name of 1. 58; for fear of 4. 128; ~ me for my part pr 201

forbare *pa. sg.* suffered to live, spared 3. 272

forbede *pr. sg. sjv.* forbid 3. 111, 119

fordon destroy 5. 20

for(e)bode prohibition 4. 194, 7. 176 (**Goddes, Lordes** ~ = God forbid that); **lawes** laws forbidding it 3. 151

forgoer harbinger 2. 187; *pl.* ~**es** 2. 60

forȝelde *3 pr. sjv.* repay 6. 279

forȝete *p.p.* forgotten 5. 404

forpyned *p.p. adj.* wretched 6. 157

forsake *1 pr. sg.* deny 5. 431

forsleues the foreparts of sleeves 5. 81

forstalleth *pr. sg.* forestalls, buys up provisions before they reach the market stalls 4. 56

forth course 3. 156

forth ford 5. 576

forth onward 5. 521

forpi on that account, therefore pr 111 etc.

forwandred *p.p.* gone astray pr 7

forward(e) agreement 4. 12, 6. 36

forweny pamper, spoil 5. 35

forwes furrows 6. 106

forwit foresight 5. 166

fote foot, step 6. 2

foule shamefully 3. 185

foules birds 5. 355 etc.

fouleth *pr. sg.* discredits 3. 153

founded *pa. sg.* created, established 1. 64

fourlonge furlong, furrow 5. 5, 424

frained *pa. sg.* asked 1. 58, 5. 532

freke man 4. 12, 156

frele frail 3. 121

frelete frailty 3. 55

frere friar 3. 35 etc.; *g. sg.* ~**s** 5. 81; *pl.* **freres/is** pr 58, 2. 182

frete eat 2. 95

fretted *p.p.* adorned 2. 11

frithed *p.p.* hedged in with trees 5. 590

fro from 3. 109, 6. 90

frutes fruits of the earth 6. 326

ful *adj.* due 2. 95

ful *adv.* full, very pr 20, 6. 45

fulle, fylle *n.* fill 1. 152, 6. 266

fyȝte resist 4. 52

fynde(n) find 7. 30 provide for pr 117; discover (in hunting) 5. 424; *pr. sg.* **fynt** (contr. from **fyndeth**) 4. 131, 7. 128; *pa. sg.* **fonde** saw pr 17, 58; *p.p.* **founden** 3. 338

gabbe lie 3. 179

gadelynges fellows 4. 51

gaf see **gyue**

Galice, Galis Galicia 4. 127, 5. 528

galle gall, bile 5. 119

gamen game, sport pr 153

gan *pa. pl.* ('began') did pr 143 etc.; *2 pa. sg.* **gonne** didst 5. 488

gange travel, walk 2. 167

garte, gerte *pa.* caused, made 1. 121, 6. 303; *p.p.* **gert** 5. 130

gate (i) way, road 1. 203, 3. 155; **heiȝe** ~ highroad 4. 42; (ii) door 5. 638

gateward porter 5. 604

gentil noble 1. 183

gerlis children 1. 33

gernere granary 7. 129

gerthes girths 4. 20

gete get 4. 141; *1 pa. sg.* **gat** 4. 79; *3 pa. sg.* **gat** (begat) 1. 33

gilte, gult offence, guilt 4. 101 etc.

GLOSSARY

girt *1 pa. sg.* threw 5. 379 (prob.
< **gurde** 'strike')

glade gladden 6. 121

glase(n) glaze 3. 61

glede glowing ember 2. 12, 5. 291

glee music pr 34

glewman minstrel, entertainer;
g. sg. ~nes 5. 353

glose gloss, commentary 5. 282

glosed *pa. pl.* interpreted pr 60

glotoun, ~town glutton 5. 310,
6. 303; *pl.* ~ones pr 76

go+*inf.* = go and 6. 30, 219, 303
etc.

God (without epithet) = Christ
1. 46 etc.

gode, good, goods property,
wealth 2. 131 etc.; *pl.* godis 4.
163; to gode to good objects or
conduct 3. 222, 5. 643; of gode
of rank, standing 2. 131, 3. 168

godelich liberally 1. 180

godly humble 5. 347

gome man 5. 541; *pl.* ~s 2. 73,
6. 219

gommes gums used as spices or
perfumes 2. 226

gon go 2. 154; *pr. pl.* gon(e) pr 43
etc.; *3 pr. sg.* goth 5. 314; *1 pr.
pl. imp.* go we let us go pr 226

gose *g. sg.* goose's 4. 36; *pl.* gees
pr 226, 6. 283

gospel (passage in) gospel(s) 1. 46

gossib friend, neighbour 5. 310

goste spirit, soul 1. 36

grace mercy (power) 4. 73; permission 3. 172; dispensation (?) 5. 52

graciouse pleasing, acceptable
6. 229

graffe graft 5. 137

graith direct 1. 203

graue inscribe = insert 3. 49;
p.p. graue stamped 4. 130

graunteth consents 2. 119, 154;
p.p. ygraunted, granted 7. 8

grauynge lettering 3. 64

grete *v.* weep 5. 386

grete *adj.* big pr 55

greue harass, vex pr 153, 6. 316;
refl. *pr. sg.* ~th becomes angry
6. 317; *pa. sg.* greued pr 139

gripeth grips, clutches 3. 248;
p.p. ~d 3. 181

gris, grys pigs, piglings pr 226 etc.

grote fourpenny piece 5. 31; *pl.*
~s 3. 137

grounde (1) earth 5. 264; (2)
? claim 5. 293

gruccheth grumbles, murmurs
6. 317; *1 pr. pl. sjv.* grucche
pr 153; *3 pr. pl. sjv.* 6. 219

grym heavy 5. 360

gult see gilte

gurdeth *imp. pl.* strike off 2. 201

Gylbe *short for* Gilbert 5. 92

gyed *pa. sg.* guided 2. 187

Gyle guile 2. 187 (pr n.), 5. 207

gyloure beguiler, deceiver 2. 120

gynnynge beginning 2. 30

gyue, gyf give 3. 181: *pr. pl.* ~eth
4. 36 (~of care for); *pa. sg.* gaf
3. 21; *pa. pl.* geuen pr 76, 5.
326; *pr. sjv. sg.* gyf 2. 120,
gyue 7. 197: *p.p.* gyue 2. 148

gyuere giver 7. 70

ȝarketh (refl.) *pr. sg.* prepares, gets
ready 7. 80

ȝatis gates pr 104

ȝe yea 3. 111 etc.

ȝe *pl. nom. pron.* ye pr 198; *acc.*
ȝow pr 199

ȝede *1 pa. sg.* went 7. 142; *2 pa. sg.*
~st 5. 504; *pl.* ȝede pr 40; *3 pa.
sg. sjv.* ȝeode 1. 73

ȝelde(n) yield, render (re)pay 5.
463; *2 pr. sg.* ~st 5. 296; *3 pr.
sg.* ~th 7. 80; *3 pr. sjv.* ȝelde
6. 129; *pr. p.* ~yng paying in
return 2. 104

ȝeode see ȝede

ȝerdes yards 5. 214; rods 4. 117

ȝere(s) *pl.* years 5. 208 etc.; ȝeris
pr 65

ȝeresȝyues annual gifts 3. 99

ȝerne *v. 2 pr. sg. sjv.* long, be eager
(for) 1. 35

ȝerne *adv.* eagerly, anxiously,
quickly 4. 74 etc.; zealously
6. 111

ȝet, ȝit, ȝut *adv.* yet, still pr 185, 1.
136; further, besides 4. 59, 6. 38

GLOSSARY

ȝeue see ȝiue
ȝif if pr 37
ȝiftes, -is gifts 3. 99, 6. 42
ȝit see ȝet
ȝiue give 7. 71; *3 pr. sg.* ~th 7. 80;
 2 pa. pl. ȝeue 4. 170; *pr. sg. imp.*
 ȝif may he give 3. 165; *p.p.*
 ȝiue 5. 390; ȝoue 2. 31
ȝowself yourselves 2. 38
ȝus yes, indeed (emphatic, answer-
 ing a question with neg. expressed
 or implied) 5. 125, 233, 643
ȝut see ȝet

hagge hag 5. 191
hailse *I pr. sg.* greet 5. 101; *pa. pl.*
 ~d did obeisance to 7. 160
hakeneyman 5. 318, see n.
half side 2. 5 etc; halue half 5. 31,
 6. 108
haliday holy day 5. 588
halidom holy relics 5. 376
halpe see helpe
halpeny halfpenny 6. 307 (cf. e.g.
 twelmonth, *Ywain and Gawain,*
 1567)
hals neck, throat pr 170 etc.
halt see holde
han see have
handi-dandi 4. 75, see n.
hansel an earnest; to ~ as a treat
 or bribe 5. 326
happe happen 3. 284, 6. 47
happes successes 5. 97
happily, happiliche perhaps 5.
 624, 626
hardiliche boldly 6. 30
harlotes buffoons, vagabonds,
 tellers of coarse stories 6. 54;
 g. pl. 4. 118
harlotrie tale-telling, coarse jest-
 ing 4. 115, 5. 413
hat(te) is named, called 5. 582
 etc.; *pl.* 5. 586; *p.p.* hoten 2. 21
hatie *2 pr. sjv.* (thou) shouldst
 hate 6. 52
haue have, take custody of *pr. sjv.*
 7. 68; *2 pr. sg.* hastow 3. 105,
 5. 310; *I pr. pl.* han 3. 48; *2 pr.
 pl.* han 6. 260; *3 pr. pl.* han 7. 11,
 haueth 7. 65 haue (of) have a

share in 5. 280; *pa. t.* hadde
 experienced 3. 284, haved 3.
 339 etc.; *2 pr. sg. sjv.* han 3. 72,
 3 pr. sg. sjv. haue 5. 580; *imp. pl.*
 haueth 1. 173
hauer oaten 6. 284
haunte practise 3. 59
he *in indef. sense* one of you 6. 138,
 7. 93
heigh(e) heiȝ *adv.* devoutly 5. 588;
 loud, loudly 2. 73, 4. 162; dear
 3. 48
heigh(e), heiȝ(e) *adj.* high, chief
 1. 162 etc.; proud 5. 67
heiȝhlich at a high wage 6. 314
hele *n.* (1) health, well-being 5. 270
 (soule *(gen.)*~salvation): cf. 5.565
hele *n.* (2) bottom crust 7. 194
hele *v.* conceal 5. 168; *p.p.* hiled
 roofed 5. 599
help(e), help ~ of provide with 1.
 17; *pa. pl.* holpyn 6. 108, halpe
 7. 6, hulpen 6. 118; *p.p.* holpe 4.
 169, hulpe 5. 633, 7. 72; *imp. pl.*
 ~ith 6. 21
hem *acc. pl.* them 7. 27 etc.; *d. pl.*
 to them 3. 345, 6. 16; ~seluen
 themselves pr 59, 3. 215
hende courteous, kind 5. 261
hendeliche courteously 3. 29,
 5. 101
hennes hence 3. 108 etc.
hente catch, seize, take possession
 of 5. 68; *pa. sg.* hent(e) 5. 5,
 6. 176; *pa. pl.* ~n 6. 1. 90
heo she 1. 73, 3. 29, 5. 632
hep, heep heap, large number pr
 53, 5. 233
her(e) their pr 28 etc.; *partv.* (of
 them) 4. 32 etc.
herberwed *p.p.* lodged 5. 233
herde *pa. sg.* heard 2. 205; *pa. sjv.*
 6. 245
hernes corners, nooks 2. 233
 (William atte Hurne, *Oxf. Hist.
 Soc.,* xvi. 25, perhaps had a
 corner shop)
herre higher 2. 28
heste commandment 3. 112; *pl.*
 ~s 7. 183
heued(e) head 5. 637; source 1. 162

heuene *g. sg.* (quasi-adj.) of heaven pr 106; **~riche** kingdom of heaven pr 27

heuy sad 5. 76

hewe servant 5. 559; *pl.* **~n** 4. 55

heyre hair (shirt) 5. 66

hiedest see **hyed**

hight see **hote**

hiȝte *pa. sg.* was named 6. 80 etc.; and see **hote**

hij they pr 43 etc.

hiled see **hele**

hitte *pa. sg.* threw down 5. 329

hokkerye retail trading 5. 227

holde trusty 6. 133

holde(n) contain 1. 118; **~** hym stay 6. 202, 7. 5; *1 pr. sg.* **holde** esteem, consider 5. 419; *3 pr. sg.* **halt (with)** support 3. 241; *p.p.* **~n** considered 4. 118, 5. 261, obliged 5. 281, 6. 96; *imp. sg.* **holde (up)** sustain 6. 217; *imp. pl.* **~th** 7. 59

hole full of holes 6. 61

holely wholly 3. 112

holpyn see **helpe**

hondreth, hundreth hundred pr 210, 5. 527

honged *pa. sg.* (refl.) 1. 68; *pa. pl.* **hongen** hanged 1. 172

honoure adorn 6. 12

hope *imp. sg.* think 5. 646; *pa. sg.* **~d** thought 1. 118

hoper seed-basket 6. 63

hoppe jump, dance 3. 199

hore *adj.* hoary 6. 85, 7. 99

hore *n.* whore 4. 166

hostellere innkeeper, ostler 5. 339

hote *1 pr. sg.* command, bid 2. 199, 6. 26; *3 pr. sg.* **~th** 3. 282, 5. 555; *3 pa. sg.* **hiȝte, highte** pr 102 etc.; *p.p.* **hote** 6. 78

hoten see **hat**

houeth *pr. sg.* hovers; **ouer ~** hovers over 3. 207

houped *pa. sg.* whooped, shouted 6. 174

houres the seven daily services of the Church 1. 181

housbonderye good management, prosperity 1. 57

houue coif; *pl.* **~s** pr 210

how ho! 6. 118

hucche chest, coffer 4. 116

hulles hills pr 5 etc.

hulpe(n) see **helpe**

huyre pay, reward 5. 557, 6. 141

huyred *p.p.* paid 6. 314

hyed *1 pa. sg.* hastened 5. 384; *2 pa. sg.* **hiedest** 3. 193

hymself, -selve itself 1. 151, 5. 221

hyne servant 4. 118

iangelers tattlers, story-tellers pr 35

iangle chatter, argue pr 130 etc.; *pr. sg.* **~th** 4. 155

iang(e)lyng(e) prattle, hubbub, gossip 4. 180, 5. 158

iape jest 2. 94; *pa. sg.* **~d** deluded 1. 67

iapers jesters, buffoons pr 35

Ich I 5. 262

iille gill, little pot 5. 346

ilke same 1.|83 ('this in particular'), 6. 164

ilyke likewise 1. 50

ingonge admission 5. 638

inne inside 6. 305

innocentz innocent folk (? children) 7. 41

inpugnen call in question pr 109; *pa. sg.* 7. 147, **impugned**

iogeloure buffoon, juggler 6. 72 (for OF. *jongleur/jougleur* see J. Orr, *Rev. de Linguistique Romane*, 30 (1965), 6)

ioutes pot-herbs, stew 5. 158

ioyntly together 2. 156

iugge judge pr 130, etc.; *pa. sg.* **~d** declared 1. 183, interpreted 7. 161

iugges judges 7. 184

iustice judge, magistrate 2. 47 etc.

iustifie (judge) vindicate pr 130

Iuwen *g. pl.* of the Jews 1. 67

kaban hovel 3. 190

kairen travel, wander pr 29; (refl.) carry themselves 2. 161; *3 pr. sg.* **~th** 4. 23; **~s** (refl.) betakes himself 5. 305

kayed fastened with a key 5. 623

kenne make known 1. 92; explain 5. 426, 7. 107; teach 1. 81; *3 pr. sg.* ~**th** teaches 6. 22, 7. 73; *3 pa. sg.* ~**d** guided 4. 43, taught 7. 133; *3 pa. pl.* ~**d** guided 5. 546; *imp. sg.* kenne teach 2. 4, 6. 24; *imp. pl.* ~**th** 6. 14

kepe maintain pr 76 etc., watch over, protect 6. 142; *1 pr. sg.* **kepe** care (for), desire 3. 278, 4. 193; *3 pr. sg.* ~**th** rules 3. 208; *2 pr. sjv.* **kepe** guard 6. 28; *imp. sg.* **kepe** guard, hold 2. 46

kernelled *p.p.* crenellated 5. 597

kerue carve, cut 6. 106

ketten *pa. pl.* cut 6. 191

keure cover, roof 3. 60

kidde *pa. pl.* showed 5. 440

kingene *g. pl.* (showing extension of ending proper to weak nouns and certain fem. strong nouns in OE) of kings 1. 105

kirke church 5. 1 etc.; **to** ~**ward** toward church 5. 305

kirtel underjacket 5. 80

kitoun kitten pr 190, 202

kitthe region, country 3. 203

knappes buttons, knobs 6. 272

knaue lad, servant, 4. 16, 5. 116; *pl.* ~**s** pr 44, 225

knitten tie pr 169

knowe, cnowe acknowledge, recognize pr 122 etc.; understand 5. 40; establish 5. 273; distinguish 6. 59; find out 6. 222; *2 pr. sg.* ~**st** 5. 183; *3 pr. sg.* ~**th** recognizes 4. 41; *3 pr. pl.* ~**þ** 1. 92; *imp. sg.* knowe 6. 51; *pa. sg.* knewe 4. 31; *p.p.* knowe 5. 648

knowing understanding 1. 136; **for ~ of** to prevent recognition by 2. 230

kokeney (small) egg: Sk notes an old belief that small inferior eggs were laid by cocks 6. 287

kokewolde cuckold 4. 164

kole-plantes greens 6. 288

konne *pr. pl.* know (how to), can 6. 70; **kunneth** know 7. 41; *2 pr. pl. sjv.* **kunne** 6. 255.

konnyng cunning, clever 3. 34

kullen kill 1. 66; *pa. sg.* **kulled** 3. 186; *1 pa. pl. sjv.* **culled** pr 185

kulter see **culter**

kynde *adj.* natural, innate pr 118, 1. 55

kynde *n.* race, species pr 186; nature, natural disposition 2. 27, 6. 166; **free** ~ gentle birth 2. 76

kyndely properly, intimately 1. 81 etc.; kindly 3. 15

kyne kine, cows 6. 142

kyngriche kingdom pr. 125 2. 130

kynne kin, kindred 2. 130; *g. sg.* **in any kynnes** of any kind 5. 273, **wolueskynnes** 6. 163

lacche catch 5. 355; get 6. 230; *pa. sg. and pl.* lauȝt pr 150, 3. 25; mastered 1. 30; *2 pr. pl. sjv.* lacche catch 2. 202

lacchyng clutching, taking 1. 101

ladde see **lede**

lafte see **leue** leave

laike play, sport pr 172

lakke (i) blame, find fault with 5. 132; *2 pr. pl.* ~**th** 3. 54; *imp. sg.* lakke 2. 47, 6. 227; (ii) be lacking 5. 465

lammas(se) first day of August 6. 291

lappe portion (*or* taste) 2. 35; *pl.* ~**s** skirts 6. 295 (v.l. 2. 35 **lippe**: see **lyppe**)

Largenesse bounty, generosity 5. 632

lasse *adj.* and *adv.* less 2. 45 etc.

lat(e) see **lete**

latter less readily 1. 197

laughen laugh, rejoice 4. 106; lawȝe of laugh at 4. 18; *pr. p.* ~**yng** 4. 153

leche physician 1. 202; *pl.* ~**s** 2. 223, 6. 275; ~**craft** healing art 6. 256

lede lead 5. 600

le(o)de man 1. 139 etc.; *pl.* ~**s** 3. 96

lede lead, guide, govern pr 126, 4. 148; draw 2. 179 (still used of carting in the Midlands); *I pa. sg.* **ladde** took 5. 251; *2 pa. sg.* ~**st** didst lead 7. 189; *3 pa. sg.* **ladde** led captive 5. 498; *imp. pl.* **ledeth** conduct 2. 134

leder(e) leader, governor 1. 157, 159

ledyng persuasion, guidance 2. 42

le(e)f *n.* piece, (small) portion 6. 256, 7. 110; leaf, page 3. 337 (fig. 5. 203); *g. sg.* **leues** 3. 337

leef *adj.* pleasant, agreeable 1. 37

legge stake 2. 34, 6. 270

legistres legists, advocates 7. 14, 59

lelli(che) faithfully, verily 1. 78 etc.

lemman lover (either sex), mistressx 2. 21, 5. 417; *pl.* ~**nes** 3. 150

lene give, grant, lend 5. 244, 6. 17; *I pr. sg.* **lene** 5. 250; *2 pr. pl. sjv.* **lene** 1. 179; *2 pa. sg.* **lentestow** didst thou lend 5. 253; *3 pa. sg.* **lent** gave 5. 203; *p.p.* **lent** 5. 254

lenge tarry, linger 1. 207

lenger longer *adv.* 1. 207; *comp. adj.* 3. 336, 5. 210

lent see **lene**

leode see **le(o)de**

lepe run 5. 578; *pa. sg.* **lepe** 2. 68, 5. 502; *pa. pl.* **lope(n)** 1. 116 etc.; *pa. sg. sjv.* **loupe** if he should escape (? < ON hlaupa: other forms < OE hlēapan); *p.p.* **lopen** 5. 198

lere face, countenance 1. 3

lere teach 1. 144; *I pr. sg.* **lere** 3. 69; *2 pr. sg.* ~**th** 3. 125, 7. 124; *2 pr. pl.* ~**n** 5. 45; *3 pa. sg.* ~**d** 1. 149; *imp. pl.* ~**th** 1. 134; *p.p. adj.* **lered** instructed 4. 11

lerned (i) *I pa. sg.* learnt 5. 203; *2 pa. sg.* ~**est** 1. 139; (ii) *2 pr. sg.* **lernest** teachest 4. 11; *3 pa. sg.* **lerned** taught 5. 302, 7. 131

lernyng lesson (= bad example) 1. 197

lese(n) lose 2. 35 etc.; *pa. sg.* **les(e)** 5. 499, 7. 158

lese glean 6. 68 (still in Shropshire) 6. 68

leste least *adj.* 3. 204; *adv.* 296

lesyng lying, (telling of) untrue tales 4. 18; *pl.* ~**es** 2. 124

lesynge loss 5. 112

lete(n), **lat(e)** (i) let, allow (not always distinguishable from iii): ~ **worth** let alone pr 187; *I pr. sg.* ~**th** 3. 136; *3 pa. sg.* **lete** (? caused) 1. 165; *3 pr. sg. sjv.* **lete** pr 155; *imp. sg.* **lat(e)** 2. 47 etc.; *imp. pl.* **late** 5. 53

   (ii) leave, forego, leave off 4. 191, 5. 26, 465, 6. 273

   (iii) cause: *pa. pl.* ~**n** 2. 158; *imp. sg.* **lat** 3. 112, **lete** 4. 20

   (iv) consider: ~ **wel by** think well of 5. 625; *pa. sg.* **lete** (liȝte of) set (small store by) 4. 161, 6. 170; *pa. pl.* **leten** pr 181, 4. 160

lette hinder, prevent, restrain 1. 156 etc.; *pr. sg.* ~**th** 3. 155, 4. 176; *pr. sg. sjv.* **lette** 5. 458; *I pa. sg.* **lette** put a stop to (1 MS. **letted**) 3. 197

letter hinderer 1. 69

letterure learning pr 110

lettre inscription 1. 49

lettred learned, lettered 1. 134, 7. 131

lettynge hindrance, delay 6. 7

leue (i) *I pr. sg.* 3. 333; *pr. sjv.* permit, grant pr 126, 5. 263

   (ii) believe 5. 45; *I pr. sg.* **leue** 4. 175, 6. 92; *3 pr. sg.* ~**th** 2. 101; *pa. pl.* ~**den** 1. 117; *imp. sg.* **leue** 5. 302, 6. 268 (*A* **loue**); *imp. pl.* ~**th** 3. 174

leue(n) leave, let alone 1. 101; refrain 3. 206, 7. 149; *imp. sg.* **leue** 5. 292; *imp. pl.* ~**th** 3. 69; *I pa. sg.* **lafte** stayed behind 3. 196; *3. pa. pl.* **lafte** left 4. 153

leue *n.* leave, permission pr 85, 3. 15

leue *adj.* lief, dear (voc.) 5. 563; *pl.* 4. 39

leue *adv.* dearly pr 163, 3. **18;**

comp. **leuer(e)** 5. 413 (**haue ~** would rather); sup. **~st** 5. 527

leuynges what was left on the ground 5. 363

lewdnesse ignorance 3. 32

lewed, lewde *adj.* ignorant 3. 38; as *n.* unlearned, lay 7. 136; useless 1. 187

lewte, leute loyalty, honesty, fair-dealing pr 122 etc.

leyde *pa. sg.* laid 5. 359, *pa. pl.* 6. 124; *p.p.* **leyde** wagered 3. 201

leyes fallow lands 7. 5

libbe live 3. 226; *pr. pl.* **~n** 5. 149; **~th** 2. 186; *pr. p.* **libbyng** pr 222, 7. 62

liche like 5. 353, 489

lief *adv.* dearly (= best) 4. 148

liflode means of life, food pr 30 etc.

lige liege 4. 184

ligge *1 pr. sg.* 5. 417; *3 pr. sg.* **~th** 3. 175, **lith** 1. 124 (lies idle 6. 165); *pr. pl.* **~n** reside, lodge pr 91; **~th** are bedded or situated 6. 15; *pr. sg. sjv.* **ligge** 5. 439; *pr. pl. sjv.* **ligge** 2. 135; **~yng** 2. 51

li3te lightly 4. 161

li3tly easily 4. 106; **ly3tlich** nimbly pr 150; comp. **li3t-loker** (< OE *lihtlucõr*) 5. 578

likam body pr 30, 1. 37

likerous pleasant, dainty pr 30, 6. 268

liketh impsl. it pleases 1. 43 etc.; with **dere, lief** and *pron.* = I, you, like: 4. 148, 6. 293

limitoures friars licensed to beg for alms within a limited district 5. 138

list *pr. sg.* impsl. it pleases pr 172, 3. 157; *pa. sg.* **~e** 1. 148; *pa. sg. sjv.* **liste** it would please 5. 400

liste strip of cloth 5. 524

listres lectors 5. 138

lith tells lies 3. 155; *2 pr. sg.* **lixte** 5. 163; see also **liggen**

lither, luther defective, vicious 5. 387; bad-tempered 5. 118

lobyes lubbers pr 55

loke (i) look, see, find out 2. 155; look up, look about pr 152, etc.; *2 pr. sg.* **~stow** 7. 136; *imp. sg.* **loke** take care 3. 269; *pa. sg.* **~d** 6. 321 (**hym lokyd** looked, appeared 5. 189);
(ii) look after, protect *pr. sjv.* 1. 207; provide, allow 2. 135; examine 2. 224

lolled hung down 5. 192

longe *adj.* tall pr 55

longe *alv.* a long time 5. 522

longeth *pr. pl.* belong, are attached 2. 45, 5. 628

lope(n) see **lepe**

lorel wastrel 7. 136

lorkynge slinking 2. 216

loseles *pl.* wastrels pr 77, 6. 124; cf. **lorel**

losengerye slander 6. 145

lotebies mistresses 3. 150

lothelich loathsome 1. 116

lotheth impsl. it irks pr 155

louedayes days for settlement of disputes 3. 157, 5. 427

loueliche loving, lovable 5. 560

loues loaves 6. 285

loupe see **lepe**

loure look frowningly 5. 132; *pa. pl.* **loured** 2. 223; *pr. p.* **~ynge** 5. 83

louryng *n.* scowling 5. 344

louye love 5. 49, 6. 211; *pr. sg. sjv.* **louye** pr 126; *pr. pl.* **louen** 1. 179

low servile 5. 139; meek 5. 560, 600; lowly 6. 230

lowed stooped pr 129

lowen *p.p.* lied 5. 95

luft worthless fellow (? thief) 4. 62

luther see **lither**

lyf (i) life 1. 202; (ii) living person 3. 292 (and *passim* in *PPl*)

lyme limb 5. 99; *pl.* **~s** 6. 126

lynde linden tree 1. 154

lyppe portion, part 5. 250, see **lappe**

maceres mace-bearers in courts of justice 3. 76

maistre master 3. 217; *pl.* **~s** 7. 184

245

maistrye dominion, sway 6. 329 etc.; *pl.* ~s masterful feats 4. 25

make (i) compose, write verse 7. 61; *pa. sg.* **made** 5. 415; *p.p.* **made** 5. 403;
    (ii) prepare *I pa. sg.* **imade** 5. 162 (cf. **yspilte, yrifled**)
    (iii) cause *pr. sg.* ~**th** 6. 208; *pr. sjv.* **make** (bring about) 4. 72 etc.; *p.p.* **maked** 7. 143; **made hymself to done** set himself to work 6. 112

males bags 5. 234

mamely mutter 5. 21 (cf. ~**ng**, v.l. of **musyng** A 8. 130)

manaced *pa. sg.* theeatened 6. 172

maner(e) (i) manner, sort 5. 25 etc.; **double** ~ two kinds (of) 2. 13; (ii) fashion, calling 6. 112

manere manor 5. 595; ~**s** 5. 246

manered conditioned; **is** ~ **after** takes after 2. 27

manlyche humane, charitable 5. 260

mannus men's pr 197

mansed *p.p.* accursed (by the Church) 2. 39, 4. 160

marchandise trade pr 63

marchen go (together) pr 63

marien arrange marriages, provide dowries for 7. 29

mase turmoil, confusion pr 196, 1. 6

masse-pans pence paid for the saying of masses 3. 223

matynes the service of psalms etc. (orig. said at midnight) pr 97

maugre ill will 6. 242; = in spite of 2. 204, 4. 50, 6. 69, 160

maunged *p.p.* eaten 6. 260

mawe stomach 5. 124

may *pr. sg.* can 5. 394

mayntenaunce support, protection (or ? rank) 5. 253

mayntene abet, support 3. 90 etc.

mede recompense, reward, bribery 3. 230 etc.

medeth *pr. sg.* pays 3. 215

meke *v.* refl. humble 5. 70; approach humbly 5. 610

melke milk 5. 444, 6. 185

mellere miller 2. 111

melleth *pr. sg.* speaks 3. 104; *pa. sg.* **mellud** 3. 36

memorye commemorative prayer 6. 97

mene intermediary, go-between 1. 158, 7. 196; *pl.* ~**s** 3. 76

mene *adj.* inferior 1. 108; mean, common 3. 596 etc.; 'small' (of ale) 6. 185

mene *I pr. sg.* speak of/refer to 5. 283; *ger.* **to** ~ to signify 1. 11, 60

mened (refl.) *sg.* complained 3. 169; *pl.* 6. 2

mengen remember 6. 97; refl. = reflect, ? be concerned 4. 94

menske honour 3. 183

merciable merciful 5. 511

merciment amercement, fine 1. 160 see n. and Yunck, p. 234

mercy (I ask) pardon (= please!) 1. 11, 2. 2; thanks 1. 43

mercyed thanked 3. 20

merke murky, dark 1. 1.

merye sweet(ly), pleasant(ly) pr 10; ? well-disposed pr 208

merchaunce ill luck 3. 166, 5. 92

meseles lepers 3. 132, 7. 102

mesondieux hospitals 7. 26

messe the Mass pr 97; *pl.* ~**s** 3. 251

Messie the Messiah 3. 301

mesurable moderate, fair 1. 19 etc.

mesure moderation 1. 35, measure 1. 175

mesurelees immoderate 2. 239

mete measure pr 214; *2 pr. pl.* 1. 175

meteless without food 7. 141

meteles *n.* dream 2. 52, 7. 143

meten *v.* dream pr 11; *pa. sg.* **mette** 7. 159

mette *pa. pl.* met 5. 522; *pa. pl. sjv.* 6. 172

meyne retinue, household 1. 108, 3. 24

meynpernour surety 4. 112

meynprise *n.* bail, surety momentarily psfied.) 4. 88: see Offord, *Parl. Thre Ages*, 295 n.

meynprise *v.* furnish (the least)
surety 2. 196

meyntene support, abet 3. 246;
pr. sg. and *pl.* ~th 3. 149 etc.

middel waist 3. 10

miȝtful powerful 1. 171, 174

mitigacioun compassion 5. 477

mnam talent 6. 243; *pl.* ~es 6. 244

mo(o) more 1. 115 etc.

moder mother 7. 196

modilich angrily 4. 173

moebles (movables) goods, pos-
sessions 3. 267

molde, earth pr 67, 2. 186, 7. 96

momme murmur, mumble pr 215

mone moon 7. 159; a lunation 3.
325

mone complaint 6. 125

monelees moneyless 7. 141

moothalle council chamber 4. 135

more in addition 7. 83; þe ~
greater than expected 5. 638

morther murder 4. 55

morthereres murderers 6. 275

morwe morning 5. 325, 6. 187

most(e) see mot

most(e) greatest pr 67, 1. 7

mot *1 pr. pl.* must 6. 291; *2 pr. pl.*
mote 1. 136, 5. 570; *3 pr. pl.*
mote 5. 257; *1 pr. sg.* most(e)
7. 106, 5. 151; *3 pa. sg. sjv.*
moste might 4. 112; mot *2 pr.
sg. sjv.* mayest thou 2. 115

mote moat 5. 595

mote summon to a law-court 1.
174, 3. 159

motoun French gold coin (stamped
w. *agnus dei*) 3. 24 (one of
2 known exx. of Eng. use, see
Speculum 36 (1961), 287

motyng pleading 7. 58

mountyng increasing pr 67

mouthen utter, talk about 4. 115;
pa. sg. mouthed 6. 240

mowe(n) *1 pr. pl.* are able pr 172,
5. 209; *2 pr. pl.* mowe have
power to 6. 40; *3 pr. pl.* mowe
3. 217; = may well 7. 97; *1 pa.
sg.* miȝte have been able 5. 120;
2 pa. sg. miȝte 3. 28, 6. 225;
myȝtow thou couldst 1. 170

moylere lady (born in wedlock)
2. 118, 131

murthe(s) entertainment pr 33,
3. 219

muryer *adv.* more delightful 1. 107

myd with 4. 77, 5. 75

myddes (*adj.* as *n.*) midst 2. 184

mykel great 5. 477; much pr 201

mys mice pr 147

mysbede *imp. sg.* injure 6. 46

myschief calamity, ruin pr 67,
4. 72; hardship 6. 208, 7. 102

mysdo transgress 3. 122; *pa. sg.*
mysdid ill-treated 4. 99; *p.p.*
done amiss, mysdo 4. 90

myseise *n.* discomfort 1. 24

myseyse *adj.* wretched 7. 26

myshappe meet with misfortune
3. 327

myssayde *p.p.* evil spoken of,
slandered 5. 69

mysshape mis-shapen 7. 95

myster employment, occupation
7. 7

na no 1. 181; ~mo no one else
3. 1; ~more never again 3. 108

nale (atte) = atten (at pen)
ale at the ale (drinking) 6. 117

nam = mnam 6. 241

nam (ne am) am not 5. 420: cf.
nere, nys

nauȝty having nothing, destitute
6. 226

ne ... ne neither ... nor pr 130
etc.

nede (at) according to need 1. 18

nede(s) necessarily 3. 225, 5. 257

nedeler needle-seller 5. 318

neighed *pa. sg.* drew near 6. 301

neiȝe nearly 3. 144, near 5. 94

nel(le) (= ne wil(le)) *1 pr. sg.*
will not pr 38 etc.; *2 pr. sg.*
neltow see wil *3 pa. sg.* nolde
6. 238; *1 pa. sg. sjv.* 5. 556

nempne name 1. 21; *pa. sg.* ~d
2. 178, 7. 153

nere (= ne were) *pa. sjv.* pr 199,
3. 134 ('if that cat/woman did
not exist' = 'but for ...')

newe anew 5. 482

247

noble gold coin (first minted by Edw. III) worth a third of a pound) 3. 45, 5. 250 (first recorded exx.; see *Speculum*, 36 (1961), 284)

noither *conj.* neither, nor 4. 130; *adv.* 5. 184

nones 'nones', dinner hour, noon 5. 378, 6. 147

nonnes nuns 7. 29

nought, nou3t(e) not pr 29 etc.

nou3t nothing 5. 489

noumpere umpire 5. 337

nouthe now 3. 288, 6. 208

now now that 5. 143

noyen harm 5. 583; *pr. pl.* **noyeth** 2. 126; *p.p.* **noyed** 3. 188

ny3t-olde a day old (so not fresh) 6. 310

nym *imp. sg.* take 6. 43; ~**meth** *imp. pl.* 6. 15

nys (= **ne is**) is not 5. 455

nyuelynge snivelling 5. 135

o(n) one 2. 30 etc; **o** colour unspotted 3. 237

obrode abroad 5. 140

of *prep.* concerning pr 100; for 2. 1 etc.; by 7. 153; = some of 6. 98; in return for 6. 129; ~**more** besides 6. 38 (gen. of thing desired)

ofsent *pa. sg.* sent for 3. 101

on in 7. 107

one only, alone 1. 170

ones, onis once 2. 227 etc.; **at** ~ at once 5. 516 (**ones** 5. 610 = ? **at ones**)

ordre order, rank 1. 104, (of knighthood) 6. 168; *pl.* ~**s** pr 58

orientales 'oriental' sapphires 2. 14

other (i) *conj.* or 3. 304 etc.; (ii) *adj.* = as well 2. 57; **none** ~ not otherwise 1. 88

otherwhile(s) sometimes pr 164, 5. 557; from time to time 4. 136

overal everywhere 2. 218

ouerdelicatly too indulgently 5. 381

ouerlede domineer over 3. 314

ouerlepe pounce on pr 199; *pa. sg.* **ouerlepe** pr 150

ouermaistrieth *pr. sg.* overpowers 4. 176

ouersen oversee 6. 115; *pa. sg. refl.* forgot myself ~**seye** 5. 378 cf. 'overseen in liquor'

oures hours of the breviary pr 97

owe *1 pr. sg.* I owe 5. 476 (see n.); *3 pa. sg.* **ou3te** ought 5. 120

paknedle strong needle used for sewing up packages 5. 212

panel (slip of parchment on which sheriff entered nn. of jurors), list of jurymen 3. 315 (cf. 'to empanel a jury')

panne brain-pan, skull 4. 78

parcel-mele ('by parts') retail 3. 81

parfourned *1 pa. sg.* performed 5. 405, 607

par(o)schienes parishioners pr 89, 5. 426

parte(n) share *3 pr. pl.* pr 81, 5. 143; *2 pr. pl.* ~**th** (see n.) share with each other 1. 180

partie part 1. 7

passe go (free) pr 155, 3. 136; *1 pr. sg.* depart 6. 205; ~**th** *pr. pl.* live 1. 7; *pa. sg.* ~**d** transgressed 1. 104, surpassed 7. 169

passynge over, above 5. 422

patentes (papal) licences or indulgences 7. 194 (< Lat. *litteræ patentes*)

paternoster-while time taken to say a P.N. 5. 348

paye pleasure: **to** ~ to his pleasure, satisfaction 5. 556

payn(e) bread 6. 152, 7. 121

paynym pagan, Saracen 5. 523

peces (pieces) cups 3. 89

pedlere pedlar, one who carries a ped (basket) 5. 258

pees peace 1. 150, 3. 220

pees pea 6. 171; *pl.* ~**en** 6. 198, **peses** 6. 189

pelet pellet, (white) stone ball 5. 78

pelure fur 2. 9, 3. 294

penaunt penitent 4. 133

GLOSSARY

penyworth amount bought for a penny 3. 256; *pl.* ~es = goods 5. 334

penyale ale sold at a penny a gallon, 'thin' ale 5. 220

perauenture lest 5. 648

percil parsley 6. 288

pere peer, equal 3. 204; *pl.* ~s 7. 16

Perkyn Peterkin, (little) Piers 6. 25

permutacioun exchange 3. 256

Per(o)nelle 5. 26; *gen.* ~s 4. 116

persones parsons pr 83 etc.

pertly boldly 5. 23; pertliche plainly 5. 15

pesecoddes peas pods containing peas (boiled whole) 6. 294

peselof loaf made from peas etc. 6. 181

peynen hem take pains 7. 42; *pa. pl.* peyned tortured 1. 169

peyred *p.p.* impaired, injured 3. 127

peys weight 5. 243

picche cut, pick 6. 105

piked *pa. pl.* = hoed 6. 113: cf. Staffs. dial. 'pike up the road'

piloure pillager, robber 3. 194

piones peony seeds 5. 312

piries pear-trees 5. 16

pitaunce allowance 5. 270

platte hire threw herself flat 5. 63

plede plead 7. 42; *pa. pl.* ~den pr 212, pleteden 7. 39

pledoures pleaders in a law-court 7. 42

plesynge gratification 3. 250

pleyed took holiday pr 20

pleyne full (? alluding to plenary indulgence) 7. 103

pleyne (refl.) complain 3. 167; *pa. sg.* ~d 6. 161; *pa. pl.* ~d pr 83

pleyntes complaints, pleas 2. 177

pliȝted (refl.) *pa. pl.* pledged, joined (thsvs.) pr 46

plow-pote 'pusher' for use in ploughing 6. 105: see n.

podyng ale thick, inferior ale used in making puddings 5. 220

poised *pa. sg.* weighed 5. 217

poke bag 7. 191 (still in dial.)

poletes pullets 6. 282

polsche (polish) make clean 5. 482

ponfolde pinfold, pound 5. 633

poraille poor folk pr 82

poret kind of leek 6. 300; ~tes 6. 288

portatyf quick-moving 1. 155

possed knocked pr 151

posternes side-doors 5. 628

potage stew 6. 152

potagere maker of stew 5. 157

potel two quarts 5. 347

pouere *n.* poor 1. 173

poundmel by pounds at a time 2. 222

pouste power, virulence 5. 36

powere armed force 4. 66; jurisdiction 4. 140; licence 6. 151

poynt ? cause 5. 15; item, condition 6. 38

prechoures *g. pl.* Friars Preachers' 4. 122

prentis apprentice 5. 202; *pl.* prentis 3. 224, 5. 317; ~hode apprenticeship 5. 256

prest priest 4. 133 etc.

prest ready 6. 199; ~est readiest 5. 558; ~ly promptly 6. 95

presumed took (on themselves) pr 109

preue put in practice *imp. pl.* 5. 43; *pa. sg.* ~d showed 7. 168; *p.p.* tested 4. 122

priked spurred 2. 189

pris price, value 2. 13

prisounes prisoners 7. 30

propre ? pertinent ? orthodox 7. 147

prouendreth provides with prebends 3. 149

provinciales (*pl. adj.*, Fr., or ? *gen. sg.* of *n.*) pertaining to *or* issued by the provincial, i.e. the head of a religious order in a district 7. 191

prouisoures persons nominated by the pope to livings in advance 2. 170, 3. 146

pruyde fine array pr 23

pryue familiar 2. 23; intimate 2. 63; ~s *pl. adj.* as *n.* secret friends 2. 177

pukketh pokes, incites 5. 620;
pa. sg. ~d 5. 643
pult out displayed 1. 125
purchace obtain 7. 186; *3 pa. sg.*
~d 7. 3
purfil(e) furred or embroidered
trimming of a dress 4. 116, 5. 26;
p.p. ~d trimmed with fur 2. 9
purs purse, bag 5. 192, 311
purtenaunces appurtenances 2.
103
put (forth) *pa. sg.* thrust, poked
(forward) 4. 47, 78, 5. 544; *pa.
pl.* (refl.) ~ten devoted themselves pr 23
puttes pits, dungeons 5. 412
pyke pilgrim's piked staff 5. 482:
cf. ~staf 6. 105
pykoys pick-axe 3. 307
pyne pain, punishment 2. 103
pynned *1 pa. sg.* fastened 5. 213
pynynge-stoles stools of punishment 3. 78

quarteroun quarter 5. 217
quitte *p.p.* paid 6. 100
quod, quatz quoth, said 3. 111,
6. 3 etc.

radde see **rede**
ragman roll pr 75 (see n.)
rakyer streetcleaner, scavenger
5. 322
rape (refl.) hasten *imp. sg.* 4. 7, 5.
399; *2 pl. pr. sjv.* **rape** 6. 120
rape haste 5. 333
rappe strike, suppress 1. 95
rathe early, soon 3. 73; compr. ~r
4. 5, 5. 263 (= first) þe ~ the
more quickly, beforehand 5. 287,
6. 120; sup. ~st 5. 342
ratonere rat-catcher 5. 322
rato(u)n (small) rat pr 158, 167;
pl. ~es pr 146
rauȝte reached, caught pr 57;
extended (= was stretched out)
4. 185
rayes striped cloths 5. 211
recche reck, care 4. 65; *3 pr. sg.*
~th 6. 122
reconforted *p.p.* solaced, 5. 287

recorded gave judgement 4. 157
recrayed *p.p.* recreant, craven
3. 257
rede (i) advise 4. 9, 29; *1 pr. sg.*
rede 1. 173, 7. 181; *imp. sg.* 4.
113; *pa. sg.* **radde** 5. 46, 125,
radde (bade, instructed 5. 485);
(ii) go over (= settle) 5. 434;
(iii) read 7. 106; *2 pa. sg.*
reddestow didst thou read
3. 257; *3 pa. sg.* **redde** 3. 334
redili easily 5. 125
redyngkyng ? lackey (only in
PPl) 5. 323 (? 'riding serjeant',
supervising reapers: *BPR*, iv. 97)
regratere retailer 5. 226; *pl.* ~s
3. 90
regraterye retail trading 3. 83
regystreres registrars 2. 173
reherce (i) declare 7. 190; *imp. sg.*
reherce 5. 182; (ii) repeat,
deliver: *pa. sg.* ~d pr 184, 5. 61
rek(e)ne enumerate 1. 22; put in
proper place 4. 177; *2 sg. pr. sjv.*
rekne reckon up 5. 277
relees discharge, remission 6. 92
relessed *p.p.* remitted 3. 58
releue aid 7. 32
religioun religious orders or
houses 5. 46 etc.
remissioun release from debt
(? with allusion to sense of
divine forgiveness) 6. 92
renable talkative pr 158 (v.l.
resonable; but Sk cfs. Nfk.
'runnable', loquacious)
rendered memorized 5. 211
renke man pr 192, 5. 399; *pl.* ~s
7. 181
renne run pr 166, 3. 213; *pr. pl.*
~n 2. 182
rental (lit. a roll recording the
rents of an estate): fig. a record
of sins 6. 92
renten endow 7. 32
rentes property returning income
3. 83
repentestow (þe) *refl. 2 pr. sg.*
repentest thou 5. 449; **repented-
estow**(þe) *2 pa. sg.* 5. 232;
repent (þe) *2 pr. sg. sjv.* 5. 263

rerages arrears of debt 5. 246

reson logic pr 167; argument, reasoning pr 175; bi ~ in order 1. 22

rest *3 pr. sg.* (contr. < resteth) is resting pr 171

restitue make restitution, restore 5. 281

retenauns retinue 2. 53

reue reeve, steward 2. 110; *g. sg.* ~s 5. 427

reulen rule 7. 10

reuthe pity 1. 173 etc.

rewarde recompense 3. 316

rewe *imp. sg.* have pity 5. 475

rewlyng rule pr 127

rewme realm, pr 177; *pl.* reumes realms 1. 95, 7. 10

ribanes rows, bands 2. 16

ribaudes profligates 5. 512

ribaudye debauchery pr 44

ribibour player on the rubible (three-stringed fiddle) 5. 322

ricchesse wealth 2. 17, 3. 90; *pl.* ~s 3. 23

riche mighty pr 18

riȝte *n.* justice 3. 238

riȝte *adj.* straight 4. 42

riȝte *adv.* straightway 4. 13; ~ so in the same way 5. 371

riȝtful just pr 127, 1. 54; *pl.* = upright men 4. 157, 3. 241

riȝtfullich properly 4. 172; justly 7. 10

rit(t) (contr. < rideth) rides 4. 13, 24; is moving about pr 171

rode rood, cross 2. 3 etc.

rolle enrol, register 5. 278

romares outriders, travellers 4. 120

Rome-renneres travellers to (the Court of) Rome 4. 128

roos *1 pa. sg.* rose, got up 5. 234

ropere rope-maker 5. 323

rored *pa. sg.* groaned 5. 398

roste roast meat pr 229

rotes roots 6. 105

Rotland Rutland 2. 110

route troop, crowd pr 146, 4. 168

rowneth whispers 4. 13; *pa. pl.* rouned 5. 333; *pr. p.* ~ynge 4. 24

roxed (refl.) stretched 5. 398

rusty filthy, foul 6. 75 (cf. *King Hart,* 930–2 and P. Bawcutt's n.)

rutte snored 5. 398

ruwet small horn 5. 348

rybaudoure teller of ribald tales 6. 75

rychen *pr. pl.* grow rich 3. 83

ryflyng(e) plunder 5. 258

rymes poems, verses 5. 402 (cf. ON *rýma,* ballad-like poem)

ryngynge ringing of church bells 3. 94

rype ready 5. 396

sadder more soundly 5. 4

sadnesse firm faith, confidence 7. 150

safferes sapphires 2. 13

safte safety 7. 36

Salamon Solomon 3. 93, 330; *g. sg.* ~es 7. 137 (Lat. *Salomon*)

salmes *g. sg.* of a psalm 3. 247

(þe) same in the same way pr 227, 3. 26

Saracenes peoples of the East, Arabs 3. 326

sarmoun sermon 3. 93

sauacioun salvation 5. 126

sauf safe 7. 51

sauȝtne become reconciled 4. 2

sauoure *n.* pleasure 7. 148

sauoure *v.* season, please (thy lips) 6. 264

sauter psalter 2. 37, 3. 247, 7. 40; *g. sg.* sauter 5. 282

sawes sayings 7. 137

say, saw see seen

s(c)hendeth *pr. sg.* harms, disgraces, corrupts 3. 154; *pr. pl.* ~n, ~th 6. 175, 2. 125; *p.p.* shent 3. 134, 4. 374

schete loose piece of cloth, e.g. skirt of a garment 5. 108

schewe see shewe

schrape *pr. sg. sjv.* scrape 5. 124

s(c)hrewe rascal, villain pr 196 etc.; sinner 5. 471; the Wicked One 1. 127

s(c)hrifte confession 5. 304 etc.

schyreue sheriff 2. 163; *pl.* shireues 2. 58

se(en) see, look at 2. 70, 4. 86;
2 *pr. sg.* sestow 1. 5; *1 pr. pl.*
seth 3. 216; *1 pa. sg.* seigh(e)
pr 50 etc., sei3 pr 230, saw
5. 9, say 5. 10; *3 pa. sg.* sei3
2. 188, seighe 5. 505; ysei3en
5. 4

seche, seke seek, visit pr 47, 7. 163;
2 pr. pl. sjv. look up 3. 344; *imp.
pl.* seketh 5. 58; *pa. pl.* sou3te 7.
166; *p.p.* ysou3t pr 50

secte suit, suite: see 5. 498 n.

seem, seme horse-load 4. 38, 3. 40

segge man 3. 63, 5. 127

segge, sei, seyn say 2. 67, 5. 617
pr 189; *2 pr. sg.* seist 6. 232;
2 pr. pl. seyne 6. 131; *3 pa. sg.*
seyde 6. 232; *3 pa. pl.* seiden
2. 151

selde(n) seldom pr 20 etc.

seleth *pr. pl.* seal 3. 147

selke silk pr 210 (silke 6. 11)

selles cells pr 28

selue himself 1. 202

seme see seem

sendal a fine silk 6. 11

sene visible 1. 147

seriaunt (Lat. *serviens regi ad
legem*) serjeant-at-law 3. 293

serke shift, shirt 5. 66

seten *pa. pl.* sat 6. 117, 195

sette plant 5. 548, 7. 6; *1 pr. sg.*
set, value, reckon 7. 194; *3 pa. sg.*
sette valued 6. 171; *p.p.* sette
placed 6. 48

settyng planting pr 21

seweth see sueth

shal, shaltow see shull

shamedest didst bring shame on
3. 189

shape arrange 3. 17; *3 pr. sg.* ~th
delivers judgement 1. 159;
causes, disposes 7. 67; *1 pa. sg.*
shope (refl.) dressed myself
pr 2; *3 pa. pl.* shope(n) established, ordered pr 122; refl.
arranged, made thsvs. pr 57

shedyng scattering: for ~ to prevent spilling 6. 9

shendeth see schendeth

shen(d)fullich shamefully 3. 275

shepe sheep pr 2

shette *pa. sg.* shut 5. 611

shewe reveal pr 106; *pr. sg.* ~th
7. 16; = suggests pr 167; *pa.
sg.* ~d 1. 72; *imp. sg.* shewe
confess 5. 373

shewyng utterance (of) 5. 385

shodde *p.p.* shod 2. 163

shonye shun, avoid pr 174; *1 pr.
sg.* shonye get out of the way
5. 169

shope(n) see shapeth

shrewe see schrewe

shrewednesse sin, wickedness
3. 44

shroudes outer garments pr 2

shryue(n) to shrive, hear confession (of) pr 64, 89; *imp. sg.*
shryue (refl.) confess 5. 373;
pa. sg. shroue (refl.) confessed
3. 44; *p.p.* shryuen 5. 309

shull etc.: *1 pr. sg.* shal shall,
must 5. 608; *2 pr. sg.* shaltow
thou must 5. 579, 6. 44; *pr. pl.*
shull(e), shullen shall 3. 34
etc.; *2 pa. sg. sjv.* shulde
oughtest 6. 49, sholdest shouldst
have to 1. 142; *3 pa. pl. sjv.*
sholde were obliged to pr 37,
2. 167; *pa. pl.* shulde(n) should,
ought to be 7. 13

sibbe, syb akin, related to 5. 634;
akin 5. 636

sight, sy3t appearance pr 16,
view 32; ? visibility 5. 499; bi
si(o)te of in view of 1. 132; ? in
presence of 2. 113

siker certain, sure 1. 130, 3. 50

sikerere more confidently 5. 509

sikerly surely 5. 547

sikul sickle 3. 306

sire father pr 189

sisoure juror 2. 164, 4. 167; *pl.*
~s 2. 62, 3. 133

sithe scythe 3. 306

sith(en), sitthe *adv.* and *conj.*
since pr 64 etc.

sit(t)henes afterwards 6. 65, 7.
25

sithes, sythes times pr 230, 5.
431, 441

sitten cost 3. 48 (cf. later use of 'stand')

skaþe injury 3. 57; wound 4. 79

sklaundre shame, disgrace 3. 57

sklayre veil (worn beneath a cap and falling on shoulders; sts. bound round head to cover chin and cheeks) 6. 7

sleen slay 3. 285; *imp. sg.* **slee** 3. 264

slepe *1 pa. sg.* slept 5. 382; *2 pr. sg.* **slepestow** art thou sleeping? 1. 5; *p.p.* ~**d** 5. 4

sleuth(e) sloth pr 45, 2. 98

slyken *pr. pl.* render sleek 2. 98

smauȝte smacked, tasted 5. 363

smerte *pr. pl. sjv.* smart, suffer 3. 167

smythye forge (passive force after do, *q.v.*) 3. 305; *pr. sg.* **smytheth** 3. 322

so (that) provided that 4. 102, 193

soffre *imp. sg.* suffer, permit 3. 92

soft mild, warm pr 1

sokene a district held in *socage* (i.e. enfranchised) 2. 110

solfe sing by note (*sol, fa*) 5. 423

somer-game midsummer celebrations 5. 413

somme *pl. adj.* some pr 31, 222; = some of 3. 13; *d. pl.* 3. 284

sompne summoner 2. 153, 3. 314

sompnoure an officer who summoned accused persons to an eccl. court 4. 167; *pl.* ~**s** 2. 58, 3. 133 (see *Speculum*, 12, 43)

sonde ? present, or message (of the text) 3. 349

songen *pa. pl.* sang 5. 346, 6. 117

songewarie interpretation of dreams 7. 148, 150 (? error for *so(u)ngnarie* (AF); rare

sonnest soonest 1. 70, 3. 281

sore sorrowfully 5. 512

sori miserable pr 45, 5. 127

sorwe harm 4. 62

soth true, 5. 282 etc.

sothe truth 4. 2, 5. 569

soth(e)ly truly 3. 189, 5. 241; assuredly **sothelich** 3. 5

Sothenesse truth 2. 24, 188

souereygne *adj.* powerful, effectual pr 159

souereynes *pl. n.* superiors 6. 82

soupe(n) eat supper 2. 96, 6. 220

soure bitterly 2. 140

souteres cobblers, shoemakers 5. 413

souteresse ? female shoemaker 5. 315 (nonce-use: *A* **sowestere**; A, V **souters wyf**)

space opportunity 3. 170

spared *p.p.* saved 5. 380

spede succeed, thrive 3. 270, 5. 601

spendeth gives freely 7. 46

sperhauke sparrowhawk 6. 199

spiceres sellers of spices 5. 311

spien examine 2. 225

spille destroy, ruin 3. 308; *pr. sg.* ~**th** 5. 41; *imp. sg.* **spille** 3. 270

spiritualte (i) spiritual character; (ii) eccl. property, dues 5. 148, 149

sprynge switch 5. 41

spynnesteres women engaged in spinning 5. 216

stable cause to come to rest 1. 120 (cf. *Ae. Legenden*, ed. Horstmann, i. 221)

stekye stick fast, be stopped 1. 121

sternly resolutely pr 183; **sterneliche** forbidding(ly) 6. 321

sterres stars 7. 160

stokkes stocks 4. 108; ? stumps 5. 585

stole stool 5. 394

stonde(n) stand 1. 121, 6. 114

streyte rigorously pr 26

streyues property of deceased aliens pr 94

stroke see **stryke**

struyeth *pr. pl.* destroy 6. 29

stryke *imp. sg.* press on 5. 586; *pa. sg.* **stroke** moved sharply forward pr 183

studye *n.* thought, studied effort pr 181

studye *v.* study, ponder 7. 143

stues stews, brothels 6. 72

stuwardes stewards pr 96

stynte cease, pause 1. 120; *imp. pl.* stynte stop, rest 5. 585 (see Zettersten, *Vocaby. of 'Ancren Riwle'*, 153)

suddenes subdeans 2. 172

su(w)eth, seweth *pr. sg.* follows, pursues pr 45 etc.; *pr. pl.* ~th 5. 60; *pa. pl.* sued 4. 167; *p.p.* sued followed, driven 5. 550

suffrance divine long-suffering 6. 146

suffre permit, allow to exist 2. 174; *1 pr. sg.* bear with 4. 1; *2 pa. sg.* ~dest 5. 490

suggestioun reason, motive 7. 67

supprioure subprior 5. 171

suren give assurance to 5. 547

surfait surfeit, excess 6. 267

sustre sister 3. 63; *pl.* ~n 5. 627

sute suit, clothing 5. 495, 504

swelte die 5. 154

swete sweat 6. 26, 130

sweyued sounded pr 10

swithe much, often, very 5. 456, 470

swonken see swynke

swowe swoon 5. 154

swynke *n.* toil 6. 235

swynke *v.* toil 5. 548, 6. 26; *pa. pl.* swonken pr 21

sydder lower 5. 193

sykenesse sickness 6. 259

syker safe, secure 7. 180

synnelees sinless, without sin 6. 232

tabarde loose coat, sleeveless, or with wide, open sleeves 5. 196

tai(l)le tally stick 4. 58 (see n.), 5. 252

tail(l)e tail, end conclusion 3. 347, 2. 185; pudendum 3. 130; *pl.* ~s roots of trees 5. 19

take (i) give 1. 56; *pr. sg.* ~s 4. 58; *pa. sg.* toke gave 3. 45;
      (ii) receive 6. 141; *pr. pl.* taken ask (w. trewlich = ask no more than reasonable wages 7. 63; *3 pa. pl. sjv.* toke (þei on) if they dealt, acted (fairly) 3. 85;

(iii) refl. *pr. pl.* taken hem meet, assemble 5. 173

tale (i) account 1. 9; (ii) talk, (lying) tale 2. 114 etc.

talwis blabbing 3. 130

tauerners *pl.* keepers of taverns pr 227

tauny dull yellow 5. 196

taxeth assesses 1. 160

taxoure assessor of taxes 6. 40

teche *imp. sg.* direct 1.83; *pa. sg.* tauȝte taught 3. 282, 6. 211

tellen *pr. pl.* count over, reckon up pr 92; *pa. sg.* tolde 3. 45

teme (1) plough-team 6. 136, 7. 2

teme (2) theme, text 3. 95, 7. 135 (? sermon) 5. 61; subject 6. 23

tempred *p.p.* attuned pr 51

tene *n.* vexation, anger 6. 119, 7. 116; trouble, worry 6. 135

tene *v. 1 pr. sg.* vex, injure 5. 432; *3 pa. sg.* tened 3. 320; refl. was vexed 2. 114

teneful harmful, troublesome 3. 345

þanne then pr 139 etc.

þat who pr 77 etc.; þat (þat) that which pr 38, 3. 347 etc.

the *1 pr. sjv.* in so the ik so may I thrive, 'on my life' 5. 228

þeiȝ(e) though 1. 10 etc.

þen than pr 147

þennes thence 1. 73, 229 etc.

þer(e) where 1. 131 etc.; ~as there where 4. 34

þerafter accordingly pr 23, 5. 223, 6. 116; in that sense 3. 186; back (to them) 5. 587

þerinne therein 1. 61

þerfore for, on account of, it 4. 54, 5. 236

þer(e)myde therewith 7. 26 etc.

þerto in addition 4. 59

þerwhile whilst pr 173; þat ilke while . . . ~ so long as 6. 165; ~s in the meantime 6. 8

þider thither 2. 161

þikke thickly, profusely 3. 156

þing (i) creature, person pr 123; (ii) ~e things 6. 212; = legal processes, suits 4. 28

GLOSSARY

pirled pierced 1. 172
pis(e) these pr 62 etc.
po when pr 176, 1. 47
po those 1, 21, 4. 40 etc.
polye suffer 4. 84
ponkynge thanksgiving 2. 148
thorw(gh) through, by 2. 41, 6. 20
thouȝte see thynketh
powȝ, powgh though 6. 36, 40
thresshewolde threshold 5. 357
threttene thirteen 5. 214
thretti thirty 5. 422
threwe *pa. sg.* threw (himself),
  fell 5. 357
prumbled stumbled (nonce-wd.)
  5. 357
prungen thronged 5. 517
thynketh (1) impsl. seems (w. dat.
  of pron.) pr 165, 227; *pa. sg.*
  thouȝte pr 6 etc.; wonder me
  ~ I am astonished 3. 182; (2)
  thynke *1 pr. sg.* intend 3. 95
tidy careful 3. 320
tikil wanton 3. 130
til *prep.* to 5. 610
tilie, tulyen labour, cultivate pr
  120 etc.; earn by tilling, procure
  6. 235
tixt(e) text 2. 121, 3. 342
to *prep.* to: to body so as to have
  a body 1. 62; to man so as to
  be a man 1. 82; to nonne who is
  a nun 5. 153; for 7. 135; upon
  5. 173; after 6. 30
to *adv.* too 6. 265
tobolle *p.p.* swollen exceedingly
  5. 84
tobroke *p.p.* broken in pieces 7. 28
tofore before, in presence of 5. 457
toft knoll, hillock pr 14, 1. 12
tokenynge token 5. 19 (in ~ of
  as a sign of)
tolled (out) stretched to 5. 214
tolleres collectors of dues pr 220
tolugged *p.p.* pulled about 2. 216
tome leisure 2. 185
toppe top, tuft of hair 3. 139
torne deprave 3. 42; be converted
  3. 325; *pa. pl.* ~d turned 5. 19;
  p.p. turned 3. 337
totorne *p.p.* torn 5. 197

toure tower pr 14, 1. 12
treieth betrays 3. 123
trauaille *n.* work, toil 7. 43
trauaille *v.* work, toil 6. 141
tresore treasure 1. 45; *pl.* ~s 7. 54
treuthe (us. psfd.) justice, loyalty
  1. 12, 6. 39 etc.; honest work 2.
  119
trewe *n.* truce, respite 6. 332
trewe *adj.* honest, faithful pr 120,
  5. 432; truthful 1. 177, 6. 52
trewlich, trewly honestly 3. 85,
  7. 63
triacle remedy, healing balm
  1. 146, 5. 50
tried *p.p.* tested 1. 85
trielich choicely pr 14
triest choicest 1. 135
troneth enthrones 1. 131
trouthe pledge, word of honour
  5. 280
trusse pack off 2. 218
tulyen see tilie
tutour warden, keeper 1. 56
tweye twice (? = more than once)
  4. 22
tweyne twaine, two 5. 32 etc.
tymbred *pa. pl. sjv.* would build
  3. 85
tyme leisure, opportunity 6. 11
tyne lose 1. 112
tynkares *g. sg.* tinker's; *pl.*
  ~eres pr 220

vchea each pr 207, 5. 116
vchone each one 1. 51, 2. 138
veille watchful one 5. 450
venesoun venison, flesh of any
  animal killed by huntsmen for
  food pr 194
venge avenge 5. 128
veniaunce vengeance 3. 258
vernicle picture showing the face
  of Christ as supposedly impressed on the *sudarium* of St.
  Veronica 5. 530
vigilies vigils, fasts 5. 416
vitaillers victuallers 2. 60
vitailles victuals 2. 180, 5. 443
vmwhile for a time, now and then
  5. 345

255

vnbuxome disobedient 2. 82

vncoupled off the leash pr 162, 206

vnder at the foot of pr 8

vnderfonge *1 pa. sg.* received
1. 76; *pr. pl.* ~n 3. 214; *p.p.*
~n 7. 171

vndernymeth reproves 5. 115

vnderstonde accept 5. 437

vneth scarcely 4. 60

vnglosed *p.p.* without explaining
it away 4. 145

vngraue *p.p.* unstamped (? =
bullion) 4. 130

vnhardy cowardly pr 180

vnkouth strange, foreign 7. 155

vnkynde without natural kindness
1. 190; unnatural 5. 276; un-
grateful 5. 437

vnlese *pr. pl.* unlock, open pr 213

vnlouely disagreeable 5. 363

vnmoebles immovable property
3. 267

vnsowen unsew 5. 66

vnthende small, poor 5. 177

vntil to pr 227

vnwittily unwisely 3. 105

vokates advocates 2. 60

vp *prep.* upon 1. 12; ~ gesse by
guess 5. 421; *adv.* open 4. 57

vpholderes sellers of old clothes
etc. (? *or* appraisers of goods, as
in Riley, *Chronicles*, 282). Cf.
'Thos. Clerc vpholder', Oxf.
Poll Tax, 1381; 5. 325

vppe imminent 4. 72

vsage practice 7. 87

vseth practises 3. 239; *2 pa. sg.*
vsedestow 5. 240

vsure-ye usury 2. 175, 5. 240;
interest 7. 83

wafrestre maker of wafers (sweet
cakes: cf. Fr. *gaufre*) = go-
between 5. 641

wage engage, give surety 4. 97;
p.p. ~d 4. 100

waited see wayte

waitynges wanton looks 2. 89

walketh *3 pr. pl.* go about 7. 96

Walshe Welshmen (lit. foreigner)
5. 324

wan went 4. 67 (v.l. went; Sk.
cites Scots use of 'win')

wanhope despair 2. 99, 5. 286, 452

wanye wane 7. 55

war aware 2. 8

wardemotes see pr 94 n.

wardes wardships or persons
under ward pr 94

ware (refl.) *imp. sg.* guard (thyself)
5. 452

wareine warren pr 163

warner warrener, keeper of a
warren 5. 316

warpe uttered 5. 87, 369

warrok fasten with girths 4. 20

Waryn a Norman Christian n.
obsolescent in 14th c. 4. 26

wateres urine 2. 224

Watt(e) short form of Walter
5. 30, 316

wawe be afoot (v.l. walke) 7. 79

wax(en) grow, increase 7. 55,
3. 300; *pa. sg.* wex 3. 328; (=
fell into) 5. 286

way, wey road 61; course 3. 17
pl. ~es 7. 27

wayte watch, look after, serve
5. 202; *1 pa. sg.* ~ed 7. 139;
p.p. ~ed 5. 551

waitynges, watchings, looks 2. 89

wayue lift up, open 5. 611

webbe (1) (woven) piece of cloth
5. 111

webbe (2) weaver 5. 215

wedde pledge, wager 3. 201, 5. 244

wederes weathers, storms 6. 326

wedes clothes 2. 90

wehe whinny 4. 22

wel much, even 5. 193; very 3. 161;
even 5. 193; much 5. 114; as
adj. 3. 65, 152 ('well in with');
þat ~ be þow mayest thou be
fortunate 6. 278

welche Welsh flannel 5. 199

wenche daughter *or* maid servant
5. 364

wende(n) wend, go 6. 60, 2. 160;
pr. sg. ~th 4. 105; *pr. pl.* ~en
pr 162; *pa. sg.* refl. went turned
aside pr 7; *pa. pl.* ~ forth set
out pr 48; *pa. pl.* wenten 4. 76;

p.p. went gone 6. 207, turned, changed 3. 280; *imp. sg.* wende go 3. 264

wene ween, imagine, think 3. 300; *1 pa. sg.* wende 5. 238; *2 pa. sg.* ~est 3. 191

wepe weep 5. 62; *pa. sg.* wep(t)e 5. 470, 480; *pa. pl.* wepten 7. 37

werche see worche

were *pa. sg.* and *pl. sjv.* should be, might be, were 5. 167 etc.

werke deed, verity 4. 146

werkmanship capacity, virility (cf. *CT*, E 1832), 2. 91

wernard deceiver, liar 3. 179

wesshen *pa. pl.* washed 2. 220

wexed *p.p.* stopped up (as with wax) 5. 351

weye *n.* weight (of cheese: 3 cwt. in Essex, 256 lb. in Suffk.) 5. 93

weye *v.* weigh 5. 204; *pa. sg.* wey3ed 5. 218; *p.p.* ~n 1. 176

weyues property without an owner pr 94

whas whose 2. 18

whennes whence 5. 532

where whether pr 171

whiche what sort of 7. 146; *pl.* 4. 25

while(s) whilst as long as 3. 28; 6. 320; þe while whilst 6. 58, 290

whoso whoever 4. 131; but ~ unless (some) one 5. 218, 6. 1

wi3te, wyght person pr 207 etc.

wi3tliche nimbly, quickly 2. 208; vigorously 6. 21

wiket wicket gate, small opening in larger door 5. 611

wikke fraudulent 5. 229

wikked bad, difficult 6. 1, 7. 27

wikkedliche falsely, 5. 204

wil *3 pr. sg.* wishes 5. 40; *2 pr. sg.* wiltow 5. 310, 6. 158 (~ or heltow willy nilly)

wille desire 2. 91; self-will 5. 596; at ~ at their disposal pr 37 (cf. 2. 147); bi ~ out of self-will, wilfully 4. 70; of o ~ with a single mind 3. 237

wise clever pr 48, 4. 69

wispe handful (of furze) 5. 351

wisse(n) teach, tell, show 5. 540, 562, 7. 127; (poss. refl.) *1 pr. sg.* wisse 1. 42, 5. 147; *pa. sg.* wissed 6. 167

wite(n) (i) know, learn 4. 139 etc.; wote *1 pr. sg.* know 5. 180, 6. 132; *3 pr. sg.* knows pr 43 etc.; *3 pr. pl.* 3. 329; *1 pa. sg.* wist pr 12; *3 pa. sg.* 5. 161; *pr. sg. sjv.* wite 5. 606; *1 pa. sg. sjv.* wiste 3. 52 etc. *imp. pl.* witeth 2. 74; wite God 5. 641, see n

witen (ii) preserve, keep pr 207, 7. 35; witen (iii) blame *3 pr. sg.* witt 1. 31 (? l. wited: *A* wytide)

with together with 2. 84 etc.; by (means of) 3. 2; ~al(le) moreover 5. 3, 307, in all things 6. 84; ~ þat provided that 5. 74

withhalt *pr. sg.* withholds 5. 559

withewyndes (*g. sg.*) convolvulus, woodbine 5. 525

(in) witnesse attestation 2. 107; attested (by) 7. 111

witt see witen (ii)

witte intelligence, wisdom pr 114, 5. 596; ingenuity, contrivance pr 156; good sense 6. 53

witterly truly, with certainty, clearly 1. 74 etc.

witty, wise, astute 5. 137

wo(o) evil 1. 167; difficulty 5. 364; as *adj.* = woeful 5. 3

woke, wyke week 5. 93, 6. 258

wol *3 pr. pl.* are willing, prepared 5. 250; *3 pa. sg.* wolde would, has desired 1. 13 etc.; *2 pr. pl. sjv.* wil 5. 54; *2 pa. sjv.* woldestow if thou wouldst 3. 49

wolle wool 6. 13; ~websteres weavers of wool pr 219

wollen *adj.* woollen 5. 215; as *n.* 1. 18

wolues-kynnes of wolfish kind 6. 163

wombe belly (cf. Scots wame) 3. 84, 193

wonden *pa. pl.* wound 2. 220

wones habitations 3. 234

wonye dwell 2. 106, 224; *3 pr. sg.* won(i)eth 1. 63, 2. 232

worche work, perform 6. 21, 120;
  pr. pl. ~th 3. 80, ~n 7. 91; *pr.
  pl. sjv.* worken 4. 146; *pa. sg.*
  wrouȝte 1. 148, *pa. pl.* ~(n) 1.
  163, 6. 111; *pa. pl. sjv.* 6. 115,
  251; *imp. pl.* worcheth 2. 133;
  p.p. wrouȝt created 7. 98
worlde state of things, life pr 19,
  6. 163; *g. sg.* ~s = worldly
  7. 125 (cf. ~ good *CA*, 8.
  9447)
worschip *n.* honour 1. 8
worschip *v.* glorify 1. 16
wortes vegetables, pottage 5. 162
  etc.
worth(e) be pr 187; *3 pr. sg.*
  worth .. will be 1, 186 etc.;
  2 pr. sg. worstow thou shalt be
  5. 622, *2 pr. pl.* worthen uppe
  mount 7. 91, *2 pr. sg. sjv.*
  worth mayest be 1. 26
wortheli splendidly 2. 8
worpier more honourably 6. 48
wowed *pa. sg.* wooed, coaxed 4. 74
wowes walls 3. 61
wratthe to enrage, anger 2. 116;
  2 pr. sg. refl. ~st makest thyself
  angry 3. 182; *pa. pl.* ~d 5. 513
wrecches evildoers 2. 194
wreke wreak, avenge (*refl.*) 5. 85;
  p.p. wroke 2. 194
wy man 5. 540
wyn wine pr 228
wynde wind (yarn on a spool)
  5. 555
wynke (uppon) sign to, 'give the
  glad eye to 4. 152; *pa. pl.* ~d
  (for the constn. cf. *CT*, F 348)
wynkyng(e) nodding, slumber
  (cf. 'forty winks') 5. 3, 368
wynneth *3 pr. sg.* earns, produces,
  by labour 6. 21: *imp. pl.* ~th 6.
  322; *pa. pl.* wonnen pr 22
wynnynge profit 5. 35, 7. 25
wyntre, wynter *pl.* winters, years
  1. 99, 3. 39
wyues women 5. 570; *g. pl.* ~n
  5. 29

ybake(n) *p.p.* baked 6. 184, 312
ybette *p.p.* beaten 4. 93

yblamed *p.p.* blamed 3. 281
yblessed, yblissed *p.p.* duly
  consecrated pr 78, 7. 13
ybore *p.p.* born 2. 130
ybounde(n) *p.p.* bound pr 178,
  5. 524
ybroken *p.p.* broken pr 71
ychose *p.p.* chosen 5. 331
yclothed *p.p.* clothed 1. 3, 2. 8
yclouted *p.p.* patched 6. 61
ycrammed *p.p.* crammed pr 41
ycrounede *p.p.* crowned 2. 10
ydel foolish, 2. 90; an ~, idly, in
  vain 5. 580
ydronke *p.p.* drunk 6. 281
yeten *p.p.* eaten 1. 152
yett see ȝit
yfolwed *p.p.* followed 3. 39
yfouȝte *p.p.* fought 6. 154
yglobbed *p.p.* gulped down 5. 346
ygo *p.p.* passed, gone 5. 207
ygraced *p.p.* thanked (*or* 'God's
  grace be on you'—Lat. *gratiae*)
  6. 126
ygraunted *p.p.* granted 7. 8
yhasped *p.p.* fastened as with
  a hasp 1. 195
yholden *p.p.* esteemed 1. 84
yhote *p.p.* named 1. 63; bidden
  2. 218
yhowted *p.p.* hooted at 2. 218
ylakked *p.p.* blamed 2. 21
yleye *p.p.* lain 5. 82
yliche like, alike 5. 494
ymade *p.p.* held 2. 43; composed,
  written 5. 507
ymaked *p.p.* made 2. 72, 6. 189
ymaried *p.p.* married 2. 39
ymped *1 pa. sg.* (en)grafted 5. 138
ympes grafted shoots 5. 137
ynowe enough 2. 162
ypassed *p.p. as adj.* past pr 189
ypliȝte *p.p.* plighted, pledged
  5. 202
yrens, yrnes irons 4. 85, 6. 138
yrifled *1 pa. sg.* rifled, robbed
  5. 234
ysein, yseiȝen *p.p.* seen pr 160,
  5. 4
yserued *p.p.* (i) served, contented
  5. 341, 419; (ii) deserved 6. 89

GLOSSARY

yshewed *p.p.* declared 2. 134
yshryue *p.p.* shriven 5. 91
ysouȝt *p.p.* visited pr 50
ysowen *p.p.* sown 5. 550
yspilte *1 pa. sg.* wasted 5. 380;
  p.p. 5. 442
ysue issue 5. 265
ytailled *p.p.* scored on a tally
  5. 429
ytermyned decided on 1. 97
ytried tried, tested 1. 133, 205

yuel (i) *adj.* hard 5. 121, 6. 50; (ii)
  adv. badly 5. 168
ywar wary, cautious pr 174, 1. 42
ywedded *p.p.* wedded 2. 42
ywonne *p.p.* won, gained 5. 93
yworth *inf.* be: lat God ~ let
  God determine 6. 84
ywounden *p.p.* wound, bound
  round 5. 525
ywrouȝte *p.p.* wrought, done
  4. 68